POLITICAL CAMERAWORK

POLITICAL CAMERAWORK

Documentary and the Lasting Impact of Reenacting Historical Trauma

D. ANDY RICE

INDIANA UNIVERSITY PRESS

This book is a publication of

Indiana University Press
Office of Scholarly Publishing
Herman B Wells Library 350
1320 East 10th Street
Bloomington, Indiana 47405 USA

iupress.org

© 2023 by David Andrew Rice

All rights reserved
No part of this book may be reproduced or utilized in any form or by any means, electronic or mechanical, including photocopying and recording, or by any information storage and retrieval system, without permission in writing from the publisher. The paper used in this publication meets the minimum requirements of the American National Standard for Information Sciences—Permanence of Paper for Printed Library Materials, ANSI Z39.48-1992.

Manufactured in the United States of America

First printing 2023

Library of Congress Cataloging-in-Publication Data

Names: Rice, D. Andy (David Andy) author.
Title: Political camerawork : documentary and the lasting impact of reenacting historical trauma / D. Andy Rice.
Description: Bloomington : Indiana University Press, 2023. | Includes bibliographical references and index.
Identifiers: LCCN 2022042920 (print) | LCCN 2022042921 (ebook) | ISBN 9780253065919 (hardback) | ISBN 9780253065926 (paperback) | ISBN 9780253065933 (ebook)
Subjects: LCSH: Documentary films—Philosophy. | Documentary films—Production and direction. | Historical reenactments—Case studies. | Motion pictures—Political aspects. | Motion pictures—Social aspects.
Classification: LCC PN1995.9.D6 R495525 2023 (print) | LCC PN1995.9.D6 (ebook) | DDC 070.1/801—dc23/eng/20221206
LC record available at https://lccn.loc.gov/2022042920
LC ebook record available at https://lccn.loc.gov/2022042921

CONTENTS

Acknowledgments   *vii*

Introduction: Reflecting on "Moments of Truth"   *1*

1. Being There Again: Reenacting Camerawork in *In Country* (2014)   *35*

2. Weaponizing Affect: A Film Phenomenology of 3D Military Training Simulations during the Iraq War   *81*

3. "Do You Want to Play a Klansman?" Lynching Photography, Civil Rights Camerawork, and the Moore's Ford Lynching Reenactment in Georgia   *120*

4. Establishing a Black Affective Infrastructure: From Lynching Performance in the Hollywood of the South to *Always in Season* (2019)   *166*

Conclusion: Toward an Embodied Social Cinema, or From Point of View to Social Sense   *194*

Filmography   *207*

Bibliography   *211*

Index   *231*

ACKNOWLEDGMENTS

ACADEMIC BOOK WRITING IS A process of condensing insights and experiences gleaned across a lot of time and countless places into a little object, wondrous to hold after so much work. Thank you to the team at Indiana University Press, especially acquisitions editor Allison Blair Chaplin, assistant acquiring editor Sophia Hebert, production editors Nancy Lightfoot and Carol McGillivray, the anonymous reviewers, and the board, for actualizing this little object. Beyond this finishing stage, it represents contributions from many people who nudged its form and ideas over years of conversations, critiques, suggestions, and affirmations. These pages pay respect to those who helped the book along its way.

First and foremost, I am honored to thank my dissertation adviser Lisa Cartwright, who taught me how to write and think in ways I never could have figured out on my own. Her notes and suggestions consistently demonstrated an incredible breadth of knowledge and speed of thought. Fifteen pages of disorganized material written in doubt would come back within the hour with her incisive details about how to sharpen phrases, signpost intellectual conversations, and rethink wobbly notions. Other comments she made would lead me to an "aha!" moment months or even years later. Somehow, she knew where I would end up before I knew where I was going. She stuck with me through thick and thin, even when my filmmaking ambitions inhibited progress on this project, and even years after I finished the dissertation and left my PhD program. Her theories of affect and intersubjectivity influenced me, too, as I suspect will be evident in the text for those who know her work.

Zeinabu irene Davis was also instrumental in helping me think through the complex relations between filmmaking, documentary, and Black experience.

She was a member of my dissertation committee, my filmmaking adviser, and then my collaborator on film projects including *Spirits of Rebellion: Black Independent Cinema from Los Angeles* (2016), a feature documentary about the LA Rebellion film movement that we coproduced and that I filmed and edited. She remains a cherished mentor in navigating the dual worlds of filmmaking and academia, and a dear friend. Working with her certainly informed ideas in this book but also altered the trajectory of my life. She evokes a heightened sense of conviction and compassion from those with whom she works, and I would like to think that I benefited from her facility in this way. Zee, I celebrate you here and try to pay it forward. Such relationships are rare.

Her commitment to collaboration also allowed me an extraordinary filmmaking experience. Through work on *Spirits*, I had the chance to meet many filmmakers I'd long admired, including Charles Burnett, Julie Dash, Barbara McCullough, Haile Gerima, Shirikiana Aina, Ben Caldwell, Billy Woodberry, Alile Sharon Larkin, O. Funmilayo Makarrah, Pierre Desir, Carroll Parrott Blue, Cauleen Smith, Bob Nakamura, Arthur Jafa, Don Amis, and Jamaa Fanaka, and scholars including Clyde Taylor, Ed Guerrero, Bill Nichols, Chuck Kleinhans, David James, Jan-Christopher Horak, Jacqueline Stewart, Allyson Nadia Field, and Shannon Kelley. I listened to conversations with these individuals mostly from behind the camera and then made sense of them at the editing station, where repeated listening to create scenes makes deep impressions. What a privilege to have learned from these brilliant minds in such a way. I am also grateful for having had the chance to meet and work with Giovanna Chesler on this project and for her introduction to cinematographer Hans Charles, who spoke with me about his approach to camerawork in a provocative phone conversation. The approach to writing in this book, especially in the second half, owes much to these filmmakers and scholars. The California Humanities Documentary Project Grant provided crucial funding for this project, and the UCLA Film and Television Archive and Hammer Museum were incredibly supportive and helpful at every stage of production.

I thank my UCSD dissertation committee members Brian Goldfarb, Patrick Anderson, Bennetta Jules-Rosette, and Roddey Reid for thoughtful comments on chapter drafts and countless conversations. Professors Ariana Hernandez-Reguant, Nitin Govil, Gary Fields, Mike Cole, Val Hartouni, Elana Zilberg, Kelly Gates, and Carol Padden in the UCSD Department of Communication and Rachel Klein, David Gutierrez, Danny Widener, Luis Alvarez, and Nayan Shah in the UCSD History Department also provided theories, histories, and ways of thinking formative to this project. The UCSD Fellowship in Global California Studies provided funding for early-stage summer research for what became chapter 2. I am grateful for nurturing and generative conversations with fellow members of my PhD program. My office neighbor Reece Peck, now at CUNY Staten Island, deserves a special shout-out, as his Gramscian interpretation of populism and working-class culture was ahead of the curve in the early 2000s, and his perspective on formalist approaches to art offered real challenges to ideas about documentary that I had taken too much for granted. I warmly solute graduate program comrades Harry Simón, Lauren Berliner, Andrew Whitworth Smith, Muni Citrin, Kim Dewolfe, Laurel Friedman, Erin Cory, Deniz Ilkbasaran, Matt Dewey, Monika Sengul-Jones, Marisa Brandt, Tara-Lynne Pixley, Stephen Mandiberg, Kelli Moore, and Yelena Gluzman, and my fellow traveler from UCSD Sociology Kelly Nielsen.

Three and a half years as the ASPIRE Fellow in Socially Engaged Media in Undergraduate Education Initiatives at UCLA opened an extraordinary opportunity for me to explore areas of film, activism, and teaching that I'd long only been able to imagine. This position offered the chance to refine chapters in the book while teaching activist documentary production and collaborating on performative documentaries. I'm grateful for the counsel and collaboration of Victoria Marks, Wendelin Slusser, Lucy Blackmar, Renee Tajima-Peña, Kyle McJunkin, Patricia Turner, Kristy Guevara-Flanagan, Jenny Jay, Cully Nordby, Raffaella D'Auria, Stephanie Pincetl, Aparna Sharma, and the staff at UCLA Libraries (especially Alicia Reilly, Doug Worsham, and Jessica Mentesoglu) who provided space, logistical support, and encouragement for our experiment in teaching media production as a component of general education within a liberal arts framework. It was a pleasure to have had the chance to speak with Vivian Sobchack while at UCLA as well. Thanks to Urban Planning, Disability Studies, Chicana/o Studies, African American Studies, and Food Studies for partnering with our production offerings. Outside of UCLA, this initiative could never have happened without the energy and know-how of social entrepreneur, film producer, and ASPIRE founder Peter Samuelson, who worked tirelessly on fundraising, publicity, and recruiting impressive guest speakers to campus. I greatly admire his ongoing efforts to improve the lives of foster youth by forming partnerships across social welfare organizations, universities, and school systems via his nonprofit foundation First Star.

At Miami University in Ohio, colleagues in the Department of Media, Journalism, and Film have provided a welcome network of support. Special thanks go to Richard Campbell, Bruce Drushel, Kerry Hegarty, Mack Hagood, Kathleen German, Ron Becker, Dave Sholle, and the Mongeese (they know who they are), as well as librarians Mark Dahlquist, Jacqueline Johnson, and Alia Levar Wegner. Colleagues Adam Rottinghaus, Rosemary Pennington, Katie Day

Good, Ann Elizabeth Armstrong, and Elena and Juan Carlos Albarrán have been wonderful friends and interlocutors over my years in Oxford, Ohio. The Humanities Center has provided valuable support for the book through their winter book proposal workshop, their yearlong Altman Fellowship to explore the theme "Truth and Lies" with fellow faculty, and Humanities Lab funding with colleague Eric Hodgson to create augmented-reality documentary work with students. Thanks to Tim Melley, Pepper Stetler, Theresa Kulbaga, and Emily Zakin for organizing these various events and keeping the humanities vibrant on our campus.

Professionally, I am indebted to scholarly organizations Visible Evidence, the University Film Video Association, the Society for Cinema and Media Studies, Poetics and Politics, and the National Communication Association for providing venues to explore the ideas developed in this book. Thanks to Danielle Beverly, Jen Proctor, Ruth Goldberg, Pooja Rangan, Jennifer Malkowski, Martin Lucas, Liz Miller, S. Topiary Landberg, Janet Walker, Hannah Rose Shell, Vicki Callahan, B. Ruby Rich, Laura Kissel, Alex Johnston, and the late Brian Winston and Jonathan Kahana for little conversations—perhaps not even remembered—that made a difference here. I appreciated encouragement from performance scholars Rebecca Schneider, Mark Tribe, Katie Johnson, Zachary Price, and Emily Roxworthy. Editors Julia Lesage and the late Chuck Kleinhans at *JumpCut: A Review of Contemporary Media*, César Albarrán-Torres at *Senses of Cinema*, Jaimie Baron and Kristen Fuhs at *Docalogue*, and Lisa Cartwright at *Catalyst* all published work that helped develop this book. An earlier draft of chapter 1, "Being There Again," appeared in *Jump Cut*, no. 58 (Spring 2018), at https://www.ejumpcut.org/archive/jc58.2018/RiceVietnamEnactment/index.html. A version of chapter 2, "Weaponizing Affect," was first published in 2016 in the online, peer-reviewed, open-access journal *Catalyst: Feminism, Theory, Technoscience* 2, no. 1, at https://doi.org/10.28968/cftt.v2i1.28830.

My thanks are also due to the filmmakers who allowed me to speak with them and study their work in depth, including Jacqueline Olive, Irene Lusztig, Meghan O'Hara, and Mike Attie. Others who generously shared their time with me along the way to completing the project include Cassandra Green, Tyrone Brooks, Charles Steele, Walter Reeves, Wade Marbaugh, Bob and Jennie Caine, and the late John Wagstaffe. To the many interviewees who remain anonymous in this book, thank you for making the work possible. Thanks as well to my filmmaking mentors Alfred Guzzetti, Ross McElwee, Robb Moss, and the late Richard Rogers and Mani Kaul in what used to be called the Department of Visual and Environmental Studies at Harvard University (now the Department of Art, Film and Visual Studies), where I spent my undergraduate years and four years as a teaching fellow. The approach to camerawork that I practice and teach retains many aspects of what I learned in this program, and parts of the book are in conversation with its philosophy. Ilisa Barbash and Lucien Castaing-Taylor's filmmaking and support for filmmaking through the Sensory Ethnography Lab and Film Studies Center at Harvard also helped me think through a variety of challenges to documentary work that are represented in this book, and I am grateful for the continued scholarly output of and about these initiatives.

Last, I want to thank my family, who inevitably make the largest sacrifice for a book to enter the world. In addition to working on a range of climate justice and public health initiatives in California and Ohio, my partner, Carla, has patiently conversed, read, moved, watched kids, cooked meals, and provided a range of emotional labor over our twenty-one years as partners. She is a brilliant force, and I am humbled to have lived the better part of my life with her. Olive and Oran, if you're reading this, you may stop here, at least for now. Thank you for keeping life fascinating and vibrant these last thirteen years. I love you guys and can't wait to see what you make and do as you grow up. Ginny, Dave, and Colin Rice have patiently listened to me talk about various bits of this book for years and provided many kinds of help, and my uncle Don and late aunt Bunny Uischner were especially gracious with housing when I conducted research in and around Atlanta. George and Marianne Blackmar are the best in-laws one could ask for. Thank you all for the support that has allowed this book to enter the world.

POLITICAL CAMERAWORK

INTRODUCTION

Reflecting on "Moments of Truth"

CHECK THE LENS AGAIN FOR dust. Frame Walter in the right half of the flip-out screen. Keep left the small group of angry whites in 1940s church clothes, backlit by the Georgia summer sun. Stay wide and high to show the three hundred Black spectators in the background across the street, witnessing. Today Walter plays "Gene," the white supremacist and former Democratic Georgia governor Eugene Talmadge, giving his 1946 stump speech in Monroe. "You tell 'em, Gene!" yells the "Talmadge Gal" in the broad red hat and the pearls, unenthusiastic in her performance. I move to find the reverse shot, a low-angle close-up of Walter, and hold the frame as he scowls (fig. 0.1). "I'd like to thank the *Atlanta Constitution* for coming out two months ago and stating plainly," he thunders, "that Talmadge is the only candidate in this election for governor who will fight for and champion the reinstitution of a white Democratic primary in the state of Georgia!"

In 1946, a week after Talmadge gave this speech, a white mob murdered common-law Black couples George and Mae Murray Dorsey and Roger and Dorothy Malcom by gunshot at the Moore's Ford Bridge just outside of Monroe.[1] Seeking justice, evidence, publicity, and fairer elections, present-day Black Georgia activists and white allies (mostly from Atlanta) annually reenact this lynching and commemorate the victims on the last Saturday in July. The evolution of their staging since 2005 has been controversial, but the reenactment organizers' sustained attention to populist discourse in American political life has proved to be prophetic as well as a public service, in part for drawing cameras like mine to document the performance. In keeping with standard practices of camerawork, I suppress my own emotional response behind the lens. Failing to do so while recording would result in intolerable camera shake and too many shame-induced tilts toward the ground. For now, just follow, just follow, just follow. Be quiet.

Figure 0.1. Video stills of Walter performing as Eugene Talmadge at the Walton County Courthouse in 2012. Recorded by the author.

Still, attentive following demands active work. Documentary camerawork is a way of being that tunes into nearby affective flow, the material base of poignant footage and cinematic structures of time. I cycle through a list of the situation's tacit commands while filming. Be cognizant of Walter's family's Klan past for which this moment stands as a perverse atonement. Be able to love his willingness to play hate here as the camera rolls and the crowd looks on with muted anger. Be mindful of the lynching reenactment scene yet to come. Be further in the future where this record of 1946 via 2012 reenactment turns into a film, maybe juxtaposed next to other moments you know and dimly consider while filming. Maybe here in this doubled documentary event is a story about ongoing right-wing efforts to suppress the Black vote in Georgia. Be aware that the shot might not be used anyway, that no one else may ever see it. Be the filmer, the editor you imagine, and the viewer you cannot know of the film not yet made, all at the same time. Be a fleshy, imperfect barometer of this chaotic, unfolding, intense set of feelings remade for today, and translate all of it through the camera for those not here.

Be there.

The mantra echoes through training, discourse about the value of documentary, and years of work, and it's hard to think otherwise in the moment. This is the harvest season, not the winter of reflection. It is the time to follow the messiness of homegrown ritual and everyday life. When I do, my footage is supposed to pledge to the viewer not to preach. The goal, in this sensory ethnographic approach to filmmaking, is to call forth the viewer's "active engagement in the generation of meaning" rather than arguing for this or that.[2] Rooted in the antiestablishment orientation of the 1960s counterculture and experiments with using lightweight, low-cost, synch-sound filming rigs to move the cinema from studio to street and site, filmers of this school tend to "seek out revelatory moments, those flashes of connection between what would otherwise be lost to flux" by closely recording daily life.[3] Yet these "revelatory moments" still aim to function as the building blocks for a politics we can't yet name (or maybe care not to label this way), and so this kind of camerawork has come to bear a relation more broadly to the affective turn in the post-2000s humanities and social sciences.[4] In Georgia, I mark my series of shots in memory for director Jacqueline Olive to consider using in her PBS film *Always in Season* (2019)—at this point, in 2012, a cinematic meditation on restorative justice rituals in communities scarred by unresolved histories of lynching, like Monroe. I've spent hundreds of similar days on this and other films, recording everyday people as they go about their business.

But the activities that take place in Monroe this day are not exactly business as usual. The performance is an intentional effort to infuse some combination of flesh and concept back into the land and air as well as the cameras nearby. And I am here filming a reenactment in part because I've lost faith in the premise of neutrality and the promise of representation on which the ethics of much documentary camerawork depends. To paraphrase Achille Mbembe's warning, twenty-first-century citizens and activists need to take seriously "the power and effectiveness of abstractions" such as theories, models, simulations, and reenactments, which "depend not so much on whether their depiction of the world is accurate as it does on their capacity *to constitute a world*."[5] In writing this book and devising its peculiar approach to the study of camerawork, affect, and the reenactment of trauma, I have found myself driven by a question intimated by Mbembe's social theory: what happens when we film simulations like the Moore's Ford Lynching Reenactment using methods designed to represent the liveliness and dignity of unscripted everyday life?

Political Camerawork: Documentary and the Lasting Impact of Reenacting Historical Trauma explores performances of the past/passed in reenactments and simulations as an angle on an unresolved debate in media studies about the status of evidence in digital culture. I focus on the affective experiences of nonfiction camerapersons and reenactors in what I am calling *simulation documentaries* like the lynching reenactment described above. Simulation documentaries are not simply films. Rather, they are reiterative, performed scenarios that both reference traumatic historical events and manage to lure documentary cameras to record live performances as events in their own right.[6] Their raw materials are the embodied, collective, live performances carried out with and for cameras in three-dimensional spaces. Attuned to the affordances of digital media distribution, the ubiquity of cameras, and the ways that journalists and documentary camerapersons like me try to follow rather than direct events, simulation documentaries aim to extend the time, space, and framing of documentary attention on an issue or subject over years of recursive performance and filming. Simulation documentaries proceed without narrative closure per se, serving over time as tools for generating particular pathways of feeling for media stories about a given event or as mediatized open-space forums for activism, learning, and social or individual growth.[7] They aim to create what John Protevi called "political affect," or "affective cognition in social contexts" distributed across individuals, ideological positions, shared somatic experiences, and local contexts invested in discursive power.[8] In simulation documentaries, camerawork and reenactment constitute key vectors for the creation and circulation of political affect and so give cause for this film studies treatment of Protevi's social concept. Case studies in this book examine such dynamics in the reenactment of the Vietnam War (chap. 1), the US military's embodied simulation training in California during the Iraq War (chap. 2), and the lynching reenactment described above (chaps. 3 and 4), as well as documentary films and media reports about each simulation scenario. I conduct close analyses of the documentaries *In Country* (Attie and O'Hara, 2014), *Full Battle Rattle* (Moss, 2010), and *Always in Season* (Olive, 2019) as components of simulation documentaries. The ephemeral reality of intense feelings and sensations experienced by actors, camerapersons, and reporters—so-called moments of truth—take evidentiary precedence here over archival sources or concepts of truths that are timeless.

I argue that in simulation documentaries such as that of the Moore's Ford Lynching Reenactment, performing bodies create the lively documentary text. Reenactors do not directly experience the traumatic past, but in performing a simulation of it, they become the carriers of its felt traces. During the reenactment performance, the road, the buildings, and the wooded landscape itself seem unusually sensitive to light for those copresent to it, like celluloid inscribing our anxious and troubled projections about this past that remains in our present. Bodies like Walter's and later those of the committed men and women who play the victims of the lynching *become* documentary for those who witness them. For a moment, through touching sacred ground in commemoration, they offer evidence of history.

The impacts of these feelings are lasting nonetheless—material, even, in digital culture. Reenactments of trauma are startling little rehearsals for death that stick with us, pain us, retraumatize us, and fascinate us. They can create something akin to what photographer Ariella Azoulay called "planted pictures" involuntarily inscribed into the body and thereby creating a "civil political space ... not mediated exclusively by the ruling power of the state."[9] These traces surge up in the bodies of performers and sometimes in copresent spectators through the ineffable energies that performance theorist Peggy Phelan associated with "liveness and disappearance" in performance.[10] For individuals who reenact events from their own lives, as with some of the nonactors in Italian neorealist films or the subjects of psychodrama therapy, the performance can be cathartic or empowering, even a "second chance" to get things right.[11] Within documentary theater adapted for film, alternatively, the reenactment of archival transcripts has allowed practitioners to explore racial and gender surrogacy as a form of critique, defamiliarize acting conventions, and highlight oppressive policies and social practices with an eye toward justice.[12] In the terms of film theorist William Guynn, "fusional moments" experienced in reenactment may facilitate a fleeting sense of insight about past lives outside of narrative interpretation, "an uncanny experience of *truth* that takes you unawares and thrusts you into a sphere where the usual protocols do not apply."[13] Perhaps most significantly, reenactment offers a way to conjure past events, experiences, and perspectives produced by asymmetrical relations of power, where recording live was dangerous or impossible. Camerawork amid reenactment aims to "reactivate" some of those energies for imagined viewers in the future in many other spaces.[14]

The films of Rithy Panh about the 1970s genocide in Cambodia, signally, have shown that documentaries premised on reenactments of traumatic history can unearth evidence and create a space for redress. As a child, Panh was deported with his family from the city of Phnom Penh to a forced-labor camp in a rural village. Though his parents and other family members died in these years, he managed to escape to France in 1979, where he learned the craft of filmmaking. Many of his films have focused on aspects of the genocide to force his fellow Cambodians as well as government leaders to reckon with it and work through their collective trauma. Panh's haunting documentary *S21: The Khmer Rouge Killing Machine* (2003), for example, excavates fragments of stories about the notorious S21 concentration camp where guards killed over seventeen thousand Cambodians between 1975 and 1979. At S21, so few prisoners survived—only three, including painter Vann Nath, who is featured in the film—that Panh had to depend on the former guards to piece together what had happened there. The film shows these now-middle-aged men acting out and explaining their former routines of surveillance, torture, and killing in the spaces where they once worked. Though they all speak throughout the film with a flat affect, a former guard named Ches unnervingly comes to life when he reenacts the nighttime routine of surveilling prisoners that he learned and honed as a thirteen-year-old boy. Film scholar and psychoanalyst Deirdre Boyle argued that this scene provided crucial evidence of the genocide long denied or suppressed in Cambodia: "Ches's reenactment demonstrates how alive Cambodia's violent past is in the psyche of its survivors, both victims and perpetrators. Denial of that past has been the national pattern for dealing with the Cambodian genocide, and Panh quietly argues throughout his film—through these reenactments—that his nation's split-off traumatic memories are the wellspring for its social pathology, violence, and corruption."[15] Adjacent to sensory ethnographic recording in its patient following of Ches as he reenacts for the camera and himself, this long take accumulates affective force at it plays in the finished film, which translated to political significance in this case. It suggests how powerful documentary evidence can be laid bare through reenactment, and how the camerawork employed during such moments inevitably participates in a nascent politics.

Yet in scholarship on reenactment, liveness in performance, and performance documentation, there is little about the body of the cameraperson almost invariably copresent with performers. I want to emphasize that in simulation documentaries, documentary camerawork is also a part of the act. In many contexts less grave than Panh's film, the notion of moments of truth must be read as ironic. The subjective recognition of something tingling the body, after all, might also characterize the spectator's adrenaline rush upon viewing the climactic action sequence in a cliché blockbuster film. A classical Hollywood plot builds toward a unique event that resolves a crisis, a scripted moment of truth functioning diegetically as the hero's unlikely individual triumph. Here the film hails its viewers as ideological subjects. Emotionally charged moments recounted and reinforced as truth in journalistic and documentary media representations, similarly, have played their part in propelling the currents of ethnonationalism, populism, and fascism, especially since 2016.[16] If a simulation documentary can steward the documentarian's quest for affecting moments, then the camerawork starts to function less like critical, neutral, or independent record making and more like a de facto public relations tool.

"Weaponizing Affect: A Film Phenomenology of 3D Military Training Simulations During the Iraq War" (chap. 2), for example, centers on the conundrum of documenting military training simulations during the Iraq War (2004–12), where following staple documentary techniques for raising critical consciousness (such as showing imagery evocative of the horrors of war) functioned instead to tap into perversely pleasurable Hollywood war movie tropes, aid the army's public relations agenda, and blunt possibilities for dissent. These training simulations also radically altered the desert landscapes of military areas in Southern California and spurred cottage industries across the region to supply Hollywood-trained pyrotechnicians and scenario writers, Arabic-speaking contract role players, and satellite-powered laser-tag accessories for standard-issue rifles in this peculiar, military-driven growth sector. Though simulations, such depictions of war are material for the ways they create new markets and infrastructures to service military-themed cultural work.

Alternatively, cases such as the Moore's Ford Lynching Reenactment show that simulation documentaries in digital culture can spur participants seeking justice (especially along the lines of race) to reclaim the physical environment, think differently about historical reality, and act in new ways, sometimes facilitating community conversation and growth. Allissa Richardson's study of smartphones and Black social movements attributes the unique power of "bearing witness while black" to long-standing sentiments of collective identity and shared struggle. For Black viewers, she explains, each videotape of police violence against a Black body points back to all such incidents, not just a singular event.[17] Her observation would extend to spectators and participants in reenactments as well, where performing bodies touch the reality of police brutality and white vigilantism through creating its sensory echoes in a historically significant place. Such witnessing, writes feminist philosopher of ethics Kelly Oliver, "enables the subject to reconstitute the experience of objectification in ways that allow her to reinsert subjectivity into a situation designed to destroy it."[18] Thinking from behind the lens, Hans Charles, the cinematographer of Ava Duvernay's *13th* (2016), who is developing what he calls a "unified black film theory," insists intriguingly that "literally the atoms that are captured [in the process of digital or analog image recording] are influenced by the bodies that are close to the camera."[19] Race mediates the experience of witnessing, the processing of pixels, and the possibilities for political transformation bound up in uses of the documentary camera. Contexts for camerawork matter, and yet they remain invisible in most finished films and thus underexplored by theorists of the image.

These starting points lead the book to pursue a twofold agenda in conversation with ongoing concerns in film and media studies, documentary theory, and performance studies. First, I offer a theory of indexicality—a concept long essential to considerations of ethics in documentary studies—centered in embodied experiences of camerawork and reenactment rather than narrowly technological understandings of photographic inscription and manipulability, which no longer serve the field. Second, I argue that in simulation documentaries (and much of digital culture by extension), camerawork itself often functions as a kind of unspoken reenactment performance of past recording practices. Across my case studies, I explore what it might mean to evaluate camerawork this way.

INDEXICALITY, SIMULATION, AND AFFECT

The book is organized around three major ideas within the framework of embodiment: the problem of the indexical trace within documentary theory, the materiality of live reenactment and simulation performance in digital culture, and embodied reenactment as an intervention into the theory behind sensory cinema practice. The conceptual framework develops in three studies of simulation documentaries in the post-2000 United States over four chapters, which all focus on collective simulations and reenactments of traumatic events. I assess the concept of media indexicality and practices of documentary camerawork, reenactment performance, and spectatorship through the lenses of performance, duration, race, and affect.

Indexicality and the Body

Political Camerawork engages questions of evidence in digital culture by bringing into dialogue two areas of post-2000 critical practice: first, camerawork in a group of nonfiction films that I am calling *sensory cinema*, and second, embodied reenactment in performance. Sensory cinema is an experimental media production practice and academic research agenda dedicated to exploring via ethnography or the representation of memory the affective and bodily dimensions of human experience. I am using the term *sensory cinema* to refer to small-crew, independent, nonfiction filmmaking practices that aim in a variety of ways to evoke or follow the lived, affective, sensorial experiences of their subjects. In ethnographic styles, sensory cinema techniques center on observational recording, sometimes in ways that include subjects' subtle recognitions of the camera, to represent vulnerable societies, ways of working, and communities for small audiences in university classrooms, film festivals, and public television broadcasts. In diasporic films and postcolonial filmmaking, sensory cinema techniques center on voice-over engagements with traumatic memory or performative staging to elicit feelings of loss and then critical reflection on a historical event or theme. These films aim to express the sensory experience of surviving trauma, exile, or displacement primarily for audiences who may share similar life experiences or relate to them in more idiosyncratic ways.[20] By *embodied reenactment*, I am referring to a collection of performance practices across the domains of performance art, simulation training, media archeology, living history, ritual commemoration, documentary filmmaking, and psychodrama in which everyday people perform historical events, memories, or archival records. Reenactors may aim to work through a personally traumatic experience, find a collective identity around the shared interpretation of a historical event, internalize procedures for action in difficult scenarios, or learn about embodied historical experience by simulating archaic material and technological constraints in the present.[21]

I engage these areas of critical practice through documentary theory, critical media theory, and performance studies on the concept of *media indexicality*, a term usually associated with the capacity of photographic media to stand as evidence of past events. In his proposal for a semiotic system, late nineteenth-century American philosopher Charles Saunders Peirce described "the index" as a sign that bears an existential bond with its object, like the finger pointing to the object of the point, the weathervane to the direction of the wind, or the footprint to the foot. In Peirce's taxonomy, indexical signs are distinct from iconic signs, which look like the objects they represent, and symbols (such as written words), which arbitrarily stand for referents.[22] The concept of indexicality was adopted into film theory by Peter Wollen in *Signs and Meaning in the Cinema* (1972), where he used it to interpret the arguments of mid-twentieth-century French film theorist André Bazin. In "The Ontology of the Photographic Image," published in his influential *What Is Cinema?* (1967), Bazin proposed that the photograph "shares, by virtue of the very process of its becoming, the being of the model of which it is the reproduction"—a proposal, in other words, that the photograph is indexical because the mechanical action of the camera physically imprints the image of the world in front of the lens on the film emulsion at the moment of exposing it to light.[23] He argued that film thus generally bore a stronger relationship to evidence and the real than did plastic arts such as painting, sculpture, and drawing. Neo-Marxist documentary theorists starting in the 1990s accepted this conceit and so saw the emergence of digital recording technologies as a challenge to the material basis of documentary film. Leading documentary scholar Jane Gaines, for instance, captured the spirit of the moment by arguing that her field should leave behind "the impossible claim to indexicality" in favor of resemblance in the context of digital media.[24] If digital images are made of the same binary data as computer simulations, in this line of reasoning, then they index an easily manipulated computer code rather than a unique moment of past time. They cannot function as documentary evidence in the same way. Many scholars still attribute the rise of performative strategies in documentary film to "digital's loosening of the referential bond" and the "weakening of photographic image integrity."[25]

Influential in setting the terms for this way of thinking was new media theorist Lev Manovich, who celebrated the affordances of digital technologies for inverting what he saw as the stilted ontology Bazin had set out for the cinema. "Given enough time and money, almost anything can be simulated in a computer," he declared in his widely read article riffing on Bazin, "What Is Digital Cinema?"[26] If cinema was "an attempt to make art out of a footprint," he argued, then digital cinema was "no longer an indexical media technology but, rather, a sub-genre of painting," an emerging condition symbolized in his article by the floating digital feather layered over a stylized crane shot in *Forrest Gump* (1994).[27] Subsequent film and digital media scholars in many subfields followed this direction to contribute important insights about nascent labor relations in the globalized digital effects industry, processes entailed in producing computer graphics for blockbuster films, narrative tendencies in the use of spectacular effects, and the impact of image manipulation in shows and films that purport to represent actual events.[28] But this direction essentially baked into the theorization of digital media a notion of "medium specificity" that failed to account for the labor and cost required to manipulate video images, factors that limited access to such techniques to big-budget studios in the early 2000s.[29] New uses of small, low-cost digital cameras in documentary production practice and everyday interactions largely went unconsidered in this time as film and media theorists speculated about potential dangers posed by image manipulation.³⁰

One exception to this general trend is Jennifer Malkowski's *Dying in Full Detail* (2017), which criticized "existing new media theory's fixation on the loss of indexicality" for failing in turn to theorize emergent, everyday trends in nonfiction production and reception.³¹ In her study of the complex political and ethical concerns inscribed in digital documentary footage of actual death—the availability of which has increased as a practical by-product of the vast proliferation of digital recording devices and distribution platforms—Malkowski found that the "drama of referentiality seems surprisingly irrelevant in the reception of digital documentary."³²

As a documentary filmmaker who learned observational and participatory recording techniques on synch-sound 16 mm film cameras in the late 1990s, I would add that the "drama of referentiality" seemed beside the point for many camerapersons, as well.³³ I remember embracing the introduction of low-cost Hi8 and then digital video (DV) camcorders, tape-based recording formats, and nonlinear video editing software such as Apple's Final Cut Pro (brought to market in 1999) for opening new possibilities to represent intimacy with precision in nonfiction film art. For documentarians working with the activist left, video production emerged as "part of a field of practices producing new subjectivities, new ways of life."³⁴ But it was difficult to imagine at the time the profound impact that the increasing number of cameras, images, and online distribution platforms would have on cultural understandings of time, space, and interaction, and by extension the kinds of subjects and styles that documentarians might pursue. I spent the years between 2001 and 2006 filming and performing in reenactment events as a reverse participant ethnographer tracking US discourses about war after 9/11, and I noticed along the way that more and more "spectators" were viewing the live reenactment performances as camerapersons wielding a range of miniature digital cameras with screens.³⁵ Sometimes they even recorded bits of themselves or family members in the foreground as mock battles (reenactments of the Revolutionary War, in my case) played out in the background. This was camerawork "in favor of connective performance rather than semantic reference," as visual communication scholar Paul Frosh put it in his insightful article about the selfie—in other words, documentary practice for pleasure, comfort, and group identification.³⁶ In digital culture, this performative episteme largely displaced or subsumed the power of a representational one, a change that had little to do with the fact that digital imagery could be altered in software programs.³⁷ Indeed, digital distribution and low-cost public screening possibilities may also catalyze the mimetic "re-enactment of tactics from elsewhere" in direct action campaigns, wherein activists screen protest videos from elsewhere to prime their bodies for potential conflicts when they take to the street. The recursive cycles of insider recording, screening of footage selects, and embodied protest in effect tether the bodily orientations of protesters to the practices of movement camerapersons.[38] This is a new wrinkle on what Jane Gaines called "political mimesis" in a thoughtful article on the relationship between theatrical documentary and social action.[39]

Already "degraded," to use a favored term of digital media skeptics, reenactment scenarios present complex and provocative case studies for thinking through meanings of the digital in which image manipulability is not a central consideration.[40] My aim in looking at camerawork and embodied reenactment here is to contribute to this debate but in doing so to decouple documentary ontology from its traditional object, the finished film, without also giving up on the concept of indexicality and the ethical claims it brings in tow. I read media indexicality as primarily affective, ephemeral, and processual rather than technological; instances of indexical signification are inseparable from experiencing bodies and may or may not have much to do with inscriptions on celluloid or digital chips. Reframing the analytic positioning from film to bodily experience also forestalls conceding the troubling point that the concept of indexicality "may have reached the limits of its usefulness."[41] I explore the experience of indexicality in the body in heavily mediated contexts, not the nature of digital cinema per se.

My study of camerawork here follows film scholars who take up the unresolved question of the trace in digital culture from a phenomenological perspective and who theorize the trace as it registers on and through the bodies of those who experienced trauma.[42] While the authenticating, indexical signs of a traumatic experience (such as repression, forgetting, heightened sensitivity to nonthreatening stimuli, and involuntary psychic reenactments) may "undermine the legitimacy of a retrospective report about a remembered incident," as Janet Walker framed this epistemological dilemma in her study of documentary "trauma cinema," the traces of traumatic experience shape future lives and constitute fields of perception in profound ways. They also have little to do with an analog or digital medium of inscription.[43]

To situate media indexicality in the body of the one perceiving the sign is to focus on matters of duration. While the video camera opens its shutter for one-twenty-fourth or one-thirtieth of a second to create an image, the body responds to phenomena in less precise, less measurable ways. A researcher looking at an old wooden projector carried town to town by a silent-era ambulatory projectionist might note with a startle the markings on the box suggestive of repeated use—stains from leather straps or indentations where the box regularly pressed against the shoulders of its carrier over the years. The surge of awareness in the researcher that cascades from these observations may be described as a form of joy or fascination at imagining the lifeworld of the former projectionist. But these are doubtful sensations. They provoke more questions than answers. What must this person have thought while walking town to town carrying "the movies"? How did they identify (or not) with the films they screened? The researcher does not have answers to such questions. Indexicality never provides answers. Indexicality provokes thought and directs attention to evidence of *something*. It changes the course of the perceiver's focus and doing. While this heightened sense of awareness may be momentary, it does not match in an isometric relation to the time required to generate the sign itself (those marks were made over a long period of the projectionist's work). In all likelihood, the projectionist did not notice these indentations in the box made by their own shoulders or did not think they were particularly fascinating. They may have indexed the need to procure a new projector if the wear inhibited use. The indentations become indexical only through this intersubjective moment of encounter when the researcher perceives them as startling.[44] Indexicality is felt in the body of the perceiver as a new, challenging, humbling space for thinking. It is a sensory unit of time. Insofar as this feeling and regard focuses on the lived experience of other humans from the past in order to preserve, analyze, or express something about them or to persuade oneself or one's contemporaries about their meanings, a "documentary poetics" might also claim them as within the field's purview.[45]

Sometimes, the indexical sign in the body requires time to emerge. One of the women who played Dorothy Malcom in the Moore's Ford Lynching Reenactment recalled a moment at the end of the event when she was lying still with her eyes closed in the grass, playing dead. A different woman sang a spiritual to conclude the reenactment for witnesses and role-players alike and offer dignity to the day. This particular actress told me she first heard the sounds—crickets, the flowing stream, the clicks of cameras—and felt the intensity of the heat. And as her mind wandered over the course of a minute lying still, she began to think about the temporality of death itself. Her attention shifted as her sense of time slowed down. Her stillness indexed an alternative trajectory. And it moved her profoundly. She attributed that powerful, nebulous, momentary sensation to the presence of Dorothy Malcom's unsettled spirit, merging with her own body just for a moment in an involuntary, eerie sense of touch. Participating in order to witness such idiosyncratic connections speaks to an ethics of reenactment, a reason why embodied performance is not simply another instance of simulation. The bodies of those living with racial trauma may channel a counterhistory in such moments, a way of being and sensing that can inform critical media practices in generative ways. Rather than reject the concept of indexicality because digital imagery can be manipulated, I consider in the ensuing chapters a cultural shift toward performative and affective forms of indexical experience and try to parse how a documentary practice might work within these parameters.

Simulation and Affect

Scholars in philosophy, neuroscience, computer science, film and media studies, history, and critical cultural theory use the term *simulation* in different ways, so I want to briefly parse several meanings associated with it. According to the *Oxford English Dictionary*, the earliest uses of the term *simulation* referred to the "attempt to deceive" or "a false assumption or display, a surface resemblance or imitation," like the play of light and shadow on the wall of Plato's cave. Between the end of World War II and the rise of computing in the 1950s, however, simulation took on a second, more value-neutral connotation as "the technique of imitating the behaviour of some situation or process (whether economic, military, mechanical, etc.) by means of a suitably analogous situation or apparatus."[46] Simulation came to connote the process of modeling events or potential events in the actual world virtually, usually through the adjustment of variables in computer programs, so as to understand, prevent, encourage, or control a range of possible future outcomes. In the philosophy of mind and history fields, the term *simulation* named the process of imagining oneself into the world of another, which proponents claimed as key to empathy, learning, and intercultural exchange. Starting in the 1990s, neuroscientists conducting fMRI research on relations between perception, action, and brain activity claimed to discover "mirror neurons," a biological mechanism that seemed to support a simulation theory of mind. Mirror neurons became similarly active when study subjects (including birds, primates, and humans) performed an action and when they watched another perform the same action. The brain itself, in other words, could simulate a particular motor action response simply by watching others perform it. Repeated instances of similar mental simulations over time, in turn, altered the materiality of the brain itself. In critical cultural theory, Sean Cubbit offered the concept of "simulation theory" in 2001 to encapsulate a strain of neo-Marxist thought that theorized the nature of exchange in a postindustrial society. Developed between the 1960s and 1990s in the work of

Guy Debord, Jean Baudrillard, Paul Virilio, and Umberto Eco as a revision of pre–World War II Frankfurt School critical theory, simulation theory in this vein asks how communications technologies such as film, television, computing, and military surveillance tools transformed everyday life.[47]

Simulation has been a particularly resonant concept within film and media studies, both because of claims that the cinema itself functions as an apparatus of simulation and because the growing place of moving images in everyday life since the development of video technology in the late 1960s seemed to suggest the emergence of a simulation society. Because dominant cinema production commodifies experiences as media objects and then extracts value (economic, political, military, and cultural) through their distribution in a sign economy, Baudrillard argued that the content and message of any given media work made relatively little impact in the trajectory of its underlying code, toward a world organized around models rather than interpersonal experiences. Moreover, mass media distribution networks facilitated the proliferation of images and ideas without much connection to productive labor, and so the balance of power in a consumer society tilted definitively to those who controlled airwaves, magazines, movies, and newspapers—favoring technologies rather than industrial workers and consumption rather than production. Any information or image commodity that could circulate in mass media, including advertisements, news programs, and Marxist ideas themselves, became tools for establishing status economies among various media consumers and groups: "Needs, affects, culture, knowledge—all specifically human capacities are integrated in the order of production as commodities and materialized as productive forces in order to be sold."[48] In this context, Baudrillard was particularly skeptical of the phenomenological method, suggesting that its focus on individual consciousness failed to acknowledge the "*directly* and *totally* collective" nature of consumption in a society saturated with advertising aimed at augmenting desire. "No theoretical analysis is possible without the reversal of the traditional givens," he claimed in *Consumer Society* (1970); "otherwise, no matter how we approach it, we revert to a phenomenology of pleasure."[49] Baudrillard revised and reconsidered many tenets from his early writing later in his career, but he did not revisit phenomenology as a means for exploring the relationship between the body, media making, and collective life, even as access to media production tools and distribution outlets expanded.

I interpret the material qualities of embodied reenactment and camerawork through the lens of affect theory, a body of humanities scholarship developed especially since the mid-1990s. In broad terms, affect theory aims to account for prelinguistic, sensorial forms of bodily intensity that shape individual and sometimes collective instances of perception, attention, and movement as well as more enduring vectors of thought.[50] Theorists often claim that affective life offers a creative, idiosyncratic terrain through which to reimagine politics, identity formation, and value.[51] In my case, affect theory offers analytical tools preferable to discourse analysis or ideological critique alone to account for the conjoined experiences of nonfiction camerapersons and reenactment performers. Indeed, camerawork and reenactment performance rarely require language-based reflection from practitioners, which is part of my rationale for writing about such practices in the context of designed, recursive simulation events. I am interested in how such practices come to cohere over time or reveal affective patterns in retrospect that do seem to have a relationship to ideology, discipline, and discourse. And I am interested as well in ways that such creative practices can help catalyze local, specific, critical forms of community infrastructure, conversation, and action—the key space for translating affective experience into new questions, unexpected collectives, or actionable agendas that exceed simulation design.

However, the wide-ranging applications of affect theory have not led to a consensus about premises for developing a field or a shared articulation of political goals. In *The Affect Theory Reader* (2010), editors Melissa Gregg and Gregory Siegworth positively characterized their subject as a "methodological and conceptual free for all" and then inventoried eight different strands of scholarship on affect.[52] Intellectual historians Brian Ott and Ruth Leys focused more narrowly on parsing two lineages of affect theory that emerged to address limitations of psychoanalytic theory and the linguistic turn of the 1980s.[53] Portions of this book draw from film studies variants of each. First, I use affect theory grounded in taxonomies of cinematic intensity described by French philosopher Gilles Deleuze in his books *Cinema 1: The Movement Image* and *Cinema 2: The Time Image*, which aim to describe how the cinema generates new kinds of affects. Phenomenologists Vivian Sobchack, Laura Marks, Jamie Baron, and Kara Keeling focused in a similar way on the experiencing body and its "incorporative capacities for scaffolding and extension" in the context of novel technologies, social dynamics, or art forms.[54] Second, I draw from a body of work grounded in evolutionary theory on motivation attributed to American behavioral psychoanalyst Silvan Tomkins as interpreted by queer theorists Eve Sedgwick and Adam Frank in *Shame and Its Sisters: A Silvan Tomkins Reader* (1995) and adapted to new feminist psychoanalytic film theory analyses of documentary by Lisa Cartwright, Belinda Smaill, and Pooja Rangan.[55]

Deleuzian affect theory proposes that art (and especially film) can serve as a philosophy beyond language, a prepersonal intensive force acting on human and nonhuman bodies alike in their processes of becoming. Deleuze created taxonomies of cinematic expressive units (movement-image, action-image, time-image, affection image, recollection-image, etc.) that were incompatible, in his view, with the phenomenological method, and so Deleuze does not theorize embodiment in cinema spectatorship. In adapting the phenomenology of Maurice Merleau-Ponty for the study of film in *The Address of the Eye* (1992), Sobchack offered the concept of the "film body" to bridge filmic text and spectator experience. The "film body," in her terms, is a "being" with capacities for expression and intention that emerge between spectator and screen as the film plays.[56] I find the distributed form of agency embedded within this idea to be well suited to the simulation documentary scenarios I analyze in this book and to camerawork in particular, which is, after all, constituted in the space between bodies, objects, and contexts rather than within an individual's mind. For Marks, who largely follows Deleuze's affect theory in *The Skin of the Film* (2000), Sobchack's phenomenological approach opened pathways for theorizing consciousness, sensation, and screen-body permeability, a "bridge to explaining how a viewer experiences images" in the context of particular "states, histories, and circumstances."[57] Her book focused on 1980s and 1990s experimental, nonfiction films by diasporic makers caught in the violent political and economic disjunctures of late twentieth-century globalization, who repurposed details from everyday landscapes, objects, and interactions in Western metropoles to center films on memories of traumatic events in their homelands. Key to understanding this work for Marks was Deleuze's interpretation of the "any spaces whatever" in numerous post–World War II European art films, where aimless and powerless protagonists wandered amid rubble without the possibility of any decisive action.[58] As the "disengagement of affective response from action" opened for Deleuze an intense, visceral, unfamiliar, affective experience of time in such films, so Marks described the "narratively thin but emotionally full" films about traumatic memory and loss by postcolonial filmmakers forced to live between two cultures. Intercultural filmmakers sought to create forms of connection between themselves and a kindred diasporic audience—touch with past bodies through film rather than on it. In this way, the intercultural cinema she named was sensory in its effect, though not anthropological in its methodological orientation. Shared affective responses to images functioned to curate a collective and perhaps a politics. In all the case studies that follow, I think through the circuits of affect that function as the locus of indexicality in digital culture—an answer to the call, as Marks put it, to focus on "indexical and nonindexical *practices* [rather] than indexical and nonindexical *media*."[59] Writing about simulation documentaries in this way thus draws on and contributes to theories of spectatorship core to film studies for a media ecological context irreducible to "screen-essentialism."[60]

A second tradition of affect theory used in the humanities is based on descriptions of affective processes from the cognitive sciences and in particular from the writing of Tomkins. Intervening in Freud's binary theory of the sex and death drives, Tomkins proposed that the human body evolved an innate "affect system" to manage motivation by mediating recursively between perception and consciousness. Tomkins theorized that there are eight affect pairs that function as endpoints for gradients of intensity of response to external stimuli, with positive affect pairs interest-excitement, enjoyment-joy, and surprise-startle, and negative pairs fear-terror, distress-anguish, anger-rage, shame-humiliation, and dissmell-disgust. Tomkins credited the early writing of Norbert Weiner (1950) on cybernetics, a field of inquiry into self-correcting machines that subsequently influenced computer science, science studies, surveillance studies, and behavioral psychology, for leading him to theorize the affect system as functioning somewhat like a loop of code hardwired into the body, "the role of consciousness as part of a feedback mechanism," in his terms. The subject seeking to maximize positive affect, minimize negative affect, and lead a rich affective life would learn over time to pursue optimization strategies within a particular social and historical context. The affect system intensified the sensorial interplay among drives, perceptions, memories, and thought processes but was not beholden to any of them in particular.[61]

Apropos of the discussion of embodying indexicality, Tomkins identified surprise-startle, one of nine affects in *Affect, Imagery, Consciousness*, as a "circuit breaker" to experiencing the flow of time as continuous. As I show in chapter 1, something like this surprise-startle affect is also central to Peirce's theory of indexicality. Tomkins described the surprise-startle affect, metaphorically, as a generally neutral response to "any visitor to consciousness who has outstayed his welcome." In documentary film production, film viewing, and performance, being startled often results from sensations that lead to a heightened awareness of contingency or stakes. We might think of this "visitor to consciousness" as an understanding of the world shaken by what has just been experienced in an encounter with a film or performance event. Becoming conscious of the history of another startles us. The experiencing subject must attend "momentarily to that massive, dense feedback from the startle response," in Tomkins's terms, with enough energy to allow for the integration of new information about the world.[62] It is a starting point for thinking about indexicality in the body and is analogous, in some respects, to the brief exposure of light to celluloid otherwise continuously existing in the darkness of the enclosed camera.

Sedgwick saw in Tomkins's writing on affect a way to theorize identity, art, and the bonds of affiliation without recourse to esoteric Deleuzian concepts, ideology critique, or the "paranoid position" of prevailing critical theory focused on naming all-powerful, world-shaping forces always hidden away from view. Through Sedgwick and her coauthor Frank's endorsement and republication of his selected writings, Tomkins reemerged as a figure of debate in fields outside his roots in psychological and cognitive science research. His work was taken up in critical areas including feminist film studies, game studies, and media ecology, among others.[63] These scholars' attention to the descriptive sections of Tomkins's writing on the affects bracketed out his overarching framework, following Sedgwick and Frank's lead to forego the "irresistibly easy discreditation" of Tomkins's underlying quest to prove the existence of a universal, innate affect system. "You don't have to be long out of theory kindergarten," they quipped, "to make mincemeat of, let's say, a psychology that depends on the separate existence of eight (only sometimes it's nine) distinct affects hardwired into the human biological system."[64]

Such bracketing was bound to attract a critic. In a provocative essay published in *Critical Inquiry* in 2011, Ruth Leys made mincemeat of Tomkins's project and the affective turn that followed it, a position she expanded into *The Ascent of Affect*, a genealogical monograph on debates over the character of emotions, feelings, and affects within the fields of behavioral psychology and cognitive science dating to the 1950s. She noted that Tomkins was more philosopher than experimental scientist and that his notion that humans are born with a self-corrective affect response system came out of his creative reading of cybernetic theory rather than extensive empirical studies with human subjects. In the hands of protégé Paul Ekman, who claimed to affirm Tomkins's ideas in empirical, cross-cultural emotion-identification tests with still photographs, this "basic emotions theory" came to orient persuasion consulting for business- and military-funded facial recognition research and the design of eye-tracking software interfaces. Leys also noted that Ekman's claims remain in dispute within cognitive science.[65]

But while Leys focused most squarely on debunking the basic emotions theory of Tomkins and Ekman, her concluding chapter assessed Deleuzian affect theorists as similarly problematic. If the aims of affect theorists working in critical theory traditions are to radically reimagine an emancipatory culture free from the blame game of political discourse, the constraints of language categories, and the disciplinary force of ideological positions, then she deemed the efforts so far to be a failure. Leys saw in the argument for the political significance of preconscious, nonintentional, autonomic affects, in effect, a paradigm that must also "mystify the realities of globalization and provide convenient support for, not a critique of, global capitalism and neoliberalism." Actor network theory, new materialism, neurohistory, and affect theory alike, she claimed, "call into question our usual understanding of human responsibility" and thereby offer an alibi to "company owners, energy traders and deregulators whose blame for the catastrophe would be attenuated."[66] In other words, while cultural theorists since Sedgwick sidestepped investigating the validity of Tomkins's claims, it is worse that, in working to affirm the irreducible uniqueness of individual subjects and the unpredictable essence of affective charges, they divested themselves from politics that could be actualized in the world. Or, to quote from Eugenie Brinkema's formidable argument for a return to close textual analysis in film studies, *The Forms of the Affects*, "the return to affect on the part of critics from wildly divergent disciplinary backgrounds... leaves intact the very ideological, aesthetic, and theoretical problems it claimed to confront.... *Affect is not where reading is no longer needed.*"[67]

I read this line of argument as less a rejection of affect research per se than a call to reengage critical language and political accountability in the exploration of such concepts when and where possible. Documentary scholar Pooja Rangan, for example, followed concepts of intersubjectivity and affect in Cartwright's writing on childhood and disability in film to offer a trenchant postcolonial critique of "immediations," her term for the realist aesthetics in participatory documentaries aiming to communicate the immediacy and urgency of humanitarian crises. She argued that such films exploit the liberal imaginary of subaltern voices speaking to in fact reify inequalities they purport to redress: "Endangered, dehumanized life not only sustains documentary, but supplies its raison d'etre."[68] When survival is at stake, she argues, underlying political issues take a back seat to a rhetoric about "saving" particular lives. The participatory documentary *Born into Brothels* (2004), for instance, follows a female British photographer who somewhat unconsciously teaches the children of Kolkata sex workers to photograph their lives as emblems of childhood innocence that might be saleable to wealthy philanthropists on an international art market. Rangan's book identifies intractable problems with humanist positions on affect, attention, perception, consciousness, and desire in a global documentary film economy creating and created through vast cultural and economic differences between film subjects and viewers.

When I write here about camerawork carried out in simulation documentaries, I aim to account for affective experiences and sensations without losing sight of political accountability. Camerawork is a form of affective labor, and in nonfiction traditions of camerawork that aim to follow everyday events and sensory textures without too many interviews or breaks in flow, it remains a responsive, quasi-improvisational craft. Camerawork seeks out moments of unpredictability and contingency within otherwise reliable structures of representational practice (framing, sound recording, movement, anticipation of editing, etc.). Moments of heightened affective intensity unfolding spontaneously in the cameraperson's field of perception tend to draw the attention of the camera. To gaze on the world is to imbue it with fascination (perhaps dangerously) and to hold it up for the regard of somewhat unknowable others in somewhat unknowable futures. In this way, camerawork draws on the kinds of affect categories that Deleuzians have identified as operational in various types of cinema (camerapersons may have these in mind as they record objects, landscapes, or unfolding activity) and on something close to the affects that Tomkins, Sedgwick, and their followers have associated with the evolution of human attention and motivation (camerapersons participate actively in interpersonal interactions by aiming the camera at and speaking with individuals who endure, explain, fight, cry, or converse).

Whereas camerapersons recording everyday life may long have envisioned themselves serving as surrogate witnesses to events for future spectators, they cannot follow the same rules and imagine to serve the same function when they record amid simulation documentaries. Simulation documentaries make use of performing bodies, props, and staging in part to direct the attention of camerapersons and then provide verbal explanations for the events just filmed. There is a danger that recording in the realist mode will be complicit by default with the aims of the simulation itself. When I write about conducting camerawork amid simulation scenarios, however, I do not operate strictly in reaction to affective sensations on site. To conduct a media phenomenology of camerawork is thus in part to invert the dictum of a filmmaker I greatly admire, Russian documentarist Dziga Vertov. "We cannot improve the making of our eyes," he wrote in 1923 amid a bout of revolutionary fervor for mechanization, "but we can endlessly perfect the camera."[69] But in writing about camerawork, I can historicize, double back, and decode the cinematic conventions in play. I can try to interpret how the cinematic lures drew my camera, question the political intent behind such designs, and speculate about what I missed in the flurry of ongoing everyday activity to be filmed. I can begin to regard the phenomenon of simulation documentary as a critic rather than a cog. I can treat my own flesh with camera extension in tow as a kind of inscriptive substrate, measuring affect performed for my camera as I record. The camera becomes part of my skin, part of my screen. I can become a theorist of camerawork performance amid simulation, striving to articulate its traps, limitations, and peculiar possibilities.

METHODS: CROSSING SENSORY CINEMA AND MEDIA PHENOMENOLOGY

My method crosses media phenomenology as applied to my own experiences of ethnographic camerawork with a genealogical approach to discourses about the real in each case study. Reenactments and simulation performances are recursive practices and so offer traces in textual and cinematic accounts about affects, attitudes, narratives, and rationales associated with recurring performance events. I piece together changing discourses about sites and practices over time through interviews with key organizers, media workers, and actors, as well as archival research and close analysis of moving-image materials and written reports.

I cross two relatively distinct strains of writing in media phenomenology. Within the field of visual anthropology, sensory ethnographic filmmakers advocate for treating film productions on the sensory textures of everyday life in diverse communities as a form of scholarship. These proponents of sensory ethnographic filming, observational cinema, and sensory vérité write reflexively about the processes of realist camerawork and editing conducted during ethnographic fieldwork for a growing audience of anthropologists who see audiovisual media offering a means to communicate the sense of other peoples and places differently than can written theory.[70] Deeply invested in the technological aspects of indexicality afforded by cameras and microphones but less concerned than film studies theorists about distinctions between celluloid and digital chips, these practitioners tend to eschew voice-over, music, acted scenes, and montage editing so as to maximally communicate the visual and aural perspective of the filmmaker while immersed in a given culture or environment. Within film studies, a group of writers largely coming from feminist theory traditions has adapted the phenomenological method (attending to the feeling of being) to write about embodied experiences of media spectatorship. Rather than focus on unmet desire and lack in spectatorship, they provide a "thick and *radical description*" of personal, contingent cinema and media experiences as tools for analyzing culture and practicing "a healthy and adult polymorphousness, a freedom of becoming."[71]

While the practices of camerawork I employ and write about in this book largely follow tenets theorized in the visual anthropology tradition, I analyze the phenomenological experience of my camerawork using the tools and techniques of the feminist film phenomenology tradition. Sensory ethnographic footage offers a useful memory aid for my writing, but as with the experience of cinema viewing, the encounter between body and cinematic code in my case studies occurs outside the field of view, in affective experience and memory. As I show explicitly in chapter 1, noninterventionist camerawork can function as its own form of reenactment within simulation documentaries, undercutting the realist rationale for observational and ethnographic recording styles. To interpret the peculiar dynamics of camerawork in simulation documentaries, then, I especially rely on feminist media phenomenology in the chapters that follow. I hedge against solipsism inherent to phenomenological and autobiographical writing by situating my phenomenologies of camerawork within archival-historical research on others' experiences of the sites in question and through semiotic analysis of others' documentary films about similar sites or situations.

ETHICAL ORIENTATION AND CHAPTER SUMMARIES

Though I theorize all three case studies in the book as simulation documentaries, spokespersons for each group account differently for the ethics of their institution's reenactment of others' traumatic experiences. It is not self-evident, after all, that playacting others' pain would—or even could—have an ethical center. How is such activity not either a form of "possessive individualism" attuned to consumption within an experience economy or a scandalous form of theft?[72] Leaders of the groups analyzed in this book are wary of such critiques and account for the ethics of their reenactments as a form of commemoration (chap. 1), training (chap. 2), or advocacy for justice (chaps. 3 and 4). These ethical accounts and their potential blind spots are important to understand as a starting point in the project, and so I offer brief explanations here as part of the chapter summaries.

For my own part, as a critical researcher and writer considering camerawork and performance practice, I am placing some measure of faith in the power of language to describe, critique, understand, and help organize lived phenomena that are often inchoate. I see this approach as ethical insofar as it minimizes risk to participants; leads the reader to new thinking about things felt, seen, and heard; and develops concepts to frame somatic, social, and psychic inequities.[73] Following standard ethnographic research practice, I use pseudonyms for interviewees unless they already had a public profile and explicitly asked me to use their actual names. On occasion, an interviewee speaking about their experience in a reenactment or simulation would recall a traumatic event from their own past, a highly unpleasant experience that can make it more difficult for some individuals to heal. In many cases, however, retelling painful stories in safe conditions can contribute to healing.[74] To this end, I tried to interview participants in places where they felt comfortable—living rooms, quiet kitchen tables, and familiar cafés of their choosing—to mitigate risks of harm. Where subjects were willing and able to participate in reenactment events in public and conduct interviews with the press, I deemed further risk of harm to their speaking about role-playing to be minimal.

"Being There Again: Reenacting Camerawork in *In Country* (2014)" (chap. 1) develops a critique of noninterventionist cinema styles in the context of simulation documentaries by conducting a close analysis of camerawork and performance in *In Country* (Attie and O'Hara, 2014). Building on insights drawn from making my own reverse ethnography feature documentary about participating with a group of Revolutionary War reenactors in New England, this chapter reconsiders assumptions about temporality and presence in observational camerawork when used to film simulation documentaries. I trace a genealogy of indexicality in reiterative labor and performance practice rather than the camera's mechanical reproducibility, which I argue better explains the function of camerawork in this film and in others by extension. I adapt Marks's theory of the "recollection-object" to identify three ways that camerawork reenacts in *In Country*, in a gestural touch on crisis coverage, an archived repertoire, and a process of psychic repair. The chapter is also in conversation with Ken Burns and Lynn Novick's *The Vietnam War*, Baron's book *The Archive Effect*, the legacy of American direct cinema, and the noninterventionist work of and rationale for the Sensory Ethnography Lab at Harvard.

The group of reenactors featured in the film, like many other units of war reenactors, espouses an ethics of commemoration. They say that they reenact the Vietnam War to honor those soldiers who fought and died for their country, and individuals' feelings about the rationale for the war itself are secondary to this concern. Many participants featured in the film are veterans, and they believe that their participation cements a kind of intergenerational bond among soldiers. It may also serve as a way for some individuals to cope with post-traumatic stress, as several tell the filmmakers in interviews featured in the film. Within the ethics of commemoration, however, there are potential blind spots to issues of inclusion, authenticity, and justice. The reenactors do not address atrocities carried out by US soldiers against North Vietnamese civilians, the flawed rationale for the war or lies the Johnson and Nixon administrations told the public about it, or the use of racist, dehumanizing, "authentic" language in the reenactment itself. From a critical perspective, these aspects of the reenactment (and to some extent the film about it) are ethical shortcomings. The filmmakers, who follow and honor their subjects in the spirit of understanding them, mostly reproduce the ethical orientation of the reenacting troupe.

"Weaponizing Affect: A Film Phenomenology of 3D Military Training Simulations during the Iraq War" (chap. 2) considers the place of camerawork and other forms of cinematic labor in the production of military training simulation scenarios during the Iraq War. Drawing from a phenomenology of my own camerawork at the Fort Irwin National Training Center during visits in 2007 and 2012, Tomkins's concept of "ideo-affective orders," ethnographic interviews, and archival research, I analyze three-dimensional military training simulation scenarios developed during the Iraq War in the Mojave Desert of California.[75] Following news reports of torture at Abu Ghraib, the US military began to implement cultural awareness training for all troops set to deploy to the Middle East. The military contracted with Hollywood special-effects studios to develop a series of counterinsurgency warfare immersive-training simulations, including hiring Iraqi American and Afghan American citizens to play villagers, mayors, and insurgents in scenarios. My primary question centers on the military technoscience of treating human bodies as variables for affective attunement in a reiterative simulation scenario.

Here, the ethical orientation of the institution in question centers on training. Spokespersons say that reenacting attacks from the recent past in Iraq to simulate potential events in the near future serves to save the lives of American soldiers. This assertion justifies all role-playing decisions within the scenarios, including those by hired Iraqi American actors and local townspeople. It is an ethics justified by a rhetoric of urgency: training soldiers to be hypervigilant about potential threats and highly distrustful of civilians may keep them alive in a war zone in the very near future. Within the military, there may be some individuals who disagree with the rationale for war or the tactics decided on by commanders, but they can rationalize their contributions to the overall effort by saying that they save lives by improving safety, cross-cultural understanding, and troop performance. This seems to be the narrative communicated to nearly all visiting journalists and filmmakers to the fort, ostensibly in the spirit of transparency and the public's right to know—at least, nearly all visiting journalists and filmers pass the saving-lives ethical rationale on to their readers and viewers. I critique this ethical orientation due to the lack of access to perspectives from Iraqi civilians living through the war, the video-game-level presentation of violence, and the staging of access for documentarians and the press to observe training.

Chapters 3 and 4 focus on the Moore's Ford Lynching Reenactment, which centers on an ethics of opposition and advocacy for justice. Organizers rationalize the reenactment of the quadruple lynching as a means of honoring the victims and seeking the arrest and prosecution of perpetrators in their names.

They also view the reenactment as part of a broader movement for Black dignity and voting rights, which motivated multiple lynchings in 1946 and remain contentious policy issues in Georgia. The reenactment is a powerful symbol that moves a particular collective to action, they say, and so they foreground descendants of lynching victims and oral history accounts of Black community elders in their staging decisions, which in turn arouse strong affective sentiments among attendees. This ethical orientation collides with those of historians who have studied this case in the archives and disagree with the historical accuracy of key points in the performed narrative, as I discuss in chapter 3. The reenactment has also fractured the once-biracial local organizing committee along the lines of race. But significantly, of the three case studies in the book, this is the one that has deployed reenactment and the indexicality of the body to achieve social change. It is the one that provides an oppositional, affective framework from which to invert dominant narratives past and present about race and criminality.

"'Do You Want to Play a Klansman?' Lynching Photography, Civil Rights Camerawork, and the Moore's Ford Lynching Reenactment in Georgia" (chap. 3) analyzes how and why this reenactment originated, changed over time, and shaped public perceptions about a crime for which little physical or photographic evidence still exists. Performance studies scholars and rhetoricians have written about this reenactment by focusing on race and memory, healing, and community reconciliation, but less on the ways that the reenactment functions as a media strategy for a social movement. I trace the reenactment as a media strategy to two divergent photographic practices: first, of spectacle lynchings in the South between 1893 and 1936, and second, of the development during the civil rights movement of a media strategy centered on television coverage. I propose that the Moore's Ford Lynching Reenactment confronts the community-making elements of the first through reappropriation and deploys staging strategies in keeping with the second. I conclude this chapter with an analysis of camerawork in Keith Beauchamp's TV documentary *Murder in Black and White* (2008) and then my own in 2012 for Olive's film *Always in Season* (2019).[76]

"Establishing a Black Affective Infrastructure: From Lynching Performance in the Hollywood of the South to *Always in Season* (2019)" (chap. 4) revisits the lynching reenactment in Georgia in the wake of the narrow and controversial defeat of the first Black, female gubernatorial candidate in US history, Stacey Abrams, in 2018. I note and consider the exponential increase in the number of cameras filming every aspect of the 2019 reenactment in a region now dubbed the Hollywood of the South for the state's success in using tax breaks to lure studio dollars to Georgia. Following Lauren Berlant, I propose thinking of the annual Moore's Ford Lynching Reenactment as an affective infrastructure, or a tool, so to speak, for contextualizing stories about Black death in the South. I then analyze the use of the Moore's Ford story in Olive's *Always in Season* (2019), which won a special jury prize for moral urgency following its premiere at the Sundance Film Festival in 2019 and aired on the national PBS documentary program Independent Lens in February 2020. I focus especially on the representation of the lynching in the film, which employs what I call an *oppositional acousmetre* at odds with the aspirations toward dramatic realism at the reenactment itself.

The conclusion, "Toward an Embodied Social Cinema," offers directions for theoretical and practical work that build on notions of intersubjectivity, distributed authorship, reenactment performance, and interracial collaboration suggested in the book. I reflect on the place of camerawork in the Black Lives Matter protests that erupted in the wake of the murder of George Floyd by former Minneapolis police officer Derek Chauvin and three others in May 2020, recorded in a single long take by then-seventeen-year-old community resident Darnella Frazier. I consider the debate that emerged within days of the publication of her video about how to characterize its aesthetics and impact, and I note the ways that the video itself inspired symbolic, memorial reenactments across the country. Framing her camerawork as a form of resistance rather than documentation or cinema vérité per se, I propose exploring how such nascent simulation documentaries express embodied social sense rather than point of view.

NOTES

1. A scandalous event in the context of nascent Cold War geopolitics made especially poignant by the fact that Dorsey was a World War II veteran and prospective voter, this "last mass lynching in America" set off months of activism, the first federal commission on civil rights, and extensive FBI investigations that amounted to nothing in the face of community silence—unbroken to this day. Talmadge won the election in 1946, and no one was prosecuted for the lynching. See a contextualization and reception study of this event in Childers, "Transforming Violence," 573–74.
2. Dai Vaughan, quoted in Lee, "Beyond the Ethico-aesthetic," 140.
3. Grimshaw and Ravetz, *Observational Cinema*, 118–19.
4. I flesh out the debate within visual anthropology over salvage ethnography, the sensory qualities of observational cinema, and affect in Rice, "Salvaging the Bees." See also Clough and Halley, *Affective Turn*; Stevenson and Kohn, "Leviathan"; Lee, "Beyond the Ethico-Aesthetic."
5. Emphasis in the original text. Mbembe, *Out of the Dark Night*, 19.

6. According to the American Psychological Association, trauma refers to "an emotional response to a terrible event like an accident, rape or natural disaster" that frequently results in shock, denial, emotional strain, or the repression of conscious memory. Maria Yellow Horse Brave Heart and Lemyra DeBruyn used the terms *historical trauma* and *historical unresolved grief* to refer to the lingering effects of sustained oppression and violence across multiple generations on a targeted group such as Jewish Europeans, the descendants of enslaved Africans and Black Americans in North America, and Native Americans that the US government forcibly displaced from ancestral lands. The place of the camera in documenting peoples who struggle to survive in the wake of historical trauma is complicated. On the one hand, as RaMell Ross put it in his poetic reflection on filming *Hale County This Morning, This Evening* (2018), "the God of the camera is a colonizer" that often ensures a "peculiar death of the imaginable" for those on the receiving end of its gaze. The camera tends to objectify human subjects and make them stand for something outside of their control, thus reproducing the winnowing of their agency in a harmful way. On the other hand, witnessing and acknowledging past wrongs has long been recognized as a starting point for creating a collective movement for justice and healing, and to this end, the camera can play a crucial part in organizing momentum and helping a community create and communicate an affirming identity or achieve shared goals. Angela Aguayo, for example, cited film reviews and materials from Black-owned company archives even during the silent era to show how national Black leaders created documentary films (no longer in existence to see as such) to "challenge commonsense thinking around race and labor," especially after the release of *The Birth of a Nation*. The tension between these two functions of camerawork in simulation documentaries is a central theme in the book, and I return to it in each chapter in different ways. As a starting point in the vast literature on the impacts of trauma and historical trauma in oppressed groups and the cinematic representation of living with trauma, see Walker, *Trauma Cinema*, 4; Ross, "Renew the Encounter," 17; Brave Heart and DeBruyn, "American Indian Holocaust"; Marks, *Skin of the Film*; Kaplan, *Trauma Culture*; Torchin, *Creating the Witness*; Van der Kolk, *Body Keeps the Score*; Malkowski, *Dying in Full Detail*; Aguayo, *Documentary Resistance*, 110.

7. See Zimmerman and De Michiel, *Open Space New Media Documentary*.

8. This line of thought follows the paradigm of "distributed cognition" (DC), a term coined by cognitive scientist Edwin Hutchins (1995) to describe "cognitive systems" that include human actors, machines, objects, and environmental contexts collaborating somewhat unwittingly on behalf of a bounded system's goal-oriented behavior. Cognition, in this way of thinking, takes place outside the individual brain and so should be studied "in the wild" (rather than in a lab) by observing and experiencing interactions among people and things. While this idea was not generally taken up as a theory or method in the field of film studies (except in Cartwright's *Moral Spectatorship* and Karen Pearlman's "Documentary Editing and Distributed Cognition" in *Cognitive Theory and Documentary Film*), I see my approach and questions as appropriate for a loose DC framework. In my case studies, I cross the film phenomenological method as applied to experiences of camerawork and reenactment with a DC-inspired understanding of context, nonhuman agency, and history as embedded in objects, landscapes, and gestures. Protevi's theory of political affect in the domain of the social and somatic provides language helpful to my overall approach. See Hutchins, *Cognition in the Wild*; Cartwright, *Moral Spectatorship*; Pearlman, "Documentary Editing and Distributed Cognition"; Protevi, *Political Affect*, xi.

9. Azoulay, *Civil Contract of Photography*, 12–13.

10. Phelan, *Unmarked*.

11. In his introduction to a key dossier on reenactment in documentary film, Jonathan Kahana noted a correspondence between the documentary films of George Stoney from the 1950s and a flurry of films released in the early 2000s, equally carried out under principles akin to those of Italian neorealist Cesare Zavattini. Ordinary people in reenactment cinema can "give themselves and others a 'second chance,'" Kahana explained of this renewed rationale for reenactment in documentary, "when psychological or social circumstances have initially prevented them from acting as they would have liked." As with psychodrama, the momentum of such "social actor documentaries," as Rowena Santos-Aquino called them, often aims at personal growth, healing from trauma, or community reconciliation through what Ivonne Marguiles characterized as "a dynamic between repetition and alienation" from which a broader viewing public might learn. Nonfiction films of this sort include *Close Up* (1990), *The Battle of Orgreave* (2001), *Bombay Beach* (2011), *Tower* (2016), and *Bisbee '17* (2017). In contrast, *The Act of Killing* (2012) uses social actor reenactment techniques with the executioners of genocide rather than everyday people to craft a critique of state corruption. Working at the nexus of social solidarity rather than social actor dynamics are recent projects including Dread Scott and John Akomfrah's *Slave Rebellion Reenactment*, a participatory, community-based reenactment of the largest slave revolt in US history staged and filmed in and around New Orleans on November 8–9, 2019, and Irene Lusztig's thought-provoking *Yours in Sisterhood* (2018), which employs the technique of embodied listening to allow contemporary women to read and reflect on letters written to the editor of *Ms. Magazine* in the 1970s. Lusztig spent years traveling across the country to cast and film contemporary readers from the towns from which the 1970s letters had been sent, documenting processes of identification with and resistance to the surrogacy required of reading. "I think there is something about simply repeating something, putting someone's words into your body enough times that you start to actually feel different," Lusztig explained. I expanded on this analysis of reenactment and memory in Lusztig's documentaries in my article "The Sense of Feminism Then and Now." See also Kahana, "Introduction," 46–47; Margulies, "Exemplary Bodies," 217; Kipper, "Emergence of Role Playing," 106; Santos Aquino, "Necessary Fictions"; Lazic, "Irene Lusztig"; Simblist, "Dread Scott's Struggle."

12. This direction for reenactment filming is more about public interest issues than social actors getting a second chance. Initiated during the civil rights and antiwar movements by groups including the Living Theatre, Open Theatre, and Teatro Campesino, documentary and verbatim theater practitioners compiled their scripts entirely from archival sources to mitigate accusations of sensationalism and subjectivity. More recent works have played with gender and race dynamics entailed in acting out transcripts. A key example of this intersection between verbatim theater and documentary film is Anna Deveare Smith's *Twilight: Los Angeles* (2000), in which she videotaped interviews with dozens of Los Angelinos responding to the Rodney King beating video, verdict, and uprising and then acted out selected transcripts of many interviewees in a one-woman performance that was later recorded for the PBS documentary. For many years, the film was used to spur role-play pedagogy in California's K-12 classrooms. The *New York Times* reprised these techniques in its "Verbatim" Op-Doc video series in the absurd deposition transcript "What Is a Photocopier?" (2014) and the staging of testimony from the police killing of Michael Brown in "The Ferguson Case" (2015). See a brief synopsis of this tradition in Odendahl-James, "History of U.S. Documentary Theatre"; Watanabe, "When Time Allows"; *New York Times*, "Ferguson Case, Verbatim"; *New York Times*, "Verbatim"; Smith et al., *Twilight—Los Angeles*.

13. Emphasis in the original text. Guynn, *Unspeakable Histories*, 2–3.

14. Perhaps especially notable in the context of this study is the post-2000 proliferation of documentary films about reenactments as components of everyday life rather than as a means to visualize events that could not be filmed. While Errol Morris's canonical *The Thin Blue Line* (1988) employed reenactment scenes to illustrate a *Rashomon*-style set of contradictions in witness accounts of a murder case, films such as *Patriot's Day* (2004), *Full Battle Rattle* (2008), *In Country* (2014), *Bisbee '17* (2018), and *Always in Season* (2019) instead employ realist camerawork and editing techniques to document people who spend portions of their lives reenacting historical events. The quotation here comes from P. Auslander, *Reactivations*.

15. Boyle, "Shattering Silence," 100.

16. In his insightful article on the documentarian's dilemma in a "post-truth society," Dirk Eitzen argued that in documentaries centered on storytelling style over information and argument, such as *The Jinx*, the ambiguity of evidence can play a helpful part in driving the plot. These films exploit ambiguity to interpolate viewers as insiders to rumor, offering "social and emotional validation" to this community now in the know. In the context of Trumpism, he is alarmed by such trends. Eitzen, "Duties of Documentary," 96. Also see a disturbing account of the reemergence of fascist rhetoric, for instance, in Stanley, *How Fascism Works*.

17. Richardson, *Bearing Witness While Black*.

18. Oliver, *Witnessing*, 98.

19. Samuel DuBois Cook Center on Social Equity at Duke University, "Film Question and Answer Session."

20. See articulations of these forms in Nichols, *Representing Reality*; Bruzzi, *New Documentary*; Rangan, *Immediations*; MacDougall and Castaing-Taylor, *Transcultural Cinema*; Marks, *Skin of the Film*; MacDougall, *Corporeal Image*; Grimshaw and Ravetz, *Observational Cinema*; Gabriel, *Third Cinema*; Rouch and Feld, *Ciné-Ethnography*; Bellman and Jules-Rosette, *Paradigm for Looking*.

21. Significant works on reenactment include Anderson, *Time Machines*; Handler and Saxton, "Dyssimulation"; Cullen, *Civil War in Popular Culture*; Walker, *Trauma Cinema*; Blatner, "Morenean Approaches"; Magelssen, "Rehearsing the 'Warrior Ethos'"; Magelssen, *Living History Museums*; Magelssen, *Simming*; Kahana, "Introduction"; McCalman and Pickering, *Historical Reenactment*; Schneider, *Performing Remains*; A. Jones and Heathfield, *Perform, Repeat, Record*; P. Auslander, *Reactivations*.

22. Peirce, *Philosophical Writings of Peirce*, 98.

23. Bazin, *What Is Cinema?*, 14.

24. Gaines, "Introduction," 6.

25. Winston, Vanstone, and Wang, *Act of Documenting*, 26.

26. Manovich, "What Is Digital Cinema?," 1.

27. Ibid., 1–2.

28. Whissel, *Spectacular Digital Effects*; Prince, *Digital Visual Effects in Cinema*; Rehak, *More Than Meets the Eye*; Winston, Vanstone, and Wang, *Act of Documenting*, 15–17.

29. With the development of consumer technologies for producing deepfakes, however, cost may be less relevant in the coming years. For example, see Rini, "Deepfakes Are Coming."

30. Many of the works from this era on the affordances of video focus on documentary, including Renov, *Subject of Documentary*; Rosen, *Change Mummified*; Wahlberg, *Documentary Time*, xiv; Belton, "World in the Palm"; Razsa, "Beyond Riot Porn."

31. Malkowski, *Dying in Full Detail*, 7.

32. Ibid., 8.

33. For example, Russian documentarian Marina Goldovskaya wrote the following reflection on filming *The Prince Is Back* (2000) on DV: "I must confess that never before did I feel so good and free as during the making of [my first digital] film.... Whenever you work for someone, you feel a sense of responsibility: they gave you money to film, and you must kill yourself to get it done on time. In this case, for the first time in my entire career, I was completely free." Goldovskaya, *Woman with a Movie Camera*, 206.

34. Razsa, "Beyond Riot Porn," 9.

35. While not the focus of this book, the experience of filming and editing my first-person documentary *About Face! Reenacting in a Time of War* (2010), about performing in reenactments of the American Revolutionary War to trace proxy discussions of war in the years after the 9/11 attacks, informs my approach to analysis here. In chapter 1, I reflect on ethical questions raised by following a realist epistemology in documenting reenactment.

36. Frosh, "Gestural Image," 1609; Hagood, "Emotional Rescue."

37. One interesting line of documentary studies research in the 2010s focused on how digital technologies afford—or even demand—the creation of new kinds of spaces and communities for screening and discussion. In some cases, the spaces are online, and the communities framed to include the technologies that enable ongoing connection. Summerhayes, for example, viewed the spatially and temporally discontinuous image mapping on the "Crisis in Darfur" website as "examples of new documentary gestures that are emerging on the web," with the people forced far from home and the images themselves together constituting an "intimate community." Zimmerman and De Michiel, on the other hand, see advantages in the digital context for foregrounding "open space," no-budget filmmaking, community events, and quickly made shorts that aim to foster dialogue about local issues of public import. Juhasz emphasized that, faced with the data-mining defaults of proprietary social media platforms, temporarily leaving digital spaces is what now creates possibilities for "realms of behaviour, interaction, and feelings that are not ownable." Jihoon Kim synthesizes a lot of this conversation in *Documentary's Expanded Fields*, a monograph that blends documentary theory and new media theory to consider interactive documentaries, multiscreen installation work, nonfiction virtual reality experiences, augmented reality works, and online vernacular activism in social movements, among other topics. See Summerhayes, "Web-Weaving," 83–84; Zimmerman and De Michiel, *Open Space New Media Documentary*; Juhasz, "Ceding the Activist Digital Documentary," 46; Kim, *Documentary's Expanded Fields*.

38. Activist-ethnographer Maple Razsa argues that the affective dimensions of the collective viewing of "riot porn" among his antiauthoritarian Croatian activist subjects catalyzed mimesis—a politics inextricable from ongoing media practices but not, in his view, thereby antithetical to "political intimacy, even love." See Razsa, "Beyond Riot Porn," 4, 23.

39. Gaines, "Political Mimesis," 84.

40. I see the concept of reenactment offering a provocative lens on claims sometimes attributed to digital devices. Anne Friedberg's protégé Heidi Rae Cooley, for instance, characterized "the moment of texting, imaging, or posting" in language that performance theorists use to describe the experience of participating in reenactment: we "materialize our feeling, our thinking, thereby actualizing ourselves as signs," she says. See Cooley, *Finding Augusta*, 48.

41. Tom Gunning, quoted in Malkowski, *Dying in Full Detail*, 8.

42. Bazin, *What Is Cinema?*; Sobchack, *Address of the Eye*; Marks, *Skin of the Film*; Margulies, "Exemplary Bodies"; Sobchack, *Carnal Thoughts*; Lippit, *Atomic Light (Shadow Optics)*; Walker, *Trauma Cinema*; Keeling, *Witch's Flight*; Smaill, *Documentary*; Torchin, *Creating the Witness*; Baron, *Archive Effect*; Malkowski, *Dying in Full Detail*; Richardson, *Bearing Witness While Black*.

43. Walker, *Trauma Cinema*, 4.

44. My thinking through the projector box, phenomenology, and intersubjectivity is a riff on and response to Cartwright, "Hands of the Projectionist."

45. Renov, "Toward a Poetics of Documentary."

46. *Oxford English Dictionary*, s.v. "simulation," accessed April 8, 2022, https://www.oed.com/view/Entry/180009.

47. See, for instance, Hayles, *How We Became Posthuman*; Mossner, "Engaging Animals in Wildlife Documentaries," 169; Goldman, *Simulating Minds*; Baudrillard and Glaser, *Simulacra and Simulation*; Cubitt, *Simulation and Social Theory*; Cross, Hamilton, and Grafton, "Building a Motor Simulation"; Rizzolatti and Fabbri-Destro, "Mirror Neurons," 223; Doidge, *Brain That Changes Itself*.

48. Baudrillard and Poster, *Jean Baudrillard*, 19, 22.

49. Emphasis in the original text. Ibid., 46.

50. Affect is an old concept in this regard, dating at least to Baruch Spinoza's *Ethics* (1677), which parsed three affects—joy, sadness, and desire—as our baseline bodily responses to stimuli in the world. More recent research on affect still considers bodily responses to perceptions of our surroundings and art, but it diverges on the particulars of how and why affect moves us. See, for example, Massumi, *Parables for the Virtual*; Gregg and Seigworth, *Affect Theory Reader*; Hagood, *Hush*; Ott, "Affect in Critical Studies."

51. Massumi reiterates this argument in subsequent publications. While highly critical of the use of affect theory by humanities scholars, Ruth Leys accepts this premise as foundational for both Deleuzian theorists and those following Tomkins's basic emotions theory. See especially the exhaustive literature review in "The Turn to Affect," a reprint of Leys's article of the same name published in *Critical Inquiry* in 2011, in Leys, *Ascent of Affect*. See also Massumi, *99 Theses*, 8–9.

52. Gregg and Seigworth, "Inventory of Shimmers," 4.

53. Ott, "Affect in Critical Studies"; Leys, "Turn to Affect."

54. Clough and Halley, *Affective Turn*, 6. See also Sobchack, *Address of the Eye*; Marks, *Skin of the Film*; Keeling, *Witch's Flight*; Baron, *Archive Effect*.

55. Cartwright, *Moral Spectatorship*; Smaill, *Documentary*; Rangan, *Immediations*; Sedgwick, Frank, and Alexander, *Shame and Its Sisters*.

56. Sobchack, *Address of the Eye*.

57. Marks, *Skin of the Film*, 150.

58. Deleuze quoted in Marks, *Skin of the Film*, 27.

59. Emphasis in the original text. Ibid., xv, 5, 28, 253.

60. New media theorist Nick Montfort began using the term *screen essentialist* in early 2000s conference presentations. Theorists of media infrastructure have since taken aim at screen essentialism in media studies to push the field beyond analyses of content and representation. While not focused on the brute, material qualities of technological artifacts, I see my project in dialogue with this gesture. See, for instance, Montfort, "Continuous Paper"; Kirschenbaum, *Mechanisms*, 31–35; L. Parks and Starosielski, *Signal Traffic*.

61. Though questions about memory and repression remain unresolved in behavioral psychotherapy, neuroscience, and psychiatry, several new research areas have built on Tomkins's work or related ideas about the influence of the autonomic nervous system on consciousness and the ways that bodily systems change in response to ordinary and traumatic life events. See Tomkins, *Affect Imagery Consciousness*, xvii, 3; Van der Kolk, *Body Keeps the Score*; Porges, "Emotion," 72–73; Damasio, *Strange Order of Things*; Mayer, *Mind-Gut Connection*. Critical perspectives on the role of a hardwired affect system in shaping attention and consciousness can be found in Leys, *Ascent of Affect*; Barrett, *How Emotions Are Made*.

62. Tomkins, *Affect Imagery Consciousness*, 273–74.

63. See, respectively, Cartwright, *Moral Spectatorship*; Anable, *Playing with Feelings*; Rose, "Silvan Tomkins as Media Ecologist."

64. Sedgwick, Frank, and Alexander, *Shame and Its Sisters*, 2.

65. Tomkins's philosophical orientation in and of itself would not likely have bothered critical theorists who used his work. But of particular concern for the queer and gender theorists embracing Tomkins's writing was his enthusiasm for the take-up of his ideas by researchers who tested them empirically, like Ekman. Elizabeth Wilson and Adam Frank's response to Leys's article in *Critical Inquiry*, for instance, downplayed affiliations between Tomkins and Ekman. Ekman had used results of his experiments to proselytize for the universality of concepts such as anger, enjoyment, and distress as tethered to involuntary facial expressions. Leys shows how Ekman and like-minded colleagues developed the Facial Action Coding System (FACS) to test emotional response to still photographs cross-culturally. Over several decades of research, this team established as dominant Tomkins's speculative claim that core emotions are hardwired and precultural within the fields of neuroscience and behavioral psychology. Leys then noted sharp critics of Ekman's methodologies such as constructivist cognitive scientists Alan Fridlund and Lisa Feldman Barrett, as well as Ekman's ties to persuasion consulting and the military. So I proceed here with caution. Frank and Wilson, "I: Like-Minded"; Leys, *Ascent of Affect*.

66. Leys, *Ascent of Affect*, 343, 347.

67. Emphasis in the original text. Brinkema, *Forms of the Affects*, xiv.

68. Rangan, *Immediations*, 1.

69. Vertov, Michelson, and O'Brien, *Kino-Eye*, 15.

70. See a summary, for instance, in Kasic, "Sensory Vérité."

71. Emphasis in the original text. Sobchack, *Address of the Eye*, xv.

72. This is the argument put forward on the ethnographic study of Civil War reenactments by Handler and Saxton, "Dyssimulation."

73. In line with precepts outlined in Larry Gross et al.'s *Image Ethics* and Pat Aufderheide et al.'s *Honest Truths*, I understand the term *ethics* to signify a set of moral values that shape research design and documentary filmmaking, including informed consent among participants, protecting the vulnerable, fulfilling obligations to sponsors, honoring the reader or viewer's trust, and creating new knowledge attuned to the researcher's interests, limitations, sense of import, and allied constituencies. As the authors of these works admit, even core values such as informed consent are approximations in research and documentary work. One's consent to be represented may change after the signing of a release form, learning more about a project, seeing one's image on screen or in print, or reading public commentary on a film or book in which one appears (at which point it's too late to do much about it). A researcher, moreover, will not likely know exactly what they will say or show about those depicted in their works until after they've had exchanges, observed events, thought a long

time, and written out their ideas. The story they tell about what they're doing and why they're doing it may change, potentially altering the terms on which consent was given. Oppositional film and research projects may also emphasize accountability to the researcher's constituency or community over and above dominant norms that the constituency perceives to be oppressive. Ethics is not one size fits all. See Gross, Katz, and Ruby, *Image Ethics*; Gross, Katz, and Ruby, *Image Ethics in the Digital Age*; Oliver, "Witnessing, Recognition, and Response Ethics"; Aufderheide, Jaszi, and Chandra, *Honest Truths*; Cartwright, *Moral Spectatorship*.

74. See a review of approaches to trauma therapy and their rationales in Van der Kolk, *Body Keeps the Score*.

75. The ethical issues entailed in filming as a form of scholarly research and documentary making are complex. In this case, the Public Affairs Office (PAO) at the Fort Irwin National Training Center facilitated my access to film training simulations that involved hundreds of soldiers. Because it is not feasible to speak with every individual about their consent to be filmed in such scenarios, the PAO grants institutional permission for the press and documentarians to film military personnel carrying out training that they deem to be in the public interest. None are identified by name in this chapter. Any individual with whom I spoke on camera granted explicit, informed consent to do so.

76. I believed that Olive's *Always in Season* had the potential to catalyze important conversations about race and historical trauma, and I came to trust her as the guiding voice for such a project. Over the two weeks I filmed for her documentary, I followed the standard PBS release and consent protocols that she was using and filmed mostly individuals that we had both gotten to know over our time working and in ways that she indicated would be useful to her project. We agreed that I could have access to raw footage for analysis from the series of shoots conducted at Moore's Ford, and she could use the footage I recorded for her film. Within the book, I use those materials for phenomenological analyses of camerawork rather than for information about subjects featured in the footage. I do conduct a close analysis of reenactments and reenactors depicted in Olive's finished film in chapter 4 that draws from publicly available sources. I know and have interviewed many people featured in the film, but I largely use these conversations as background for analysis.

ONE

BEING THERE AGAIN

Reenacting Camerawork in *In Country* (2014)

INTRODUCTION

During the early years of the Vietnam War, while reflecting on camerawork unrelated to the conflict, direct cinema filmmaker Ricky Leacock compared the cameraperson recording everyday life to the voltmeter measuring electrical current. "You design your voltmeter so that very little goes through it," he said. Leacock's ideal cameraperson was copresent with subjects but barely there as a being, concentrating on framing, exposure, focus, and reacting with his camera and his body to live events in their unfolding. "We say we are filmmakers, but in a funny sort of way *we are the audience*. We do not have the burden of a director," he proposed.[1] Numerous critics have taken issue with the aspiration to neutral, quasi-scientific observing in statements like these, but documentary filmmakers still refer to the unique, evidentiary value of *being there* with a camera to justify their practice. Meghan O'Hara, for example, explained her role as a filmmaker on *In Country* (2014), a feature documentary about Oregonian men who reenact battles from the Vietnam War (fig. 1.1), in similar terms to me: "I think we tried to give people watching the film the experience we had being there, as best we could, and used all these cinematic techniques that try to give people that feeling."[2] Privileged proximity to subjects and a willingness to follow their activities with a camera whither they go, this statement suggests, generally reveal valuable cultural insights about the individuals observed. Explicit reference to the filmmaker's body, their politics, or their need to make films relatively quickly for university tenure just gets in the way of that—even betrays a "whiff of cynicism" that contributes to a post-truth discursive context, for some.[3] But in O'Hara's peculiar case, the reenactors' deep investment in collective, embodied mimesis as a route to authentic feeling and discovery about the Vietnam War quite literally shaped how she and coproducer/director

Figure 1.1. The Vietnam War reenactor subjects of *In Country* pose for photos at a parade and allow boys to hold their M-16s, likely a combination of replicas and decommissioned period weapons. Courtesy Mike Attie and Meghan O'Hara.

Mike Attie's observational camerawork could be done. Unlike some other units of reenactors, the subjects of *In Country* perform only for one another and not usually for general audiences or outside observers. Not included in the diegesis of the film is the fact that O'Hara and Attie were dressed as Vietnam-era war correspondents, the reenactors' condition for the filmmakers' access to make the documentary. In other words, the filmmakers had to reenact in order to be there (fig. 1.2).

Being there with a camera so as to avoid the need for staging and reenactment was the explicit goal of 1960s direct cinema and observational cinema practitioners like Leacock, who preferred nimble 16 mm synch sound rigs to the enormous 35 mm studio cameras and the awkwardness of having film subjects "do that again" after setting lights and frame. But the *In Country* filmmakers reenact as filmers with nimble cameras simply to have access to observe, for the first time, the reenacted moments from the Vietnam War. Even though the *In Country* filmmakers do not script the events that they film or direct their subjects about what to do, there is a distinction between the epistemology of their camerawork amid reenactment and that long associated with the observational recording of daily life. There is a tension between the subject, a war reenactment performance of a past event with life-and-death stakes, and the filmmakers' instincts to make the film about the reenactment itself using vérité

Figure 1.2. Filmmakers Meghan O'Hara (*top left*) and Mike Attie (*top right*). The production stills (*middle and bottom*) show the two filmmakers dressed as 1970s war correspondents to roleplay while also recording their documentary. Courtesy Mike Attie and Meghan O'Hara.

methods, which emphasize being there with a camera to attend to events in the present. A reenactment does not follow a "crisis structure" in which the people in front of the observational camera negotiate actual war, unresolved policy issues, or competition in elections, sports tournaments, and spelling bees.[4] Neither does a reenactment offer the observational camera a means honor everyday work and social life for people living in precarity, long an argument for "transcultural cinema" in visual anthropology.[5] Perhaps because neither trajectory was on offer for filmers of this reenactment, the directors admitted in retrospect that their vérité strategy failed on its own terms. "We thought the reenactment would be a little more self-sufficient than it was," O'Hara reflected, that "if you could take [viewers] there you'd see all the layers that we were seeing."[6] But vérité filming turned out to offer a different way to express the layers of reenactment and their connection to the impacts of war in this case, largely because Vietnam-era TV camerapersons filmed in more or less the same way Attie and O'Hara did at the reenactment.

Below, I aim to make sense of this tension by considering camerawork as a live performance practice rather than passive-recording or "voltmeter" work. I argue that the vérité cameraperson's decisions at the moment of recording are indexical gestures touching camerawork of the past. Perhaps because of its inextricable connections to recording, the live act of camerawork has not been considered as a kind of performance through the lens of performance theory, which focuses on liveness and disappearance—qualities theorized to be resistant to image economies premised on camerawork. But performance theory offers analytical tools that may be applied in new ways to questions about the indexicality of the image at the point of production, questions that have long been central to film studies and documentary studies. To paraphrase performance theorist Rebecca Schneider's argument about the materiality of reenactment performance, "a gesture, such as a pointing index finger [or way of pointing the camera while recording], can itself be a remain in the form of an indexical action that haunts (or remains) via live repetition."[7] *In Country* is a limit case for thinking about camerawork as a kind of reenactment performance. It's rare that a film literally has camerapersons reenacting as they record footage (though pushing such a position explicitly offers an intriguing potential avenue for practitioners). But I suggest in this chapter that the return of 1960s-style direct cinema and observational camerawork in institutions such as the Sensory Ethnography Lab at Harvard or the slow cinema movement celebrated at prestigious film festivals often constitutes a reenactment practice, or something like it, in digital culture.[8]

This is not the way that nonfiction filmmakers working within the sensory turn have characterized what they do. Aspirations to be a camera-wielding voltmeter (even one who sticks a hand in the frame on occasion, asks the infrequent question, or drops in a line of voice-over about the troubled look of a subject) so as to more appropriately disappear have changed about as much since the 1960s as men's tuxedos worn to the Academy Awards—that is, with a few exceptions, not too much.[9] In any case, the long takes in observational cinema are in the contemporary moment the antithesis of voltmeter-ish at the point of reception. They tend to shock or disturb viewers—and sometimes in a thought-provoking way—by forcing them to attend to everyday life imagery in a timescale out of synch with the fast-paced editing typical of digital commercial fare. In this context, watching such a film is like participating in a reenactment. It is long, slow, and focused on minute details of lived experience. From this vantage, long takes of pastoral life as received by urban viewers who have no firsthand experience of farming or animal husbandry, such as the forty-five-second close-up of a sheep chewing its cud at the start of *Sweetgrass* (2008, Barbash and Castaing-Taylor), are performative before representational. Like a reenactment, these observational shots conjure temporalities already lost and offer a method to ruminate on details about what such life-worlds might have been like. In filming a reenactment, however, the *In Country* makers found these techniques to be unsatisfying for getting at what their subjects were thinking as they performed. In following men in costume walking through the woods for a weekend before returning to a humdrum workweek on Monday, they found themselves making something closer to a high-production-value home movie for the reenactors, or maybe a collective reenactment of archival footage they'd all seen.

Archives and online video sites remain awash in cinematic materials depicting the Vietnam War. Though more than fifty years in the past, the Vietnam War remains vivid in American collective memory, even as fewer people remain who lived through it. The existence of reenactments testifies to the war's enduring mythology in American life and to a collective desire to return to it in some way, which produces its own effects on those who participate. History played over and over again by reenactors becomes personal; reenactment blends myths of state violence and the intensity of war experience with muscle memory in the body and, perversely, affective sentiments associated with comfort, joy, friendship, and national belonging. Vietnam also seems to return unbidden to discourse and policy making in times of foreign policy trouble. At the time of release, for instance, stories in Ken Burns and Lynn Novick's eighteen-hour PBS series *The Vietnam War* (2017) led critics to identify parallels with then-ongoing conflicts in Afghanistan and renewed nationalist hubris.[10]

Nonetheless, films and archival materials about the Vietnam War, like Burns and Novick's series, situate the conflict as of the past and claim the authority to tell from the use of archival evidence and in-depth, first-person interviews. Jamie Baron's theory of the "archive effect" aptly describes the popular reception of Novick and Burns's work as well as many other historical documentaries. Materials that viewers experience as found footage from the distant past in *The Vietnam War* produce a "temporal disparity" between present-day interviews and historical events.[11] As with Burns's previous war films, *The Vietnam War* draws its storyline and affective power from combining personal interviews, photographs from family albums, revelatory behind-the-scenes recordings of key figures in presidential administrations, and archival film materials and still photographs recorded by journalists who were there in Vietnam in the 1960s and 1970s. The authorizing power of the state institutions that once maintained archives, regardless of whether Novick and Burns gathered their materials from such places, informs the viewer's experience of archival footage in this context. While some viewers may see parallels to other conflicts in these stories, the film aims to communicate something of cultural value about the past.

When the *In Country* filmmakers concluded that their observational recording alone "fell flat" after the first edit, however, they came to rely on archival footage in a way quite different from Novick and Burns's film.[12] *In Country* hewed closer to what Baron called "archive affect" than the "archive effect" described above. "Archive affect" expresses of "the overwhelming sense of time's passage and of all that has been irrevocably lost to the present," rather than a grand narrative about past events.[13] Like New Historicists who looked within archives for oddities, contingencies, exceptions, and moments of antidisciplinary unruliness that could illustrate the fragmentary nature of archival reconstruction and the vital importance of interpretation and deconstruction in historical writing, a number of nonfiction films of the 1990s and early 2000s reappropriated archival footage, photographs, and sound recordings—or just fabricated them in cases of archival absence, as in Cheryl Dunye's *The Watermelon Woman* (1996). These films often created for viewers an overwhelming feeling of time having passed, or the loss of possible reconstruction of past lives due to gaps in the archive, especially along the lines of race, ethnicity, gender, and sexual orientation. These films aimed to conjure for the viewer the feeling of loss and disappearance that Phelan proposed to be the ontology of performance.[14] Likewise, *In Country* follows its reenactor subjects to situate the Vietnam War very much in the here and now of performance, where we know that the reenactors' careful media consumption has prepared them to achieve intense feelings of connection with the past as they play. The "proliferation of indexical documents outside of official archives" into spaces such as YouTube here seems to have been internalized by the reenactor subjects of this film, who have watched numerous documentaries, YouTube clips, and Hollywood films about the Vietnam War and then projected bits back out in the woods during their reenactment.[15] As they walk together through the foliage in Oregon to commemorate soldier forefathers, they also become gun-toting flaneurs seeking out a range of grisly delights—the inverse of those late nineteenth-century flaneuses of Anne Friedberg's description in *Window Shopping* (1991), who learned consumer desire and the cinematic gaze by walking past the tantalizing window displays of early malls.[16] Part of the appeal of reenacting is in the getting away from ubiquitous images, cameras, displays, shopping windows, and desk work, but walking in the woods does not mean leaving behind cinematic structures of desire. In the name of commemoration, reenactors project those longings to touch the past onto each other and into the trees, where simulated dangers may lurk.

So what happens when documentary camerapersons participate in this live performance projection while also recording it? The cinematic perceptual process layered on the woods during the reenactment turned out to be a surprising and revealing resource for the filmmaker-reenactors, who may have been misled initially by voltmeter-talk about the location of indexicality in their project. Claims on being there to witness high-stakes events were inaccurate if not misleading in this case. Rather than imbuing the film with the authority of being there, observational footage in *In Country* indexed the repetition of gestures and movements from the past—like what performance theorist Diana Taylor called "the repertoire"—here immediately archived by recording as building blocks for recreating a collective martial psyche exploring masculinity and anxieties about the specter of its loss in the present (fig. 1.3).[17] Observational-ish camerawork turned out to be a useful tool for evoking a martial psyche in reenactment, but less so for representing events and affective textures as such.

The aim of this chapter is to chart out a theory of indexicality that accounts for the idiosyncrasies of camerawork and editing in this film, which I see as applicable to simulation documentaries more broadly. Following a synopsis of the film *In Country*, I develop this argument in three major sections. First, I reflect on my own experience as a documentary cameraperson who made a film about participating in Revolutionary War reenactments. I point out limitations of reenactment as a documentary method—and vérité camerawork as a method for documenting reenactment—with an eye toward a reading of *In Country*.

Figure 1.3. Archival footage of soldiers on patrol in Vietnam (*top*) juxtaposed with observational footage recorded in the Oregon woods (*bottom*) calls attention to collective memories about the meaning of the war in *In Country*. Courtesy Mike Attie and Meghan O'Hara.

Second, I revisit documentary studies writings on the concept of indexicality to excavate qualities of subjective perception in Charles S. Peirce's 1895 essay on this particular category of sign, connect these qualities to Laura U. Marks's theory of recollection-objects, and flesh out implications for theorizing camerawork in simulation documentaries. Third, I engage performance theory and Baron's writing on archive affect to analyze the relationship between observational footage and archival materials across the filmmakers' process of making the film. I frame examples of camerawork as gestural recollection-objects that touch crisis coverage, an archived repertoire, and processes of psychic repair, and I suggest how this ostensibly observational, third-person omniscient footage came to function as an emblem of a collective martial psyche. In the conclusion, I revisit the ethical rationale of commemoration and the limitations it embeds into both reenactment events and filmmaking efforts like *In Country* that follow them.

SYNOPSIS OF *IN COUNTRY*

Though *In Country* follows a group of men from Oregon who reenact battles from the Vietnam War, the opening five minutes of the film do not foreshadow the unfolding of this story. We are instead led to believe that we are watching an observational film about soldiers five years into the Vietnam War in real time who are about to undertake a deadly mission. A somewhat insecure and informally dressed officer under a tent rallies a group of ten or so US soldiers, and then a unit leader debriefs his men on the plan to destroy weapons caches in a lightly patrolled "VC area." High strings in the background cue us to potential dangers as we see the men wade across the river in water up to their thighs, step through the brush with weapons drawn, and spot an enemy encampment through the leaves by the river. "We came upon their Vietcong camp," whispers one soldier into a radio. There is a straight cut to a shot of other US soldiers hiding by a nearby road, who copy the message.

One whispers to the camera that he's relatively old at twenty-four and doing his second tour with "no end in sight." In the close-up, his face expresses concern. Then the eerie soundscape fades out, and the film tips its hat as being of reenactment and anachronism rather than Vietnam. The soldier we just heard waves hello to a large, 2005-ish red pickup truck with a dog in the flatbed as it rolls by his position. An ironic, '60s slideshow-style title-card reading "IN COUNTRY" comes on screen set to the opening of Count Five's classic 1966 rock track "Psychotic Reaction." The ensuing music montage juxtaposes archival footage of army basic training in the late 1960s with shots of the reenactors preparing their props and food for the reenactment. This dynamic introduces a key mechanism for advancing the narrative through the rest of the film, which employs archival footage as markers of the past that remain in the present. But the moment for affectively dropping film viewers into the world of Vietnam has now passed. All subsequent footage of these characters dressed in 1960s army garb reads as documenting performance rather than events of war. In some respects, this opening "fiction" is the only moment in the film in which the viewer sees the environment as the reenactors attempt to experience it through their role-play.

The film's narrative structure centers on a single reenactment that takes place over a weekend in Oregon, but from the opening scene on it draws from a variety of sources for footage. Scenes made from footage of other times and places spin out from the storyline of the reenactment almost like memories triggered unexpectedly by details in the performance. Seven sequences of archival clips of journalists' and filmmakers' 16 mm films of US soldiers in training and Vietnam during the late 1960s and early 1970s, which depict actual death, suffering, and malaise, function as complex affective and visual points of comparison to the reenactment. In some cases, they seem to stand in directly for the memories of one or another reenactor who undertakes a similar task in the reenactment. In others, they extend a scene of walking or waiting at the reenactment into Vietnam and then back, employing editing techniques that suggest unities of time, place, and action while using footage created nearly fifty years and seventy-four hundred miles apart. Interviews with the reenactors focus on why they participate in the hobby as well as personal reflections on war, PTSD, and reintegration into civilian life.

The film also includes observational footage of the reenactors' everyday lives with families, friends, and contemporary military units, as well as home-movie footage of several reenactors' deployments to Iraq and Afghanistan, providing a survey of motivations for participating in the hobby. Joel Kinney, a Vietnam War memorabilia collector, describes with fascination how the aroma of "bug juice" (slang for the plastic bottles of DDT-laced insect repellant issued to US soldiers during the war) compels veterans' psychic returns to tours in Vietnam. Iraq War army veteran Charles "Tuna" Ford plays soldier with his small children in the grass of a fenced suburban backyard. Later, we see footage of him detonating a bomb in the Iraqi desert—"Fucking tight," he sighs—recorded by a fellow soldier in the passenger's seat of their Humvee. A South Vietnamese Army (ARVN) reenactor named Vinh Nguyen, a Vietnamese American who fought for the ARVN with the US military in the 1960s and then immigrated to Oregon after the war, says that he reenacts to "revisit the image of what I was in the past." Hayden "Bummy" Baumgartner fought in Vietnam as a young man in 1970–71 and reenacts "to go back" while also advising younger members of the group on uniform authenticity. Lucien "Doc" Darensburg, who served as a medic during the Iraq War and now plays one as a reenactor, talks on camera about the difficulties of coping with PTSD. Matt Kinney, the manager of a Portland brewery who has no affiliation with the contemporary military, reenacts to live out "that childhood love of playing war in the woods." And high school student David "Cricket" Safina-Massey states that he has enlisted to join the marines once he turns eighteen. Matt Kinney and Cricket serve as foils to reenactors with past military experience and soldiers pictured in archival footage in Vietnam.

References to 1960s songs, Vietnam War movies, historical footage, and training manual details recur in interactions among these men as they prepare their uniforms and gear and then perform in the reenactment itself. When Nguyen arrives at the encampment, for example, he and Joel Kinney exchange bear hugs and the exuberant salutation "Good morning, Vietnam!"—a joking reference to Nguyen's ethnicity as well as the eponymous 1987 movie starring Robin Williams as a comedic, irreverent Armed Forces radio host during the Vietnam War. Other soldiers decorate their helmets with designs, flowers, and slogans reminiscent of the conflicted characters in Stanley Kubrick's *Full Metal Jacket* (1987), a dystopian farce about the inadequacy of military training to aid a doomed unit of American soldiers in Vietnam. One reenactor wrote "Sock It To Me" in bubble letters on the back of his helmet, a term with such a convoluted history in popular culture that it is difficult to pin down the referent here for what seems to be a self-reflexive critique of the war and the soldier's reluctant, helpless place in executing it.[18] Using a chalkboard in a makeshift classroom under a tent, Joel Kinney teaches racist, Vietnam-era slang to the other reenactors through occasional references to fiction films and encourages his fellows to use the terms when they role-play. The first night under the tent, the group screens *Easy Rider* (1969) together while smoking cigarettes.

On the second day, the reenactors patrol the woods and participate in brief gunfights with the Vietcong, played by several men dressed in black sweatsuits. The patrol, gunfights, and simulated deaths segue to deeper vignettes with the reenactors and the story of Tuna's deployment to Afghanistan. Footage from Vietnam, Iraq, and the reenactment intercuts more regularly, without further setup or explanation, as though all events exist in the same plane of time. When Nguyen captures two reenactors playing the Vietcong, for instance, a close-up on his face cuts to a brief montage of armed ARVN soldiers standing uncertainly over presumed communist enemies in Vietnamese villages. The return to Nguyen's close-up in the reenactment leads the shots to read as something like a sequence of unbidden memories. When it starts to rain at the reenactment by the evening of the second day, Nguyen's subtitled voice-over in Vietnamese validates this interpretation. The reenactment weekend concludes in the rain with the reenactors sharing a beer together back at the camp. The film ends with Tuna's return home from Afghanistan to his family and the unit of reenactors marching together in a small-town parade as a small boy in camouflage fatigues looks on.

RECORDING REENACTMENT: A PERSONAL TAKE

Between 2002 and 2005, I conducted a reverse participant ethnography and filmed with a group of New Englanders who reenacted battles from the American Revolutionary War as eighteenth-century British soldiers, commonly referred to as Redcoats. My documentary, titled *About Face! Reenacting in a Time of War* (2012), explored how discourses on the then-contemporaneous war in Iraq circulated through the bodies of those who played the part of America's "first enemy" in reenactment performances.[19] It was a documentary about something like what Michel Foucault called "biopolitics," about how state power is reproduced and enforced at the level of the subject body, though I could not have articulated those concerns when I started the project.[20] In hindsight, my twenty-two-year-old self was drawn to the subject because of the way the reenactment projected onto the world the contours of cinematic drama—lavish costumes, events that gestured at life-and-death stakes, complex points of identification, possibilities for humor, and clear timelines. The reenactments, in other words, were designed to attract cameras, and I fell for the lure. I dressed as a Redcoat and played the role of an eighteenth-century infantryman in battle reenactments and training sessions to make the film. The experience led me to places that I did not expect and at times into positions in which I was uncomfortable. My body projected a set of narratives about national identity with which I had significant and growing qualms, but I struggled to make those critiques while also maintaining my sense of responsibility to the reenactors, who dedicated a lot of time and effort to helping me.

There is a similar tension in the *In Country* filmmakers' claim to have made a film about "understanding" this group of Vietnam War reenactors. Cultural historians Brenda Boyle and Jeehyun Lee argued that at least some of the reenactors in the film have structured their performances of individual personhood and trauma to prevent engaging with "the complexities of military and foreign policies, the history of Viet Nam's anticolonial struggles, or the ethics of the whole affair."[21] That Joel Kinney, the founder of the Vietnam War reenacting group shown in the film, described in the *In Country* bonus features his first experience seeing the film as "kind of like a father seeing his child portrayed in a positive manner" does little to dispel Boyle and Lee's critique.[22]

In my case, reenactment posed additional, practical challenges to filming. To maintain the appearance of an eighteenth-century soldier, I was not permitted to film while playing a role. I would videotape at events where I was not required to appear in uniform, and during one particularly large reenactment, my group permitted me to wear a well-concealed spy camera. But I usually had to rely on other camerapersons to film those events. As a participant, I was able to experience and speak at length with many reenactors about their strategies for thinking deeply about the struggles and everyday lives of eighteenth-century people. These perspectives were at odds with most media reports about the reenactments of that era, which often rehashed narratives about using "morally just" violence from the past to rationalize US imperial ventures in the present. But they also did not adequately address the question of why participants reenact. Verbalized answers to this question are too pat in many cases, or grounded in feelings not easily translated into words.

My film eventually came to historicize the rise of US reenactment in the 1960s and 1970s as a reactionary social movement within the broader turn from political to social history. Emblematic of what postwar cultural historian Michael Kammen called "heritage syndrome," early war reenactments in the United States strengthened social ties among white male participants, made use of the newly built highway system to draw vast numbers of car owners to events, and perpetuated a narrative about American identity that many participants then perceived to be under threat. Commemoration events around the centennial of the Civil War (1961–65) and the bicentennial of the Revolutionary War (1975–81) happened to coincide with the era of the civil rights movement and the Vietnam War, and discourses about reenactment mirrored broader cultural divisions. A former Confederate reenactor with a unit called "the Blackhats," for instance, included in his online memoir a photograph of him and his buddies in costume with segregationist presidential candidate George Wallace in 1963 and acknowledged that "some Centennial events bore an uncomfortable similarity to white resistance." John Hope Franklin, the late scholar of Black history, lamented in 1962 that the states of the former Confederacy had "entered into the observance—one could almost say celebration—with greater enthusiasm than the states in other parts of the country," a foreboding sign that "as a nation and as a people we have never faced up to the full implications of our expressed ideals and goals."[23] While Revolutionary War reenactments centered less on racial conflict, a number of participants started as Civil War reenactors, and many units wrote discriminatory policies into their charters barring the participation of women and nonwhite men under the auspices of historical authenticity. Good teeth were okay. The unit I joined only changed this race and gender policy in the 1990s, around the time when Vietnam War reenacting groups began to form.

Much of my film focused on a reenactor with German and Native American ancestry who had served as a sniper in Vietnam and Desert Storm and communicated about his experiences to me through references to popular films such as *Apocalypse Now* (1979), *Rambo* (1982), and *Enemy at the Gates* (2001). His experiences as a soldier seemed to give him unusual affective tools through which to understand battles of the past. When we once stood together on what seemed to me yet another empty historic battlefield, for instance, he told me that just being there "made the hairs stand up on the back of [his] neck." The hairs on the back of my neck did not stand up even after he explained to me what the attack must have felt like for those soldiers who once held their ground where we now stood. I just did not have a lived experience to draw on in conjuring such a response to this nicely mowed patch of grass.[24] And I doubt that my recorded images of this individual and the grass we looked at together could have done much affective work for viewers who are more like me than him. While I learned a great deal from this reenactor, recording such sentiments using mostly observational shooting methods fell short of my goals. We were not being there in the same way, and what was worth making a film about was *his* way of being there, not mine. I leaned heavily on conversational filming and voice-over to communicate, sometimes speculatively, about what could not be seen. The filmmakers of *In Country* dealt with a similar problem in a different way, as I detail below.

Reenacting and filming reenactment did open for me a way of thinking about documentary as a form of experience rather than a genre of film. Reenactment experience generates something like what Vivian Sobchack and later Baron called "a documentary mode of consciousness," here applied to the performed world rather than the screen.[25] Sobchack wrote about documentary consciousness as being like the mentality of the apprentice, searching the screen for cues to learn things of cultural importance. Similarly, reenactors who role-play as Redcoats in their leisure time are learning from the same manual as their eighteenth-century referents. The sensations that reenactors feel in doing so—of the body as mechanical parts, the camaraderie of common purpose, the unity of action, humanity as a machine—seem to comingle text and body, the indexical connection to the past created as these contemporary people collectively follow old directions. Reenactors often describe experiencing the strong and yet puzzling sensation of "period rush" as they perform, partly conscious of the here and now and partly imagined into a body of the past. As Schneider put it, "times touch" through the body's performative citations.[26] For me, such moments provoked abiding questions about the nature of connection, discovery, and the ethics of historical understanding—core concerns of documentary theory—rather than answers about what past lives were like. While the rest of this chapter is not about my own experience as a reenactor, I inevitably draw on those insights and experiences in analyzing the filming and reenacting of the Vietnam War in *In Country*.

To touch back on the theoretical argument sketched above, the production process behind *In Country* exposed a shortcoming in a notion of indexicality rooted so firmly in technology and the image. While filmmakers Attie and O'Hara used digital technologies to record images and sounds of the reenactment, they somewhat unconsciously followed 1960s and 1970s analog documentary tenets grounded in faith that the image could represent events. The directors never considered manipulating frames or shots in postproduction beyond basic editing and color correction. Yet the subject of the film itself is already a step removed from representation, already an image of war shorn of fear and death and built to feel cinematic.

In other words, the material connection between the image with stakes and its subject was broken before Attie even turned his digital camera on. The purported loss of indexicality has nothing to do with the digital or analog image itself. However, the US men featured in the film—like the Redcoat reenactors with whom I participated—do aim for indexical touch with the past through their documentary method of choice: shared, reiterative reenactment performance. The filmmakers reenacting as 1970s camerapersons also shared a perceptual orientation with their predecessors, but in ways that they only came to appreciate later. In doing so, ironically, they came to express and perceive indexicality differently than did the predecessor documentarians they emulated. Below, I trace a history of the index alternative to the one typically used in documentary theory but better suited, I argue, to account for camerawork in simulation documentary scenarios like this one.

MEDITATIONS ON A ROLLING GAIT: PERCEPTION AND INDEXICAL EMBODIMENT

Many documentary theorists worried that the rise of digital imagery starting in the early 1990s posed a crisis for the field. Authors including Bill Nichols, Mary Anne Doane, and David Rodowick found the concept of indexicality useful for emphasizing the materiality of the image and the ethical obligations of spectators who understand existential connections between events in the world and images of such events. Each warned that the referential, evidentiary quality of film as opposed to other plastic arts erodes with the turn from analog film to digital media. Doane even called *digital media* a contradiction in terms, as digital creations aim toward the erasure of medium specificity rather than establishing physical, material limits for exploration through a particular art practice. They argued that digital photographs and moving images were essentially made of code and exhibited a "fantasy of immateriality."[27] Software programs such as Photoshop were made of the same immaterial stuff and could alter digital images without detection, potentially throwing the ethics (and thereby existence) of documentary premised on photographic inscription into crisis.

As I discussed in the introduction, this technological understanding of media indexicality entered film theory through Peter Wollen's interpretation of Peircian semiotics. His reading of indexicality as created through the mechanical action of the camera depended especially on one oft-quoted passage from Peirce's brief survey of indexical signs in his 1895 essay "The Theory of Signs," in which Peirce characterized photographic technologies as indexical: "Photographs, especially instantaneous photographs, are very instructive, because we know that they are in certain respects exactly like the objects they represent. But this resemblance is due to the photographs having been produced under such circumstances that they were physically forced to correspond point by point to nature. In that aspect, then, they belong to the second class of signs, those by physical connection."[28]

Peirce understood the process of composite photography, in which multiple negatives were seamlessly spliced together to make one image, but downplaying the subjective, expressive dimensions of photography was in keeping with the spirit of late nineteenth-century social science, a moment in which these disciplines staked claims in the academy as inheritors of the natural sciences.[29] What was useful to discern from observation was not anecdote but "physically forced" patterns that evidenced universally applicable truths about human experience. Many of the examples that Peirce provided to illustrate his concept of the index (the bullet mold, weathercock, sundial, barometer, plumb bob, yardstick, etc.) were mechanical tools used to measure natural forces and decode such patterns. The indexical relation of these tools to the forces that shaped them in turn exerted its own kind of force on the thoughts of the subject regarding them. "We are forced by the law of the mind" to think that the weathercock points in the direction of the wind, Peirce stated.[30] Subjectivity had little to do with it.

Doane's *The Emergence of Cinematic Time: Modernity, Contingency, the Archive* (2002) posited that this way of thinking about the cinematic apparatus was one symptom of a transformation in the meaning of seeing in the late nineteenth century that influenced Peirce's semiotic philosophy. Doane connected Peirce's ideas about indexicality to growing cultural suspicions about the inadequacy of human vision to perceive the world accurately. Debates in that era about the possibility of representing movement and duration, Doane observed, "indicate that the issue here is one of representing what we *cannot* see—time."[31] Doane argued that the invention of archival technologies such as cameras, museums, typewriters, and phonographs was imbricated in the emergence of a new way of seeing time in the world that was invested in "the contradictory desire of archiving presence."[32] The tools of science had the power, it seemed, to preserve for reflection the instantaneous events of everyday life that before had passed unrecorded. Doane described how nineteenth-century scientific belief in the concept of the afterimage, the idea that the human retina retained the ghosted contours of the seen on its surface after exposure to light, both explained the eye through the metaphor of the camera and testified to the imperfection of the eye as a documentary apparatus. The film camera recorded sequences of images without such flaws.

Peirce likened the concept of the afterimage to the relation between presence and thinking more broadly. Thought was a kind of afterimage of perception, held in the mind for reflection while the senses processed other, less striking perceptions. The indexical sign was closest to the sensation of instantaneous presence for Peirce, but as such, Peirce argued that it was also furthest from human thought. Any thought, like the afterimage on the retina, existed only through an interval of time and with the enabling copresence in consciousness of other thoughts. Because the indexical sign existed in contiguity with its object, it seemed the most objective of his sign categories and therefore the least human. It had no existence itself outside of the thing to which it referred. Peirce's index was therefore a sign, in Doane's terms, "evacuated of content; it is a hollowed-out sign."[33]

The very inhumanity of the photographic index also promised its validity, rationality, and potential, ironically, to make present again the irrational, idiosyncratic, and inexplicable qualities of living that escaped conscious perception, memory, or external control.[34] This remains the central premise of observational camerawork. If film was a "hollowed-out sign," then it functioned for spectators like an opening through which one might behold the indexical traces of the historical world. It could make past time palpable in the present. In this way of thinking, film could reenact in the theater past moments or events that spectators had not experienced personally and so draw them into new ways of conceiving their relationship to the world and their capacity to change it. The medium promised the spectator a means to transcend the everyday self through this relationship of responsibility with representations on screen. In film studies, the term *indexicality* still refers predominantly to the technological processes of mechanical reproduction that create possibilities for evidentiary connection between photograph and world. Documentary theorists have debated indexicality in the digital context by centering analysis on technologies including digital cameras, simulation programs, video games, and animation rather than embodied experiences in a forum such as historical reenactment. In one suggestive departure, Doane posited that the photographic frame itself served as an index in a second aspect, as a deixis focusing attention in the present. She argued that in film studies treatments of indexicality as photochemical trace, this performative aspect of the indexical sign "is frequently forgotten."[35]

Here I want to revisit Peirce's writing on the index, which offers a broader definition of the concept than the one typically used in film studies. And in excavating the implications of his other examples for my analysis of *In Country*, I intend to center indexicality in the experiencing body over the image. This is not to dismiss image-making practices culturally marked as documentary, which might be grouped by their shared intention toward conjuring touch with the past in a variety of ways. Indeed, the ubiquity of images in our everyday lives forces us to internalize contents, cultural conventions of spectatorship, and practices of image making and so cannot be ignored. They are vital to the creation and experience of the Vietnam War reenactments, for instance.

But I do claim that documentary experience need not—indeed cannot—start in the image, photographic or otherwise. While the makers of *In Country* filmed in an observational style and did not manipulate their footage in postproduction, the records of reenactors in the woods were not the focal point of evidence that registered as such for the filmmakers. Rather, they found touch with the past unexpectedly, more like in Peirce's offhand example of a man with a rolling gait than in his more often quoted characterization of the photograph.

In his taxonomy of the index, Peirce included examples of indexical signs that had less to do with scientific instruments than with the subjective sensation of being startled by particular perceptions. In one instance, he considered his perception of a man's "rolling gait" as an indexical sign: "I see a man with a rolling gait. This is a probable indication that he is a sailor."[36] Between the two sentences "I see . . ." and "This is a probable . . . ," there is a tacit personal question: Why did this man's walk strike me as notable? It compels Peirce to offer an explanation. It also arises from an observation of performative behavior, in Judith Butler's sense of the term—that is, the repeated activities, gestures, or ways of thinking that produce, reinforce, and reify identity over time. The performative utterance or gesture brings a situation into being rather than describing a thing that already exists, and so it may constitute a politics.[37]

Peirce refers to the reiterative labor process—working as a sailor—that might have caused the rolling gait in the late 1800s. But the grounds for the indexical sign to emerge at a moment in Peirce's mind did not develop quickly for the man who walked this way. If indeed the gait was the occupational by-product that Peirce deduced, then the rolling gait indexed a life at sea. The gait perceived in an instant by Peirce touches the accumulation of this past time. Like Roland Barthes's concept of the punctum as "that accident [in the photograph] which pricks me," Pierce experiences a startling sensation at the moment of observing the rolling gait and thinking this thought.[38] There was likely nothing startling about the style of walk for the man doing the walking, and it was not obvious that the rolling gait should register as a sign in a different context, perhaps closer to the docks, where it might simply be the way "we" walk. It is a striking way of moving to Peirce and then perhaps to us as readers aiming to be in synchrony with his description. When he marks this man's walk as a "rolling gait," we readers can understand the startling aspect of what Peirce calls indexical signs, even if we cannot exactly envisage the reiterative walk cycle of Peirce's probable sailor of a now bygone era.

Peirce's example suggests a theory of thought centered on the psychic experience of reenactment. Here is the startling experience of perceiving difference that one can then explain only through imaginative speculation about a past and further research or thinking. The walk is evidence, but what it points to beyond the fact of difference remains unclear. It catalyzes further consideration of this man and the set of life conditions that led him to walk this way. Touch with the sign *rolling gait* is compelled and affective. It is a surge without codified meaning in Peirce's body, generated intersubjectively and leaving him with work yet to do. We might further wonder how long Peirce took to come to his moment of perceiving difference, whether he stared at the fellow, and what kind of a look the man might have shot back at him. Peirce leaves us no indications about such events in his one-line description of this example of an indexical sign. He moves on briskly. But I raise these questions here to suggest how such chained acts of perception shape the trajectory of future thinking and behavior. They have material effects, especially when a camera is involved.

The process of perception, affect, and thought entailed in Peirce's example describes standard practice in much documentary work—especially camerawork. Unexpected, contingent details emerge in the field of perception, beckoning further exploration and attempts at discovery. The cameraperson may sense with a repressed ecstasy a revelatory, ephemeral moment unfolding in front of the lens as they record that will one day become a moment for spectators to regard on the cinema screen with mirrored fascination.[39] The cameraperson regards the present from a position of disparity relative to subjects because of this thinking about a future moment of reception, the inverse of what Baron identified as the "temporal disparity" experienced affectively by the documentary viewer regarding archival footage from their present moment of viewing.[40] The cameraperson is trying to make the good bones of the good film, the kind of footage or scene that will allow for rough alignment of their affective experience with that of the viewer sometime down the road. Ethnographic filmmaker Jean Rouch, for example, explained his craft in such terms in an interview conducted in 1980 for a retrospective of his work. He described seeking out in his camerawork "these privileged moments that you yourself feel through your viewfinder" that might enable him to enter an out-of-body "cine trance" in rhythm with life's unfolding contingencies. Transference of this trance was his explicit goal, he explained: "For me, the second moment—which is the moment of truth—is when I am at the editing table, and without my having forewarned her, the editor in front of the little viewing screen stops, rewinds, and looks again."[41] If the editor catches the moment unprompted, he suggests, then so will the spectator of the finished film. It is often the case that the pleasure of viewing and re-viewing direct-cinema and cinema vérité–style documentary also depends on the process that Pierce and then Rouch intimate in these examples.

But more to the point for the case of reenactment, the rolling gait opens up a way for Peirce to perceive accumulated time in the present as a startling absence. In this way, it bears a strong relation to examples of what Marks called "recollection-objects" in diasporic films, which functioned as fetishes for felt durations of time or traumatic memories. Marks posited that fetishistic objects "condense time within themselves" such that "in excavating them [through photography and film], we expand outward in time." Viewers understand this expansion affectively as accumulation rather than as a narrative or discourse. This way of thinking about the fetish, Marks explained, crossed the Marxist understanding of the fetish as labor and movement transformed into a commodity with the psychoanalytic understanding of the fetish as memory partially cathected as affect onto an object. Marks emphasized the importance of indexicality in any account of the documentary real through the metaphor of the fossil, as well as the inevitably subjective, unobservable apprehension of the indexical reality in a given object through the metaphor of the fetish. "The fetish, by partaking physically of the thing it represents, threatens the idea that only the distance senses"—sight and hearing, the staples of empiricism—"lend themselves to knowledge.... Thinking fetishistically allows us to take embodied knowledge seriously." Marks's proposal for considering embodied knowledge, in other words, critiques notions of individual subjecthood and mind-body dualism: "To be dependent upon an object affirms not only the materiality of one's body but also the incompleteness of one's self."[42] Peirce's example of the rolling gait also suggests as much without fleshing out these implications.

By way of example, Marks analyzed Rea Tajiri's *History and Memory: For Akiko and Takashige* (1991), a haunting experimental documentary about Tajiri's mother's experience of forcible displacement and incarceration at the Poston camp in Arizona during World War II. Tajiri's mother seems unable to tell her daughter much about her years at Poston, and Tajiri finds few photographs of her ancestors' time there. Incarcerated Japanese Americans were not permitted to have cameras. Seeking evidence that might flesh out her mother's story in the face of this absence, Tajiri travels to the camp and correctly intuits her way to the space where her mother had lived. She removes a single piece of tar paper from the roof of the building and takes it with her, envisioning it as a silent, fossilized witness to the lives of those once incarcerated there. Though it is an artifact with neither lens nor image, Marks interpreted the tar paper to be photographic in its punctum-like effect within the film: "One could say the piece of tar paper, having been exposed to those events, 'photographed' them and just needs to be developed: rectangular and gray, it even looks a bit like an old photograph." Like the landscape at a reenactment site in the midst of performance, the tar paper carries accumulated affect within it for idiosyncratic moments of perception, as in Tajiri's film. There is, in fact, a clinical, overhead photograph of the piece of tar paper included in *History and Memory*, as if its trace on the screen will allow it to evoke stories that it cannot tell. Done according to the conventions of forensic and archeological documentation, the overhead camerawork isolates the tar paper in the frame and directs viewer attention. Viewers (and especially Japanese American viewers) may sense affective power in this piece of tar paper for its once physical proximity to the incarcerated at Poston. It is metonymic in the context of the film, an indexical sign that operates through the affective "transfer of presence" rather than a symbolic transfer of meaning.[43] In this way, the recollection-object functions like the body in long-duration performance art or reenactment, both thing-it-itself and something else in contiguity with the body diffused through performance out into the space. "Metonymy is additive and associative; it works to secure a horizontal axis of contiguity and displacement," Phelan wrote of the body in such works.[44] The tar paper touched and touches a particular "cryptic history" of oppression in the context of Tajiri's video and compels reflection and sense-making from the touched who see it, thereby affectively identifying a collective in their shared sense of overwhelming loss.[45]

I must say here that it is not self-evident that the tar paper should index the experience of incarceration in this way. The piece of tar paper itself, after all, had remained unnoticed in the roof of the barrack for forty years. If the tar paper was a photograph "waiting to be developed," as Marks put it, then it was Tajiri's performance of removal, forensic recording, and emplacement within the film that guided the photographic paper through the chemical baths in the darkroom. Tajiri's labor functions performatively to create the tar paper as an archival object and indexical sign.[46] This object, such as viewers receive it, is a chunk of cinematic time in the film body, not the tar paper itself. The tar paper in the film is a gestural recollection-object. It is as much a performative act to restore dignity to Tajiri's ancestors as a thing in itself.

Though *In Country* represents cultural memory and explores the place of the sensorium in reenactment and film, it is not a project that looks too much like those of the diasporic makers that Marks discusses, such as *History and Memory*. The archive of imagery about Vietnam, after all, is extensive, dense, and thoroughly reconsidered, albeit US-centric, to judge from *In Country* and *The Vietnam War* series by Novick and Burns. War materiel and the things soldiers carried are available for purchase by collectors. The makers' instincts to use observational recording techniques to document subjects and their initial positions as outsiders to the group of reenactors run against the strong sense of distrust of visuality and archives learned by the diasporic filmmakers that Marks considers. Being there wasn't an option for them. But *In Country* is a project about intercultural encounters—between veterans and civilians, past and present, Vietnam and Oregon—that lend Marks's theories explanatory power here.

For example, *In Country* includes a scene about a recollection-object that functions at a slant to the tar paper in Tajiri's film, the bug juice that Vietnam memorabilia collector Joel Kinney describes in an interview with the filmmakers. Here, Attie and O'Hara record as Kinney frames the metonymic significance of this item. "These Vietnam veterans that come over here, the first thing they'll do is grab a bottle of bug juice," he says as he sits down into an interview frame in a room of his house filled to the brim with war paraphernalia used by the US military in Vietnam. Attie and O'Hara set up this conversation with a montage of objects in the room, including a wide shot that prominently features a Confederate flag on the wall. There are "survival cards" to avoid illness in Southeast Asia, helmets, hunter-green lockers, framed military medals, knives, ammunition, guns, and hundreds of uniforms, among other things. None except the bug juice function in the film quite like Tajiri's tar paper, however. These objects are curios rather than witnesses to absent history, at least in this context. Kinney proceeds to reenact what Vietnam veterans do with the bug juice when they visit his house: "They'll open it up—this happens every time—and they'll go [he smells the open bottle], 'Oh my gosh.'.... And it takes them right back to the rice paddy, in 1967. [pauses] How powerful is that?" He acknowledges that just watching the veterans smell and trip "gets me sucked in, too, and I was never even there."

Like the tar paper, the bug juice "condenses time within itself" and hails in the smelling a particular collective that shared a difficult experience.[47] But this recollection-object encodes a different politics than the tar paper, in part because the film gives over the interpretation of the bug juice to Kinney himself. Kinney seems to regard such memory events as collector's items. They are an extension of the room itself, in a way, experiences encoded in his memory that touch veterans' efforts to remember and perhaps to cope or heal by remembering. He sees one after another "man with a rolling gait," he seems to suggest, fascinated at each turn by veterans' expressions of being overwhelmed at their renewed awareness of the passage of time in the present and perhaps an unstated ambivalence about what they've lost. That he gets "sucked in" demonstrates a desire for something akin to "archival affect" of Baron's description, the "shudder . . . deeply entwined with historical desire, the desire to know and/or 'experience' history." She was writing about reasons why viewers seek out novel footage of World War II, but such shudders are core to why many war reenactors participate in their hobby. They may frame what they are doing as a commemorative practice, but it is also an effort to ward off banality and the humdrum routines of civil society by seeking out an authentic form of masculinity. The intergenerational troupe of reenactors featured in *In Country* suggests that there is a desire to know, reconnect, and keep alive a particular kind of martial masculinity to this end, to reexperience or reimagine the intensity of war through reenactment. When the camerawork itself follows men like Kinney expressing curious enthusiasm for his role in triggering veteran memories, it also gets "sucked in" by that desire.

Later in the film, however, the filmmakers' camerawork itself functions as a recollection-object rather than as an apparatus for recording the fetish objects of collectors. The filmmakers came to distrust their own archive of observational records to tell the story, after all, and so had to root around for other ways to express sensory experience and memory. Extending Marks's analysis of the tar-paper scene, we might ask when gestures like that rolling gait or reenactment performance or camerawork within it might function like the piece of tar paper she describes. Reenacting is a temporal fetish for traumatic historical events and a route to embodied knowledge. Moments of perception in performance partake physically of movements once carried out by others; in reenacting those gestures, the time of the present may seem to expand. We enter the logic of accumulated pasts in the present rather than linear narrative time. And in reenactment, the gesture of camerawork offers a latent means to express this fetishistic accumulation of time. The reenactment of observational camerawork also "condenses time within [itself]," to return to Marks's characterization, like the tar paper waiting for exposure in the right semiotic context to function metonymically.[48] Such camerawork in reenactment may be narratively thin, but it offers affordances to become affectively full. In this manner, chunks of Attie and O'Hara's footage edited into scenes and juxtaposed with archival footage and home movies came to function as recollection-objects in the finished film. They become gestural records, encoded in the film as embodied recollections rather than as evidence of events.

To recap, Peirce described as indexical an experience that was mildly startling for him, an encounter with difference that compelled him to imagine an explanation. This subjective experience depended on Peirce's reading into the performed but historically conditioned movements of another subject, an intersubjective encounter. This kind of indexicality reemerged in media phenomenology and performance theory grappling with language to express the condensation of time in media objects and bodies, as well as the startling, overwhelming sense of loss entailed in experiencing such signs at the point of reception. Peirce expanded at greater length shortly thereafter on startling, ephemeral indexical signs: "A rap on the door is an index. Anything which focuses the attention is an index. Anything which startles us is an index, in so far as it marks the junction between two portions of experience. Thus a tremendous thunderbolt indicates that *something* considerable happened, though we may not know precisely what the event was. But it may be expected to connect itself with some other experience."[49]

"Anything which focuses the attention" must mark its difference from other things for the subject perceiving it. There is a suddenness to perceiving these indexical signs—the rap at the door, the thunderbolt—that compels attention. Shifting to the domain of camerawork (and by extension film viewing experience), a cameraperson waits amid subjects before the lens for the emergence of something as striking as the rap on the door. It is perhaps a detail that others present or subsequent viewers might not notice or might notice differently. And why this something as opposed to that something demands attention is as difficult for filmmakers to articulate in the moment as it is for reenactors to explain the appeal of what they do. In both cases, without the perceiving subject to experience this something, this indexical sign will not emerge. Indexicality is embodied as an experience before it is thinkable as inscribed on this or that. And so the particulars of the perceiving bodies matter.

What is more significant for indexical perception than image manipulation, then, is the vast proliferation of screens and photographic images in everyday life. Photographs are more often banal than wondrous, as commentators in the nineteenth century described them being, and the tricks of manipulating photographs are commonly understood. The frame in the screen may focus attention, but it does not necessarily mark a "junction between two portions of experience" or indicate that anything considerable has happened. An early example of the implications for this changed context is described by Australian cultural theorist and self-acknowledged "media baby" Meaghan Morris in her now-seminal "Banality in Cultural Studies" (1988) in an anecdote about an unexpected interruption in her own television viewing. "This was not catastrophe on TV—like the Challenger sequence," Morris reflected of the incident, "but a catastrophe of and *for* TV. There were no pictures, no reports, just *silence*."[50] It was the absence of televised indices of catastrophes in other places that indexed something catastrophic looming in Morris's own locale. The loss of the television signal, the indexical trace of catastrophe, worked on Morris performatively by evoking the sensation of liveness, the visage of her own disappearance, and "something like a *truth*."[51] What startled her was an affective sense of the limitations of her own body—its medium specificity, to recast Doane's use of the term—and the unknown series of historical events that enabled this moment of silence and mortality in the present.

This indexical form of perception remains at the heart of documentary film practice, though it has little to do with technology per se. The indexical signs that constitute a reenactment, we might say, are gestural recollection-objects. They are the instances when the bodies in performance generate archive affect or the overwhelming sense of witnessed, absent history like that cathected onto the tar paper in Tajiri's film. Considering indexical perception opens possibilities for thinking about the interplay of various subjectivities and a situated theory of the index. Within this framework, we may theorize an indexical relation inhering in a felt, bodily sensation mediated through a photograph, weathervane, plumb bob, bullet mold . . . or embodied performance. The perceiving subject momentarily senses the past activities of another being, other beings, or another ecosystem in an intersubjective engagement. We may also consider the possibility that the presence of moving images, however horrific or sensational their contents, may not in themselves produce the sensation of their indexicality in a particular viewer. What startles a viewer into rumination on history is contextual and contingent. It has no necessary relationship with a photograph. Neither should documentary theory.

WALKING IN THE WOODS: TRACES OF RECORDING IN *IN COUNTRY*

I have argued above that, as a live performance practice with object-creating capacities, camerawork can create gestural recollection-objects. Here I apply this theory of indexicality to three different examples of camerawork in *In Country* as they are reconstituted in the finished, edited film. In practical terms on the ground during the reenactment, Attie and O'Hara's camerawork followed a great deal of walking in the woods, as this is indeed a staple activity of war reenactment. *In Country* in turn dedicates a good deal of screen time to shots of the reenactors toting replica (or perhaps actual) M-16s loaded with blanks and patrolling the Oregon foliage, a routine that seems to offer little in the way of filmable stakes. In the examples I analyze, aspects of Attie and O'Hara's camerawork that function as reenactment take priority over the observational ethic of being there to represent unfolding events. I frame these gestural recollection-objects as functioning to index crisis coverage, an archived repertoire, and psychic repair, concepts that will recur in analyses of other simulation documentaries in the rest of the book.

Crisis Coverage

In her article on information, crisis, and catastrophe on television news, Doane described the crisis as "a condensation of temporality. It names an event of some duration which is startling and momentous precisely because it demands resolution within a limited period of time." Subsequent writers have referred to camerawork carried out in such unresolved scenarios as *crisis coverage*, noteworthy for what it suggests but fails to show. Crisis coverage indexes chaos through off-screen sounds and the inscribed records of movement as the cameraperson ducks, hides, or fails in efforts to film through smoke and dust. But such footage falls short of visualizing events external to the body of the cameraperson, who may be confused or under threat. Things are up in the air, both aesthetically and, perhaps, politically. When the cameraperson feels safe enough to again frame their images with intention and an outward-directed gaze, the moment for creating such a gestural object has passed. Crisis coverage nonetheless indexes affectively by implying what might have just passed unseen, as I aim to show in subsequent chapters in this book.[52]

About an hour into *In Country*, the filmmakers and their subjects are ambushed by several other reenactors playing the Vietcong, and the film shows the transition from the controlled follow-shot of the reenactors on patrol to a crisis-coverage movement record of Attie diving into the weeds. At the sound of gunshots, the image on screen loses its mooring to the cameraperson's eye. The moment in the performance and the record of this moment that we film viewers see here touch precedent events in complex ways. Perhaps the reenactors on screen suddenly imagine being in a firefight Vietnam, or perhaps audience members watching the finished film think back to viewing embedded reporting of battles in Iraq; blurry, uncontrolled footage of protest events turned violent; or the fictionalized helter-skelter camerawork employed in the opening scene of *Saving Private Ryan* (1998). Perhaps it's some of all four. We viewers are literally lost in the weeds by the side of the road, taking in camerawork not visibly focused, momentarily, on anything in particular in front of the lens. The referent for the camerawork is unstable, a "severed index," to refer back to Schneider's term.[53] It becomes a gestural recollection-object of crisis coverage (fig. 1.4).

Of course, Attie, the observational cameraperson diving into the weeds, knew that he was not in real danger. This is perhaps an obvious point, but it is nonetheless worth noting for its aesthetic significance. Shooting from the grass was one choice among many at Attie's disposal. He could have rushed into the trees to catch a few shots of the opposing army or moved around to the front of his subjects to record their faces instead of settling for plants and backs. We might think of the camerawork as a kind of "unprivileged camera style," to refer to ethnographic filmmaker David MacDougall's phrase for a camera that attempts to mimic the perceptual and cultural sensibility of the subjects.[54] Attie's rationale for the choice he made indeed seemed to express something like this logic. "When you're shooting, you want to be respectful of the event and also to some extent playing along, and that's the part of the war correspondent. You know you want to keep cover, you want to lay low because I think it would ruin it for them if I was standing up getting the ideal angle of the firefight," he said.[55]

Perhaps in diving down into the grass, Attie was being a good reenactor, that way of being that direct cinema and observational cinema practitioners have long resisted if not reviled as anathema to the serendipitous, immediate, spontaneous phenomena that the skillfully wielded camera could reveal when rolling—voltmeter-style—amid everyday life. But since Attie and O'Hara had to act in order to record the reenactment according to observational tenets (proximity to subjects, following rather than directing activities, and accepting everyday activities as events to record), their bodily orientations

Figure 1.4. Cameraman Mike Attie dives into the weeds when he and the reenactors he records are "ambushed." Courtesy Mike Attie and Meghan O'Hara.

are at odds with Leacock's theory of the observational cameraperson as faux-invisible recorder or audience member. "During the event, we were totally immersed in their fantasy world," O'Hara and Attie wrote in an online article about the process of making the film for the *Daily Beast*: "At certain moments they even talked to us as if we were actually reporters from the 1970s. When we were outside in the field, we didn't ask them about their real lives. We reserved questions about their home life and experiences in Iraq for after the reenactment was finished in order to stay in character and fully inhabit their fantasy."[56] Compared to an observational filmmaker like Frederick Wiseman, in any case, Attie and O'Hara were not recording their institution to provide a third-person-omniscient impression of presence. But they did mean to communicate a kind of commitment to the film concept premised on copresence with subjects and attunement to their culture. It is a way to say that the film should follow subjects whither they go, even into the weeds of everyday minutiae, while downplaying the political views of the filmmakers themselves. Attie and O'Hara say they share an affinity with this epistemological orientation. In an interview with me, O'Hara recounted one of their "founding myths as film collaborators" in these terms: "It's not that either one of us don't care about films that could change the world, obviously, but I said to [Mike], I was like, you're so clearly not in this camp of people trying to make lasting change through a film, and he was like, yeah, well, I don't feel like I know the answer."[57]

The problem with this spirit of being there with its presumption of humility and neutrality, as Trinh T. Minh-ha, Brian Winston, Michael Renov, Fatimah Tobing-Rony, Jill Godmilow, and many others have pointed out, is that it occludes choices and sociohistorical forces: the choice to focus on a war reenactment instead of a more urgent subject—or even those reenactors who play the Vietcong.[58] There was the need for two young filmmakers seeking academic jobs in a tough market to produce a cinematic feature documentary somewhat quickly and cheaply, as well as the fact that the reenactment offered ready-made production value, aesthetics of the outdoors, the hot-button theme of masculine vulnerability, and the "sexiness of the Vietnam War," in O'Hara's terms.[59] Intimate observation, even carried out from a place of love, can function as a kind of voyeurism that neglects "accountability for the ethical/political relationships that ethnographic and other documentary filmmakers co-construct with the subjects whose lives are central to their films."[60] And a key tenet of critical race and gender theory (unfairly attacked in the culture wars that unfolded after the 2020 election) holds that claims to neutrality often rationalize the norms of power in practice, such as the tacit and sometimes explicit racism, sexism, and nationalism that creeps into war reenactments under the banner of historical realism or commemoration.[61] To follow and record such subjects as a means to understand them teeters close to simply projecting their values when the records find their way into a finished, edited film.

Moreover, reenacting the Vietnam War in the Oregon woods may offer cinematic capital in the form of outdoor aesthetics, controversy, and eccentricity, but the stakes of reenacting are in many cases internal to individual reenactors or invisibly and intersubjectively present in the space between performers who share desires for connection with a lived past and commit themselves to discovering or repairing something ineffable. The observational camera cannot directly visualize these affective forces. And though there is crisis coverage, there is no organic crisis structure to follow that might allow a documentary to graft off this trope of Hollywood narrative, as in the 1960s direct cinema films about election primaries and school segregation standoffs produced for television by Robert Drew.[62] At the end of their shooting and first major round of editing, Attie and O'Hara worried that they had instead fallen for the illusion of reenactment or the allure of simulation. They had a film about costumed men with replica guns walking in the woods who then returned to their regular jobs. Notions of indexicality as mechanically reproduced photographic image inscribed on film or chip had led their documentary to a dead end. Somehow, Attie reflected, "you never really had a sense about what Vietnam was."[63]

But reenacting being there as Vietnam-era journalists offered an unusual indexical possibility to the makers of *In Country*. It was almost as if by accident and through the coincidence of a shared ethic of camerawork with 1960s filmers of war—a shared rolling gait, if not the same analog film rolling through the same kind of gate—their footage bore the potential to touch something of the past lingering in the present, like the tar paper Marks described as waiting to be developed. This was touch not by the cameraperson's image to the world in front of the lens but by the cameraperson's unconsciously reenacted practices of recording to those of camerapersons of the past. This archived repertoire, as I am calling it, opens out from the record of a singular event to encompass the weight of feeling a collective past that still bears down on the present.

An Archived Repertoire

In her ethnographic study of performance art and protest performances in Latin America, Diana Taylor distinguished between the archive, or the resources accumulated and guarded by the state as the official repository for telling stories about the past, and the repertoire, or the kinds of stories, performances, and sayings that circulated via word of mouth—for instance, among copresent protesters risking life and limb to hold an oppressive state to account for disappearing their friends and relatives. The repertoire could change over time but constituted a repository of cultural memory for keeping a particular cause alive outside the purview of police crackdowns or state surveillance. The ability of the live performances to dissipate without an archival trace and re-form in other, more advantageous times and spaces was to the protesters' advantage. Attie and O'Hara were not protesting when they filmed the Vietnam War reenactment, but they were participating somewhat improvisationally in a live performance, much as documentary camerapersons following everyday life long have. It just so happened that their repertoire for camerawork—archived by default as movement and framing choices once the live performance of recording was complete—happened to match the repertoire practiced by camerapersons working in Vietnam and accessible as a vast, informal archive scattered across online video distribution sites circa 2014. Several years into producing the film, Attie and O'Hara realized they could cut relatively easily between their own footage of the reenactment and archival footage recorded in Vietnam. Now in the editing stage, Attie and O'Hara could draw from, juxtapose, and reconstitute this peculiar, archived repertoire of camerawork for their own film, recasting their observational long takes into a densely layered evocation of absent pasts in the present.

A scene early in the film demonstrates how this technique transformed their footage of a reenactment into archive affect, that overwhelming, thunderbolt-like experience of indexicality that the viewer feels coursing through their body. The reenactors are on patrol, and no firefight has yet happened. There is then a sequence of shots of waiting in the woods of Oregon. One reenactor, echoing 1968, places a daisy in his helmet. The reenactors sit and pass the time. The montage ends with a profile close-up of a soldier smoking a cigarette, subtly different from the previous shots in the sequence. The foliage in the background has changed, the colors are softer, and the image is grainier. Then comes an aerial shot that follows the logic and rhythm of the spatial montage as though showing the terrain in the same area at the same time from above. But the texture of the footage feels as though it is from another world. It is no longer the crisp HD video, and the verdant rice fields below are not the Oregon woods. This is archival footage of rural Vietnam recorded from a military helicopter, presumably sometime during the Vietnam War. The disjuncture between the continuous observational recording and editing style and the self-conscious temporal rupture across this cut infuses the sequence with weight, difference, and stakes. *This* is Vietnam. The being there of these shots is that of the war correspondents of the 1960s or 1970s, reappropriated in the editing room by contemporary filmmakers who had role-played as those correspondents and found their own footage of reenactors lacking on its own. But because their viewers' entry point to the archival footage is through the contemporary reenactors behind and in front of the camera, they are primed to understand both the performance activities and the shots they are about to see as nodes along an ongoing continuum of time, a continuum they now enter as spectators of the film. Like the reenactors themselves, viewers can now "experience of the uncanniness of history simultaneously both as an absence and a presence in the present," as Baron describes this perception of archival footage as metonym for the past.[64]

In one thread of discourse about the meaning of war for the teenagers who come of age within it, soldiers prove masculinity through the trials of battle and endurance in spaces outside the comforts of civil society. It is striking that the camerawork featured in the montage of Vietnam here matches the hardening imagined vital to masculine success. As the voice of a soldier reads a letter home about arriving in Vietnam amid a lightning storm, the camerawork seems to regard skulls on pikes, hacking through bush, and bodies collapsed in exhaustion with equal clinical detachment. Two soldiers carry a shirtless man between them who appears to have fainted. "I can't walk through that kind of stuff all day," says a voice off-screen. The image cuts to a ¾ shot of a different man lying on the ground, awake but dazed, and the cameraperson zooms in to an extreme close-up of his face as a cold, off-screen male voice, presumably the journalist, asks, "What does it do to you?" The question implies that the core of the journalist's interest is not in the soldier's well-being (unlike, for instance, "How are you feeling?") but rather in the way that this particular conflict and physical environment test manhood.[65] "Well, try to name something it doesn't do to you," the soldier responds. The frame holds on the face of this dazed individual for a beat before the cut. Another soldier's voice reads a litany of uncomfortable sensations—"The heat, the stench of the air, the sick feeling in your stomach day after day, the smell of body odor, and the choking dust in your throat"—as the montage on screen illustrates the repetitive, monotonous quality of the everyday difficulties to endure. The camerawork betrays a fascination with it all, a sense of disparity with life at home not yet expressible other than through these disciplined observational recordings. The camerapersons show the events, and their bodies disappear. Soldiers walk through the bush and past the camera, each shot taken at a different time in a different place and featuring a different face. A wide shot shows a soldier in the middle of a stream, water up to his neck, holding his rifle above his head as he crosses—a point of reference we can cast back to an early shot in the film of the reenactors wading across a river in Oregon. A soldier sits and waits as the sound of gunshots drones faintly in the distance, off screen. Then there is an interview with a soldier featured in the 1970 CBS television documentary *The World of Charlie Company*. "It's like pure hell," he starts. "I mean, like, a lot of guys, they hunted back in the world before they come over here. They come over here, they stay out anywhere from eighteen [days] to a month. Bugs biting on us, crawling all over us. You sleep on the ground, and you know, you're humping all day long. A lot of guys, you know, they change opinion about being out in the woods. A lot of guys say if they go back to the world, they won't go out in the woods for anything, hunting or any other reason."

As the soldier speaks, a montage loosely illustrates what he is saying, with soldiers slapping bugs, lying on the ground, hiking, and rustling in bushes as the talking ends. It appears that the soldiers are setting up an M18 Claymore antipersonnel mine that reads "FRONT TOWARD ENEMY." There is a close-up of the mine on the ground, wires protruding in several directions from its top. Then there is a straight cut to a Claymore mine in the hand of a reenactor in Oregon, nearly identical to the one featured in the previous shot but crisper in the HD footage and sans wiring. If we miss this detail, we still quickly catch on that we're back in Oregon. The reenactors are going about activities of their own in the woods, digging foxholes and relaxing in hammocks. We recognize them. But we as the audience understand what they are doing differently now. We have been transported elsewhen and elsewhere by the footage of Vietnam, where the proximity of death is palpable, the circumstances are grave, and the camerawork tacitly participates in the ritual of an old American rite of passage to manhood.

As the high schooler Cricket finishes his foxhole, the off-screen voice of O'Hara says, "You told me yesterday that this was one of the better experiences of your life. Do you still feel that way?" He responds, "Yeah, for sure," as a lower third identifies him as "David 'Cricket' Safina-Massey, High School Student." O'Hara asks him to explain what he likes about it. He replies, "I don't know. It's real. You have to work to get it done. It's not like Boy Scouts where everything's like, oh, you know. This is how it would be if it were actually real. Stuff actually happens. But yeah. This is perfect." Cricket is away from home for the reenactment, spending time with men who have served in the Armed Forces. These veterans have complex views of their war experiences, but in general they express pride in their service and the ethos it represents. At moments, they seem to use their time reenacting to work through difficult memories of war together. They accept Cricket as one of them. At the end of the scene, Cricket discloses that he has enlisted in the marines, which he will join after graduating from high school the next spring (fig. 1.5).

Cricket's character embodies the figure of the naive young man who envisions military service as the route to authentic masculinity, only tested thus far in the sensory real of reenactment. Variations of this coming-of-age theme have played out in many US cultural narratives from novels such as *The Red Badge of Courage* (1895) to policy documents such as *The Moynihan Report* of the 1960s to films such as *The Hurt Locker* (2008, released during the US occupation of Iraq) to war reenactment scenarios dating to the early 1960s. There is a great deal of symbolic poignancy in its invocation here, primed as we are by the archival snippets of soldier experiences from Vietnam. There is a scary truth to contemplate about the effects of simulation in Cricket's underexplored conviction of reality in reenactment—at least compared to the Boy Scouts—and in his future trajectory as a marine, where we imagine him if unlucky finding his own way to a "pure hell" that might make these Oregon woods anathema should he return. At his luckiest, he has still signed up to be an executor of US war policy. Little of this scene, to return to the central argument about indexicality in documentary, stands on the observational footage alone. The brief conversation between Cricket and O'Hara startles largely because of the context provided by its juxtaposition with the archival montage, by the match in the archived repertoire of camerawork across two different times.

To return to Baron's theory of temporal disparity in uses of archival footage, most historical documentaries in which the viewer perceives archival footage produce the archive effect. The documentary appropriates the archival filmic

Figure 1.5. An archival montage of soldiers in Vietnam describing and living through traumatic scenarios, represented here by a young soldier who recounts hearing the cries of wounded US troops while being pinned down after an ambush (*top*), is juxtaposed in the film with scenes of reenactor David "Cricket" Safina-Massey (*bottom*), a high school student who reveals that he has enlisted in the marines. Courtesy Mike Attie and Meghan O'Hara.

traces of a past traumatic event to give clout to a retrospective story about that past. Soldiers recounting their experiences in war, for instance, carry the power of immediacy rediscovered in the present, tacitly drawing social authority from the institutions that have deemed these artifacts and not others worthy of preservation. The film then expresses, in Baron's take, the "authority that adheres to the archival document as evidence."[66]

Something like authority or gravity clings to Attie and O'Hara's reappropriation of archival footage, which frames the Vietnam War as historical and mythic. But this use of archival footage cuts against the social authority of the film's reenactor subjects here. In the montages of archival footage, the anonymous soldiers on screen stand in for the quagmire of Vietnam and the existential crisis the war posed to prevailing ideas about the virtues of loyalty and patriotism. Attie and O'Hara's editing breaks up the close-to-the-ground reportage of 1960s journalists to emphasize affect, fragmentation, and lyricism in the soldiers' brushes with death. Individuals appear, but we learn little about the context of their stories. They add up to a general feeling about the hardships and losses of the Vietnam War, an archive affect. In this way, *In Country* aligns more closely with the New Historicist approach to representing the past than with a film like *The Vietnam War*, which aims at a grand narrative. The reenactors may imagine the archival films they've watched authorizing aspects of their dress and decorum as they perform, but as viewers of the film, we do not share their orientation to archival footage.

When the film returns to Oregon, the afterimage of Vietnam that remains in the viewer's consciousness undermines and undercuts Cricket's statement, who knows reenactment and the Boy Scouts but not war. In contrast to the anonymous soldiers who appear in the archival montage, moreover, Attie and O'Hara clearly identify individuals in the unit of reenactors by name, profession outside the hobby, and personal reasons for participating. The film's presentation of reenactors, in other words, is at odds with the film's use of archival footage from Vietnam. Impressionistic montages of archival footage communicate social types and tropes, functioning as a gestural recollection-object about Vietnam, to refer back to Marks's term—"an irreducibly material object that encodes collective memory."[67] The shots from the archival footage accumulate in density but do not progress. They are affectively full but narratively thin, like the tar paper from Poston in Tajiri's *History and Memory*, a sign of absent presence that overwhelms. The camerawork at the reenactment may not represent indexical events (it is footage of the banal), but the repertoire of camerawork—largely unchanged since the 1960s in framing, pacing, and commitment to stoic, voltmeter-ish observation—matches the archived repertoire, allows for intercutting, and creates a temporal disparity in which viewers may regard the values and blind spots that undergird the reenactors' efforts to keep this past alive. Viewers of *In Country* can feel the presence of the absent past now more like the reenactors themselves.

The contrasting juxtaposition across archival footage and reenactment record also creates one of the film's moments of critique. This time now touches that one through collision or temporal disparity, but what surges up in the metonymic feeling is somewhat undetermined. We could say that by taking responsibility for making his body the echo of a Vietnam-era soldier through details gleaned from training manuals, war materiel, documentary films, history books, video games, and Hollywood Vietnam films, Cricket becomes a living document of the Vietnam War for the long duration, cinematic documentary he observes in his head as he and the other reenactors play out their scenario over the weekend. What seems clearer is that the feeling of "collective effervescence" for the particular but unknowable past that Cricket plays further melds to his own future identity as a marine.[68] His perception of Vietnam in the reenactment as real is certainly felt and earned, in a way (he is outside digging holes and camping in the woods), but it is more significantly future-oriented and ideological in its investment. In the continuity-disjuncture played out across camerawork from these two different times, the film makes the ideological orientation clear. The stakes of the reenactment have to do with the passing on of ideas about masculinity and military service.

Psychic Repair: Reenactment, Camerawork,
and Working Through

Drawing from Tomkins's writing on the affect system, Eve Sedgwick critiqued the "strong affect theory" undergirding the "hermeneutics of suspicion" that prevailed in much critical theory of her era and prior ones, which fixated on the exposure of hidden forces said to determine social life (discourses, the unconscious, performativity, superstructure, etc.). The "paranoid position" characterized by "terrible alertness to the dangers posed by the hateful and envious part-objects that one defensively projects into, carves out of, and ingests from the world around one" augmented fear and anger, encouraged strategies of avoiding "bad objects," and thereby short-circuited any possibility for repair, nourishment, and growth. She argued in favor of "weak affect theory" that applied only to local contexts but effectively mitigated anxiety and paranoia within them.[69]

Reenactment in therapeutic scenarios can help bring about what she calls "reparative practices" more typical of "weak affect theory," a conceit central to psychodrama therapy, for example. Working through difficult family relations or traumatic experiences via the reenactment of different subject positions, in dramaturg-turned-psychiatrist J. L. Moreno's praxis, helped create the tools for the individual to expand their understanding of a feared object or traumatic event and then learn to live with it more peaceably. Sometimes, the filming of psychodrama reenactment scripts, as in William Greaves's fascinating cinematic experiment in revolution *Symbiopsychotaxiplasm: Take 1* (1968), plays a role in a collective working through as well. The observational footage of the crew discussing whether to rebel, if this is the right word for these records, folds into a communal process of reflection and growth in Greaves's film.[70]

Something like this reparative dynamic emerges in *In Country* through the character of Doc, a former army medic filmed participating in his first Vietnam War reenactment (fig. 1.6). In a key scene, he tends to a fellow reenactor pretending to have been killed during a firefight. According to Attie and O'Hara, Doc sprang into action to evacuate the reenactor's body from the "battlefield," radio in to a nearby "medevac" for a pickup, drag the reenactor down a long hill, and carry him over his shoulder to the agreed-upon evacuation point some distance away. The process of extracting the living reenactor from the woods was strenuous and time consuming—excessive for the goal of playing war, thought Attie and O'Hara while filming him. This was Doc's rolling gait, so to speak. When Doc finally rested the body on a gurney affixed to the ATV medevac, the "dead" reenactor was immediately allowed to come back to life and rejoin his unit. The pure expenditure of energy in Doc's performance startled Attie and O'Hara, like the echo of a traumatic symptom passed across bodies. They recorded this event through a series of long takes that may have expressed something about temporality and conventional media pacing when deployed at length in niche art film contexts, but in making these shots they perceived something else that did not quite translate into the footage of the reenactment on its own. The psyche, especially in scenarios involving trauma, tends not to reveal much to the gaze. But by the end of their editing process, Attie and O'Hara had reoriented their outward-facing observational footage from that day to face inward as evidence of Doc's ongoing efforts to work through PTSD from experiences tending to wounded comrades in Iraq. Sometime later, they interviewed him for several hours at his home and conversed with him about his role-play as a Vietnam-era medic. Doc made the connections to his own traumatic memories of serving in Iraq and his struggles with returning to civilian life. His sparse, reflective voice-over about insomnia, memories of dismemberment, nightmares, and struggles with despair play in the finished film beneath Attie and O'Hara's footage of Doc's reenactment performance, home movies that Doc and his unit recorded in Iraq, and a shot of US soldiers in Vietnam dragging the body of a dead comrade up a riverbank—the only such image in the film. The scene suggests that at least some of the reenactors use the shared scenario of playing war as a space for healing and contemplation rather than nostalgia alone.

Though the filmmakers originally sought to make a film by being there to record events in the present, the subject of reenactment itself (to return to the argument at hand), with its affective evocation of past time always returning in the present, changed their perspectives on the temporality of their ostensibly observational footage. "We decided to make a film that only existed in the present tense," O'Hara explained to me, as if channeling Phelan's ontology for

Figure 1.6. Scenes featuring medics tending to men killed in action in Vietnam (*top left*), Doc tending to a wounded man in Iraq during his deployment (*bottom left*), Doc thinking (*top right*), and the Vietnam War reenactors performing death and evacuation in Oregon (*bottom right*), juxtaposed in *In Country* (2014). Courtesy Mike Attie and Meghan O'Hara.

performance or Freud's "mystic writing pad." "We did think a lot about how it was a way in which to say all this history exists in the present moment, like each of these moments has all of those moments kind of built into them."[71] In other words, the filmmakers' efforts to stave off the banality of their observational footage led them to act like reenactors even during the editing of their film, scouring archives, documents, and home movie footage to seek out moments of connection to their recordings. The temporal disparities created through juxtaposition—a "double helix" structure, in O'Hara's terms—might yet create for viewers of their film that overwhelming affect that comes from perceiving loss in the present. But unlike the individual revisiting traumatic memories (as suggested in the scene with Doc), the film as a whole can range across a sprawling array of video recordings made by many other people in many other contexts. If the footage registers as traces of the psyche in the finished film, then it is a collective psyche that it aims to touch.

CONCLUSION

I have argued in this chapter that observational camerawork alone failed to reveal contingency or stakes in footage of the reenactment event in *In Country* but that framing the camerawork itself as a reenactment of practices dating to the 1960s embedded a latent form of touch with the past—an embodied, affective indexicality—into the footage. Through editing for archive affect that was also core to the reenactors' desires and goals, the camerawork itself came to constitute gestural recollection-objects, to adapt Marks's term, here by turns fetishes for crisis coverage, an archived repertoire, and a process of psychic repair. None of these outcomes have much to do with being there to record events in the present as an omniscient observer. Indexicality in this case starts in the bodies in performance in front of and behind the camera and has to do with the extended work of researching and watching film about Vietnam to facilitate the charged perception of absent time in the present of performance. As with Pierce's example of the man with the rolling gait, such moments of embodied indexicality startle and humble. They can open space for new ways of thinking.

Yet the ethic of nonintervention is still central to *In Country* in ways that limit its capacity to critique the subculture of war reenacting or create too many open spaces. In part, this has to do with the intensely personal focus of war reenactment. The film mostly honors the commemorative mission of the reenactors and their desire for a sensory experience of past martial sacrifice, which the filmmakers illustrated through the juxtaposition of archival and observational footage. Kinney, the leader of the group who was featured in the scene of smelling bug juice, wrote an extended explanation on their website to answer the oft-asked question "But why do we do it?" He noted that Vietnam was "an infantryman's war" in which "the grunt bore the brunt" of suffering and public criticism from the "professionally sensitive," though of course the grunt had no say in policy decisions or their missions. The goal of the group is to honor the grunts "in understanding, in preserving his memory and in keeping their collective spirits alive," he explains:

> We exist to say "thank you" to the true fighting men who fought and bled in Vietnam. They are our credentials. The freedom they bought for us in a far off land is beyond any feeling of gratitude that we can express. We cannot thank them enough.... We freely admit that reenacting is also a serious hobby from which we derive a sense of satisfaction that cannot be matched by watching ESPN and chowing down on a bowl of potato chips. If we are to live vicariously through the lives of other men, then we choose to live through the lives of the true heroes of our nation.[72]

What Kinney offers here for Vietnam veterans, ironically, is something like what Thomas Waugh called an ethics of "oppositional film practice" in his writing about accountability in queer film of the 1970s and 1980s. Rather than follow normative cultural mores about accountability to a general audience, Waugh argues that an oppositional ethics must first and foremost account for the needs, perspectives, and concerns of an aggrieved, activist constituency threatened by law, prejudice, or impoverishment. "My reasoning is that the film-makers' decision to dramatize the universality of homophobic discourse threatening their constituency takes precedence over the film-makers' responsibility to homophobes," Waugh quipped.[73] When Kinney expresses an ethics for the grunt here, he is essentially giving over accountability for representing the Vietnam War to those American infantrymen who fought in it and the needs they may have in the present for therapy, respect, or validation. There are ways that these young men were victims of circumstance, but it is also clear that some burned villages, killed and mutilated civilians, and executed prisoners of war, like those men featured in the documentary *Winter Soldier* (1972) about the war crimes hearing that took place in Detroit in the winter of 1971. It was met with skepticism upon its completion, and no broadcaster aired *Winter Soldier* in its era; the film only came to screen in select art house venues in 2005.[74] Moreover, the reenactment has nothing to say for the Vietcong or those in Vietnam (except Nguyen's poignant reflections) who had no choice but to live through this war and occupation. To write that reenactment is only about gratitude for "true heroes" and an undefined notion of "freedom they bought for us in a far off land" is to mistake reactionary nostalgia for public service. It is dangerous. In what turned out to be a prescient line about this kind of force in the reception of archival war imagery, Baron observed that "nostalgia has a frightening power to shape political movements that seek to 'return' the individual, the nation, or the world to an idealized past that obscures history's darker side."[75] Kinney's statement seems to argue for commemoration without the necessary reflection. In aiming to follow its subjects' perspectives in this simulation documentary scenario, *In Country* mostly allows the commemoration ethic to stand.

To their credit, Novick and Burns focused their interviews with former American soldiers and infantrymen who fought with the Vietcong on hard-earned reflections about the dark side of that war, perhaps none more poignant than veteran John Musgrave's analysis of the meaning of youth in such circumstances. *In Country* also suggests a critique of the warrior ethos proffered to the nation's young, both in the scene with Cricket that follows the archival montage in Vietnam and in the last shot of the film, where a boy looks on at the Vietnam reenactors marching in a parade. Temporality in a reenactment points forward and backward simultaneously, after all, and here the film suggests this. It is not hard to imagine Cricket deployed to Syria, Sudan, Lebanon, Iran, or somewhere else yet to be identified as requiring brutal American civilization.

Cricket the reenactor gestures back to other young American men who enlisted to fight in Vietnam. But these striking moments with Cricket do not add up to a reflection on the past, at least not the way that Musgrave reflects. He joined the marines at about the same age as Cricket, and by his own account, he did so with about the same level of introspection and expectation. He spoke in Burns and Novick's film about wanting adventure, hardship, and patriotic duty. But later in the series, Musgrave reflected on the nature of youth, confusion, and racism in war and learning hatred for the enemy:

> I saw a Marine step on a bouncing betty mine, and that's when I made my deal with the devil. And I said I will never kill another human being as long as I'm in Vietnam. However, I will waste as many gooks as I can find. I'll wax as many dinks as I can find. I'll smoke as many zips as I can find. But I ain't gonna kill anybody. Turn a subject into an object. Racism 101. It turns out to be a very necessary tool when you have children fighting your wars. For them to stay sane doing their work.[76]

Musgrave's confession about his linguistic strategy for turning subject into object bears ominously on Kinney's presentation of period-correct slurs to use in the reenactment, represented in the film. Musgrave explains how the language of dehumanization can work to justify killing; in the reenactment (and *In Country*), the teaching of this language reads as a quirky farce. We are left to wonder whether Cricket in his likely current deployment will find himself reenacting this particular lesson, the deepest and darkest motif in the repertoire of America's collective memory. It is a flaw of the reenactment and the film about it to fail a harder interrogation of such moments, but it is also part of a more general trend in films that participate in simulation documentaries, which often short-circuit access to key voices in the stories they purport to embody. In the next chapter, I consider more contemporary simulations/reenactments in the military, focusing on cultural awareness scenarios constructed and carried out in the early 2000s by the US Army during the war in Iraq, where stories and narratives about training face similar kinds of limitations.

NOTES

1. Blue, "One Man's Truth," 409.
2. O'Hara, interview.
3. Balsom, "Reality-Based Community."
4. See especially studies of television producer and 1960s filmmaker Robert Drew, who offered the "crisis structure" argument for direct cinema. Mamber, *Cinema Verite in America*; O'Connell, *Robert Drew and the Development of Cinema Verite in America*.

5. See this strain of argument especially in MacDougall and Castaing-Taylor, *Transcultural Cinema*; Balsom, "Reality-Based Community"; Grimshaw and Ravetz, *Observational Cinema*.

6. O'Hara, interview.

7. Schneider, *Performing Remains*, 37.

8. For assessments of sensory filmmaking and slowness in post-2000s art films, see Lee, "Beyond the Ethico-aesthetic"; De Luca and Jorge, "From Slow Cinema."

9. Notable films associated with this renewed sensory orientation in nonfiction filmmaking include *Sweetgrass* (2008), *Terrace of the Sea* (2009), *Foreign Parts* (2010), *The Iron Ministry* (2014), and *Into the Hinterlands* (2015), all from the Sensory Ethnography Lab at Harvard, and *Honeyland* (2019) from North Macedonia. Scott MacDonald wrote a hefty monograph on "the Cambridge turn" in ethnographic film and personal documentary with sections on the Sensory Ethnography Lab, whose practitioners pursue an ethics and aesthetics largely grounded in the traditions of observational cinema practice. They have argued that this approach, unlike written theory, foregrounds affective textures and experiences through and beyond individual sense perception. Some of these films are indeed exceptions. The flagship journal *Visual Anthropology Review*, for instance, dedicated a full volume of scholarly essays to *Leviathan* (2015), an austere feature largely recorded with miniature action cameras placed on masts, poles, and the bodies of New England fisherman at work. Journal editors Lisa Stevenson and Eduardo Kohn characterized the film as "groundbreaking. By decoupling voice from any stable narrative perspective, it allows the viewer to be made over by a world beyond the human. It is, we argue, a form of dreaming—a modality of attention that can open us to the beings with whom we share this fragile planet. As such, *Leviathan* gestures to a sort of ontological poetics and politics for the so-called Anthropocene." The film still largely follows the observational tenets of nonintervention and sensory immersion, and it expresses what Christopher Pavsek critiqued as "a visceral distrust of words or discursivity, a *logophobia*." In any case, these films eschew reenactment as subject and method, and none of the writing on observationally informed camera practice has looked at this kind of work through such a lens. "Voltmeter" still gets closer to it, even if the cinematic instrument measures current a bit differently. See select articles on this body of work at Pavsek, "Leviathan," 4; Stevenson and Kohn, "Leviathan," 49; MacDonald, *American Ethnographic Film*; Lee, "Beyond the Ethico-aesthetic."

10. Burns himself addressed the question about lessons learned, the obligations of storytelling, and possible parallels to draw about wars without endings: "Our job is just to tell the story, not to put up big neon signs saying, 'Hey, isn't this kind of like the present?' But we know historical narratives cannot help but be informed by our own fears and desires. The tactics the Viet Cong and also the North Vietnamese Army employed, as well as the Taliban and Al Qaeda and now ISIS, suggest an infinite war—and that's why you hope that lessons of Vietnam can be distilled." See, for instance, Klay, "Ken Burns."

11. Baron, *Archive Effect*, 106.

12. Attie, interview.

13. Baron, *Archive Effect*, 159.

14. Phelan, *Unmarked*.

15. Baron, *Archive Effect*, 102.

16. Friedberg, *Window Shopping*.

17. Taylor, *Archive and the Repertoire*.

18. Following Aretha Franklin's use of the term as an emblem of Black female empowerment in her 1967 song "Respect," "Sock It To Me" became the famous tagline of a recurring misogynist motif on the TV variety comedy show *Rowan and Martin's Laugh-In* (1968–73). At the end of the show, a dancing, bikini- or miniskirt-clad woman (usually Judy Carne or Goldie Hawn) would sensually declare that it was "sock-it-to-me time." An unidentified party off-screen would then douse her with water, open a trap door beneath her feet, or visit her with some other indignity. US soldiers in Vietnam wrote variations of the term on their helmets as an expression of longings for sex and as a dubious metaphor for their unenviable (and possibly feminized) position on the ground in Vietnam. The phrase was also reappropriated in the film *Fight Club* (1999) when the unleashed id character Tyler Durden (played by Brad Pitt) wears the slogan on a white T-shirt, replicas of which consumers may still procure from dozens of online outlets. See, for instance, one rendition on a Brad Pitt mannequin from a company based in Japan at "Screen Accurate FIGHT CLUB 'SOCK IT TO ME' Sweat T-shirt," Max Cady, accessed October 6, 2021, https://www.maxcady.com/e/socke.htm. See also Rowan & Martin's Laugh-In, "Sock It to Me."

19. I was surprised at how far the visage of Redcoat soldiers traveled in the three years after 9/11. The group of reenactors I joined and documented also appeared in a PBS American Experience documentary about Revolutionary War reenacting called *Patriots Day* (2004), at the 2004 Democratic National Convention in Boston, and in a permanent, $16 million exhibit at the Smithsonian Museum of American History in Washington, DC, titled "The Price of Freedom: Americans at War." Commissioned shortly after September 11, 2001, during a time of heightened jingoistic sentiment nationally, the exhibit covers every major war or conflict that involved US soldiers between the mid-1700s and 2003. The Smithsonian paid groups of Redcoat reenactors—including the one I had joined—to stage the massacre of Lexington colonists for their film cameras, recording the event from perspectives simulated to be those of minutemen on April 19, 1775. As of 2022, the edited video loop still served as the centerpiece for the first area of the exhibit. When visitors standing between wax sculptures of two Lexington minutemen press a button labeled "Push here to start," a video of Redcoat reenactors appears on a screen facing the museumgoer. The Redcoats on-screen launch into a one-minute frontal attack, complete with the bayoneting of the camera-lens-turned-viewer-perspective. The visceral experience is meant to represent the start of the US Revolutionary War for museum visitors of all ages, and it plays almost continuously every day while the museum is open. My feelings about briefly appearing on-screen in it remain conflicted. The film is accessible at AndyRiceFilms, *About Face!*

20. Articulated in Michel Foucault's 1975–76 lecture series "Society Must Be Defended," biopolitics refers to a set of impersonal mechanisms of state control set on subjects, who then became their front-line enforcers. These include categories of illness and perversion, sexuality, liberal economics, and law, among many others, that in turn become rationalizations for professionals, soldiers, bureaucrats, wardens, police, and so on to enforce on the body as discipline and then self-discipline. Foucault, *Essential Foucault*.

21. B. Boyle and Lim, *Looking Back*, 10.

22. *In Country: Reenacting the Vietnam War*, "Bonus Features," DVD, directed by Mike Attie and Meghan O'Hara (Film Movement, 2015).

23. Some accounts date the start of the hobby of war reenacting to 1950, when a Smithsonian employee who proclaimed himself a "true Southerner" asked a fellow black-powder enthusiast from the North to set up skirmishing events between "Yanks and Rebs."

These were marksmanship competitions in which collectors of Civil War–era, muzzle-loading rifles shot breakable targets. Such gatherings caught on with other collectors, the number of skirmishing groups swelled, companies began manufacturing replica muskets for hobbyist use, and by the early 1960s, participants had formed a national organization and bought land in Virginia to host one-thousand-person events. Many moved into war reenacting with the one hundredth anniversary of the Battle of Bull Run in 1961, the opening salvo of Civil War commemorations. The loosely scripted reenactment included over four thousand reenactors, a hundred thousand spectators, National Guardsmen paid to dress as Union and Confederate soldiers, and US Army officers who guided logistical maneuvers throughout the four-hour event. State committees, politicians, historians (some reluctant), and enthusiastic white hobbyists organized reenactments regularly over the next five years, leaving a legacy partly about honoring soldiers who fought and died in war and partly about reaffirming some participants' own racist convictions for "killing the n----rs!" as one group screamed at a nighttime reenactment campout shortly after the Mississippi Klan killed Freedom Summer activists James Chaney, Andrew Goodman, and Michael Schwerner in 1964. Not all reenactors agreed with the politics of these Southern units—many reenacted to honor ancestors who fought for the North, for instance, and Black Americans still reenact the Massachusetts Fifty-Fourth featured in the film *Glory*—but the act of re-creating the events helped keep the Lost Cause alive, as well. North-South Skirmish Association, "About the N-SSA"; Stanton and Belyea, "Their Time Will Yet Come," 273; Kammen, *Mystic Chords of Memory*; Franklin, "Century of Civil War Observance," 103, 105; Kimmel, "My Recollections"; United States and Civil War Centennial Commission, *Civil War Centennial*, 14.

24. Marks, *Skin of the Film*, 119–20.
25. Sobchack, "Toward a Phenomenology," 246; Baron, *Archive Effect*.
26. Schneider, *Performing Remains*, 168.
27. Nichols, *Representing Reality*; Rodowick, *Virtual Life of Film*; Doane, "Indexicality"; Doane, "Indexicality and Medium Specificity," 143.
28. Peirce, *Philosophical Writings of Peirce*, 106.
29. Winston and Tsang, "Subject and Indexicality."
30. Peirce, *Philosophical Writings of Peirce*, 109.
31. Doane, *Emergence of Cinematic Time*, 89.
32. Ibid., 82.
33. Ibid., 92.
34. Doane developed this idea further in a subsequent article, "The Object of Theory" (2003), about the attraction of the concept of indexicality in film in the context of a modernity dominated by "highly technologically mediated rationalization." In her reading of Paul Willeman's work on cinephilia, Doane insisted that what cinephiles came to value and believe in about the indexicality of the film was the medium's capacity to represent contingency, the traces of life beyond the control of direction, mise-en-scène, or the performativity of roles: "The lure of contingency is that it seems to offer a way out, an anchoring point for the condensation of utopian desires. It proffers itself as a way out of systematicity." Doane, "Object of Theory," 85.
35. Doane, "Indexicality and Medium Specificity," 136.
36. Peirce, *Philosophical Writings of Peirce*, 108.
37. Stella Bruzzi's *New Documentary* (2006) uses Butler's concept of the performative to analyze first-person documentary films that follow a character playing a part, like Nick Broomfield's scandal-hunter persona. Counter to theories that documentary represents

history, she argues that "documentaries are performative acts whose truth comes into being only at the moment of filming." I see her analysis as appropriate for interpreting these parts of Peirce's writing on the index as startle and pursue a kindred line of thinking in this book through analyses of camerawork and reenactment. Bruzzi, *New Documentary*, 10.

38. Barthes and Howard, *Camera Lucida*, 26.

39. See, for instance, a passage on "the ecstasy of the filming-body" in MacDougall, *Corporeal Image*, 27.

40. Baron, *Archive Effect*, 31.

41. Rouch and Feld, *Ciné-Ethnography*, 153.

42. Marks, *Skin of the Film*, 77, 119–20.

43. Runia, quoted in Baron, *Archive Effect*, 162.

44. Phelan continued to distinguish metonym from metaphor in keeping with the account in Baron's writing on archive affect. She could have been writing about the cameraperson's aim to disappear during filming: "In performance, the body is metonymic of self, of character, of voice, of 'presence.' But in the plenitude of its apparent visibility and availability, the performer actually disappears and represents something else—dance, movement, sound, character, 'art.'" Phelan, *Unmarked*, 150.

45. Marks, *Skin of the Film*, 82.

46. In his consideration of performances carried out through documentation rather than with a copresent audience, Philip Auslander described the "performativity of performance documentation" in similar terms. He referred especially to Vito Acconci's *Blinks* (1969), a series of photographs that Acconci snapped when he blinked while walking unnoticed down a city street with an outward-facing camera. Without an audience there to see the walk down the street, the "live" performance occurred only when the visitor to the art gallery regarded the grid of nine photographs Acconci took hanging there on the wall. In the context of this kind of performance art, the performativity of camerawork becomes an explicit object. Though the performativity of the take is less explicit in *History and Memory* (the stakes are higher for subjects in Tajiri's film than in Acconci's banal walk down the street), the case is similar to Tajiri's tar paper. P. Auslander, *Reactivations*, 21–40.

47. Marks, *Skin of the Film*, 82.

48. Ibid., 82.

49. Peirce, *Philosophical Writings of Peirce*, 108.

50. Morris, "Banality in Cultural Studies," 17.

51. Ibid., 20.

52. Doane, "Information, Crisis, Catastrophe," 252.

53. Schneider, *Performing Remains*, 139.

54. MacDougall and Castaing-Taylor, *Transcultural Cinema*, 200.

55. Attie, interview.

56. O'Hara and Attie, "Vietnam War Never Ended."

57. O'Hara, interview.

58. Minh-ha, "Totalizing Quest of Meaning"; Winston, "Documentary Film as Scientific Inscription"; Renov, *Subject of Documentary*; Rony, *Third Eye*; Godmilow, "Kill the Documentary."

59. O'Hara, interview.

60. Ginsburg, "Decolonizing Documentary," 42.

61. See an introduction in Delgado and Stefancic, *Critical Race Theory*; on race in reenactment, see Bates, "Good Ol' Rebel."

62. *Primary* (1960) focused on the Democratic primary contest between John F. Kennedy and Hubert Humphrey, and *Crisis: Behind a Presidential Commitment* (1963) focused on the conflict between Alabama governor George Wallace and the Kennedy administration over the integration of the University of Alabama. In both cases, a crisis structure was built into unfolding scenarios in which the filmmakers could anticipate the temporality of the conflict and characters to film along the lines of a Hollywood fiction feature that could "move you and shake you and leave you a different person almost," as Drew put it, even if the documentarians could not know the outcome of the crisis in advance. Mamber, *Cinema Verite in America*; O'Connell, *Robert Drew*, 35.

63. Attie, interview.

64. Baron, *Archive Effect*, 162.

65. It is noteworthy that similar interests in the effects of martial endurance trials on the body and the senses animate news stories about early 2000s military simulation training carried out during the wars in Iraq and Afghanistan (discussed in chapter 2).

66. Baron, *Archive Effect*, 18.

67. Note that I am referring only to *In Country* in this example. Other Vietnam films including Lynn Novak and Ken Burns's series *The Vietnam War* (2017) feature interviews with individuals whom we see pictured as younger selves in archival footage. In *In Country*, alternatively, we see several of the Vietnam War reenactors in their own archival footage taken during the Iraq War. Marks, *Skin of the Film*, 77.

68. Building on the concept of the social that he developed in *The Rules of Sociological Method* (1895) and *Suicide* (1897), Durkheim argued in *Elementary Forms of Religious Life* (1912) that participants in group rituals like reenactments created a collective form of energy—a "collective effervescence"—that was inaccessible to the individual members going about their everyday lives. The collectively witnessed and enacted rites "changes the conditions of psychic activity," Durkheim argued, so that the "experimental proof of [the practitioner's] beliefs" could emerge. With each recursive cycle of collective ritual performance and reflection, the objects of group focus seemed to accumulate greater auratic power, which in turn served to strengthen community bonds, compel mutual accountability, and reinforce values. Durkheim, *Elementary Forms*, 416.

69. Sedgwick, "Paranoid Reading and Reparative Reading," 128.

70. See especially chaps. 4 and 5 in Murphy, *Rewriting Indie Cinema*.

71. O'Hara, interview; Elsaesser, "Freud as Media Theorist," 100–101.

72. Kinney, "Mission Statement."

73. Waugh, "Lesbian and Gay Documentary," 253.

74. See the film and notation about its reception in the DVD release from 2006: Winterfilm, Vietnam Veterans against the War, and Milliarium Zero, *Winter Soldier*.

75. Baron, *Archive Effect*, 169.

76. Ward et al., *Vietnam War*, 214.

TWO

WEAPONIZING AFFECT

A Film Phenomenology of 3D Military Training Simulations during the Iraq War

THE VIETNAM WAR REENACTORS DISCUSSED in chapter 1 impose nostalgia on a murky and at times disgraceful military past in the name of commemoration. Simulation training for modern war fighting, the subject of chapter 2, imposes political affect on the present and future. This chapter critically considers the relation between simulation design and human experience through the analysis of three-dimensional military training simulation scenarios developed between 2003 and 2012 at the Fort Irwin National Training Center (NTC) in the Mojave Desert of California (fig. 2.1). Activities here are recursive, cinematic, situated in physical space, premised on embodied reenactment, collective, and speculative in significant ways, and so I analyze the site as a simulation documentary.

During the occupations of Iraq and Afghanistan and after the Abu Ghraib prisoner abuse scandal broke in March 2003, the US military overhauled its force-on-force training paradigm in favor of cultural awareness and cultural terrain.[1] The military contracted with Hollywood special-effects studios to develop a series of counterinsurgency warfare immersive-training simulations, which included hiring Iraqi American and Afghan American citizens to play villagers, mayors, and insurgents in scenarios. My primary question centers on the military technoscience of treating human bodies as variables in reiterative simulation scenarios like these. I analyze interviews with soldiers and actors, my own experiences videotaping training simulations at the fort, and the accounts of many other visiting journalists and filmmakers across time. I argue that the stories participants tell about their simulation experiences came to constitute one key outcome of the simulation itself. Moreover, these stories functioned to blunt dissent, neutralize the impacts of graphic war imagery, and aid the fort's long-term efforts to retain clout and funding in the face of

Figure 2.1. One of three camera operators records a training simulation at the Fort Irwin National Training Center in 2012 (*left*). Simultaneously, a technician in a media center nearby (*right*) records video streams for later review by soldier trainees. He also follows a director's commands to emit smells, broadcast sounds, and ignite small explosions as the scenario unfolds. Recorded by the author, with permission from the Fort Irwin National Training Center, Barstow, CA.

wars whose intensity fluctuated. Expanding on the concept of the film-body as a distributed system of being that expresses perception and intention, I treat the ongoing cinematic performances at the fort as a kind of simulation-body unbounded by skin.[2]

"Despite the fact that cultural knowledge has not traditionally been a priority within the Department of Defense (DOD)," argued Montgomery McFate, a trained cultural anthropologist who became a key architect of the military's turn to culture, "the ongoing insurgency in Iraq has served as a wake-up call to the military that adversary culture matters."[3] The army introduced cultural awareness training to a new manual in 2004 that built on older concepts of the warrior ethos. The new training regime meant to instill in each soldier the autonomy and quick-thinking capacities needed to negotiate the uncertainties of urban, insurgent warfare on behalf of US interests.[4] In coordination with the new emphasis on cultural terrain, the NTC constructed thirteen mock Iraqi and Afghan villages to simulate locations, social conditions, and everyday life practices characteristic of emerging counterinsurgency war zones. These sites served as the final training grounds for American soldiers before they deployed to war zones in Iraq and Afghanistan. For two weeks, the army, contracted special-effects technicians, and scenario writers from the Hollywood film industry orchestrated simulated improvised explosive device (IED) attacks, suicide bombings, beheadings, sectarian infighting, protests, raids, and sweeps for four thousand soldiers finalizing their preparations for deployment. Army forts and marine bases across the country began to build such simulation sites, all hiring Arabic-speaking Iraqi American actors (and later Pashto- and Dari-speaking

Afghan Americans) to play mayors, villagers, police chiefs, mothers, aid workers, and so on to enhance the cultural realism of their scenarios.[5] In effect, the military extracted from these diasporic subjects a staged, embodied enactment of support for America's invasion of their native countries.

Rather than expanding on the obvious irony of this scenario, I examine the complex experiences afforded by the site simulations among these civilian subjects as well as the troops in training, the mix of military and civilian staff members who managed the sets, and the media and academic visitors (including me) who have documented the Fort Irwin simulations. I contend that when the army began to operate embodied training simulations focused on cultural awareness and counterinsurgency, it was almost hard-wired to adapt old instincts for domination and control to this new, intersubjective context, raising a series of questions about culture, learning, and critique. "A key element in our consideration of political affect," writes John Protevi to this point, "is the triggering of affect programs such as rage and panic." These programs turn the individual and social body into "a self-preserving agent capable of emergency action" but forestall the kind of self-conscious curiosity that facilitates cultural exchange, mutuality, and growth.[6] What do troops learn about culture and cultural exchange, then, through a cultural awareness training regime that still treats "the enemy" as embodied subjects? How do different role-players make sense of their experiences in the training simulations in relation to their prior life experiences, and what meaningful patterns emerge from their accounts? And why would the public affairs office in this fort welcome—and even cultivate—visits from journalists, television news reporters, artists, and documentary filmmakers to assess worst-case-scenario training that on the surface makes visceral the failure of US military policy in Iraq and Afghanistan?

In many journalistic accounts, scholarly studies, and documentaries about the fort, somewhat incredibly, the spectacular display of violence, blood, chaos, and bodies serves as evidence of progress rather than failure within the military in the wake of Abu Ghraib.[7] "I sensed a genuine desire on the part of Army and Iraqi staff to make things right," concluded one performance-studies scholar after spending a day immersed in rehearsals of IED attacks at the fort.[8] My analysis, however, is not an endorsement of the training. I am not in a position to evaluate whether cultural awareness in simulation training demonstrates an essential change within US military institutions in keeping with the interests of Iraqi and Afghan civilians. Rather, I propose below that the manufacture of media fascination and positive reporting is part of the simulation's design—and is significant to the survival of this fort. Finding new ways to cooperate with reporters on military-friendly terms is in keeping with strategies since Vietnam for controlling journalism about US wars.[9] In the context of pervasive cameras in the United States and abroad, the military's vision of a future of endless small-scale urban warfare against insurgent enemies facing poverty and environmental collapse, the routines of torture in secret military prisons, the rise of "militainment" news and video games, and the pervasive use of drone strikes that sometimes kill civilians, I argue that it is imperative to see the military's experiments with managing affects in immersive, cinematic simulation performances as a new kind of weapon executing old ends and not a new iteration of clean, "virtuous war," in the ironic phrase of military-simulation scholar James der Derian.[10]

At its core, this chapter considers the cinematic mechanics entailed in weaponizing affect. Like the shock-and-awe campaign in miniature, the war-movie cultural awareness spectacles at Fort Irwin are intended to disorient and soften those immersed within them—troops and visiting journalist-filmmakers alike—so that they are primed for official explanations on hand to account for the real of their intense affective sensations. Kara Keeling offers a theory of cinematic clichés, which she argues can be internalized and projected on the world as "common sense" filters for perception and attention. At Fort Irwin, the cliché of the stoic, masculine action-film protagonist who must harden himself to sadness and grief also centers troop learning priorities and teaching methods, limits the range of soldiers' encounters with Iraqi and Afghan role-players, and offers a familiar schema for visiting journalist-filmmakers to follow in their own documentary stories. Action-cinematic narratives in the movies and simulation-training scenarios alike typically end before the aftermath of urgent action, short-circuiting the need to process suffering, remorse, and loss. In addition to their supposed role in simulating adversary culture and facilitating troop learning, in other words, cinematic techniques serve a military public-relations strategy to mitigate dissenting journalism and subvert critique amid disastrous wars.[11]

FILM PHENOMENOLOGY WITH CAMERAS AND THE SIMULATION-BODY

Cameras and performance have played a key role in war campaigns, dating to Matthew Brady's photographs of corpses on battlefields arranged before his lens during the American Civil War, but the Iraq War featured an unusually wide array of camera operators who created photographs, moving images, and spectacles to be photographed for very different ends.[12] Photographs of atrocities have not necessarily communicated dissent or moral indignation. Below,

I offer an account of how the visual records of bloody, violent displays at Fort Irwin have in fact undermined possibilities for their use in critique. I draw on film theorists of affect and intersubjectivity to think through the centrality of cinema-industry tropes in the construction of the training simulations and the porous boundaries between action-film depictions of war and the subjective perceptions of participants in the training simulations to interpret the real and the fake of their experiences. Affect theorist Tarja Laine argues that the orientation of the cinema viewer to the screen epitomizes the ephemeral yet continually reconstituted space "where the 'outside' of the collective experience becomes the 'inside' of the subject's psychic life."[13] My research on Fort Irwin suggests that many young soldiers who have not yet gone to war have internalized these cinematic outsides and drawn from formative cinema-viewing and game-play experiences as a basis from which to judge the affective realism of their military training. In this light, the cinema is not exactly an ideological apparatus of mechanical reproduction or an illusion machine playing on insatiable unconscious desires but rather a matter of affects that drives those in charge of Fort Irwin to conform the landscape to their trainees' common-sense orientation to the world. I intend to emphasize, however, that it is not just soldiers but also visiting camerapersons, journalists, and documentarians who understand war imagery at least in part according to the clichés of entertainment cinema.

My analytical approach draws from the film phenomenological method discussed in the introduction. While Vivian Sobchack writes from the position of a viewer in a cinema theater, I write from my experience as a cameraperson in a three-dimensional, cinematic war-simulation space inhabited by various actors. I visited Fort Irwin in 2007 and 2012 to document and observe training simulations. I return to my footage here to help recall events that I might otherwise have forgotten, failed to notice, or needed to analyze further but also to reflect on the performativity of being a documentary cameraperson in the context of this intersubjectively produced simulation experience. This simulation documentary was well prepared to manage the variable of the visiting journalist-documentary filmmaker. To avoid the trap of putting faith in being there with camera, I situate my phenomenological analysis in a historical study of 250 news reports written about the fort over a period of roughly twenty years (1989 to 2018), as well as three articles published in performance studies journals and a feature-length documentary film titled *Full Battle Rattle* (2008).[14] I also analyze interviews I conducted with a former soldier who rotated twice through Fort Irwin and with a white Barstow resident who donned a burqa to play an Afghan woman. Patterns emerge.

The patterns suggest that the simulation itself has agency and shapes human affective experience within it in significant and sometimes alarming ways. Phenomenologist Maurice Merleau-Ponty grounded his understanding of experience in the human body's capacities to perceive stimuli and express intention, qualities that Sobchack ascribed to the "film body" that emerged in the space between a film and a viewer in a screening. What I am calling the *simulation-body* denotes a spatially distributed system that perceives stimuli and expresses intention in performance, here in performances that change slightly over time to keep the fort relevant and funded. The human bodies, communications networks, scenario scripts, vehicles, mock towns, and so on constitute so many variables for the simulation-body to manage toward the aims of its own economic, political, and cultural reproduction. I consider the traces left by the simulation itself across time in the archive of film and journalistic reports, the desert landscape in the transition from force-on-force combat to counterinsurgency war, and accounts of participants who have passed through simulation training. Synthesized, the traces indicate the ongoing development of something akin to an affect system motivated to pursue survival goals. To sharpen the implications of my central point here, I treat the journalist-documentarian as a variable to be controlled by various other elements within the distributed simulation-body, not as an observer to be ignored. The simulation itself always already accounts for the journalist-documentarian who attempts a neutral evaluation of training simulations.

Though it is unbounded by skin, the NTC simulation-body consistently executes an affective strategy centered on avoidance and mystification of the feared object, here the enemy that the military constructs, defeats, and then augments across time like an endless and increasingly elaborate action scene. Lucy Suchman, citing Judith Butler, refers to the figure of the enemy in US military-training simulations as a limitation to cultural awareness: "The intelligibility of the body includes always its 'constitutive outside,' those unthinkable and unlivable bodies 'that do not matter in the same way.'"[15] In the military, the two terms for "those unthinkable and unlivable bodies" are *enemy* and *civilian*, with the former category figured as threatening and immoral and the latter as antithetical to the disciplined, hypercapable, action-oriented soldier body.[16] This institutional hubris is in tension with the fact that the US military remains somewhat accountable to civilian oversight, which can constitute an existential threat—especially during a messy counterinsurgency war rife with mistakes and scandals such as Abu Ghraib. Public-relations strategies since Vietnam have aimed to lead US civilians to identify with US soldiers and the activity of soldiering, as opposed to the civilians and enemy combatants they have killed.[17] Part of this strategy has entailed attempts to control journalism, which I tether below to my account of stories about Fort Irwin. The simulations serve as training for troops about to deploy, but they also seem to function as quickly recognizable, close-to-home, good-enough stories for visiting US writers and filmmakers who cannot or would rather not undertake the hard, expensive, controversial, and dangerous accounting needed to assess the efficacy of such methods in Iraq and Afghanistan. This is a devil's bargain. Starting from a phenomenology of my own documentary camerawork at Fort Irwin and a genealogy of discourses on the real in articles about desert-based military training, I come to suggest a more general problem for documentary practice and reportage in the context of simulation documentary, one with particularly high stakes in times of war.

"STITCH LANE," 2007

"Turn the camera off," the army sergeant tells me. Several unscripted flames are searching for unconsumed materiel on the driver's side of a mangled charcoal Humvee spattered with red stains. This army officer, known at Fort Irwin as a tactical controller (TC),[18] is about to veer from standard protocol to fix the problem. The TC grabs a plastic container filled with fake blood and uses it to douse the fire as twelve other TCs, a Fort Irwin public-relations guide, and several members of the media look on. Satisfied, the TC politely informs me that I can resume videotaping. Smoke continues to billow into the air from three canisters hidden behind the wheels of the "bombed" Humvee—canisters designed for use in scenes like this one.

We are at the closest training site to the public affairs office at Fort Irwin NTC: Medina Wasl, a mock Iraqi village comprising thirteen cargo containers fashioned with faux siding to resemble homes in rural Iraq, as well as a mosque, a pen with goats, and a market, all aligned along a central dirt road. The Humvee serves as the focal point of the most often observed and practiced training simulation here, dubbed "Stitch Lane" by the army. The simulation depicts the aftermath of an IED attack—complete with $60,000 "SimMan" medical dummies dressed with bloody lacerations and scattered across the street, Iraqi villagers wailing over an injured family of three in a black sedan struck by shrapnel from the explosion, and a confused army private stumbling through this scene, alternately calling for a medic and his mother. Troop trainees must "stitch" and evacuate the wounded quickly and safely.

My shock at being immersed in the dimensionality and chaos of this environment blends with a perverse sense of fascination, familiarity, and even comfort at the resemblance it bears to a Hollywood action-film set, maybe with a touch of horror thrown in. I wind my way through this action-film documentary-ish performance with a video camera of my own, both impressed and confused by my access to the damning scene as an early-stage graduate student. Troops in training are tasked with quickly securing the area around the blast, assessing injuries to soldiers and civilians, stopping massive bleeding while warding off insurgent sniper attacks and car bombs, and evacuating the injured to a secure forward operating base set up in the desert several miles from the village. All participants in the simulation wear MILES laser-tag vests, which perceive signals emitted from guns or roadside bombs that approximate the ballistics and physical trajectories of actual weapons. When a suicide bomber detonates close to the American soldiers, a TC with a "God Gun," a light-blue physics calculator fashioned after a handgun, "shoots" each casualty to assess the extent of their simulated injury or death. It is, in short, a complex machine for generating affective sentiments of fear, shock, shame, and also video-game-style joy. During their two weeks at Fort Irwin, troops practice this scenario three or four times, with TCs observing their performance and stage-managing insurgent attacks based on the soldiers' failures to follow proper procedures. TCs try to "kill" all the new troops in early renditions of this exercise should they take more than ten minutes to carry out the evacuation. This time, a suicide bomber drives a truck through an unprotected alley to the scene and detonates, killing all the soldiers and civilians.

At the end of a simulation, the troops gather in a communal space in front of a television screen—the central courtyard of the village "mosque"—as a TC shows video of their performance and leads a discussion about how to improve the next time. The emphasis here is on procedure (how to secure the perimeter of the IED site, identify wounds, apply a tourniquet efficiently, load bodies into the medevac truck, and so on), but unspoken is the development of positive affective sentiments among the soldiers who learn together. The soldiers bond through this ritual before a mainstay of domestic architecture, the television, which functions not as a window on reality but as a mediator of their relations with one another and perhaps a reminder of home. Video viewing in this spatial arrangement is a historical practice and a comforting form of expressive experience they all share. And in any case, performance before cameras is vital to their mission as the executors of empire in an age of ubiquitous media, as the scandal of Abu Ghraib ironically suggests.

The significance of performing affective qualities before the camera is exemplified later, when the army arranges for two particularly charismatic and friendly Iraqi American actors to sit with me for interviews. They say that they try to play a role in "saving lives" in their native and adopted countries by teaching young American soldiers about the cultural nuances they will encounter once in theater. One, a Chaldean Christian liquor store owner from San Diego who immigrated to the United States in the 1970s and last visited Iraq in 1986, states that "this is reality; we're not playing games with it. We're using real Iraqis": "We act like them, we get mad like them, we yell out just like the Iraqis, we tell them get the hell out of my country, 'cause you're not helping—we do everything just like in Iraq 'cause they should know. That's what they're gonna face. I talk to lieutenants who have been in Iraq already when they come here. They say, hey, flashback. This is the same. We give them the same thing."[19]

I later discover that he has conducted more than fifty interviews for the press. He also appears in many photos on a wall at the public affairs office, including one with former president George W. Bush. I see this wall on the day I am leaving the fort and pan my camcorder across the photographs of other journalists who have passed through this place, labeled by name and institutional affiliation: Market Road Productions, Australian TV, a newspaper from Berlin, Armed Forces Info Services, Christian Broadcasting Network, Danish National TV, History Channel Modern Marvels, Deutsche Welle Television, French Radio, State Dept. Press Tour, Sacramento TV, the BBC, and dozens of others. Six to twelve media institutions visit for every rotation, the public affairs officer tells me. "Then they go on my wall of shame," he quips. I am surprised when he points out the newest image, a photograph he had taken of me, unaware, the day before. He tells me that keeping photographs on the walls helps him remember all the people he has met, and he reiterates again how much he likes journalists. I like him, too. He has told me many good stories today about the history of the fort, his own life as a military reporter, the Iraqi American actors he has met, and the pedagogical aim of all the simulation scenarios that we watched together. But as I leave the office and begin the thirty-mile drive through the desert between Fort Irwin and Barstow, I cannot shake the thought that all of us media visitors hang there like so many hunting trophies.

Being trapped in this literal and metaphorical "desert of the real" is a confusing sensation. It is not clear, after all, that visions of chaotic violence, civilian death, and physical destruction like those I had just documented should function to promote a war effort. Noor Behram's haunting forensic photographs of the rubble and innocent victims of US drone bombings in Pakistan, for instance, testify to the ongoing significance of documentary imaging of atrocity for raising awareness, indignation, momentum for protest, and policy change. "I want to show taxpayers in the Western world what their tax money is doing to people in another part of the world," he explained. Behram had a network of friends in northern Pakistan who called him when they saw or heard about drone bombings. He would then travel to the site of the attacks, sometimes minutes after the event and sometimes several days later in villages that were difficult to reach. His images reveal a stark contrast to the depictions of drone attacks as an emblem of "clean war" as reported in the United States. He accumulated over 100 photographs of children, over 620 of women, and countless images of men killed in the attacks in addition to medium-shot portrait photographs of shocked survivors holding the casings of hellfire missiles—the kind fired from drone planes and American helicopters. "For every 10 to 15 people killed, maybe they get one militant," he said. "I don't go to count how many Taliban are killed. I go to count how many children, women, innocent people, are killed." It is significant (and troubling) that Behram's photographs first came to attention in the United States and Europe through art exhibitions rather than press outlets.[20]

The US military, applying similar ideas about the power of documentary images to opposite ends, has pressured journalists in Iraq not to publish graphic photographs of the actual dead.[21] But at Fort Irwin, the explicit depiction of violent events that the army treats as representative of actuality and predictive of future experience, gory, bloody, and merciless throughout, in fact seems to short-circuit energy for dissent and anger in the near term—my own and that of the other journalists on the wall of shame.

Over months of reflection, I came to understand the scenes of violence at Fort Irwin, the accounts of Iraqi American actors, and the public affairs officers' explanations, which seemed to anticipate my strong affective responses, as aligned with incremental policy changes dating to the 1960s designed to control depictions of American wars and suppress dissent. Roger Stahl, for instance, argues that the rise of military-industrial-entertainment collaborations since the Vietnam War, and especially since the early 2000s, co-opts war imagery for pleasurable, interactive "militainment" products and military recruiting. Economic pressures on journalism wrought by the consolidation of corporate news media outlets (from fifty in 1983 to five in 2003) and the rise of cable and twenty-four-hour news channels incentivized the production of low-budget, opinion-based talk shows and dependence on the briefings of Pentagon public-relations personnel over in-depth investigative reporting. Publishing graphic war photographs could endanger ongoing access to these officials, so most news organizations did not do so.[22]

The unfortunate result has been the ceding of war imagery almost entirely to the entertainment industry, where images of killing and the killed tend to drive action and plot rather than reflection on suffering. Narrative films about masculine war heroes who successfully solve problems through violence and first-person shooter games "invite one to project oneself into the action," in Stahl's phrase.[23] Building on such trends, Fort Irwin produces immersive environments designed to arouse strong affective responses from participants, including those of journalist-documentarians. The codes of action-entertainment cinema and military-themed video gaming—complete with reductive depictions of the culture of the other—are then deployed to define interpretations of graphic violence. In other contexts or historical moments, such scenes might have served to discredit a war effort or show a lack of cultural knowledge. But here and now, the circulation of intense, negative affect functions as an evolving weapon—one calibrated, as I explore below, by narrative cinema techniques.

CULTURAL AWARENESS OR AWARENESS OF CINEMATIC CULTURE?

Central to the mechanics of this affective system are ideas about realism, a contested and endlessly debated term in film studies. I understand realism to signify a regime of production and evaluation that works within industrial cinema conventions to translate the look and feel of an original event into representation. Classical narrative cinema conventions usually stand as normative.[24] Realism of this sort seeks to induce deep identificatory investment across the triad of camera, actor-subject, and spectator through narrative momentum and the disavowal of production apparatus via continuity editing—historically the object of strong critique in feminist psychoanalytic film studies for embedding the male gaze into the structure of narrative film itself. Thus, paradoxically, realism expresses what Keeling called hegemonic "common sense" in a media-saturated society. The cinematic real simultaneously aims to play up the appearance, manner, and affective resonance of a thing that exists, once existed, or could plausibly exist in the world and to present it in such a way that an imagined demographic of viewers can recognize this resemblance and integrate it into their preexisting worldview. Media consumption itself shapes worldview, however, and perceptions of realism may bend over time toward seductive presentations of preternatural strength, beauty, and wealth. Viewer engagement with narrative, character motivations, or genre conventions—characteristics of what Ien Ang called "psychological realism"—takes precedence over social representativeness in shaping that preexisting worldview. When realism succeeds by its own terms, then, a spectator may comment about the experience of seeing a film as believable or convincing without articulating the assumptions from which this sense of the real emerged, sometimes even in the full awareness that their sense of this reality directly contradicts social facts.[25]

In the context of Stitch Lane, participants' experiences of realism play on broadly shared understandings of Hollywood action tropes for manufacturing drama, affect, and audience investment, even if—or perhaps especially because—the immersive scenario references war events that spectators and participants alike imagine to have had mortal corollaries in Iraq or Afghanistan in the recent past. As in the Vietnam War reenactment discussed in chapter 1, there are moments in the simulation that do conjure sensations of touch with some unknowable war experience now newly considered in the performance.[26] In this light, the drama of the simulation scenario affectively stitches together the trauma of the IED explosion as an actual world phenomenon, the narrativization of such events through Hollywood techniques, and the training of anxious troops in the present who know movies but not war for the contingencies of a future that may bring actual wounds. These three sutured temporalities function to solidify bonds of camaraderie in troops who must confront the specter of bodily harm through performances in which they stand at once as subjects and objects for their fellow performers, including Iraqi and Afghan role-players. All function simultaneously as subjects and objects of the cinematic realism operational in the simulation, a style of realism vested in the visualization of the wound above all. Cultural awareness training, in short, proceeded first through the awareness of a dominant cinema culture shared among military officers and troop trainees, though not necessarily among the Iraqi civilians they might encounter in the future.

Embedding such visualizations within narratives affects soldiers and actors, as I show below, but also visiting observers to the fort like myself. How are we new arrivals to make sense of a training spectacle designed to overwhelm the senses? Military spokespersons stand at the ready to offer explanations for the shocks: train like you fight; inoculate against stress; weed out the bad-apple troops who might kill civilians; teach troops cultural awareness so they don't misunderstand gestures, expressions, and gender norms; and so on. Over time, Medina Wasl became not just a site for training soldiers but also a showpiece for the army's new, public-relations-oriented framing of itself as a progressive cultural institution adapting to the conditions of insurgent war. This has been an effective strategy, not least because the desert itself has functioned for so long as a US-military-scale kind of media screen. An army adept at transforming the desert to the warfare demands of the moment simply focused its resources on a new kind of ideological truth, that of performance for cameras during the war in Iraq.

THE TRANSFORMATIONS OF
THE DESERT OF THE REAL

In the latter half of *America*, Baudrillard wrote about the landscape and culture he encountered while traveling through the southwestern United States. He marveled, somewhat horrified, that California's freeways, suburban supermarkets, theme parks, and housing developments existed on land that was essentially like the deserts just a few hours to the east, where life itself seemed impossible. He was especially captivated by the experience of driving through the Mojave, which he interpreted as a metaphor for the forces of simulation at the center of American culture. "The simulacrum is something you can simply feel here without the slightest effort," he wrote. "It is Disneyland that is authentic here! The cinema and TV are America's reality!"[27] When he wrote about the "desert of the real" in *Simulacra and Simulation* (1994), he was describing a social condition in which the copy, instrumentalized toward the ends of profit and empire, preceded the possibility of a preexisting original. Sanitized of archaic, ritualistic, and mystical qualities, these copies simply reproduced a normative code, stretching lifeless in all directions like the endless Mojave Desert. Building on such a desert was fundamentally meaningless, for Baudrillard. When the United States Army constructed its premiere training facility on land in the Mojave Desert, it was acting literally according to the metaphor by which Baudrillard characterized American society more broadly. The lure of the desert was its pliability to metaphor, its seeming lack of visible history and ongoing life.

While Baudrillard viewed the desert as the quintessential symbol of American culture, however, the US military envisioned it as the ideal site for producing otherness, an endeavor that changed in inflection in response to historical circumstances across time. Before 2004, the army used the spacious and remote desert land of Fort Irwin to train specialists in force-on-force tank warfare. General George Patton directed armored-vehicle maneuvers on land in the Mojave Desert starting in the early 1930s in anticipation of the United States entry into World War II, and he orchestrated the training of tank battalions there for the campaign in the deserts of North Africa in 1941–42.[28] After World War II, the land was used minimally until 1981. After the Arab-Israeli War, the formation of OPEC, and renewed strategizing for a potential ground war against the Soviet Union, the US Army designated this land as the Fort Irwin National Training Center. Studying tactical decisions made in the Arab-Israeli War convinced military planners that practicing full-scale mobilizations would be crucial to implementing an effective military strategy in the case of an actual war. For military strategists of the time, the vast stretches of flat land in the Mojave Desert approximated the topography of the flat eastern plains of Germany, the anticipated site of an initial ground battle against the Soviet army should the Cold War détente have broken down. The remoteness of the landscape, moreover, allowed the army to drop "anything but nuclear weapons," in the terms of one officer, and fire live rounds of tank ammunition on target ranges without alarming civilian populations.[29] By 1982, the American soldiers stationed at Fort Irwin were performing as an enemy army—the "Krasnovians"—that employed Russian tanks and small arms and simulated Soviet military tactics. Rotations of US Army tank battalions would engage in mock battles against the Krasnovians that stretched over dozens of miles of desert.[30]

At the end of the Cold War in 1989, military officials struggling to justify continuing military expenditures and journalists who visited Fort Irwin attributed new meanings to its desert backdrop. One article reported that the Krasnovians had begun shifting between playing "Samarians" modeled after Saddam Hussein's army in Iraq, "Atlanticians" based on Cuban infantry units, and "Hamchuks," an unfinished project to simulate the army of North Korea. At the time, the army was also studying the military forces of Libya, Iran, Algeria, and several other, smaller third-world nations to develop more simulations. While army personnel were still training to fight against the technological capacity of a conventional military foe, these developments suggested the representational trajectories afforded by the desert and the Soviet weaponry already on hand. "Everybody and his brother bought the Soviet equipment," said one Fort Irwin officer interviewed in 1992.[31] Commanders at Fort Irwin settled on emulating the army of Saddam Hussein in 1989 because the army deemed the Republican Guard to be the third most threatening to the United States at that time, and because the Iraqis used Soviet arms already available at the fort, a significant cost savings.

As the army designed its new enemy, the discourse about the military value of the fort began to shift, emphasizing its screen-like quality and barrenness over its size. The scale of the fort was said to facilitate the testing of technologies that linked widely dispersed individual soldiers through computer networks, and the harsh desert environment was frequently likened to the landscape in Iraq. Articles indicate that the army tested out "smart bombs," rifle-scopes that doubled as cameras, and night-vision binoculars equipped with data screens that automatically communicated real-time information about troop locations and the movement of enemy combatants. Officers argued that these "Nintendo" technologies would reduce Americans' exposure to risk in a ground war without front lines and an easily discernable opposing army.³² As American soldiers amassed in Saudi Arabia in preparation for the invasion of Kuwait, journalists visiting Fort Irwin deemed the desert landscape significant for its incompatibility with civilized living. One reported that tank battalion trainees at Fort Irwin suffered from "immense loneliness" when staying in the desert for extended periods, as they were used to living "in moderate climates amid water, greenery and other people." Excepting those from "western Nebraska or Kansas," quipped an army major quoted in this article, trainees were "spooked" by the undifferentiated landscape that offered few visual cues with which to gauge distance.³³ "The environmental stresses alone present a tremendous challenge," reflected one combat psychiatrist who had served during the Persian Gulf War. "The desert is like the far side of the moon. Everything becomes arduous."³⁴

Though inhospitable, the desert was also seen to be a socio-geographical formation suited to the projection and enactment of hyperreal fantasies of war quite like the ones actually mobilized during Desert Storm. The desert, after all, has been flexible to a particular army truth: "The big point is you need something that stands in stark contrast to your own," said Colonel Patrick O'Neal to a visiting *Washington Post* reporter in 1992, who was raising questions about the utility of simulating tank warfare after the fall of the Soviet Union. "You need an enemy."³⁵ The convergence of entertainment paradigms and war-making technologies sutured the training carried out in the desert to a new ideal of "clean war," executed via cameras from a distance and witnessed by spectators who did not feel the suffering of those on the ground. "*The desert is a screen* where all is exposed to the searching eye of an adversary employing the full array of object-acquisition systems," wrote cultural theorist Paul Virilio in an essay about the Gulf War of 1990–91 in *Desert Screen*.³⁶ The most significant battles were occurring on and for broadcasters like CNN rather than territory, he argued, aided by the facility with which the flat desert landscape could serve as a metaphor for the television screen. "The screen is the site of *projection of the light of images*—mirages of the geographic desert like those of the cinema," he explained. "*The screens of the Kuwaiti and Iraqi deserts* were to be linked with the *television screens* of the entire world, thanks to CNN."³⁷ Virilio here completed the conceptual transformation of the desert from a space large enough to accommodate tanks to the archetypal apparatus of the culture industry. One could say that the metaphor of the screen also guided the transformation of Fort Irwin after 2004. Seen through the instrumental gaze of the military, the desert functioned as a screen for the projection of an operational imperative, to harden and mechanize its fleshy components. This combination of factors played out on and through the bodies of performers in the simulation, who were filmed and engaged in cinema production from a variety of perspectives.

Fort Irwin became the Rhode Island–sized screen on which the army produced its peculiar brand of realist drama, its thirteen mock Iraqi villages too dispersed to be seen by individuals on the ground without the aid of technological instruments such as databases, digital maps, coordinated scenarios, surveillance cameras, and twelve teams of specialized operators. Commonsense scenarios for training centered on the emergence of the IED in Iraq. The focal point of Stitch Lane, the IED was the weapon that catalyzed the shift from combat operations to makeshift municipal governing. A story that ran in the *New York Times* in February 2006 reported that the Pentagon was tripling its spending, to $3.5 billion that year, on strategies for mitigating the impacts of "homemade bombs," armaments to which were attributed over 90 percent of the army's casualties up to that point in the war. Counting attacks on Iraqi civilians and security units allied with the United States, there were 5,607 reported incidents with IEDs in 2004 and 10,593 in 2005, of which the military was able to detect only about 40 percent. Most of the spending on strategies, the article reported, was to fund a "combat laboratory" at Fort Irwin, dubbed the "IED Center of Excellence."[38] This laboratory and the simulation scenarios that developed through it played a central part in the training rotations in the ensuing years while also producing something like entertainment content— characters, charismatic actors, storylines, anecdotes from the front, and bomb defusing techniques—for a variety of media visitors to the base. Numerous articles feature a role-player named Tim Wilson, "a former tank commander who shed his uniform for a bisht (gown) and kaffia (head-dress)," according to one article, to play "Monsour Hakim," a friendly hot dog vendor by day who spent his nights making IEDs for the insurgency.[39]

By November 2006, the army had spent $6 billion on efforts specifically aimed to neutralize IEDs, yet these weapons remained the army's central problem. Official figures released on October 21, 2006, listed 1,034 American deaths and 11,231 injuries caused by IEDs—50 percent of the total in Iraq and 30 percent in Afghanistan.[40] General Robert Scales argued that satellites were not useful in this new war environment, which depended overwhelmingly rather on the operations of "small units" working on the ground. Everyday activities such as trash pickup assumed vital military importance, as trash on the streets and "dead animals" provided places for insurgents to hide IEDs.[41] American soldiers working in urban areas had started paying local Iraqi civilians to pick up trash in streets where IEDs had been found in the past, as much a cost-saving measure as an intercultural negotiation.[42] The army developed a version of the simulation training scenarios called XCTC, or the "exportable combat training center," which could be set up across the country at a savings of about $10 million per rotation. This model quickly became pervasive.[43] "All of our Army regulations, all of our training manuals, are completely changed," observed one soldier for a *New York Times* reporter at Fort Irwin in May 2006. Another added, "We're pretty much fighting ghosts."[44] By February 2006, SWET procedures, or "Sewage, Water, Electricity, and Trash," were the focus of many simulations.[45] Army officers began making visits to the LAPD "to learn how they fight crime and deal with gangs," information that they believed would help track the production of homemade bombs in Iraq.[46] An article written in the spring of 2006 reported that counterinsurgency training, virtually unmentioned in 2004, occupied about 45 percent of the soldiers' time at Fort Leavenworth, Kansas. The shift in training emphasis also transformed the landscape of forts throughout the country, leading then-commander of coalition forces in Iraq David Petraeus to remark that Fort Leavenworth was "now scarily like the Sunni Triangle."[47] The emphasis in articles shifted from "military operations" and "decapitation" to "nation-building" and "cultural terrain."[48] "When we came into this town, the battle scenario reminded me of the movie 'Black Hawk Down,' a film about the chaos in Somalia," said one army officer about his first impressions of Medina Wasl.[49] Still, as of 2012, the IED remained the central weapon used against American troops in Afghanistan.

The military's shift to cultural awareness training after 2004 in response to the threat of IEDs created a new cottage industry in Southern California to service the cinematic and theatrical production needs of bases. Army veteran Jamie Arundell-Latshaw and her husband, for instance, started a small storefront business in the predominantly Iraqi American Chaldean community of El Cajon in San Diego to connect the US Army to Arabic speakers who could play roles in simulation training exercises. Between 2006 and 2009, as annual revenues of their company (called Lexicon, Inc.) increased from $101,943 to over $14.4 million, the couple also contracted to provide Arabic-speaking translators, interpreters, and cultural educators for dozens of high-profile military and intelligence agencies throughout the country.[50] Strategic Operations, a subsidiary of San Diego–based Stu Segall Productions, opened for business in 2002. Known previously for producing the San Diego–based TV crime drama *Silk Stalkings* and soft-core pornography, Stu Segall Productions partially transitioned into the military training simulation business after 9/11, when the action film and television industry "took a bit of a nose dive," in the words of one company executive. While the company does not disclose its earnings publicly, a spokesperson acknowledged growing at a rate of 60 percent per year between

2002 and 2011.[51] According to the Fort Irwin public affairs office, as of 2012, Strategic Operations was responsible for producing almost all the pyrotechnics special effects for the training simulations at the base.[52] Strategic Operations contracts with dozens of other security and paramilitary institutions as well.

Incremental changes to simulation scenarios since 2004 have aimed to magnify the sensorial cues that produce the sensation of shock, bewilderment, or disgust in trainees, even where these representational effects might exceed the volume and visual display that a soldier could see in actual combat. "Hyperreal," in fact, is a moniker that Strategic Operations has claimed with pride, going so far as to use the word as a trademark on its webpage about "Combat Wound Medical Effects." During the war, the page read, "Truly 'next generation' in detail, realism, dynamics, and scope; Strategic Operations Inc. (STOPS) calls it Hyper-Realistic™." A photograph of a young actor wearing a Middle Eastern–style headscarf and looking skyward to display a gaping, bloody protrusion from chin to thorax and as wide as his neck accompanied the text. In addition, following the lead of Strategic Operations, Fort Irwin began to hire amputees to play the victims of IED attacks in simulation scenarios in 2008. These actors wore full-body, flesh-colored latex suits that gushed fake blood when punctured. Each suit cost approximately $25,000, a savings from the completely synthetic $60,000 "sim-man" of previous simulations that also enabled for greater drama on the field of simulation.[53]

These are expensive effects, and their use in training simulations offers visiting reporters and journalists a great deal of free production value for their projects. Simulation scenarios generated by the military mimic commercial forms of dramatic realism while intimating actual life-and-death stakes that documentary filmmakers and institutions of journalism tend to deem worthy of reportage. It is a gift, a spectacle covered by the alibi of public interest. These training simulations thus seem to offer a readymade answer to a long-standing journalistic dilemma: how to integrate the drama of a good story into reports about issues of public concern. And it is cheap to cover. Instead of traveling to Iraq, hiring interpreters, risking their lives, and spending weeks of uncertainty developing stories about life in a war zone, filmmaker-journalists journey to Fort Irwin from Los Angeles for a day trip or short overnight and leave with a range of dramatic, affect-inducing storylines on which they can graft timely metanarratives about war, culture, and stagecraft. For its part, the army offers journalist-visitors courteous and affable guides from the public affairs office; easy access to charismatic role players, polite soldier trainees, and amenable commanding officers for interviews; and proximity to simulation performance events for observation or even in some cases participation. Army spokespersons reiterate statements about the necessity of counterinsurgency warfare in the present, the importance of audiovisual realism to effective training, and the value and patriotism of ethnic role players who cultivate soldiers' proper performances of American nationalism. Filmmakers and reporters communicate these opinions in their work, and everyone seems to win. The soldiers are better prepared for handling terrorist attacks and cultural negotiation, California and its cultural industries receive federal funding to provide the military with cinematic expertise, the Arabic and Afghan Americans have well-paying jobs that allow them to express love of their native countries and American patriotism at the same time, the army itself can claim ownership of the story, and journalist-filmmaker visitors offer their supporting institutions entertaining, cheaply produced, saleable narratives that touch on issues of public concern. None of this includes or really even considers the views of Iraqis and Afghans dealing with social instability and the US occupation of their countries on the ground.

The pattern of talk about realism at Fort Irwin, to return to the theme of this section, best aligns, oddly, with Linda Williams's theory on "body genres," those categories of film such as horror, pornography, and melodramatic weepies that elicit involuntary, physiological response.[54] Her emphasis on excess over narrative efficiency speaks to the spirit of simulation design, even though her interest in tears avers from the kinds of bodily responses sought after in a military training regime. The excess of the weepy, after all, has no place in the soldiers' projection of common sense upon their shared, but dangerous world. Rather, the hard landscape of the desert makes way for the logic of closing down one's emotional and affective range, as in the action genre. And in this action-adjacent context, the realism of bodily response demands other fluids.

INDEXICAL PUKING: AFFECTIVE REALISM IN REPORTS ON SIMULATION TRAINING

I have argued in the section above that the army's transition to counterinsurgency training was a matter of pragmatism rather than a transformation of value. Nonetheless, the descriptions of sensations required to produce "stress inoculation"—the staging of shocks to daze, overwhelm, and scare participants in training along the way to affective hardening—shifted during the Iraq War toward dramatic accounts of personal, action-cinematic experiences and their fascinating impacts on bodies. Journalists' narratives came to read like a cross between phenomenological description and Hollywood script: "Pop-pop-pop-pop-pop-pop! BOOM!" wrote one. "Toomer popped off a round—and then his gun jammed, at the worst possible time, just like in the movies."[55] The *New York Times* feature published in 2006 likewise connected the action-cinematic ethos at the fort to realism, authoritatively demonstrated in this account by soldiers' embodied responses to their new training regimen: "With actors and stuntmen on loan from Hollywood, American generals have recast the training ground at Fort Irwin so effectively as a simulation of conditions in Iraq and Afghanistan over the past 20 months that some soldiers have left with battle fatigue and others have had their orders for deployment to the war zones canceled. In at least one case, a soldier's career was ended for unnecessarily 'killing' civilians."[56]

The figure of the soldier who "unnecessarily" kills civilians plays an important part in this story and many others—a peculiarity worth analyzing. I interpret two meanings to the recurrence of this figure. First, it implies the narrative of the progressive army, monitoring its troops for bad apples who may misrepresent US interests in theater by committing atrocities. The line suggests that the army will not deploy a soldier who demonstrates an unnerving lack of calm in a simulation, though it is worth noting in this context that the military did not systematically count civilians killed in Iraq and Afghanistan until 2007, judging from reports that I address below. Second and more to the point, in the news story, the soldier who kills civilians functions as evidence for this visiting journalist that the cultural awareness training simulations are working properly. The public affairs officer at the fort tells the reporter that the simulations are so realistic that they have induced "battle fatigue," puking, and killing sprees to prove that the training approximates an intense war experience. The training indexes something about war! The reporter then conveys this juicy information to readers.

Somehow, across the institutional transition from force-on-force training to cultural awareness, the figure of the puking, pathological, traumatized soldier body remained the index of functionality in journalistic evaluations of military training. Puking indexed training effectiveness differently, however, in the era of cultural awareness than it did in that of desert training for tank warfare. Quotations from senior officers offer rationales for extreme training of this sort that shift away from environmental conditions and toward culture. In 2004, when the US Army still emphasized force-on-force training, Brigadier General Robert Cone of Fort Irwin stated, "We want our commanders to say that it's harder at the National Training Center than in war. . . . We put them in a tent where it's 100 degrees, there's dirt in their computers and they haven't had a shower for a week and see how they function. We want to put them under stress and see how they cope."[57]

Cone emphasized the realism of the training in terms of the soldier's bodily response to the harsh desert conditions, but he did not mention culture as part of this environment. Four years later, comments from Fort Irwin commanding officer General Dana Pittard emphasize sensations of alterity (which we may hesitate to characterize as culture) over the physical environment: "The kind of towns, the urban towns we're creating, the signs, it must hit all five of your senses. You must see Iraq and Afghanistan. You must smell it. You must touch it."[58] A feature published in 2007 affirmed that this kind of sensorial realism was key to the new regime of cultural awareness military training—and to writing about such training. "'It's realistic to the point where soldiers pass out, throw up, turn white and start shaking,' said Sgt. Mark Ramsey, an Iraq War veteran and Hollywood stuntman who helps plan the training mission."[59] Ramsey, of course, was referring to the sensations of fear and shock that troops experienced amid referents to the sensorial environment of Iraq and surprise insurgent attacks, not simply the heat of the desert.

Newly at stake here, in other words, is an affective realism, the production of real feeling in the bodies and psyches of the troops—a realism of involuntary bodily responses to cultural phenomena that startle, frighten, and disgust but never nurture or comfort. While spokespersons for the army argue that these simulations "inoculate [soldiers] against stress"[60] and thus allow them to function more effectively in scenarios where lives may be at stake (a conceit of this training that I examine at length below), it is also the case that phenomena that arouse intense affects, particularly those that routinely defy explanation and trigger fear, force those who experience them to undertake specific coping strategies. They repress dissonant sensations or search out explanations for the negative affects they feel. Associations between IEDs and the smell of kabob seem practically inevitable here, arguably undercutting claims about the liberalizing persuasion of the cultural awareness regime. But it's worth taking a step back to theorize the affective strategy behind such training. Below, I draw from Silvan Tomkins's writing on the affect system to tease out the recursive relationship between affect and consciousness in this simulation-body.

SIMULATION AND THE AFFECT SYSTEM

"How should one devise an automaton to simulate the essential characteristics of the human?" asked Tomkins in a piece of writing on the workings of the affect system. Tomkins was inspired by the capacity of computers developing in the 1960s to operate through a feedback system and saw a parallel to this process in the relation between memories of experiences and consciousness in human thought. Simulation machines offered an apt analogy, for Tomkins, to the mechanics of what he called the affect system. In theorizing what the affect system was, Tomkins suggested that the answer might be found in identifying what the computerized automaton was not. He asked what elements of programming an automaton would need to be improved to make it act more like a human, concluding that a central problem with the computer simulation was its inability to track its own motivations to survive across time. "The automaton must be motivated," Tomkins stated. "It must also be motivated to reproduce itself... if we are interested in the problem of human simulation, the race of automata must be perpetuated not only by knowledge but by passion." An automaton that could feel pain, guard its own integrity against overzealous interlocutors, and reproduce itself would function as an organism with a drive system, "a characteristic of all forms of life." A human automaton, Tomkins continued, would also require an affect system, or "a number of responses [to stimuli] which have self-rewarding and self-punishing characteristics."[61] He included among these affects excitement, joy, fear, sadness, shame, anger, and contempt, each of which could vary in terms of duration and intensity. The "phenomenological quality" of these self-rewarding and self-punishing affects were hard-wired into humanity across evolutionary time and cultural context, in Tomkins's theory. Humans evolved to want to maximize positive affect and minimize negative affect. They desired to live in such ways that minimized the inhibition of affect of any kind and still enjoy the power to control their own affective lives. Affects mediated between perceptions and consciousness as an intensifying filter, playing the indispensable counterpart to reasoning and action. But the affect system was also shaped by a sensory-affect-memory feedback loop that was responsive to lived experience over time. Tomkins likened the affects to technologies for the ways they extended and transformed external stimuli. "The fragmentation and amplification of man's capacities by automata has been the rule," he explained: "The next and the final development of simulation will be an integrated automaton—with microscopic and telescopic lenses and sonar ears, with atomic powered arms and legs, with a complex feedback circuitry powered by a generalizing intelligence obeying equally general motives having the characteristic of human affects. Societies of such automata would reproduce and care for the young automata."[62]

Fort Irwin resembled this "final development of simulation." Army forts such as Fort Irwin secured funding, or self-reproduction, by demonstrating that their training simulations helped US troops survive when at war. The way to ensure the survival of the fort's affect system, ironically, hinged on its capacity to create images that could induce in its human components the affects associated with looming death. The visible evidence of stress, fear, and disgust at Fort Irwin is central to its claims to improve the survival rates of soldiers. Such images suggest to visitors and evaluators that the fort can habituate soldiers to the intense affects of war, thus limiting the power of affective responses to gore and fear that can impede judgment in actual battle. Fort Irwin must also anticipate war scenarios of the future, or at least make a case that their training paradigm remains relevant in times of peace. Images at Fort Irwin thus have a dual aim in relation to the fort's survival. By coincidence, Tomkins named the aims of consciousness within the affect system *Image*. The aggregate of sensory, memory, and affective imagery processed through consciousness comprised the organism's Image, its understanding of purpose and direction: "In the case of predominantly habitual action it is the rule rather than the exception that affect plays a minimal role."[63]

Habitual action in military simulation training, ironically, operates through an intensely punishing kind of Image; it hunts for strong affective response. An ex–Marine Corps noncommissioned officer, "Greg," who rotated through Fort Irwin on two different occasions while on active duty, reflected in an interview with me that the training he received was overwhelmingly intended to make soldiers fearful, suspicious, and on edge. "The commanders want to instill a certain fear in you to keep you sharp, to keep you edged, to keep you ready," Greg explained. Pedagogy emphasizes that no procedure or action carried out by troops deserves a commander's positive praise. "Bottom line is that it's just never going to be good enough, no matter what," Greg said. "Their reward system is through negativity. . . . I didn't realize that until I stepped out of the military and got into this profession, fitness, which is more about positivity."[64]

He recalled an incident in his training that occurred several days after a suicide bomber had killed US soldiers in a mess hall in Iraq. One of his commanding officers lectured Greg and his unit of two hundred marines about the need to be vigilant about the activities of contract workers, even those that they knew and liked personally. The commander left the room, and several minutes later, a female janitor whom the marines knew by name entered the conference room with a large trash can. "When she walked out of the room, she left a trash can there," Greg recalled. Several minutes later, he walked over to the trash can, peered over the top lip, and saw a simulated bomb made of gallon milk jugs and some wires: "I was like, aw, shit. This would take out everybody, like 90 percent of the room. And they all looked at me, and I tried to shove it out of the door and it popped. From the backside, the commanding officer walked in, and it was a 'gotcha' kind of thing. It was an eye-opener for everybody. It was like, I don't think we're ready for this. It's an intangible kind of thing, a fear."[65]

Greg further explained the affective response that this moment induced in him. While acknowledging that he felt shame for "letting everybody down," he also connected the moment he saw the fake bomb to a traumatic experience from his childhood. As a ten-year-old, he had seen his father beaten at a bar by a man he described as a burglar, and seeing the "bomb" in the trash can triggered the return of that memory to consciousness, he told me. It was "almost like a feeling where you just want to tuck up in a cave and hide," he said. "Again, it's a moment where you feel so hopeless. You had absolutely no control over this."[66]

Greg's story raises questions about the line between the reenactment and simulation of trauma. On the one hand, the sensory experience of discovering the fake bomb led to the involuntary negative affect of despair and replaying in his mind a traumatic event from his childhood. Somehow, *this* touched *that*. The tenor and shift into the present tense in his telling of this story bears the marks of reenactment, a strategy for coping with traumatic memory. But the event that catalyzed this reenactment was his reflection on finding the simulated bomb in the trash can. When the simulation event occurred at Fort Irwin, it indexed for the entire group of marines a specific moment of the recent past as directly as a photograph, while also suggesting an emergent strategy being deployed by insurgents that would likely impact this unit when they deployed to Iraq in the near future. The relatively brief time between the actual IED explosion in the mess hall in Iraq and its simulation at Fort Irwin was key to its affective power for this group of marines. This was a reenactment of current news and a training simulation simultaneously. In this context, the bodies of these marines in training touched something of the bodies of those who had died in the bomb attack affectively, if not literally. The bomb in the trash can was the recollection-object that hailed the unit as a collective and condensed time. It could have been them. Greg's response, "I don't think we're ready for this," was perhaps the desired pedagogical outcome of the bomb simulation. But in the idiosyncratic case of Greg, the doubt he expressed about his ability as a marine also touched one earlier moment of intense humiliation and fear.

Tomkins argued that a subject exposed to repeated and unremitting humiliations can internalize the feeling of self-contempt that others project onto him or her. The subject that such conditions produced, in Tomkins's description, resembled the military's avowed ideal of the good soldier, "learn[ing] to have contempt for those who surrender too easily and to avoid defeat at any cost lest he suffer self-contempt."[67] Tomkins suggested that there is a monopolistic tendency in the affects of contempt and humiliation if they are not confronted, assuaged, or worked through. Repeated experiences of these negative affects produce in the subject what Tomkins called a "strong affect theory" that serves as the foundation of ideological thinking: "It is the repeated and apparently uncontrollable spread of the experience of negative affect which prompts the increasing strength of the ideo-affective organization which we have called a strong affect theory."[68]

"Strong theories" about how the world works harden over time into what Eve Sedgwick, building on ideas of Sigmund Freud and Melanie Klein, called the "paranoid position." This corresponds most closely with the principle of avoiding negative affect, the defining strategy of military training and defensive infrastructure. Avoidance strategies cut the subject off from a range of encounters with potentially shaming, humiliating, or misunderstood objects that have in the past overwhelmed the psyche, and so these strategies further mystify the objects. This leads a strong theory position to claim more and more objects as applicable within its purview over time, because the power to control affective experience is defined increasingly by avoidance.[69] It seeks almost automatically to expand its power through boundary marking, and this can be contagious to others who follow a similar affective strategy of avoidance that is not counterbalanced by positive affective experience, such as fellow soldiers forced to endure drill and then threat. Moreover, positive affect can come about in the process of working to counter the negative affect by avoidance or anger, as was the case with the soldiers' staging of photos at Abu Ghraib. In these cases, the object associated with the strong affect theory of avoidance becomes central as well to the experience of a restrained positive affect. Total destruction of the source of negative affect leaves a kind of vacuum at the center of affective life.

Materializations of cinematic affect accumulate on the land in places like Fort Irwin. Cinematic structures here homogenize processes of identification and becoming for the ends of military capital, "even to make that violation feel good," in Keeling's terms.[70] Certainly for soldiers, the strong negative affects of training reinforce boundaries between us and them and work against the notion of openness in intercultural exchange that one might think to be central to cultural awareness engagements. Performance scholar Zack Whitman Gill argues that this kind of training in fact reinforces a "martial heterotopia" defined by a "warrior ethos" parallel to but set apart from (and above) civilian life: "While an Army soldier demonstrates the qualities that comprise the Seven Core Values [loyalty, duty, respect, selfless service, honor, integrity, and personal courage], a civilian is constructed as the opposite. Every moment of a recruit's existence in the Army affirms this absolute difference, through a series of performances that immediately and visually discard the lax and disorganized lifestyle of the civilian."[71]

Gill's analysis of the training at Fort Irwin as a permanent rehearsal, detached from and contemptuous of civilian life at home and abroad, would seem to dovetail well with Keeling's theory about the projection of cinematic common sense and Tomkins's writing on strong affect theory. Military scripting does not produce a value-neutral simulation in which participants can envision future scenarios by tweaking abstract variables. This is a simulation, rather, that intends to encode through cinematic techniques a set of values and presuppositions into its human variables for an ideological outcome. Whereas Sobchack likens cinematic consciousness to plastic surgery ("We have all had 'our eyes done,'" she quips), the Fort Irwin simulation-body aims to colonize the sensory-affective organization of individuals within its space.[72] And visiting journalists and filmmakers who follow the norms of neutral reportage are easily subsumed as variables within this system, time and again moved by the affective force of witnessing simulation scenarios and interviewing soldiers to then reproduce as "consciousness" the military-friendly explanations on hand.

CRITIQUE OF AFFECTIVE REALISM

Bonnie Docherty, a researcher at Human Rights Watch who specialized in questions of disarmament and limiting civilian casualties during war, published an earnest and detailed study of the training simulations and their relation to the practices of soldiers once deployed in theater. Her account (*"More Sweat... Less Blood"*) threw into question the recourse to affective realism in public-relations material and news reports about the efficacy of training at the fort. Docherty positioned herself as a spokesperson for improving military training to reduce civilian casualties and was allowed unusually extensive access to the fort and its personnel. She visited the fort three times over the course of four years of research and pored through forty thousand pages of training manuals and documents about army lessons learned. In line with the reports of other visitors, Docherty emphasized the importance of realism in her study, but she found it lacking at Fort Irwin. The towns were too small and the Iraqi role-players too few to simulate the sense of threat that they engendered for troops once deployed. She said it was a problem that only American soldiers stationed at Fort Irwin played the insurgents, as soldier trainees quickly learned to distinguish between Arabic speakers who took on cultural roles and insurgents who did not speak Arabic. The simulation scenarios themselves were not varied enough in intensity or goals. Encounters with Iraqi role-players were still minimal. And the rules of engagement taught and practiced at Fort Irwin did not always overlap with international humanitarian law, in her estimation. She insisted that "troops must receive reviews that consider not only military success but also civilian casualties," a factor not evaluated in army engagements in Iraq until September 2007, four and a half years after the start of the war. While Docherty quoted veterans who experienced flashbacks to their combat experience while participating in simulations, she did not accept these comments as evidence of the kind of realism she deemed most important to cultural awareness training. "The different views of NTC's realism are in part attributable to whether or not a trainee had been to Iraq," she observed. Her field research corroborated the views of one battalion commander she interviewed, who said that "those who had not been in theater were 'relatively unfazed [by the realism. To them, it's] a training exercise.'" She concluded that the realism advertised by the military as its training product and relayed by most visiting journalists and filmmakers in their representations of the simulations remained elusive. "The new trainees' lack of reaction is disconcerting since NTC's role is to awaken them to what lies ahead," she concluded.[73]

The public-relations officer who guided my first visit to Fort Irwin later talked with me on the phone about the dilemma the army faces in getting the attention of its young trainees. "If it's not on video," he said, "then it didn't happen."[74] He explained that for a generation of recruits who grew up playing video games and watching war films, the baseline standard of assaultive sounds, smells, and actions that could induce the sensation of affective realism—the stated key to pedagogy at Fort Irwin—was extreme. This problem was partly of the military's own making. In military-sponsored video game series such as *America's Army*, *Call of Duty*, and *Halo*; recruiting depots set up in public schools; advertisements aired during sports broadcasts; Hollywood action movies endorsed by the military such as *G.I. Joe* (2009) and *Iron Man* (2008); and the controversial Army Experience Center opened in a Philadelphia shopping mall, extreme, graphically depicted, reactive violence predominantly functioned as a form of exciting entertainment.[75] Offering gaming experiences as part of the army brand, in addition to suggesting that army life might lead to such adventures, aided recruiting within the army's key demographic of low-income, frustrated young men. It was also an ethos at odds with the notion of cultural awareness. As one sergeant noted in unnerving frustration about the shift to cultural awareness in 2004, "You train a guy to kill, and then you tell him to go hand out water and not to shoot anybody unless he's shot at."[76] Within this context, it is not surprising that some of the soldiers viewed the embodied training simulations as just another drill to endure. Moreover, and perhaps more to the point, commanders' assumptions about such preexisting attitudes led them to develop worst-case-scenario simulations, to perform simulated gore and violence that exceeded what soldier trainees would likely see in combat. To achieve the affective realism that would open the space for soldiers to feel the consequences of their actions and the possibilities for their own deaths, in other words, would mean creating scenarios that were not representative of their future lives.

It is worth saying a bit more about the kinds of realism claimed as operational at the fort and the problems that these claims pose for evaluation by outsider journalists and filmmakers. Visitors have no way to judge whether this kind of training is effective at reducing civilian casualties, facilitating cultural exchange, or saving the lives of American soldiers during deployment. Beyond this, the evaluators who most matter, Iraqis and Afghans living through wars who must deal with the presence of American troops in their home countries, are not available for comment about the realism of military training. Instead, Iraqi Americans (most of whom left the country in the 1970s), soldier trainees who have not deployed but have played video games, and veteran soldiers whose traumatic experiences of war lead them to experience flashbacks in the midst of much more mundane, everyday sensations stand as authorities on realism in reports and films about the fort. While these participants may be well intentioned and open, they are also following orders. They manage procedural realism: the reality of written military codes about how to move down a narrow street as a unit, perform guard duty, inspect cars at checkpoints, and "kick down doors," to use the phrase of one army mechanic. While these concerns are practical and relevant to the everyday activities of soldiers and are useful to see and improve upon video review, they have little to do with Iraqi or Afghan culture.

What is significant here is the relation between the affective experiences induced by the simulation scenarios and the official interpretations on hand to account for them. Military spokespersons use the term *culture* to describe differences in customs, beliefs, and behaviors that troops will encounter in Iraq and Afghanistan, but in practice the sensory experiences of otherness produced in the simulations are very much about the conjuncture of army and cinema customs, beliefs, and behaviors. Viewers and participants who have not been exposed to graphic depictions of violence tend to have more pronounced visceral responses to the training simulations. One middle-aged, white woman from the nearby town of Barstow, whom I will call Jane, accepted a job as a part-time role-player at Fort Irwin around 2008. I interviewed her in 2012. In rotations of troops who were destined for Afghanistan, she wore a burqa and played the second wife of a rural Muslim Afghan man (his actual wife, Jane's actual friend, played his first Muslim wife in the simulation). Though Jane knew very little about Afghanistan or Muslim culture, the army allowed her and other local American women to play these roles because, according to script, they said nothing in public, remained anonymous beneath the burqas, and simply followed their husbands.[77] Arabic- and Pashto-speaking role-players were more expensive to contract, so as many roles as possible were played by enlisted army members and local civilians who needed part-time work. As a result, role players like Jane entered the simulations with a very different set of experiences of war imagery and expectations about war representations than most army trainees. Witnessing the performances of indexical touch with war events moved her. Jane recalled seeing for the first time one of the amputees who played a bomb victim in the Stitch Lane simulation (fig. 2.2). "To me it was so realistic that I just started crying," she said:

> He was yelling where was his leg, and the next thing I know I'm just crying because I'm wondering where his leg's at. Just sitting there, and you're like, oh my god, it's how they must feel when they're out there and they lose their leg.... My dad didn't really let me watch war movies, so my first time out here, I didn't know we had amputees, so I cried a lot my first rotation. They made me stay over there because I really was ... I was devastated. I don't know a lot about war. So when I'd seen it, it was very scary.[78]

Jane said she gradually learned how to cope with the display of violence and blood because she needed the job and because she accepted her officers' interpretation of what she had seen: many soldiers had lost limbs in Iraq and Afghanistan, so it was crucially important that they experience something of what these moments are like before deploying. Here, again, the simulation-body of the fort brought Jane's strong negative affective response into line with the position of the overall military mission. Repeated exposure to simulations of traumatic events—here an odd parallel to the logic in therapy for "prolonged exposure" explored in Marisa Brandt's research on reenactment in PTSD recovery—blunted Jane's potentially political, visceral reaction to the visage of the aftermath of an IED attack as devastating, scary, and sad.[79] By hardening herself to the intense affects of fear and disgust that overwhelmed her at first, Jane came to believe she could help soldiers better perform their jobs. "I got to where I understand that the concept out here is to help [American soldiers] come back alive," Jane explains: "I have to learn to do it because it's my job. And so I waited a couple days and I came back, and the more you come back and you see it, you see you're helping soldiers. They come in, and you know that hopefully what they learned while you were here is going to bring them back alive. So that made me feel really good about what had first freaked me out."[80] Jane's

Figure 2.2. Video stills of the "Wounded Private" (*left*) and Afghan role players (*right*) acting in the Stitch Lane training simulation, 2012. Recorded by the author with permission from the Fort Irwin National Training Center, Barstow, CA.

reaction to the horror of seeing an amputee, and her subsequent acceptance of the military's interpretation of its meaning, mimic the logic at the center of many documentary and journalistic interpretations of the training simulations.

Absent their own critical intervention, these reports convey a message sympathetic to the military mission. "I sensed a genuine desire on the part of Army and Iraqi staff to make things right by teaching the troops about the changing face of the cultural and political landscape in Iraq, and a deep resentment toward those who act poorly, as in the case of the alleged Blackwater massacres," wrote one performance ethnographer after visiting the fort.[81] Like the embedded reporters who "objectively" related sympathetic stories about humble and patriotic American soldiers on the ground in Iraq, these visitors in effect assumed what digital-media theorist Elizabeth Losh described as a pragmatic rhetorical stance. Losh ascribed this position to critics of the US wars who nonetheless accepted military contracts to program virtual-reality training games such as *Tactical Iraqi* and *Virtual Iraq*.[82] These programmers argued that the games' missions to teach the Arabic language and Muslim culture and to aid treatments of PTSD, respectively, outweighed the fact that the military had funded the games and might misuse or reappropriate their work for other ends in the future. While I appreciate the nuance of this position for the designers of such programs and scholars who write about military affairs, it is not the place from whence to evaluate training outcomes. Perhaps the author quoted above was intending to give pause to an audience of academics who would regard military activity as a de facto negative component of collective life in the United States, or perhaps they were acting out what they saw as ethical ethnographic practice by affirming the legitimacy of the pragmatic position of his Iraqi American subjects. This is, indeed, the dominant framework in journalistic accounts of the fort, and their article overall offers a more detailed account than most from which to draw such conclusions. But focusing on being there as opposed to the longer history of the fort itself or the potential ramifications of the shift from conventional warfare to cultural awareness has led many visitors to overestimate the truth value of proximity to the cinematic events and people described. Reports read as though the author had not been a part of the show, and yet they resemble the public-relations material that the military itself has generated.

The same could be said about the nationally televised feature documentary on the Fort Irwin training simulations, *Full Battle Rattle* (2008), by Jesse Moss and Tony Gerber. While the filmmakers state in material about the film that they personally opposed the war, and while it is the most comprehensive exploration of the experiences of individuals in the training simulations (soldiers and actors alike), it foregrounds intimacy with subjects employed by the military, presence at simulated performance events, and the stories of participants over structural critique. Thus, while the style of the film retains faith in the camera to communicate the phenomenological experience of fake war and all the complexities the endeavor entails (much like *In Country*, discussed in chap. 1), it also by design gives a great deal of control over the production of affect and the interpretation of its political import to military spokespersons, who orchestrate for the participants in the simulation, the filmmakers, and the spectators of the finished film. Absent a story from the perspective of Iraqi civilians that follows soldier trainees once they are deployed (a far more difficult, hazardous, and expensive project to undertake), the filmmakers must acknowledge a measure of complicity in the military campaign and its continuance, despite their stated intentions to the contrary. For years afterward, the public-relations office at Fort Irwin still showed the film to introduce the look, feel, and rationale of the simulations to groups of tourists who visited the fort to see a live training exercise.[83]

CONCLUSION: STITCH LANE, 2012

Like the US economy, the Fort Irwin simulation-body has equated survival in an era of cultural awareness with growth. When I return to the fort for a second visit, I am again taken to this area—Medina Wasl, now reimagined as an Afghan village called Ertebat Shar—to witness the performance of Stitch Lane from a press box above the now-paved central street. The village has more than two hundred structures and has become by far the largest on the fort (fig. 2.3). Concrete barricades line the street, and buildings feature more elaborately detailed facades and awnings. Hooded men push carts of plastic toys

Figure 2.3. Video stills of the staging ground for the Stitch Lane training simulation, 2007 (*top row*) and 2012 (*bottom row*). The explosion that initiated the simulation in Medina Wasl in 2007 can be seen in the top right frame; the explosion in this same space, renamed Ertebat Shar by 2012, can be seen on the bottom left. Recorded by the author with permission from the Fort Irwin National Training Center, Barstow, CA, 2007 and 2012.

and melons through the street, occasionally followed by a figure in a burqa or a goat. A statue stands in the center of the town, a replica of the Princess of Hatra erected in 238 CE in the city of Al Hadr, Iraq. Though the town is now meant to simulate Afghanistan, the statue remains. The circumference of the statue's base and the concrete barricades that surround it prevent anyone from standing too close, and TCs and their contracted pyrotechnicians can hide large gunpowder charges there and detonate them safely, a sensory-story element they are loath to give up (fig. 2.4). A plaque on the base of the statue indicates that it was constructed "in appreciation of the American Soldier, the true protector of democracy" by Strategic Operations, the San Diego–based production company that presumably avoided bankruptcy through the fulfillment of such contracts.

Professional army videographers record the training events from three different angles using large cameras with expensive zoom lenses. Their footage is compiled, marked, and integrated for use in after-action reviews at a communications center hidden in the village. Soldiers will watch selections from the footage later at a newly built, climate-controlled movie theater instead of the interior of a faux mosque. Two contract employees monitor the feeds on a computer screen and cue the sounds of gunfire, the call to prayer, livestock, screams, and so on at the command of the lead TC. They can also release smells into the center of the village, including burning flesh, "dragon's breath," coffee, roast beef, jasmine, sewer, apple pie, gunpowder, and vomit.[84] All the footage that they record is sent wirelessly by way of microwave transmission to a larger communications center and server on the post. Through a radio lavalier I attach to the head TC, I hear stage directions before they unfold in the town as the action begins. He conjures snipers out of myriad windows, summons a suicide bomber to the center of the city street, and directs insurgents to fire from their locked-down positions until they are hit. "Give them a Hollywood ending," he says to one. The insurgent stands in a window and shoots as many of the American soldiers as he can before the receptors on his laser-tag vest beep to indicate that he has been killed. The duration of the firefight stretches on, nearing forty-five minutes as other civilian tourists on an NTC Box Tour look on with me from the covered platform. We are confined to the space for our own safety, and it is as though we are pioneer spectators to a new form of hypermasculine super-CinemaScope filmmaking.

Immersion in action-cinematic simulation, however, is a difficult place from which to explore adversary culture or offer a critique of military activities already visible within the simulation itself. Indeed, media visitors to the NTC became a key asset within the simulation over time. The public affairs office at

Figure 2.4. Video stills of the Princess of Hatra statue and placard, 2012. Recorded by the author with permission from the Fort Irwin National Training Center, Barstow, CA.

the fort anticipated the norms of journalistic and documentary practice, the allure of cinematic display, and the influence that their interpretations could have on the stories their guests would tell about simulation training. In the midst of shocking and disorienting simulations of worst-day-ever scenarios, public-relations officers, TCs, and particularly gregarious Iraqi and Afghan American actors offered quick, on-message explanations of the need for such scenarios to save lives and the virtues of the military's new, culturally aware approach to warfare. Reporters, scholars, and documentary filmmakers visiting the base have reproduced both the phenomenological novelty of taking in the cinematic spectacle firsthand and the military's explanation for these innovations as emblematic of enlightened, virtuous war-making, although they are inappropriate indices for the efficacy of cultural awareness in theater. This consistently reproduced result—one way in which the military is weaponizing affect in an era of counterinsurgency war—foregrounds a difficult dilemma for documentary practices in the context of increasingly ubiquitous simulation technologies. The documentarian can be anticipated by the simulation and enfolded within its logic.

Cultural performance in the context of military training, in short, is not by default progressive, humane, or just. The affective strategy that emphasizes avoidance, mistrust, and contempt of potential enemies remains a part of army camaraderie, and it is structurally incompatible with the objective of intercultural engagement. Counterinsurgency warfare rather demands cultural performance to function as one weapon among many.[85] Amid ubiquitous cameras, cultural performance cannot simply be the domain of Special Forces who have long functioned in the US military as collaborators in guerrilla wars in distant locales. The attacks that most devastate the army, in this case, are the journalistic reports of war that reveal the scope, manner, and long-term effects of unnecessary civilian deaths. From the perspective of the US military, as the lack of punishment meted out for Abu Ghraib attests, the crime is not in the killing or the torture but in the leaked photographs of the killed or the tortured.

Ruminating on the photographs of Behram, media theorist Lisa Parks suggested that the nature of camerawork in the digital era has rendered covert war difficult, if not impossible.[86] It is a provocative assertion and leads to two further thoughts about the dynamic between digital photographic media and embodied performance. First, covert war must hide itself in the context of ubiquitous cameras in different ways. It must take place in remote, highly secured prisons like those photographed from miles away in the work of Trevor Paglen, or, as the Russian influence operations on the 2016 election in the United States suggest, in exploiting design parameters in algorithms and cybersecurity protocols.[87] Second, the presence of cameras produces the internalization of the cinematic in an institution such as the US military, which in turn drills these values into individual troops. Cinematic performance is here a weapon that short-circuits the oft-assumed power of documentary exposure to work toward justice. Rather, the rules by which documentary practitioners play—faith in following subjects or foregrounding their statements over voice-of-God narration, belief in proximity to subjects as a route to truer representation, discerning organic narratives in subjects' lives to allow their nuanced characters to emerge—are easily subsumed by Fort Irwin's simulation-body as vehicles for political affect.

But if oriented toward justice and advocacy rather than military training, a simulation documentary can create open spaces for public dialogue about structural inequalities as well. One advantage of thinking about indexicality through the body in performance is that everyone has a medium for inscription. At the Moore's Ford Lynching Reenactment in Georgia, participants use their media—and all the epidermal affordances with which they come—to participate in activism together. I turn my attention to camerawork in this case study next.

NOTES

1. For an overview, see the chapter on cultural terrain in González, *Militarizing Culture.*
2. Sobchack, *Address of the Eye*, 139.
3. McFate, "Military Utility," 43.
4. Sewall et al., *Counterinsurgency Field Manual*, viii, 1–2.
5. Public affairs officer, personal interview.
6. Protevi, *Political Affect*, 46–47.

7. To foreshadow a point to which I return at length later in the chapter, many of the reports and films I consider here position the cinematic gore and violence in simulation training as tools for hardening troops to the realities of battle as well as reining in impulses to abuse prisoners or kill civilians. The visage of Iraqi dress, décor, and everyday activity serves in these stories to emphasize the seriousness with which the military is taking culture in the midst of chaos, a connection I will critique. See Filkins and Burns, "Mock Iraqi Villages"; Magelssen, "Rehearsing the 'Warrior Ethos.'"

8. Magelssen, "Rehearsing the 'Warrior Ethos,'" 68.

9. Roger Stahl identifies the formation of the all-volunteer army, the official press conference, the embedded reporting scenario, and the interactive first-person presentation of troop experiences as entertainment as parts of a sustained effort since the 1960s to blunt dissent, decouple citizenship from soldiering, and create "large scale press integration into a system of Pentagon public relations." Fort Irwin welcoming reporters to observe training fits into Stahl's critique of "militainment," and I touch on his larger argument below. Stahl, *Militainment, Inc.*, 15–16, 23.

10. Looking back from the perspective of 2021, *The U.S. Army and Marine Corps Counterinsurgency Field Manual* of 2007 articulates scenarios that have in many respects come to fruition in the Middle East–North Africa region, among others. The manual ruminates on the fact of 9/11, the failing wars in Iraq and Afghanistan, and the specter of 2.8 billion young, jobless city dwellers living in poverty throughout the globe by 2015, coping with "overcrowding, pollution, uneven resource distribution, and poor sanitation," and ostensibly recognizing an allure in radical ideologies that identify the United States as a key culprit. The introduction of the manual predicts a long, low-intensity war against an entity like the Islamic State: "America is at war and should expect to remain fully engaged for the next several decades in a persistent conflict against an enemy dedicated to U.S. defeat as a nation and eradication as a society." Sewall et al., *Counterinsurgency Field Manual*, viii, 1–2; Der Derian, *Virtuous War*.

11. In *The Witch's Flight* (2007), Kara Keeling adapts the term *common sense* from Antonio Gramsci's *Prison Notebooks* to articulate the ways that collectives of various sorts understand and act on the meanings of the media they consume. Keeling, *Witch's Flight*, 19–23.

12. For a consideration of the production process of Brady's photographs and its relationship to the industrialization of war, see Trachtenberg, "Albums of War."

13. Laine, *Shame and Desire*, 10.

14. I relied extensively on the NewsBank: Access World News database for news stories about simulation training, which I accessed in July 2011 to download articles for analysis in intervening years. Subsequently, I read a small number of articles about the fort published between 2016 and 2018 to flesh out the arc of its post-2000 history.

15. Suchman, "Configuring the Other," 8.

16. See a veteran's description of this dichotomy in Gill, "Rehearsing the War Away."

17. Stahl, *Militainment, Inc.*

18. When I visited the fort in 2007, these trainers were called *operational controllers*. In 2012, the army referred to them as *tactical controllers*. To avoid confusion in this chapter, I refer to them throughout as *tactical controllers* (TCs), but this is not necessarily the case in other works about the fort created before 2011.

19. The rhetorical emphasis on realism is ubiquitous in my interviews, a point to which I return in my analysis below. Role-Player 1, interview.

20. Though Behram began photographing and videotaping the victims of the United States' secret drone war in the Federally Administered Tribal Areas of Pakistan in 2004, his photographs came to attention only with an exhibition in a self-made street stand for journalists in Islamabad in 2011, followed by a story published in the German publication *Spiegel Online* in 2011. Behram was also profiled in *Wired* magazine in 2011, after twenty-seven of his photographs were featured in a show in London called *Gaming in Waziristan*. Trevor Paglen, a geographer and visual artist who has done extensive research on the invisible aspects of American militarism, extreme extradition practices, and torture, curated a show in March 2012 at the Kansas City Art Institute, *On Watch*, that included some of Behram's photographs. See stories and select photographs at Ackerman, "Rare Photographs"; Kazim, "Drone War in Pakistan"; Walters, "Parrhēsia Today."

21. The case of photojournalist Zoriah Miller, who published images of marines killed in a suicide bombing in 2008, highlights the complexities entailed in press access, representation of war, and embedded reporting. Spokespersons for military units have embraced embedded reporters' positive stories about the everyday lives of soldiers. However, they claim that published photographs of Americans killed in action provide their enemies with intelligence about the effectiveness of their attacks, violate principles of informed consent, and offend soldiers' families. Miller argues, conversely, that the images are vital to communicating to American readers about the physical and emotional costs of the war. The fact that his photographs shocked viewers when suicide bombings happen every day, he concluded, "says that whatever [the military is] doing to limit this type of photo getting out, it is working." Since the publication of the photographs, no military unit has permitted Miller to embed. As war casualties increased, fewer US units allowed embedded journalists to accompany them to battle sites. Kamber and Arango, "4,000 U.S. Deaths."

22. Stahl, *Militainment, Inc.*, 14.

23. Ibid., 3.

24. On realism in industrial cinema, see especially Bordwell, Staiger, and Thompson, *Classical Hollywood Cinema*.

25. Ien Ang's seminal reception study *Watching Dallas*, for instance, discusses the phenomenon of "psychological realism" in relation to European fans' responses to the American TV soap opera *Dallas*. Audience members identified with the dilemmas of the show's protagonists even though they were aware that the degree of wealth and drama were not representative of American society on the whole. Ang, *Watching Dallas*. Keeling, *The Witch's Flight*.

26. See the discussion on "archive affect" in chapter 1, drawn from Baron, *Archive Effect*.

27. Baudrillard and Turner, *America*, 104.

28. See J. Harris, "Short History of Fort Irwin."

29. Rogers, "Nevada Soldiers Help in Training."

30. Public affairs officer, personal interview.

31. Lancaster, "At Army's Training Center."

32. Komarow, "Cybersoldiers Test Weapons."

33. Levins, "War."

34. Jurgensen, "Stress under Fire."

35. Lancaster, "At Army's Training Center."

36. Emphasis in the original text. Virilio, *Desert Screen*, 20.

37. Emphasis in the original text. Ibid., 135.

38. Schmitt, "U.S. Tripling Fund"; Gutierrez, "Training Stop."
39. Mueller, "Preparing for Urban Warfare"; Filkins and Burns, "Mock Iraqi Villages."
40. Dorsey, "Government Has Spent $6 Billion."
41. Komarow, "Unexpected Insurgency."
42. Ibid.
43. Paylor, "Replicating Iraq."
44. Filkins and Burns, "Mock Iraqi Villages."
45. Gutierrez, "Training Stop."
46. Mueller, "Graduate-Level Training."
47. Cuningham, "Training Leader."
48. Mueller, "Graduate-Level Training."
49. Ibid.
50. M. Harris, "Fillmore Couple's Firm."
51. Vizzo, "Purposeful Chaos."
52. Public affairs officer, phone interview.
53. While the "Combat Wound Medical Effects" are no longer posted on the company website, as of 2022 there was a page featuring comparable products. See Strategic Operations, "Medical Products."
54. Williams, "Film Bodies: Gender, Genre, and Excess."
55. Thevenot, "Duty Calls."
56. Filkins and Burns, "Mock Iraqi Villages."
57. Santschi, "Uncertain Future."
58. Rather and nomorenarcissism, "U.S. Military Future 1."
59. Vargo, "Destination Iraq."
60. Lavell, "Advances in Training."
61. Sedgwick and Alexander, *Shame and Its Sisters*, 41–42.
62. Ibid., 43.
63. Ibid., 45.
64. Greg, interview.
65. Ibid.
66. Ibid.
67. Tomkins, *Affect Imagery Consciousness*, 481.
68. Ibid., 460.
69. Sedgwick, "Paranoid Reading and Reparative Reading," 128.
70. Keeling, *The Witch's Flight*, 25.
71. Gill, "Rehearsing the War Away," 144.
72. Sobchack, *Carnal Thoughts*, 49.
73. Docherty, *More Sweat . . . Less Blood*, 4–7, 20.
74. Public affairs officer, phone interview.
75. The $12 million center, which closed in July 2010, offered visitors eighty gaming stations, helicopter and Humvee simulators, and a space for managing enlistments. Located between an arcade and a skate park, the center became a flashpoint for protesters troubled by the army's endorsement of graphic violence in first-person shooter games targeted at children. See Cousineau, "Surveillant Simulation of War," 518–20; Matheson, "Flashy Army Recruitment Center"; González, *Militarizing Culture*, 16.
76. Thevenot, "Duty Calls."
77. Jane, interview.

78. Ibid.
79. Brandt, "Simulated War."
80. Jane, interview.
81. Magelssen, "Rehearsing the 'Warrior Ethos,'" 68.
82. Losh, "Palace of Memory."
83. A public affairs officer communicated this information to me during my visit to the fort in 2012. Every month, the army leads several "Box Tours" for members of the public to see the "worst day ever" a soldier might encounter in Afghanistan. In 2012, tickets cost around fifty dollars. "If you're interested in experiencing how America's war fighters train before they deploy, book a tour today!" the site read at the time. As of 2020, NTC tours were open to the public, free, and limited to only five visitors at a time. The tour very much resembles a Hollywood war movie, as I suggest in the conclusion of this chapter. See US Army, "NTC Community Box Tours."
84. Technician, interview.
85. Overall, the military moved away from cultural awareness as the wars in Iraq and Afghanistan decreased in intensity. In 2012, the army began to shift from counterinsurgency to what it called *decisive action training*, a combination of conventional force-on-force warfare techniques, counterinsurgency, and police procedures. In the words of one *Army* writer who visited NTC in 2013, "Decisive action includes pretty much everything from armor fights to humanitarian operations (simultaneously) with insurgent forces and criminal gangs thrown into the mix along with the need to gain the trust and fight alongside friendly coalition forces, and it includes an increased emphasis on the tenets of Mission Command." By 2021, NTC officers emphasized "preparation for conflict with established 'near-peer' or 'high-end adversary' nation-states at the full brigade level" to lobby for more land on which to carry out maneuvers. Steele, "Decisive Action Training," 30; Sterenfeld, "Army Seeks to Expand."
86. L. Parks, "Coverage, Media Space, and Security."
87. Paglen has employed extreme zoom lenses to photograph from great distances secret prisons in Afghanistan (*The Black Sites*, 2006) and then-classified US military compounds (*Limit Telephotography*, 2012). The necessity of documenting such sites from miles away creates artifacts in the image that come to index relations of power. Paglen describes these sites as follows in text for *Limit Telephotography*: "Many of these sites are so remote, in fact, that there is nowhere on Earth where a civilian might be able to see them with an unaided eye. In order to produce images of these remote and hidden landscapes, therefore, some unorthodox viewing and imaging techniques are required." See Paglen, "Limit Telephotography."

THREE

"DO YOU WANT TO PLAY A KLANSMAN?"

Lynching Photography, Civil Rights Camerawork, and the Moore's Ford Lynching Reenactment in Georgia

TO REPEAT AND REVISE THE introduction of this book: on July 25, 1946, at the Moore's Ford Bridge just outside of Monroe, Georgia, a white mob brutally lynched two Black couples who worked as sharecroppers, George and Mae Murray Dorsey and Roger and Dorothy Malcom. The perpetrators—who may have included at least one Georgia police officer—were never prosecuted.[1] Both to work through the lingering trauma of that event and to compel the arrest and prosecution of the three to twelve surviving suspects in the case who still lived unpunished in Walton County, Black civil rights activists and white sympathizers from the region began to reenact the lynching in 2005. Over the ensuing sixteen years, the reenactment evolved in relation to changes in the status of renewed investigations into the cold case and sometimes in response to new forms of media coverage. There are no credible eyewitness accounts of the lynching itself available to the public and no known photographs of the violent acts that took place that day.[2]

Those who wish to piece together the story of the quadruple lynching in Monroe must speculate. Truth exists below the surface, in the land, or, for some, in the spirits of the dead that pass by the living on that site as a breeze. But souls do not speak in juridical language. They cannot prosecute, and with each passing year, it seems less likely that the living will be able to prosecute either. This absence both motivates and complicates the organizers' stated ethical rationales for staging the reenactment, which center on justice for victims and advocacy for Black dignity and voting rights. Long-standing anger among Black activists and white allies about unpunished white-on-Black violence does not abate, after all, and the lynching remains a powerful symbol. When speakers at the reenactment mention the deaths of Maceo Snipes, Lynn McKinley Jackson, Trayvon Martin, Sandra Bland, Lennon Lacy, and many others, they emphasize the fact that the Moore's Ford lynching was not an isolated incident. Each touches the others affectively. It is through the ritual of gathering and reenacting, as Diana Taylor noted, that "performed, embodied practices make the 'past' available as a political resource in the present."[3] This is the point.

The murders touch a common-sense experience among many Black audience members whom have seen friends and family die or lived through close calls themselves.[4] Affective evidence at the reenactment is close to the event that occurred, the recollection-image of an affect-laden symbol of trauma like those discussed in chapter 1, or gossip that might be true.[5] This "poetic repertoire of metonymic expansiveness," to use the thoughtful characterization of performance rhetoricians A. Susan Owen and Peter Ehrenhaus, better serves the inclusion of a broader Black community than "a repertoire of archival restraint" in which the details of theatrical presentation strictly follow documented presence in archival sources. Archival sources in towns where lynchings occurred are notoriously unreliable. In this way, the reenactment creates and augments affective evidence for "moral witnesses" who gather to memorialize those who have died.[6] Cultural anthropologist Mark Auslander, who has been writing about the reenactment for many years, recalled a conversation to this effect that he had with an attendee in 2017. Rather than speak about the arrest and prosecution of the 1946 lynchers (long the stated purpose of the reenactment), his interviewee, "Janet," described the reenactment as a "funeral procession" for all Black victims of police violence. "But don't you see," Janet said to him, "it wasn't just a reenactment, now, this time around. It really was a funeral procession, for all of them. For Trayvon, for Eric Garner, for the Emmanuel church-people. For Sandra. We're here today for all of them."[7] The common thread of their Blackness compelled affective touch, for Janet, and in quoting her perspective, Auslander affirms that something like it has extended to him.

These performance scholars describe how the Moore's Ford Lynching Reenactment creates a liminal ritual space through which a collective finds strength and some participants find personal healing, redemption, or catharsis.[8] I argue here that it also offers an event to be observed and recorded in minute detail. This section considers the evolving and heterogenous media artifacts created about this story and its reenactment. To the discomfort of many, the reenactment inevitably repurposes and redirects certain community-making aspects attributed to historical spectacle-lynching events.[9] Claiming the Christian spirit of an eye for an eye, lynch mobs between 1893 and 1934 would theatrically reenact the purported crime on the body of the accused or a surrogate for the accused in front of thousands of white spectators. Mobs carried out mutilation and castration for stabbing, immolation for arson, or penetration by hot poker for rape, and then lynchers, spectators, and their children would pose for postcard photographs with the bodies of the victims to cement a community premised on the tenets of white supremacy. The intergenerational trauma inflicted on Black southerners and differently on white perpetrators from these events remains raw and unresolved.

While the reenactment at Moore's Ford memorializes lynching victims who were not photographed—a private lynching rather than a public one—it also confronts the history of spectacle lynchings through the reappropriation of their form. Organizers understand the power of photographs, stories, and videos of the reenactment when they circulate beyond the town of Monroe in Walton County, Georgia. They know the power of framing civil rights protest actions in biblical terms to garner support from the network of Black churches in Georgia and beyond. And over time, I argue here, the creation of dramatic scenes amenable to recording became a key goal. In chapters 3 and 4, I analyze how and why camerawork came to constitute part of the "performative repertoire," to recast Taylor's term, of the live reenactment events. I argue that the organizers of the reenactment were savvy to think in this way. Spectacular photographability of bodies in live performance was the movement's route to the archive, to becoming an accessible infrastructure in the digital world. As with the objectives of civil rights campaigns of the 1950s and 1960s, the staging of the reenactment created a national and international profile for the unsolved Moore's Ford lynching case that was useful to all others like it while possibly sacrificing some aspects of archival fidelity and interracial dialogue about the lynching in the town of Monroe. For its recursivity, spatiality, photographability, focus on performing bodies, and speculative claim on the historical real, I am categorizing the Moore's Ford Lynching Reenactment as a simulation documentary.

I argue here that the transformation of the reenactment from a local, biracial community effort to promote healing to an event organized and carried out mostly by Atlantans with almost no participation from local whites has a lot to do with steps taken over time toward enhancing the reenactment's photographability. In this way, the reenactment hearkens back not only to a quadruple lynching that occurred just before the start of the civil rights movement and the widespread adoption of television but also to the media strategy that the movement developed over the course of ensuing activist campaigns of the 1950s and 1960s with television coverage in mind. I suggest in the next chapter how the growth of the media industry in Georgia has influenced this reenactment performance and its relationship to activism.

This section of the book, in short, pursues a deeper understanding of simulation documentary through a close analysis of the Moore's Ford Lynching Reenactment and the complex questions it raises for camera-wielding spectators, filmmakers, and organizers alike. Why did the reenactment continue year after year, and how and why did it change over that time? Given key organizers' roots in civil rights movement activism and the vital role of news cameras recording white-on-Black violence in that struggle, what is the place of cameras in this reenactment? What do cameras do to the tenor of the live performance, and how does the performance itself anticipate the presence of cameras and direct their attention? And given that the most popular reenactments in the US depict major battles of the Civil War—which often downplay the central place of slavery as the historical catalyst for the participants' weekend activities—how have Black and white Georgians responded to the existence of a lynching reenactment? In a media ecosystem that tends to reward attention to lurid visuals and shocking headlines characteristic of true-crime docudramas, should we theorize the reenactment as part of this genre or as an extension of civil rights movement activism? Is the reenactment primarily a live event or a vital means to keep the lynching story at the top of the results in a Google search for "Moore's Ford"? In other words, what kind of a tool for struggle does the reenactment become beyond the charged moments of liveness and copresence characteristic of the performances themselves?

I aim to answer such questions in the final two chapters of the book. The first (chap. 3) describes the reenactment and its history and then excavates the place of camerawork in representations of spectacle lynchings from 1893 to 1936 as well as common-cause TV news recording during the civil rights movement campaigns from 1955 to 1965. This chapter largely draws on secondary sources by historians who have written on one or the other of these topics, which I see as the two lineages of image making germane to interpreting media objects that have incorporated or covered aspects of the Moore's Ford Lynching Reenactment. In the last part of this chapter, I analyze camerawork in recent films about the Moore's Ford lynching, including my own during the 2012 reenactment, when I first attended as an ethnographic researcher and cameraperson for Jacqueline Olive's feature documentary *Always in Season* (2019). Chapter 4 argues for theorizing this annual reenactment as an affective infrastructure, drawing from an ethnographic description of nearly ubiquitous attendee camerawork at the 2019 reenactment and a close analysis of the representation of the lynching reenactment in Olive's finished film, where it serves to recast by metonymic juxtaposition the official ruling of suicide in the 2014 death by hanging of Black North Carolina teenager Lennon Lacy.

DO YOU WANT TO PLAY A KLANSMAN? REFLECTING ON CAMERAWORK, RACE, AND ROLE

"Do you want to play a Klansman?" The first time I spoke with the director of the Moore's Ford Lynching Reenactment in 2010, she asked me the question that now serves as the title of this chapter. Then she dangled a lure for an early-stage graduate student: "You'd have a whole book to write about that experience." She explained to me that whites from Monroe generally refused to participate in the performance, so they needed more nonlocals to complement the white thespians from Atlanta who annually volunteered to play the major parts, such as Walter as Eugene Talmadge and the social justice activist and playwright who portrayed the head Klansman. Even progressive whites from Atlanta and Athens were hard to recruit, she told me. One who had played a Klansman later could not remember what had happened during the performance. This is a symptom of trauma.

Black participants faced other kinds of dilemmas. In the early years, the Black actors who played the Malcoms and the Dorseys were middle-aged locals who grew up during the early years of desegregation, when white kids threw rocks at them coming and going to school. A couple of the male actors were distant relatives of the lynching victims. Thinking back to these childhood experiences and painful memories helped them channel the terror they imagined the Malcoms and the Dorseys feeling at that moment. The reenactors suffered minor traumas to play the parts because they were angry, tired of living in fear, and hopeful that the arrest and prosecution of surviving members of the lynch mob would improve morale in their community. But for several years after their performances, some of these actors found themselves frozen out of job opportunities without any explicit explanation as to why. They were also in their mid-fifties or older. After 2008, most of the Black actors also came from outside the area. They were in their early twenties, closer in age to the Dorseys and the Malcoms at the time of their deaths, and they watched documentaries about the civil rights movement to prepare where personal memories of childhood did not offer adequate affective intensity.

I considered playing a role but came to agree with one colleague who said that this would be "a bad way to introduce yourself to the community" when seeking honest conversations on the reenactment with local Black and white people. I did not like the prospect of appearing on camera as a Klansman lyncher either, so I declined the invitation and instead partnered with film director Jacqueline Olive for two weeks to observe the reenactment from behind a camera while filming for her documentary *Always in Season* (2019). As I suggested in the introduction, being there with a camera gave my fieldwork a different angle than previous ethnographers of the reenactment who had focused on community performance, rituals around death, and racial trauma in American life. I argue that the Moore's Ford Lynching Reenactment is a media strategy as well. From this vantage, I reinterpret the question that the director asked me in our first conversation. To be white and filming in this context, I suggest in the last portion of this chapter, may be a tacit yes to the reenactment director's question about playing a Klansman. If noninterventionist recording of the Vietnam War reenactment fell flat for want of stakes (chap. 1) and similar kinds of camerawork undermined dissent and served the military's public relations goals at Fort Irwin (chap. 2), then camerawork at the Moore's Ford Lynching Reenactment diverges from the promise of neutral representation in another way: observing with a camera reproduces the perpetrators' view of a hate crime. For the viewers of this footage in a finished film, at least, footage recorded while next to white Georgians playing a lynch mob seems to produce the ocular experience of playing a Klansman. It turns out that there is a whole book to write about that experience. But as I discuss in chapter 4, Olive and her editors found an unconventional way to avoid this trap.

While I note certain staging decisions and trace out their consequences in this chapter, I do not believe that the organizers of this event should apologize for seeking out the lifeblood of camera and press. They are essential components of movements for structural change in our world and keys to the instructive successes, as I see them, that have cascaded from the annual commitment to stage the reenactment since 2005. Unlike others who have written about the case itself, I am not in a place to help solve it or to bring about prosecutions of those who committed the murders in 1946. Some small form of redemption may be on offer for the descendants of suspects and the neighbors who know them who choose to speak publicly, or possibly to a judge or two who can decide to release the grand jury transcripts for the case.

During fieldwork, when Black interviewees would sense my limitations and politely ask me questions about my motivations, I would make the case for activist scholarship in the context of higher education. A media studies scholar must make choices about where to direct limited research time and energy, a privilege associated with university life. Research on lynching history and the contours of its reenactment can be used to lead students—especially in predominantly white institutions—to sit uncomfortably in histories of racial oppression, Black anger, and white complicity that may complicate a faith in American Dream narratives that some bring into the classroom. The months and weeks when I write about the reenactment, I regularly experience nausea and depression—visceral responses that Ann Cvetkovich via Cornel West describes as emerging when "a privileged form of hopefulness that has so often been entirely foreclosed for black people is punctured."[10] The contradictions entailed in writing about a civil rights lynching reenactment while living with the privileges associated with whiteness give rise to these feelings, which are not to be confused with Black sadness. Nonetheless, broad support for reparations for communities impacted by racial violence requires broad affective understanding of the ongoing damage wrought by slavery, lynching, Jim Crow, and more tacit forms racial discrimination and of the strategies that local or regional leaders now pursue to bring about awareness, justice, memorialization, reconciliation, healing, and policy change. My research aims to serve as a tool for facilitating such goals and to consider connections between reenactment, media, and politics. There are ways to bridge this study with contemporary writing on structures of mass incarceration, voter suppression, and police violence against Black Americans. This case study, like the reenactment itself, can work within a range of operations, so to speak.

Through the interpretation of Black history that it enlivens before cameras, in short, the reenactment functions as an affective infrastructure for many causes, not just the prosecution of this lynch mob.[11] This availability of the lynching reenactment for politics speaks to one leader's insistence on characterizing the reenactment as a movement, not an event. Many of the reenactors—and especially the white reenactors—say that the story should become a movie or a program to be performed on stage in schools rather than on the locations in which the lynching and ancillary events occurred in 1946. I argue in this section that this movement is inseparable from media production, distribution, and consumption, much like the civil rights movement before it, but that the power of such media objects depends on the annual coming together of organizers, activists, actors, and community people to reenact. To transpose the reenactment to institutional spaces would give it a greater physical scope but depoliticize the performance as being of the past rather than the unresolved present. It is the fact of copresent bodies annually performing this ritual on the site of actual unresolved, violent death that renews its indexical charge and justifies ongoing media representations. The ritual is a way to cope with death collectively that is nonetheless attuned to cinematic sensibilities.

INDEXING CINEMATIC DEATH "DOWN HOME"

Representing natural death in the cinema presents a problem of duration, as the process of dying slowly across time ill suits Hollywood content and pacing preferences. In everyday life, moreover, urbanites tend to shutter death and dying away into nursing homes, hospitals, and care facilities such as hospice. Many of us do not see a lot of it in person. Yet we also long to make sense of death and dying as beings approaching this status, and so we turn to media depictions, which offer seemingly endless simulations of violent death. In fictional cinema, Vivian Sobchack observes, "violence gives death a perceptible form and signifies its ultimate violation of the lived body." But because death is a taboo subject in modern societies, she argues that spectators need an ethical rationale to witness actual death in documentary. The act of filming death must also signify love, helplessness to prevent it, or an effort to intervene if spectators are to judge the looking as ethical.[12]

These alibis for gazing at death in documentary film, I would add, apply to witnessing the reenactment of the Moore's Ford lynching, though no one literally dies. The staging encourages witnesses to see the reenactment as an act of love, an acknowledgement of helplessness to prevent what happened, and an intervention into the wanton murder of Black people simultaneously. And they are shown the violent and violating deaths that occurred through tropes of violent, abrupt death in fiction filmmaking, "the most effective cinematic representation of death in our present culture" for Sobchack.[13]

In the context of reenactment, the setting of the Moore's Ford Bridge indexes the lynching that once occurred there. The subtle movements of leaves in the trees, the flying insects, and the river are like particles of silver halide on the emulsion behind the closed shutter, waiting for human perception to compel their becoming indexical signs of something, of violent death still lived with. As evidence of affective history, the landscape at Moore's Ford is timeless even though the adjacent road is now paved and the wooden bridge has been replaced with one of concrete. Like a photograph with scratches or the yellowish tinting of age, this landscape stands the perceptual test of time for participants in the reenactment, spectators, and locals who know something about the lynching that once stained it. The landscape becomes cinematic—and documentary, I would add—during the live, acted performance of the lynching itself in the presence of witnesses. It is a fleeting recollection-object jolting affective response like the tar paper in Rea Tajiri's *History and Memory* as well as a "documentary space" in these moments, to paraphrase Sobchack's film theory. The site is "constituted and inscribed as ethical space: [in the midst of performance] it stands as the objectively visible evidence of subjective visual responsiveness and responsibility toward a world shared with other human subjects."[14]

The indexical quality of the landscape conjoins with the "collective effervescence" of the ritual reenactment to lend poignancy to the performance of death and killing by actors.[15] The racist ideology at the core of the lynching tradition, of course, produces relations with these deaths that are quite unlike the viewing of other cinematic deaths where racial animus is not so evident. These are deaths that index deeply personal sentiments of sadness, anger, and need for solidarity for many Black spectators who witness the reenactment and actors who play roles within it.

bell hooks' phenomenological insights about her experiences with death and dying as a "down home" Black southerner complement the framework that Sobchack sets out in her documentary theory of representing death. Black people living "in the midst of racial apartheid" did not have the luxury of keeping death at a distance. "Growing up, I learned to respect the reality of dying, not to ignore or make light of it," hooks stated. She recalled church songs that framed death as a transitional state between two kinds of embodiment rather than an event to fear. The objective result of death was not a corpse to behold but a spirit to feel in the presence of a community: "Many southern Black people have held to the belief that a human being possesses body, soul, and spirit—that death may take one part even as the others remain." She suggests that this tripartite understanding of the subject in death has enabled African American believers to confront death without feeling overwhelmed. But like Sobchack, she identified the lifestyles of Black urbanites (including her own) as structurally antithetical to these traditional rituals for expressing grief and working toward healing after death. "Just the pace of life in cities makes constructive prolonged mourning in the context of community nearly impossible," she states. Given these circumstances, hooks argued that Black women needed to take an active role in creating the spaces for their own healing. "Individual Black women must ask ourselves, 'Where are the spaces in our lives where we are able to acknowledge our pain and express grief?' If we cannot identify those spaces, we need to make them."[16] In this section of the book, I suggest how the reenactment of the Moore's Ford lynching creates a space for acknowledging pain and expressing grief especially for Black female participants. But I hold to the claim that this is also a cinematic space layered on the down-home one that it appears to be. The Moore's Ford Lynching Reenactment, in this vein, lends itself to attention within the serialized, transmedia environment of the early twenty-first century—a feat largely due to the long-standing strategic work of civil rights movement field secretary and former Georgia state representative Tyrone Brooks, without whom the reenactment would never have come into being.

WHY REENACT: A SYNOPSIS OF THE MOORE'S FORD LYNCHING REENACTMENT

Brooks regularly recounts the origin story of the reenactment in public speeches. On April 4, 1968, he was a field secretary for the Student Nonviolent Coordinating Committee (SNCC) working in Monroe to gather more details about the lynching case when he learned of Dr. Martin Luther King Jr.'s assassination in Memphis, Tennessee. In the wake of this personal and national trauma, he committed himself to carrying out King's strategy to pursue the arrest and prosecution of perpetrators of cold-case lynchings like the one that had taken place in Monroe. King had intended to travel to Monroe several weeks after his stop in Memphis, Brooks emphasizes, to bring awareness to the failed FBI attempt to prosecute the case in 1946. Along with a local activist group called the Moore's Ford Memorial Committee (MFMC) that formed in the late 1990s, a group associated with Brooks, the Georgia Association of Black Elected Officials (GABEO), participated in April 4 marches on the Moore's Ford Bridge to commemorate the assassination of Dr. King. At the event in 2005, former Alabama state senator Charles Steele, the lead organizer of the annual reenactment of the 1965 march across the Edmund Pettis bridge in Selma, suggested to the Georgians that they reenact the Moore's Ford lynching. Sensible that a reenactment would bring media attention to the case and extralocal pressure on residents of Walton and Oconee Counties to come forward with information about the perpetrators, Brooks mobilized his network of political allies and leaders in the Black church to organize a reenactment of the lynching on the last Saturday in July 2005.[17] As with vintage civil rights actions, the one-day event attracted worldwide attention. Organizers and participants appeared in interviews about the case on CNN, on NPR, in the *New York Times*, and on *Democracy Now!*, among others. Longtime activists involved in pursuing the case in collaboration with the Georgia Bureau of Investigation (GBI) and the FBI said that in the wake of the reenactment, more people came forward with relevant information about the lynch mob than they had in decades.[18] GABEO has sponsored a reenactment of the lynching annually since then, though without ongoing official support from the MFMC.

Over the years, the annual reenactment came to include a full day of educational, spiritual, and political activities meant to contextualize the lynchings, pay respects to the Dorseys and the Malcoms, and highlight connections to contemporary violence against Black Americans. Though the reenactment is free and open to the public, attendees are typically over 90 percent Black. Many have returned multiple times. The day begins at noon at the First African Baptist Church in Monroe, where Georgia-based reverends, civil rights activists from across the South, lawyers and investigators working on the case, and representatives of GABEO speak to the attendees about why they organize the reenactment of the Moore's Ford lynching. Keynotes have included C. T. Vivian, Charles Steele, and Stacey Abrams. Speakers discuss the history of racial oppression in the county and nation, the connection between the reenactment activities and the civil rights movement as led by Martin Luther King Jr. in the 1950s and 1960s, and the importance of holding political officeholders accountable to notions of justice derived from United States law and the Bible. Sometimes descendants of the Dorseys and the Malcoms speak in the morning session, and in recent years, descendants of lynching victim Maceo Snipes (1946) and relatives of possible lynching victim Lynn McKinley Jackson (1981) have also participated.[19] The presence of these families in official proceedings demonstrates a shared feeling about Black death and systemic failure to protect Black bodies.

The entire group then caravans by car to the grave sites of the Dorseys and the Malcoms and three sites in the county where key incidents related to the lynching occurred in 1946. At each location, organizers explain the context and social significance of events that took place there before volunteer actors reenact these scenes. Several of these reenactment vignettes are performed in highly trafficked public spaces in and around Monroe so that Black and white locals encounter them as they go about their everyday routines. The troupe first reenacts Roger Malcom's stabbing of his white landlord, Barnett Hester, who may have been having an affair with Dorothy Malcom. Some local elders interviewed decades after the lynching say that Malcom was pregnant at the time and suspect that this was the source of the dispute. In the first three years of the reenactment, reenactors performed the stabbing scene in front of the actual house where the incident occurred and in full view of the Hester descendants, if they chose to look out the window. When the Hester family demolished this building site and demanded that the reenactors stay off their property, organizers decided to avoid the potential for violence and began staging this scene in the church before the group departed for the Malcom and Dorsey grave sites.[20] Next comes the reenactment of the speech given by segregationist gubernatorial candidate and Klan ally Eugene Talmadge to local sympathizers on the front steps of the Walton County Courthouse Annex in downtown Monroe.

Talmadge ran his 1946 campaign on a promise to suppress the Black vote, visited Monroe several days before the lynching to give a stump speech, and reportedly offered immunity to anyone "taking care of the negro."[21] Starting in 2018, the reenactment has followed the speech with a scene in which Black citizens trying to vote in 1946 confront a mob of angry Talmadge supporters, who cross epithets characteristic of 1946 vernacular with phrases voiced in post-2016 conservative media outlets. Then the group walks a brief distance to the old jail site where the Dorseys' white landlord, Loy Harrison, bailed out Roger Malcom. Dorothy Malcom and the Dorseys accompanied Harrison, and in the reenactment, the actors playing these roles stage a happy reunion before the five head off ostensibly for the Harrison farm. Last, the spectators and actors caravan by car twelve miles northeast of Monroe to a property near the Moore's Ford Bridge, owned by a local who allows the group to park there. All who can walk the last half mile in the late July Georgia heat to the site of the final performance. The day culminates in the evening around 5:30 with the brief but emotionally draining reenactment of the lynching scene, which takes place very near the original site by the Apalachee River. The four actors playing the victims then remain "dead" on the ground as a singer performs a spiritual for the group (fig. 3.1). Altogether, the day's events take approximately six hours. The lynching reenactment itself takes about four minutes. But that four-minute reenactment produces in graphic and controversial detail likenesses of the blood, the mob, the guns, and the corpses associated with the brutal murder of two Black couples before spectators and camerapersons. Documentary videos of at least thirteen of these reenactments have been uploaded to YouTube, where they remain accessible as of September 2021.

Reenactment participants, locals from Walton and Oconee Counties, and outside observers continue to debate whether the annual commemoration events are historical reenactments, theatrical productions, passion plays, key markers of a nascent political movement, therapeutic rituals, an emergent kind of grassroots art practice, or disastrous echoes of spectacle lynchings. Laura Wexler's *Fire in a Canebreak* (2003), published before the first reenactment, was at that time the most rigorous archival account of the 1946 lynching and its subsequent legacy in Walton and Oconee Counties.[22] Writing the book as a detective story in the tradition of Truman Capote's *In Cold Blood* (1965), Wexler aimed to coax out a deathbed confession or two from suspected surviving members of the lynch mob. She was unsuccessful in breaking the local wall of silence about the case, but her book usefully represents what is gained and lost by interpreting the story primarily through archival documents and on-the-record interviews. In her conclusion, she articulated two different ways

Figure 3.1. Video still of the conclusion of the 2012 Moore's Ford Lynching Reenactment. The reenactors who take on the roles of the Malcoms and Dorseys are visible playing the dead in the bottom left corner of the frame. Photography by Justin Schein. Courtesy Jacqueline Olive.

of remembering the lynching itself. "For many Black people," she said, "the lynching was the most horrific thing that ever happened in Walton or Oconee counties, but for many white people, it was mainly an annoyance, an event that smudged the area's good name." Her white interviewees often asked her why she would want to "drag this thing up." Some felt that even gesturing to the kind of hatred that fueled the original lynching would do no one any good. Others, she said, implied in the way they asked her this question that they didn't understand why anyone would make a "fuss over four dead Black sharecroppers." The degree to which the collective memories of the event itself remained segregated, for Wexler, suggested "the extent to which racism has destroyed—and continued to destroy—our ability to tell a common truth."[23] Other critics argued that the goal of arrest and prosecution validated the Brechtian local flavor of the early reenactments and symbolized the ongoing struggle against institutional racism. Art critic and documentarian Martin Lucas, for instance, described the reenactment in 2006 as a new form of vernacular public art better suited to critical political engagement in the "society of the spectacle" than trying to participate in "enlightened discourse among equals" in an imagined public sphere.[24]

Scholarship on the reenactment published since 2010 downplays the espoused rationale for the event in favor of reading its contours through the lens of ritual and repair. Julie Buckner Armstrong writes about the lynching reenactment as serving "a therapeutic function" in line with the development of "slave tourism" sites at Middle Passage departure dungeons in Ghana, Underground Railroad recreations in Indiana, and experiential exhibits of slave ships at museums such as the National Great Blacks in Wax in Maryland.[25] She sees the Moore's Ford reenactment in line with the tradition of the Judeo-Christian passion play because it employs stepwise "movement through space" and the "theme of redemption" to "transform into something sacred the evil that happened in their own backyards" (fig. 3.2).[26] Instead of engaging the messier historical narrative that Wexler tells, Armstrong contends, the reenactment presents the victims of the lynching as archetypal martyrs. She suggests that the script followed in the reenactment of the lynching at Moore's Ford shows how "communities can and do conflate incidents" as stories about lynchings travel from place to place and become entangled in one another as legends, distilling the most poignant and lasting details into a hybrid story aligned with the community's affective sense of the things that can be true.[27] Auslander frames the annual reenactment as a ritual in which Black and white participants are "trying to work out, and at least partially resolve, a set of underlying conundrums such as the status of the dead in U.S. society." He argues that these reenactment performances of traumatic historical events "often lead to unexpected moments of profound dialogue and exchange across putative lines of race and difference" and so offer members of historically antagonistic social groups a direction for reconciliation and healing.[28] Through performance, white and Black reenactors share responsibility for reengaging the affective energies of a collectively repressed traumatic event and so offer themselves and witnesses to their acting a chance for grieving and self-expression. Megan Eatman proposes that the reenactment shows how there is a "complex role that inadequate archives can play in memorial practices," where rhetoricians who historically focused on language might begin to study "rhetoric *in situ*."[29]

No detail proved to be more divisive than the organizers' decision starting in 2008 to stage Dorothy Malcom as having been pregnant at the time of the lynching. White MFMC members who had participated enthusiastically in essay competitions and commemoration events at the grave sites of the Dorseys and the Malcoms in the late 1990s and early 2000s, including the late Richard Rusk, son of Vietnam-era secretary of state Dean Rusk, expressed wariness about staging the reenactment at all, fearful that it would damage local goodwill for other activities. All white MFMC participants dropped out in the year or two after the 2007 reenactment—some with bitterness and anger. After the lynch mob murders the Malcoms and the Dorseys by gunshot, in this version of

Figure 3.2. Video still of spectators walking the last half mile to the Moore's Ford Bridge for the reenactment. Photography by Justin Schein. Courtesy Jacqueline Olive.

the script, one of them lacerates Dorothy's stomach, pulls out the "fetus" from under Dorothy's shirt (a Black baby doll), holds it up in the air, and says, "Is this good, boss?" to the leader of the gang. "Yeah, that's good," he responds; "let's go have a drink." The henchman drops the doll onto the adult actors playing the Dorseys and the Malcoms, and the mob walks away. Brooks christened this figure "Justice Malcom" in a naming ceremony. "We now name this baby Justice, denied Justice in death, he is accorded Justice in the hereafter," he said.[30]

Historians Wexler and Anthony Pitch noted in their books that they found no evidence for a pregnancy in archival materials. They both believe it should be there if the detail were true. Photographers and reporters from Black newspapers such as the *Chicago Defender*, the *Pittsburgh Courier*, and the *Atlantic Daily World*, among many others, visited Monroe after the lynching to try to piece together what might have happened, deduce motives, and report on the extent of the brutality. Black reporters described the sizes and numbers of gunshot holes in the bodies, lacerations, breasts that were removed, eyes that were shot out, bones that were broken, and differences across the corpses (one noted that only Mae Murray's face remained unmutilated).[31] The NAACP, moreover, sought to use the Moore's Ford case to catalyze changes in the ways that lynchings could be prosecuted. In 1946, lynching in the South could be tried only in state courts as murders, where all-white juries were sure to acquit perpetrators. Dan Young, the Monroe undertaker and NAACP activist who prepared the victims' bodies, was interviewed by multiple newspapers in 1946. He was in regular communication with associates of Walter White, then the head of the NAACP in Washington, about new developments in the lynching case and the six-month-long FBI investigation. White had been advocating for legislative change to lynch laws for the NAACP for decades, and a case could be made that he would have wanted to publish widely about the brutal killing of a pregnant woman and her fetus—he had done so before in his own reporting as a young field operative on the case of Mary Turner, a pregnant woman brutally lynched in Quitman, Georgia, in 1918.[32] But there are no written traces to suggest that Young communicated this information, if it were true, to anyone in 1946. Pitch emphasized that "the only references to Dorothy Malcolm's alleged pregnancy, among 2,790 transcribed interviews conducted in the year of the crime, are in eleven lines out of 3,723 pages devoted to FBI activities.... On both occasions the speakers relied on hearsay, passing on gossip and what they had overheard." Representative Brooks regularly says that Young was the person who told him that Malcom had been seven months pregnant at the time of the lynching, but Young's daughter told Pitch that her father "never did mention anything about [Malcolm's pregnancy]" to her. Convinced that this detail was false, Pitch regarded its repetition in the annual reenactment as "a mockery of the truth, inflaming untold numbers through the broad reach of social media."[33] The depiction of Malcom's pregnancy remains a key element of the reenactment script, and the placard about the Moore's Ford lynching posted on the highway a mile from the bridge where it occurred mentions Dorothy Malcom's pregnancy as a historical fact.

The organizers are aware that historians remain skeptical about the pregnancy, but they feel that the story should honor the memories of those in the community over archives long regarded as untrustworthy on matters of racial history in the South. "They said, oh yeah, Dorothy was pregnant. She was big! Really. And that was the source of the confrontation between Barney Hester and Roger, that, hey, this my baby or your baby?" one told me. He said he had spoken to relatives who corroborated elders' stories as "common knowledge."[34] The *New York Times* report on the first reenactment likewise quoted a community elder named Flosse Hill who recalled hearing about the lynching on the radio: "Noting that she and the pregnant woman, Dorothy Malcom, were about the same age, Ms. Hill said, 'They say her baby's still living somewhere,' referring to the persistent rumor that the baby was cut from Ms. Malcom's body" and raised by a family elsewhere.[35] Others have speculated that because Dorothy and Roger Malcom were not legally married, the NAACP made a calculated decision to play up George Dorsey's military background and elide the detail about Malcom's pregnancy. And reflecting on her research about the Turner lynching, Armstrong acknowledged that official archives in Lowndes and Brooks Counties in Georgia contained no documented evidence of the pregnancy in Turner's case and little about a spate of lynchings that occurred that week. One white archivist from Quitman who claimed to be the descendent of the county sheriff, Armstrong wrote, "told me that no lynchings had ever happened in Brooks County." But the county museum she managed happened to have mysteriously lost the microfiche for the local newspaper—only for the summer of 1918—to a fire. As if to validate the spirit of the organizers' approach to history at Moore's Ford, Armstrong found evidence of the lynching of Turner only after a Black man died in police custody of a "brain hemorrhage" from either falling and hitting his head or sustaining a blow at the hands of a white officer, and the town divided along lines of race that were impossible to ignore. Black residents talked to Armstrong about the lynching and their anger over its obscurity in white-controlled institutions. "My uncle took me to where it happened when I turned thirteen and told me to watch out for white people," one young student told her.[36] Similarly, a longtime activist in Monroe who had been the target of two attempted lynchings told me that such incidents likely exceeded those that appeared in the press. He recalled witnessing old Black men break down in tears—and "black men didn't cry back during the day," he interjected—when they talked to him about their own experiences as young men. Some mentioned one or another friend who "left town" after a minor altercation with local whites only to turn up months later as "these bones out there in the wood" discovered by wintertime rabbit hunters. "You know, the Moore's Ford lynching is the one that's been mentioned and talked about, but you have to listen to them old folks," he said. "This was a way of life here in the south."[37] In popular culture, DNA evidence validated a story passed down orally through generations of Black people that Thomas Jefferson had fathered the children of the enslaved Sally Hemmings. Yet it is also the case that "communities can and do conflate incidents," as Armstrong suggested: "As the Moore's Ford story traveled through private discourse, it took on the quality of urban legend: it became the story of what happens to women who get lynched in Georgia."[38] I accept from all of this that some key details of the story behind the reenactment remain unknown and unknowable, charged with affective significance, and problematic for scholarship centered on ritual renewal and community cohesion. The uncertainty is a key constitutive element of racial violence. Uncertainty also inhibits political activism and building effective social movements, as historians of science Naomi Oreskes and Erik Conway argue in their exposé on climate denial among scientists on the fossil fuel industry dole, *Merchants of Doubt*.[39] I believe that some combination of these concerns, though unstated, have played a role in decisions to include the pregnancy in the script.

Here, I diverge from the focus on the performance as a live community event in favor of reading a media strategy within the reenactment. The distinction between archive and repertoire, while useful for thinking through matters of state-sanctioned historical preservation and community resistance, in practice makes it difficult to account for organizers' aims to attract media attention—attention enmeshed in the economics of translating lived memory into nascent archival materials for Black Twitter, legacy news outlets, advocacy publications, and films. While I agree that staging on unmarked, public places helps frame the reenactment performance through an ethic of political accountability rather than tourism or theater, it is equally vital to show how organizers' strategies for the extension of story and affect center on attracting and anticipating media coverage. The locations where organizers stage reenactment performances ordinarily bear no markers about the lynching and related events that once took place there, but a Google search in 2020 for "Moore's Ford" reveals only stories about the lynching. It is a notable victory for the organizers of the annual reenactment event. And I do not see their media strategy, in the broader context of the civil rights movement, as necessarily antithetical to—or even separable from—the affective jolts that circulate among audiences at reenactment events as they work through trauma. This is, in fact, close to the playbook that activists such as Brooks learned starting out as teenagers in the civil rights movement, when the goal was to get on television rather than Google. I next consider two image-making practices in relation to the reenactment: lynching photography and television camerawork during the civil rights movement.

LYNCHING AND SPECTACLE: THE LYNCHER'S CAMERA AND THE MAKING OF MODERN COMMUNITIES

While Puritan colonists hung the ungodly in public executions and early American military officers lynched soldiers for wartime misdeeds, the term *lynching* came to refer to vigilante acts of racial terror in the era of photography and then narrative film.[40] The term itself likely referred in its earliest usage to Charles Lynch, a Revolutionary War–era militia officer from Virginia who persuaded the Continental Congress in 1780 to pass Lynch's Law to forgive his extrajudicial wartime imprisonment of Loyalists and poor treatment of Welsh miners in the state. By the 1830s, the few archived uses of the phrase *lynch law* generally referred to the vigilante administration of corporal punishment in rural areas that locals tended to deem just and fair, if also somewhat outside the letter of the law. The many brutal murders of enslaved Black persons on antebellum plantations were not referred to as lynchings. Documentation of the murder of Francis McIntosh, a mulatto man from Missouri burned to death by a white mob following accusations that he murdered a deputy sheriff in 1840, clearly connected racial prejudice to the term *lynching*. But the practice of lynching really accelerated in the wake of the Civil War with the efforts of white supremacist Democrats and Ku Klux Klan groups to terrorize Black citizens seeking to exercise their right to vote, punish interracial sexual relations, and cement community identification in the South along the lines of race. After the *United States v. Harris* (1882) Supreme Court decision declared that lynching should be tried in state rather than federal courts, the Klan hoods came off, and lynchers began posing for photographs with the bodies of those they murdered. White photographers created postcards out of their lynching images, which local participants bought and mailed to friends and family. The 1893 lynching of Henry Smith in Paris, Texas, inaugurated a new era in this grim history, when a crowd of fifteen thousand gathered to participate in the torture, dismemberment, burning, and photographing of this seventeen-year-old boy who was accused of killing a three-year-old white girl. Historian Grace Elizabeth Hale identified this "first blatantly public, actively promoted lynching of a southern Black by a crowd of southern whites" as the "founding event in the history of spectacle lynchings."[41]

Though these were less frequent than the so-called private lynchings of the previous decades, organizers of spectacle lynchings used modern technologies and infrastructures emerging across the late nineteenth and early twentieth centuries—railroads, mass market commercial newspapers, telegraphy, and photography—to publicize lynchings, facilitate travel to lynching sites, photograph the murders, and profit from the national dissemination of images and stories for weeks and years to come. Spectacle lynchings were both crimes exacted on actual Black and brown bodies (and white bodies on occasion) and powerful metaphors for broadly projecting the meaning of community in urbanizing locales. Photographs of the Smith lynching circulated via newspapers, postcards, and traveling curiosity shows across the country in the decade after 1893, with some even accompanied by sounds supposedly recorded as Smith burned and screamed. While it is unlikely that the mob recorded live audio of the event in 1893, this probably reenacted sonic documentary experience was indexical enough for at least one fairgoer who heard it.[42] Curious about how the then-new sound technology functioned, Black antilynching activist Samuel Burdett wrote about trying on something like an audio headset at the Seattle fair in 1901 to experience the story of the lynching of Henry Smith. "Oh, horror of horrors!" he recalled in *A Test of Lynch Law: An Expose of Mob Violence and the Courts of Hell* (1901). "Just to hear that poor human being scream and groan and beg for his life, in the presence and hearing of thousands of people, who had gathered from all parts of the country about to see it."[43] Literature historian Jacqueline Goldsby summarized the dilemma that Burdett lived with in the wake of his regretful decision to consume this carnival show. The exhibit "confused Burdett's perception of his relation to the murder scene," she noted: "Was viewing the simulation a way to protest the lynching, or did watching amount to a vicarious act of complicity with the southern mob? How different could Seattle and Paris, Texas be if the deaths of Black people were openly sought out as public events worth seeing and without the risk of legal reprisal?"[44]

I would add to Goldsby's sharp question about the complicity of beholding lynching imagery the powerful place of sound objects in Burdett's indexing the event in memory, subsequent thought, and written account, a point to which I return in subsequent analyses of lynching events on film.[45] The question of complicity might also be asked of the Moore's Ford Lynching Reenactment, which functions still to augment the story through a spectacular simulation, albeit from an intention to reclaim narratives about lynching victims for Black dignity and justice. Both Burdett's account and the Moore's Ford case quickly get to the heart of the difficulties faced by Black filmmakers in representing lynching. To rephrase Goldsby's insight, if white urbanites across the United States could consume lynching imagery at carnival shows, then what strategies of representation might Black activists pursue to break entangled circuits of community identification, dehumanization of the Black body, and even pleasure among uncaring or sympathetic whites? Historian Ashraf Rushdy found a pamphlet by a participant-witness to the Smith lynching that aimed to sell "a lifestyle and land, values and venues, based exclusively on the lynching." Advertising land in Paris, Texas, at two dollars per acre, the pamphlet author welcomed anyone to move to town who would "lose a week in hunting down and bringing back and burning alive any wretch of any color or clime, who is base enough to steal and outrage and murder any man's child."[46] The writer regarded the well-publicized torture and burning of a Black male teenager as a point of civic pride.

While the boast reflects poorly on the author and his ilk, we might also read the tone as a sign of a society in crisis. In her cultural history *Lynching and Spectacle: Witnessing Racial Violence in America, 1890–1940*, Amy Louise Wood presented evidence that white supremacy was a contested ideology in the late nineteenth and early twentieth centuries. As towns and cities in the

South were "lurching into modernity," they encountered new possibilities for interracial class alliances.⁴⁷ New factories in the South attracted working-class, single men—Black and white—as well as the attendant gambling halls, saloons, and brothels, which middle-class families and strivers identified as morally threatening and responsible for upticks in crime. Northern Republicans' abandonment of Reconstruction in the late 1870s tilted the balance of force in negotiating these tensions toward white supremacy and away from nascent interracial class solidarity. The figure of the "Black brute" and his insatiable appetite for white women emerged time and again in white supremacist discourses of this period, and served among southern whites to justify the brutality and public nature of lynchings. Wood argued that spectacle lynchings were in part responses to these shifts in the agricultural economy, voting rights for Black Americans, and the threats that both represented to the old patriarchal order of the antebellum slave South. They were meant to compel white southern solidarity across class lines. "Lynching spectacles, in this respect, did more than dramatize or reflect an undisputed white supremacy or attest to an uncontested white solidarity," she concluded. "Rather, they generated and even coerced a sense of racial superiority and unity among white southerners across class, generational, and geographic divisions."⁴⁸ The performativity of spectacle lynchings aimed at possession, that is to say, not persuasion. To be white and present at lynching was to be hailed as part of a community that was possessed by the values of white supremacy.

And in this context, to be white and viewing lynching photographs removed in time and place from the event depicted was to understand a particular kind of voyeuristic invitation, a solicitation not altogether different from window shopping in the new malls of growing cities or going to the movies.⁴⁹ Quoting the words of a young, white, southern girl who spoke to a reporter of "the fun we had burning the n----rs," Barbara Lewis suggested that the possessive power over witnesses to such events was "pleasurable and strong, vital enough to last a lifetime; vital enough to motivate the keeping of a photographic reminder of a lynching in the family album for years and years where it could be periodically fingered in an evocation of nostalgic memory."⁵⁰ Photographs of lynchings and representations of lynching in motion pictures, especially in D. W. Griffith's heinous but commercially successful Klan epic *The Birth of a Nation* (1915), even served to "affirm and authenticate" white supremacist ideology as a consumer good in this period.⁵¹ The film employed what David Bordwell, Janet Staiger, and Kristin Thompson would come to characterize as the "classical Hollywood style" to induce audiences to identify with fictional Klan founder Ben Cameron, even (or especially) when he lynches a Black Union soldier named Gus and leads an army of gun-toting KKK horsemen to intimidate Black citizens from voting. This scene eerily reenacted on film events that had occurred in Wilmington, North Carolina, in 1898 after the publication of an editorial by white supremacist Rebecca Latimer Felton about how the community was too "soft" on Black men accused of raping white women.[52]

Kara Keeling connected the rise of the cinema around this time to W. E. B. Du Bois's 1903 prediction that "the problem of the twentieth century is the problem of the color line." Following Deleuze, she used the term *the cinematic* to designate "images and processes that are perceptible via film" as sensory motor schemas, clichés, and occasional challenges to conventional thought "but that can be said to have appeared in other arenas contemporaneous with film." While she focused this insight on the emergence of Black feminist liberation in cinematic images starting in the 1960s, her theory of the cinematic also helps explain the power struggle over representations of lynching in film and photography in the first four decades of the twentieth century as distilled in the aesthetics and social impacts of *The Birth of a Nation*.[53] On the one hand, the rise of the feature film through this mechanism caused incalculable damage, both through the actual formation of KKK units nationally in the years after 1915 that conducted actual lynchings of thousands of Black Americans and through the standardization of damsels, heroes, and monsters reducible to—or translatable from—racist stereotypes across the subsequent hundred years of Hollywood film production.[54] *This* touches *that*. Lynching spectacles did not just destroy Black lives, in the words of Lewis, but actively created "an effigy or trace of the power of whiteness."[55] Through photography, lynching escaped the bounds of locality and the lived experience of memory, exacting a psychic toll across generations of Black families and the communities in which they lived. The cinematic apologia for lynching on behalf of a white supremacist nation vastly extended the reach and material consequences of that trace.[56] Current scholars estimate that at least 4,742 Black persons were lynched between 1882 and 1968; across the fifty years between 1880 and 1930, a Black person was lynched approximately once every five days.[57] Many more were executed through "legal lynchings" (accelerated trials and executions for Blacks accused of crimes), the private actions of white southerners, and "n----r hunts" in which victims' bodies were never found.[58]

On the other hand, the spectacle lynching and its manifestation in Griffith's film also served as documentary evidence of criminality, ignorance, and moral depravity in the hands of the newly formed NAACP—and increasingly for the nation. Though unsuccessful at thwarting the distribution of the film, Black Bostonian newspaper editor William Monroe Trotter of the *Guardian* organized mass direct action resistance to protest the film's content, distribution, and ideology in a manner that anticipated strategies to be employed during the civil rights movement of the 1950s and 1960s.[59] In direct response to *Birth of a Nation*, Oscar Micheaux's feature *Within Our Gates* (1920) foregrounded the pain of an aspirational and virtuous mixed-race educator traumatized by the lynching of her adoptive parents, whom the film represents as framed for a murder they did not commit. In melodramatic fashion, Micheaux repurposed Griffith-style parallel editing to intercut the climactic lynching scene with the protagonist's near rape by her white biological father, who stops only when recognition of a birthmark on her chest reveals to him who she is. Though underfunded; widely banned for its frank depiction of racial violence, miscegenation, discrimination, and lynching; focused on bourgeois Black life; and lost for a period of years after its release, *Within Our Gates* modeled a "fascinating and cogent response to the racist accusations" of Griffith and other works of the plantation genre, in the terms of Michelle Wallace.[60] Micheaux may have been influenced by Black playwrights including Angelina Weld Grimké and Alice Dunbar-Nelson, who wrote and staged one-act lynching plays in the early twentieth century that humanized Black male lynching victims and told stories about how their families survived afterward. "While the mob's efforts centered on Black death," observed theater historian Koritha Mitchell, "African American dramatists helped their communities to live, even while lynching remained a reality that would not magically disappear."[61] NAACP president Walter White regularly used lynching postcard photographs and reports in the press to pressure Congress to pass antilynching legislation.

By the time of what historians now deem to be the last spectacle lynching, that of Claude Neal in Marianna, Florida, in 1934, even the Hollywood studios had begun to turn the conventions of the classical narrative style toward identification with victims rather than perpetrators of lynching. In Wood's assessment, a notable measure of the inversion had to do with camerawork. While the Hays Code of 1934 forbade the depiction of racial violence on screen (and, to the horror of Black film critics such as journalist Roi Ottley, led to bizarre scenes that seemed to justify the mob lynching of white gangsters in *Barbary Coast* [1935] and *Frisco Kid* [1935]) and studios generally avoided political topics that might arouse censure from white southern audiences or Black viewers, several prestige films of the 1930s and early 1940s including *Fury* (1936), *They Won't Forget* (1937), and *The Ox-Bow Incident* (1943) critically dramatized scenarios of lynching from the perspective of victims.[62] Especially notable was Austrian émigré director Fritz Lang's *Fury* (1936), his first American film. Trained in the German Expressionist style of the 1920s and internationally known for his silent-era dystopian science fiction epic *Metropolis* (1926) and the proto-film-noir murder mystery *M* (1931), Lang crafted a brooding allegory about lynching that featured an innocent white male protagonist wrongly imprisoned for kidnapping in a fictional midwestern town. It was loosely based on the lynching of Jack Holmes and Thomas Thurmond, two white prisoners held for kidnapping and murder in a San Jose, California, jail in 1933 who became subjects of a national newsreel story. Newsreel camera operators had captured a few shots of the mob in front of the building prior to the San Jose lynchings and then interviewed several witnesses to the event and created a two-minute story that played alongside entertainment shorts before feature films in theaters across the country.[63]

Unlike the experience of watching a spectacle lynching as a participant or distant newsreel cameraperson, Lang exploited shot–reverse shot scene construction to synthesize close-up impressions of sadistic onlookers to the nighttime burning of the town jail that imprisoned Joe Wilson, who was wrongfully detained while on his way to rendezvous with his fiancé. The low-angle, demonic flickering light on the faces of a grinning mother holding her child, a man casually eating a hot dog, and cackling male townspeople were intercut with Wilson peering out the bars of his jail cell through smoke and flames and extreme close-ups of Wilson's fiancé, Katherine, staring in horror directly into the lens, as if at the film viewers themselves; these images combined to "offer a panoptic visual experience of the lynching," writes Wood, "that transcends the limitations of individual sight."[64] The gritty camerawork, coupled with the eerily silent crowd and the sound of the crackling fire, communicated an affectively persuasive "indictment" of the white cinema spectators themselves, to use the word of 1930s movie reviewers. The film also incorporated scenes of newsreel journalists cranking away at the unfolding lynching as they excitedly (and damningly) speculate about the national prospects for their sensational documentary recordings.[65] Wood cited one reviewer who wrote that the burning-of-the-jail scene was "so realistic that when flames leap up . . . and encircle the caged victim, you actually smell the burning flesh."[66] And even though the film scrupulously avoided any direct mention of race, then–NAACP president White enthusiastically endorsed the film for the way it laid bare the community's collusion in silence and the feelings of bitterness, cynicism, and sorrow that the films' protagonists expressed. Alongside lynching photographs, he believed that such a cinematic indictment could pressure Congress to see the necessity for passing federal antilynching legislation.[67]

The spectacle lynchings that had once enforced white supremacist commitment among copresent white spectators, in other words, became a liability once such communities came under national scrutiny for their claims to moral and intellectual superiority. "Lynching spectacles, which had once served to substantiate and normalize white claims to moral superiority," in Wood's terms, "now served as documentary and incontrovertible evidence of just the opposite, even when encountered in Hollywood melodramas."[68] Black activists, artists, and critics created the frameworks through which white Americans could interpret lynchings as fundamentally unjust and oppressive, even if it did not lead to widespread agreement among whites about racial equality. The shift was nonetheless significant. By the late 1930s, southern leaders had been forced to disavow lynching practices, at least publicly. Indeed, southern whites made concerted efforts to bury the evidence of their crimes and to move on with life as though the horror and embarrassment of this period had not happened at all—even going so far as to remove records of lynchings from town archives.[69] Images of Black celebrities such as Louis Armstrong, Lena Horne, and Paul Robeson and athletes such as Jackie Robinson took precedence in popular culture in the 1940s, as the projection of a narrative about an inclusive American society better suited geopolitical strategy during World War II and the Cold War.[70]

It was partly for this reason that the unphotographed, brutal lynching of the Malcoms and the Dorseys at Moore's Ford Bridge in 1946 caused such a scandal. Situated between the period of spectacle lynchings that circulated in the mass press between the 1890s and 1930s and the era of television and the civil rights movement of the 1950s and 1960s, the Moore's Ford lynchings stood as a unique embarrassment for the postwar Truman administration as well as a demonstration of the ongoing political effectiveness of secretive, unpunished white supremacist terror in the South. While the lynching took place in the secluded woods outside of agricultural Monroe rather than in a city square, it was meant to send a message to returning Black war veterans who now understood more of what life was like outside of their oppressive Jim Crow hometowns and to prospective Black voters preparing to cast ballots in the statewide election of that year. Then-seventeen-year-old Morehouse sophomore Martin Luther King Jr. wrote a letter to the editor of the *Atlanta Journal Constitution* about the spate of lynchings in Georgia culminating in this one, excoriating the white establishment for "kicking up dust" about interracial relationships instead of focusing on justice for the lynched and "basic rights and opportunities" for Black citizens.[71] Extensive news stories in the Black and white presses about the lynchings, broadly publicized $10,000 rewards for information leading to arrest and prosecution, and a six-month FBI investigation failed to yield a single indictment in the case.[72] It retained a sense of unresolved, suppressed, affective potency across subsequent generations of Black Georgians. But in 1946, there was not yet an effective mechanism through which to mobilize mass protest among Black citizens, especially in hostile pockets of the deep South. That would come later, after the lynching of fourteen-year-old Emmett Till in 1955 and his mother Mamie Till Mobley's savvy decision to provide to the press a stunning portrait photograph of her living son from Christmas in 1954 while demanding an open casket at his funeral so that press photographers could document his disfigured corpse. The juxtaposition shocked viewers across the country and persuaded many young Black men to begin participating in political resistance movements. "It would not be going too far to say that Mobley thus invented the strategy that later became the [Southern Christian Leadership Conference's] signature gesture," reflected television historian Sasha Torres, "literally *illustrating* southern atrocity with graphic images of Black physical suffering, and disseminating those images nationally."[73] In a context of minimal Black control over cameras or television distribution networks, it turned out to be a strategy suited to its time. I next turn to the second major influence on the media strategy of the Moore's Ford Lynching Reenactment, the common-cause camerawork of the civil rights era.

COMMON-CAUSE CAMERAWORK AND CIVIL RIGHTS SUBJECTS: A COMPLEX HISTORY

Across the late 1950s and early 1960s, leaders of the civil rights movement came to see television coverage of protest activities as central to achieving their political goals. When King declared in the wake of televised police violence against marchers on the Edmund Pettus Bridge in Selma, Alabama, that "we no longer will let [white men] use clubs on us in the dark corners. We're going to make them do it in the glaring light of television," he gave public voice to a key strategy previously kept private.[74] So as not to appear calculating, King rarely mentioned the media in public speeches except through allegorical references to illumination or light shining forth on the evils of racist violence. Television historians working with his archives have since characterized him as becoming by necessity "an accomplished public relations operative" and "an excellent television producer" behind the scenes.[75]

Torres, for instance, described how press coverage of the Montgomery Bus Boycott transformed the movement's vision of what the relatively new medium of television could be and do for it. At first, church leaders resisted having their names and photographs in newspapers and on television for fear of reprisals including murder, intimidation, arrest, and job loss from segregationist whites with political power. But they came to see advantages to broadcasting their message and demonstration plans. Television coverage in the Montgomery campaign communicated to Black citizens who might have missed announcements at church or in flyers, helped recruit new participants by showing them a potential image of themselves as agents in public life, consolidated a civil rights press corps, helped King become a movement star on the national stage, and showed how nonviolent protest and images of Black suffering could forward movement goals in the context of the Cold War United States.

Television programs about movement events, moreover, could function as training materials for future campaigns, such as the *NBC White Paper* program "Sit In" (1960) about the Nashville student movement that successfully desegregated lunch counters in the city. Youth enthusiasm for such bold direct action campaigns spread quickly across the South, made for dramatic television, and inspired countless young Black people to join the movement.[76] By the time of the Project C campaign to desegregate businesses in Birmingham, Alabama, in 1963, movement organizers had internalized the schedules and content demands of broadcasters in the orchestration of their demonstrations, the brevity of their messaging, and the presentation of dignified and orderly "civil rights subjects" who would read as sympathetic to an imagined national audience of middle-class white viewers.[77]

Aniko Bodroghkozy, however, cautions against accepting the argument made by veteran TV producers in their memoirs that television was "the chosen instrument of revolution." The relations between white camerapersons working for national news agencies and Black activists who lived in the South were complicated. Black activists were not, after all, the primary consumers sought by the brands that purchased television advertising and wanted access to an increasingly national audience. By the early 1960s, over 90 percent of households in the US had at least one television.[78] Torres thus described the relationship between the movement and the television networks as one more of "common cause" than allies in revolution. At a time when the networks were reeling from quiz show scandals and fearful that new FCC chairman Newton Minow's description of television as a "vast wasteland" portended government regulation for their industry, expanding public affairs programming and following the civil rights movement offered a low-cost way to address broadcasters' political and economic problems. It showed that they could serve the public interest by covering a serious, topical, unresolved social issue to inform national discussion and provided a chance to manufacture a national consensus (at least for an imagined white, middle-class audience) on the meanings of racial difference acceptable enough for southern network affiliates to put on the air. Bodroghkozy argues that before 1963, news broadcasters neither did "the bidding of even the most moderate of civil rights groups, nor was television bent on always demonizing and dismissing the segregationist position."[79] Rather, many television documentaries emphasized the perspectives of white moderates in the South and characterized civil rights advocacy groups including the NAACP as militant to appease the sensibilities of white southerners. In the end, it was just not tenable to positively spin the positions of southern segregationists as white police, Klansmen, teenagers, and even mothers carrying babies insulted and beat Black protesters, children, and reporters alike in public.

While movement leaders did not like the fact that they faced violence in advocating for their own dignity, they understood the propaganda value of what movement historian Adam Fairclough described as the presentation of "*dramatic* violence rather than *deadly* violence" on television and did not shy away from courting it. Student Nonviolent Coordinating Committee leader James Forman recalled seeing Wyatt Walker, organizer of the 1963 Birmingham campaign, "jumping up and down in elation" when he watched the footage on the evening news of police spraying firehoses at child protesters.[80] Photographs and footage quickly made their way onto Russian and Cuban media outlets, troubling the Kennedy administration's Cold War case for America's unique brand of freedom and justice. "The events in Birmingham and elsewhere have so increased the cries for equality," Kennedy stated in a radio and television address shortly thereafter, "that no city or State or legislative body can prudently choose to ignore them."[81]

This sequence suggests a broader pattern that the movement leaders came to recognize. When television cameras recorded southern brutality for broadcast to viewers in other parts of the nation and world, it placed pressure on federal agencies and elected officials to do something, perhaps even to change racist regional laws. And the prospect of eroding local control further enraged southern white segregationists. Through these recursive cycles of protest, reactionary hostility, and national or international news coverage, network television came to symbolize "the newest manifestation of modernity and consumer culture extending its lines into the deepest reaches of the South."[82] Like the railroads did fifty years before, television created national markets and sensibilities at odds with dominant white assumptions about racial difference in such southern locales. Television, conjoined to the civil rights struggle, came to constitute another technology through which "outsiders" would chip away at their taken-for-granted white power structure. Here, the dynamics of simulation documentary worked somewhat toward the ends of racial justice.

On the ground, the presence of cameras led civil rights activists to recalibrate their strategies and assessments of risk. Thinking about the logistics of media coverage, movement leaders such as Southern Christian Leadership Conference (SCLC) operative Andrew Young came to favor large group demonstrations in city or town centers relatively close to airports. For instance, he worried that the 1964 SNCC-led voting rights campaign in rural Mississippi now known as Freedom Summer would fail because its diffuse geographical scope would be difficult to film. "The presence of national media was virtually the only inhibitor of official violence, and you simply could not get that kind of attention for people in dozens of towns in Mississippi," he said.[83] Birmingham activist Ruby Hurley recalled her work for the NAACP in the 1950s being more dangerous than 1960s campaigns "because when the eye of the press or the eye of the camera was on the situation, it was different." Camerapersons working for national broadcasters, noted Torres, signified "a kind of safety net for those in the movement, who mention them frequently in oral histories and movement memoirs."[84]

Indeed, even the infamous televised brutality of Selma marchers known as Bloody Sunday was tame compared to untelevised incidents of mob violence. The violence was worse for the 1961 Freedom Riders in Anniston and Birmingham, Alabama, and Montgomery, Mississippi; volunteers and SNCC workers associated with voter registration campaigns in rural Mississippi from 1961 to 1964; and nighttime demonstrators in Marion, Alabama, in 1965, where white reactionaries and state troopers shot out the lights of press corps camera crews so that they could not record the ensuing melee, including the murder of World War II veteran Jimmie Jackson. Yet the police violence in Selma remains iconic in collective memory and a key catalyst for the passage of the 1965 Voting Rights Act because of the unique circumstances in which it was recorded and viewed. ABC interrupted the primetime broadcast premiere of Stanley Kramer's Academy Award–winning film *Judgment at Nuremberg* (1961), which included harrowing newsreel footage recorded in concentration camps, to show footage from Selma to its audience of forty-five million Americans. Viewers saw Alabama police officers led by the notoriously violent Sheriff Jim Clark donning Nazi-esque helmets and gas masks and wielding truncheons as they walked briskly toward the multigenerational line of Black citizens gathered to march for the right to vote.

Clark may have believed that reporters were far enough away from the scene so as not to be able to record the violence. He and Governor George Wallace had agreed that the beating of protesters should be a "live event" and not one to play on the evening news. Apparently, Clark underestimated the mechanics of telephoto lenses or the acousmatic power of visual obfuscation coupled with sound—the screams of fleeing marchers, rebel yells and epithets of troopers and white bystanders, firing of gas cannisters, the low thump of truncheons on flesh, horse hooves galloping on pavement—to communicate a story about unnerving and inequitable power.[85]

The acousmetre, in the writing on off-screen voice by Michel Chion, bears a kind of ethereal power for its invisibility, for its resemblance to the subject's experience of the mother's voice in the womb or the psychoanalyst's questioning during therapy. While the voices in the Bloody Sunday scene signify terror rather than nurture or repair, the mechanism of transcendent power still seemed to function. "The footage at the beginning of the confrontation was disturbing because it so clearly showed white brutality," Bodroghkozy noted. "This subsequent footage was disturbing for what it did not show."[86] The blurry footage, shaky handheld camerawork, distant views, and incoherence that signify "crisis coverage," Torres argues, "are in fact the formal markers of the political process that is unraveling before our eyes: the loss of the camera's control of the image is one of the things that tells the audience that political control, too, is up for grabs."[87] Something similar was on the mind of John Lewis from his position at the head of the line of marchers, something telling about the way that movement veterans had internalized the television apparatus and the camerapersons copresent with their bodies at risk. "You could hear the news photographers' cameras clicking," he recalled, "and I knew that now it was starting, that cycle of violence and publicity and more violence and more publicity that would eventually, we hoped, push things to the point where something—ideally, the law—would have to be changed."[88]

We might say that the clicking of the cameras, like the thunderbolt of Peirce's description, indexed a process of attention shift. For Lewis, camera sounds initiated a social script that was both prologue and uncertain epigraph, a social form then nascent in its becoming. The clicks and whirrs of the new, portable synch-sound 16 mm cameras, even when wielded by the overwhelmingly white, male press corps, touched an infrastructure for exchange far beyond but also intimately connected to the policeman's club coming down on him. *This* touches *that*. Lewis claimed to have understood these gestural indexical bonds even then, when his own survival was uncertain. For viewers, it was something like a televised documentary rehearsal for death—volatile, piercing, uncontrolled, and now a part of them as the community it hailed. Torres suggests that there is in fact an intimate, if unexplored, relation between the emergence of television news formats and the imperatives of Black political struggles through which the conventions of news coverage came into being. These connections course through media frames about Black life and movement struggles against violent Black death through to the early 2000s, when those now-elder statespeople of the civil rights movement began to stage the reenactment of the lynching at the Moore's Ford Bridge. There was something enduring about the courting of the camera to record these events, even such that one actress told me that as she played Dorothy Malcom lying dead on the grass by the Apalachee River, she remembered first and foremost hearing the clicks and whirrs of so many cameras wielded by the spectators, just like John Lewis had. Only at that moment of the reenactment, the camerapersons were mostly Black citizen-attendees making up for the absence of photographic imagery from 1946.

Having scooped its competitors with the Selma story, ABC resumed the film about German guilt in the brutalization and murder of Jewish Europeans. Special reports soon followed on CBS and NBC for their millions of viewers.[89] This event cemented Lewis as an icon of the civil rights movement, became the subject of Ava DuVernay's breakout studio feature *Selma* (2014), provided pressure for passage of the Voting Rights Act of 1965, and gave cause for commemorative reenactments on key anniversary dates, including one with thousands of marchers on the fiftieth with then-president Barack Obama leading the way. It started young Henry Hampton, a twenty-five-year-old northerner who made his first trip south for the march in Selma, on the path to becoming a filmmaker, founding Blackside Films, Inc., producing the watershed fourteen-hour documentary on the civil rights movement *Eyes on the Prize* (1986), and training a generation of Black and white activist filmmakers.[90] And the annual Selma commemorative march across the bridge led by then–SCLC president Charles Steele, in fact, inspired the activists who sponsored essay contests on the Moore's Ford lynching to try staging their own reenactment in 2005. It is worth noting that Steele's good friend Brooks, the longtime state representative who spearheaded the decision to reenact the lynching, worked for a dozen years as the communications director of the SCLC under Ralph Abernathy after the assassination of King. In this position, he learned the SCLC's media strategy and became one of its leading architects through the turbulent 1970s. While historical accounts of the SCLC identify this period as one of decline for the organization's effectiveness, it remained active and influenced Brooks's approach to politics when he began his thirty-year run as a Georgia state representative in 1980.[91] He understood the importance of media coverage and the value of control over media framing for movement success. And thinking about the playbook for media-savvy civil rights movement campaigns of the 1960s— dramatic but not deadly violence, cultivating a reliable and sympathetic press corps, campaigns close to big cities made up of daylong actions sustainable over long periods of time, clear and succinct goals to articulate in public with an eye toward long-term movement benefits that might cascade from pursuing them—it is not hard to see parallels in the Moore's Ford Lynching Reenactment. With this backdrop in mind, I briefly trace media representations of the reenactments next.

REPEAT AND REVISE: FILMING REENACTMENTS OF THE MOORE'S FORD LYNCHING

In her short essay "Elements of Style," playwright Suzan-Lori Parks explains her approach to theater-making through the metaphor of the "repetition and revision" structure of jazz. "With each revisit the phrase is slightly revised," she riffs. "Through its use I'm working to create a dramatic text that departs from the traditional linear narrative style." Repetition and revision "creates a drama of accumulation" rather than action. Instead of a three-act play with rising action, climax, and denouement, works such as *The America Play*—an absurdist meditation on Black subjectivity and the myth of Lincoln's assassination set in what the notation calls "an exact replica of the great hole of history"—repeat key actions with subtle variations in language, gesture, and scenario. The reenacted pattern functions in the play as a gestural recollection-object, to return to the analysis from chapter 1, a narratively thin but affectively full evocation of the presence of absent history. A Black protagonist called the Foundling Father makes a living off his passing resemblance to the late Abraham Lincoln by allowing white customers, time and again, to choose from an assortment of cap guns to reenact the assassination of the president that he plays, evidently a cathartic act for them. Each repetition of this mythic moment further undercuts heroic associations with Lincoln by dint of their serialized, iconic repetition. What emerges over the course of the play is a melancholy aura about the Foundling Father whose access to history is in and through this theatrical performance, perhaps followed on for audience members by new ways of thinking about the past. "Since history is a recorded or remembered event, theatre, for me, is the perfect place to 'make' history," Parks has explained—"that is, because so much of African-American history has been unrecorded, dismembered, washed out."[92] A "great hole" at once describes the fragmentary archive available for reconstructing Black American history and constitutes a point of reference through which to reinterpret national myths picked apart by the play. In this context, looping, repetition and revision, and circular conceptions of time resemble thought and attempts to survive trauma, subverting myths about being great.

Documentary camerawork follows a repetition-and-revision structure, too, but unlike Parks's narratives, it often remains a hidden part of the work process along the way to making a film. Kristen Johnson's *Cameraperson* (2016) is a rare exception. The film reconstructs the filmmaker's life as a hired cameraperson on dozens of films through the presentation of affectively intense footage she remembered. The accumulation of moments she chooses in this context works somewhat like Parks's repetition-and-revision logic, charging the recordings with a sense of her psyche as well as the things in front of the lens. It offers a unique view into the subjectivity created by a lifetime of camerawork for hire. Usually, if footage does not help move a story from A to B, takes too long to unfold, or centers on the cameraperson more than the film subject, it ends up on the cutting-room floor, meaningful only to the cameraperson who noticed a look or the peculiar move of the arm far afield from the ostensible plot. Such odd little moments don't always line up with general structures of communication within the cinema, which do repeat time and again.

A term for one key repetition-and-revision structure of camerawork is *shot–reverse shot scene construction*. This is a technique drawn from principles of continuity editing in fiction filmmaking, but shot–reverse shot logic applies differently to unfolding and unscripted life events. Many life events themselves follow a repetition-and-revision structure (planting seeds in a garden, doing the dishes, knitting a sweater, practicing a sport, typing at a computer, etc.) that allow the cameraperson to film a similar set of actions from multiple camera positions. One take from this side, one take from that side, then cutaways and close-ups of actions. Rinse and repeat. In scripted cinema and television, viewers of the shot–reverse shot scene intuit flow across ruptures in camera position so long as characters remain oriented in a single space and dialogue and emotional tone follows on sensibly as continuous interaction; in unscripted documentary camerawork that anticipates the reappropriation of these continuity editing principles, disjunctures in camera position enable the editor to seamlessly compress time to accelerate story (to elide one or another ungainly conversation that might lose audience attention, for instance), clarify process (as with close-ups of hands, products, and complex machines in Frederick Wiseman's many factory scenes), or shift from one to another character's point of view. Close-ups enhance the visibility of objects, actions, and gestures and can help bridge otherwise awkward cuts from one thing to another, and so they become staples of coverage recording. Side one, side two, cutaways, and close-ups. This orientation to time and ongoing activity often shapes how a cameraperson perceives while at work.

I wrote about one way that a shared orientation to repetition-and-revision camerawork structured a drama of accumulation in my analysis of *In Country* in chapter 1. Ostensibly observational camerawork reenacts camerawork there and functions as an emblem of the psyche remembering or encountering ideas about war. Shot–reverse shot crosses time rather than space, affectively charging the sense of continuity rather than alienating viewers from it. Now I consider what this shot–reverse shot structure of filming has meant within and across different recordings of the Moore's Ford Lynching Reenactment. Unlike Parks's plays that disavow realism and refuse linear narrative, it is worth noting that the Moore's Ford Lynching Reenactment presents a clear, linear story for political ends. It does aim and claim to be filling an archival gap, and so a repetition-and-revision structure for camerawork is already beholden to this linear script within footage from a single year of recording. However, the conventions of shot–reverse shot scene construction, as I discuss in the next chapter, allow for creatively reworking this linearity over many years of filming. Below, I begin to lay the groundwork for how this reworking takes place in my case study in chapter 4, Olive's *Always in Season*.

The first filmed reenactment of the Moore's Ford Lynching predated the first public reenactment in 2005. As the Moore's Ford Memorial Committee carried out small, locally based initiatives in the late 1990s and early 2000s, documentary filmmaker Keith Beauchamp began work on *The Untold Story of Emmett Louis Till*, which was released in 2005. Though Till's was officially deemed a cold case, Beauchamp's interviews suggested that there may have been as many as fourteen individuals involved in the brutal murder of the Chicago teen. Beauchamp's film presented enough new evidence to catalyze a national dialogue about justice and accountability in such cold cases and persuaded the Justice Department to reopen the Till file to seek further prosecutions.[93] In addition, Congress initiated dialogue on what became the Emmett Till Unsolved Civil Rights Crime Act of 2008, which provided annual funding for investigations of unresolved, racially suspicious, pre-1970 cold-case murders. Encouraged, Beauchamp proposed a series of television documentaries for TV One on four other cold-case lynchings called *Murder in Black and White* that aimed, similarly, to educate the general public about the crimes and uncover new leads for investigators. He focused on the cases of World War II veteran Lamar Smith (1955), truck driver Willie Edwards (1957), voting rights activist Reverend George Lee, and the quadruple lynching at the Moore's Ford Bridge, which brought him into contact with the key organizers of the MFMC just before the group began to splinter. Each *Murder* program coupled filmed reenactments of the crimes with expert and witness interviews, explanatory voice-over, and archival images from newspapers and stock sources.

The *Moore's Ford* episode is as notable for what it features as for what it excludes. Even though presented as a TV crime reenactment docudrama—a genre notorious for dwelling on lurid detail—the film generally avoids graphic depictions and descriptions of injuries. One interviewee, for example, struggles on camera to find the language to describe the victims' bodies: "They were [pause] bones were broken. You know, they were [pauses and shakes head] there was torture before being shot." In line with the sensibility of this careful Black pastor from Georgia, the image track of the film never presents photographs of the bodies of the victims, and the commentary focuses more on how the particulars of the case relate to structures of white supremacy. The film asks why a brutal quadruple lynching remained unresolved and unprosecuted given the wealth of local gossip about it and interpolates the viewer as possibly confused or underinformed on this point. Though working within the conventions of brisk cable television pacing, sound stingers, mood music, and the slow reveal of key details, the film proposes to answer this structural question for the viewer.

Notably, the reenactment created to visualize the lynching echoes the crisis-coverage aesthetic I touched on differently in chapter 1 and my analysis of the Selma TV footage above. Here, of course, crisis aesthetics is a stylistic choice rather than a matter of uncontrolled framing or unprivileged camera style. The image floats and blurs because the director and cinematographer deemed the aesthetic appropriate to the affective experience they sought to craft for viewers, or perhaps, as Torres suggested of the Selma footage, for the sense of political disruption baked into this style of seeing. The sequence concludes with brief close-ups of several gun barrels pointed in the direction of the camera lens—a striking reverse shot here—to simulate the perspective of the lynching victims, and then the sound of the executioners firing as the image tilts from a holstered gun to the profile shot of a white man wearing a sheriff's hat, leaning against a car with arms folded. The images of the actors playing the victims are brief across this scene, and we do not see them here or elsewhere in the film after they have been shot. Neither do we see the victims tortured, though interviewees such as the one above state that this occurred. Beauchamp made these films to help pressure for legal changes to cold-case prosecutions and lynching laws, not to fascinate an audience per se. Though Beauchamp's films visualize and consider lynchings, it would be a mistake to categorize them as spectacles.

Beauchamp's film is thus different in its orientation to the lynchings from another widely discussed public cultural work of this period, the exhibit *Without*

Sanctuary: Lynching Photography in America organized by postcard collector James Allen starting in the year 2000. The one hundred postcards from the early 1900s, which featured photographs of spectacle lynchings, drew capacity crowds at exhibit venues in New York City and beyond. Photographic reproductions of mutilated bodies and joyous, hand-scribbled notes from participating whites were damning bits of long-hidden evidence that scandalized audiences, catalyzed academic conferences, and guilted the US Senate in 2005 into issuing an overdue official apology for failing to enact federal lynching laws. Problematically packaged as a sixty-dollar coffee-table book now in its fourteenth edition, *Without Sanctuary* also circulated these photographs once again as a bizarre collector's item, here perhaps to illustrate one's social justice sympathies. While the project raised awareness about the extent and brutality of lynching, it nonetheless reproduced a one-sided way of looking. There are no reverse shots, so to speak, for these lynching photographs. It is troubling that though the NAACP had pushed Congress to pass antilynching legislation to no avail in the 1920s, 1930s, and 1940s and had regularly published testimonies of struggling Black families related to persons who were lynched across the first half of the twentieth century, it was the exhibit of historical pro-lynching souvenir postcards in 2000 that compelled popular response. "When we pause to ask why," cautioned Mitchell in the introduction to her monograph on one-act lynching plays, "we find that the nation has again allowed the archives left by perpetrators to eclipse all others."[94]

The postcard views alone say nothing about the trials, tribulations, and dilemmas faced by families and communities who lived with lynching, issues considered by Black female playwrights of the early 1900s chronicled in Mitchell's book. Their plays avoided the representation of violence that de facto dehumanized Black bodies. The contemporary reembodiment of a lynching spectacle staged by Black men and women from the South at Moore's Ford, then, reopens the question about the thorny relations among spectacle, possession, and empowerment discussed in this chapter. On the one hand, reenacting a racial atrocity of the past as a spectacle conjures these old tropes of white supremacy and the feelings of terror, oppression, and guilt associated with them. But the reenactment at Moore's Ford Bridge is effectively a one-act lynching play organized by Black activists, performed outside rather than on a proscenium, that centers on the graphic depiction of violence. It includes discussion of the impacts of lynching on victims' families and the broader community but also aims to render the violent atrocity visible and recordable, like the staging for a lynching actuality film a century after the actuality genre's peak. It is complicated. And part of the complication, as I have laid out in this chapter, stems from the dual aim of the reenactment itself: to facilitate community healing while also (following the civil rights movement playbook) attracting extralocal media coverage to help pressure for change. It is a realist theatrical performance that gauges, perhaps accurately, the kinds of aesthetics that will jolt a general American public into attention.

For her own part, Olive has said that seeing the *Without Sanctuary* postcard photographs led her to explore lynching history and its impacts, albeit with a sensibility aligned with Mitchell's and those of Black female playwrights of the early 1900s. When I met her, Olive had been working on a documentary for several years about restorative justice rituals in towns where lynchings had once occurred. Funding for the project was tight at the time. She was focusing especially on three contemporary cases: the Moore's Ford Lynching Reenactment; the construction of a commemorative sculpture in Duluth, Minnesota, on behalf of Black lynching victims Elias Clayton, Elmer Jackson, and Isaac McGhie; and the peculiar case of the Klan-themed clothing store and museum in Laurens, South Carolina, known as the Redneck Shop, deeded by a repentant former KKK Grand Dragon to Black civil rights leader and lynching victim descendant Reverend David Kennedy. Olive had also recorded Danny Glover reading newspaper advertisements published in Florida in 1934 to announce the public lynching of Claude Neal, a Black man tortured and killed in front of a crowd of ten to fifteen thousand following accusations that he murdered a white woman. Driven to explore how justice and healing could proceed in communities scarred by lynching histories, Olive had compiled dozens of hours of footage with key community organizers in each case and had even constructed a virtual restorative justice forum in the then-popular massively multiple online role-playing world *Second Life*. She had traveled to the lynching reenactment in Georgia the year before and established a network of contacts in the area. As part of my graduate work, I had a small grant to pay for housing, food, and camera equipment for several weeks of ethnographic research. Olive and I decided it would be mutually beneficial to pool resources and work together when and how we could. This was two years before the death of Lennon Lacy, the teenager who would become the central focus of Olive's documentary and whose story other camerapersons filmed. Over our two weeks together in Georgia, we filmed rehearsals, interviews, and the reenactment itself, repeating that shot–reverse shot structure time and again. Rehearsals make it easy—just shift position between iterations one and two and film from the opposite direction. Find key close-ups and cutaways on the third round, some response for that initial line the head Klansman yells each time he slams the hood of the car, "We want that n----r Roger!" Follow discussions among actors about how to say the lines and block the scenes in medium shot. Provide numerous options for an editor to pluck out this or that character, this or that event, this or that way of regarding race and history here. It's a rehearsal for me, too, so I'll be ready on the day of the reenactment. Head Klansman in close-up for "On the count of three, fire!" The actors playing the Malcoms and the Dorseys in wide shot by the time he gets to three, with the spectators in the background of the shot as they fall to the ground. Shot–reverse shot.

On the day of the reenactment, I am one of two white, male camerapersons that record for Olive's film, and we silently coordinate with one another like complementary improv musicians. As the car rolls up to the Moore's Ford Bridge to start the reenactment, I film the audience as the other cameraperson moves in close to the action of a scene that I had filmed the week prior in rehearsal. One of the actresses set to play a victim had to attend a funeral, so a new reenactor takes her place. Three or four other professional-looking camerapersons whom I do not know also circle around the unfolding action and film it. The actors pretend not to notice any of us. Many members of the audience also record the scene on smartphones and digital camcorders from their place in the crowd.

Having seen several rehearsals, I anticipate events and move into position to film them clearly and close in. I pan the crowd looking on as the second cameraperson walks backward in front of the reenactors, who scream and yell as they jostle with controlled chaos to the designated lynching site by the Apalachee River. I record the head Klansman in medium close-up as the late-afternoon sun lights the trees yellowish behind his beige fedora and face in shadow. He points at the four victims and intones, "We are doing this for the preservation of our race!" Framing, light, and the complex blend of anger and sadness in his voice register in my memory as I film the completion of this line, and I think in the moment of recording that this is a potential clip for the finished film. I whip pan to a wide shot of the scene approximately as he sees it, with his mob pointing their toy guns at the reenactors who play the Malcoms and the Dorseys, huddled together and crying (fig. 3.3). I want the camera to record the mock-transition from life to death in the performance, with the panoply of witnesses here in the background memorializing the moment with their own cameras. The editor may cut from any segment of the close-up of the Klansman to around this moment my frame settles, when the troupe will again reenact the lynching by gunshot. I am now close to the reenactors playing the lynch mob—more or less a part of the circle they have formed around their victims, as if the camera embodies the view of a lyncher. It is not something I think about in the moment, when I am preoccupied by foreground-background relationships

Figure 3.3. Video still of "Head Klansman" during the Moore's Ford Lynching Reenactment of 2012 (*top*) and reverse shot with reenactors in the foreground and spectators in the background (*bottom*). Recorded by the author.

in the frame. The high angle allows for the spectators to remain visible in the background of the shot. I will record cutaways of faces of spectators later, I tell myself, so that I do not miss this key moment of action. To witness the moment of death, after all, seems to be the purpose for being here today. The head Klansman yells, "Fire!"

The moment itself plays quietly. The CD track of gunshots is barely audible coming from the tiny portable stereo in this relatively vast, open space where the reenactment unfolds. The guns are toys with orange plastic caps over the muzzles. Cameras audibly click as the actors gingerly lower themselves to a blanket on the ground and close their eyes. As the white reenactors move in toward the victims, I prepare for the next action in the scene and zoom in on the stomach of the actress who plays Dorothy. In the raw footage, the frame holds uncomfortably as the actress searches the folds of her skirt for the doll, but I anticipate that the editor will cut the seconds ticking away for the moment when she pulls it out. In the here and now of recording, I concentrate on focus, exposure, and framing, and not on what it means to film this particular detail. Camerawork follows action, and this action will happen only once today. I record a clear medium close-up of the Black baby doll as it is pulled out from beneath Dorothy's dress. "Is this good, boss?" says a white actor who holds the doll aloft for the benefit of the distant spectators. The collective gasp is audible. Whether or not Malcom was pregnant in 1946, this shot will communicate the orientation of the stage-play to this detail. For her part, Olive has recorded interviews with local elders who tell her that Malcom was pregnant.

Combined, the second cameraperson and I record enough details from the event to create a comprehensive documentary scene from an omniscient point of view. Disjunctures in space and time from one shot to another will disappear beneath the momentum of the story itself once the most compelling frames are artfully edited into a sequence. Shot–reverse shot scene construction will condense the time. The variety of views and participants and the thick realism of gesture, dress, Georgia foliage, and sweat will offer viewers a profound learning experience about what being here is like. But it turns out that neither I nor the second cameraperson recorded the reverse shot that would have positioned the camera with the reenactors playing the Dorseys and the Malcoms. In retrospect, it seems like a significant oversight. Beauchamp's documentary *Murder in Black and White*, which featured a reenactment of this event staged for the camera rather than for a live audience, includes several point-of-view shots with gun barrels pointed toward the camera lens (fig. 3.4).

There were reasons not to record from the place of the Dorseys and the Malcoms. To position a camera among the Black reenactors would have interfered with the sightlines of spectators to the live performance, and for many Black attendees, their space in that moment is sacred. It is not a location for a white cameraperson to occupy. But the absence of their perspective complicates the orientation toward omniscience intended in the footage—an orientation often intended in documentary footage recorded in the realist mode. Looking on the bodies of the lynched from among reenactors playing a lynch mob eerily reproduces something like the view of the lynching photographer of the early 1900s. These images do not mean the same thing or the same way in the context

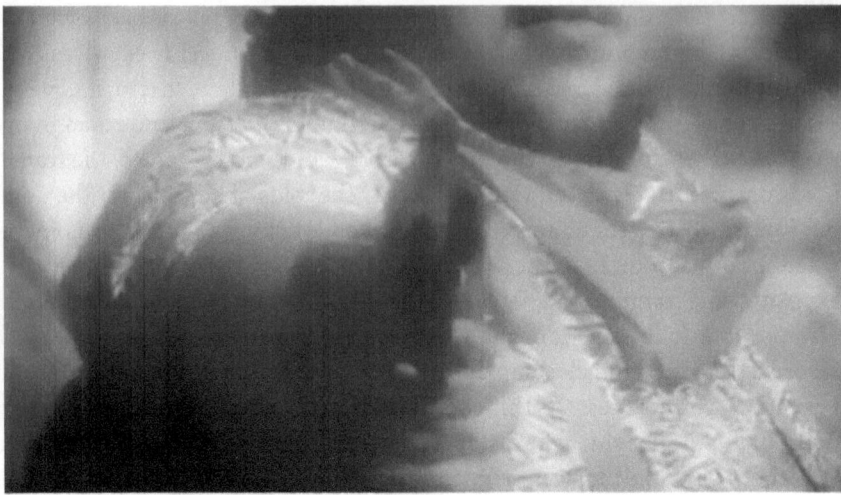

Figure 3.4. Frame grab of the lynching scene from the Dorseys' and Malcoms' point of view in *Murder in Black and White* (2008).

of the reenactment, given its oppositional political goals. But neither do such images communicate anything like Black subjectivity in this moment. Years later, a little of this footage ended up in Olive's film. It played a part in the expression of indexical perception in her film. But she devised a better strategy to foreground white accountability and Black experience in her documentary than either of her camerapersons following shot–reverse shot filming of the live event. This is the subject of the next chapter.

NOTES

1. A man named Clinton Adams came forward in the early 1990s to tell a story about witnessing the lynching while hiding in a nearby cotton field as a ten-year-old boy. He claimed to have been traumatized by what he saw and scared for decades to say a word about it. He most recently agreed to do a videotaped interview with the *Atlanta Journal-Constitution* at the Moore's Ford Bridge, where he mentioned seeing the car of at least one Georgia police officer at the scene. See Atlanta Journal-Constitution, "Clinton Adams Recalls."

2. Laura Wexler's *Fire in a Canebreak* (2003), which is based on archival documents about the case, interviews with locals, and newspaper reports from the Black and white presses in 1946, questioned the credibility of the two main eyewitness accounts, those of Loy Harrison and Clinton Adams. Harrison was driving the vehicle that was stopped by the lynch mob, but investigators in 1946 deemed him likely to have been part of the lynching and so distrusted his account. Details in Adams's story changed over time, and by his own description, he would have been some distance from the lynching when hiding in the field, if he were there. Wexler, *Fire in a Canebrake*.

3. Taylor, *Archive and the Repertoire*, 68.

4. For instance, a key organizer of the early reenactments, Bobby Howard, tells a story about his mother's home being firebombed by a local Klan group, among other attempts on his life. He has spoken to others in the area who were convinced that people who "left town" were actually killed somewhere in the woods and never discovered. Such experiences and fears create a common sense at odds, in many respects, with the logic of the archive or the constraints of documentary evidence. For Keeling, common sense at odds with cliché suggests "the condition of possibility for the emergence of alternate knowledges that are capable of organizing social life and existence in various ways, some of which might constitute a counterhegemonic force." See NBC News, "Looking behind Tragedy"; Beauchamp, *Murder in Black and White*; Keeling, *Witch's Flight*, 19–20.

5. Dirk Eitzen argues that viewers' emotional experiences of storytelling are akin to the pleasures of being on the inside of gossip. In asking why viewers flocked to long-form series such as *The Jinx* on HBO, he proposes that the answer "does not lie in evidence, information, truth claims or anything else that they present or represent. It lies, instead, in the emotional appeals that documentaries *make* to viewers. These emotional appeals speak to particular social dimensions of viewers' experience. In this regard, they bear a striking and illuminating resemblance to the appeals of gossip." See Eitzen, "Duties of Documentary," 102; Marks, *Skin of the Film*.

6. Owen and Ehrenhaus, "Moore's Ford Lynching Reenactment," 88.

7. M. Auslander, "Contesting the Roadways."

8. Owen and Ehrenhaus use the phrase *Moore's Ford Lynching Reenactment* to refer to the subject of their research. I find the term suitable and so reuse it here for clarity and consistency. Owen and Ehrenhaus, "Moore's Ford Lynching Reenactment," 72.

9. Key books on spectacle lynching include Hale, *Making Whiteness*; Goldsby, *Spectacular Secret*; Rushdy, *End of American Lynching*; Wood, *Lynching and Spectacle*; Malkowski, *Dying in Full Detail*.

10. Quoted in Owen and Ehrenhaus, "Moore's Ford Lynching Reenactment," 78.

11. The term *affective infrastructure* appeared in Lauren Berlant's essay on "the commons" to describe unfamiliar "placeholders for our desire" that might "hold out the prospect of a world worth attaching to": "What remains for our pedagogy of unlearning is to build affective infrastructures that admit the work of desire as the work of an aspirational ambivalence." Anthropologist Hannah Knox used the term in her study of politics in Peru to refer to "the embodied, affective relationship that people experience with material forms" as well as "the ways in which things carry latent stories of their entangled pasts, and the manner in which stories are activated and projected forward into forms of pressure." My use of this term builds on affect theory as articulated in previous chapters as well as media studies on infrastructure that I describe in chapter 4 in ways akin to Knox's description. See Berlant, "Commons," 414; Knox, "Affective Infrastructures," 368.

12. Sobchack, *Carnal Thoughts*, 238.

13. Ibid., 238–39, 249–50.

14. Ibid., 248; Marks, *Skin of the Film*, 119–20.

15. Durkheim, *Elementary Forms*, 416.

16. hooks, *Sisters of the Yam*, 100–104.

17. Organizer, interview.

18. One dilemma of the reopening of the FBI investigation into this case, however, is that this information has not been made available to the public. As a result, statements of progress

in the case function much as details about the lynchings themselves have since the 1940s. They are rumors that beg for speculation and imaginative interpretation. At least in the short run, such rumors inhibit rather than facilitate the collective desire for closure on this case. Harvey, interview.

19. Lynn McKinley Jackson, a Black army private from Monroe who disappeared in August 1981, was found hanging from a pine tree in the woods of nearby Social Circle, Georgia, in December. His death was ruled a suicide, but civil rights leaders remain unconvinced. To quote from a report on this troubling case, "The coroner said he found no signs of foul play. However, there was no suicide note and to reach the branch from which his body was found hanging, Jackson would have had to climb 20 feet straight up a pine tree with no intervening branches and wearing ordinary sneakers." Jackson was also dating a white woman at the time of his disappearance whose family was suspected to have ties to white supremacist organizations in Georgia. See, for instance, Smith Broady, "Hanging Near Social Circle."

20. For a description of the 2008 staging of the stabbing scene in front of the Hester farm, where "the family is hostile to the Reenactment," see Owen and Ehrenhaus, "Moore's Ford Lynching Reenactment," 82. By 2011, this scene was staged in the church instead.

21. Quoted from the J. Edgar Hoover files on the case in Pitch, *Last Lynching*, loc. 733 of 5025, Kindle.

22. There are, in fact, two Laura Wexlers who have written about the history of race, gender, and traumatic incidents in the United States. As of 2020, the Laura Wexler to which I am referring here taught in the MFA program in creative nonfiction at Goucher College in Baltimore, Maryland, not in the American studies program at Yale University.

23. Wexler, *Fire in a Canebrake*, 266–67.

24. Lucas, "Resistance and Public Art," 18.

25. Armstrong, *Mary Turner*, 167.

26. Ibid., 168–69.

27. Ibid., 170.

28. M. Auslander, "'Give Me Back My Children!'"

29. Eatman, "Loss and Lived Memory," 155, 164.

30. M. Auslander, "Holding On."

31. Wexler, *Fire in a Canebrake*, 73–74; LaFlore, "On-the-Scene Story."

32. White, a light-skinned Black man with a southern accent, passed as a white visitor to Quitman, Georgia, to investigate a series of lynchings that took place there in 1918, spending time in barbershops, stores, and other places where men gathered. He reported finding that local whites were anxious to brag about their roles in various incidents of racial violence. Turner was one of eleven Black sharecroppers from the area who were lynched after a Black field hand named Sydney Johnson allegedly shot and killed the white farmer Hampton Smith over a wage dispute. Johnson also shot Smith's pregnant wife in the arm and was accused of rape, probably falsely. Retaliatory violence against Blacks in the area was brutal. Early reports by the white press explained that Mary Turner had made "unwise remarks" to the mob that had lynched her husband, Hayes Turner, the day before. Specifically, she was reported to have stated aloud that she would take the mob to court for lynching her husband, who she claimed was innocent of involvement in the Smith affair. But before White's report, no mention had been made of Turner's pregnancy. His published report included the names of all eleven of the victims, sixteen members of the lynch mob, and the following, extremely disturbing description of the lynching of Mary Turner: "At the time she was lynched, Mary Turner was

in her eight [sic] month of pregnancy. Her ankles were tied together and she was hung to the tree head down. Gasoline was taken from the cars and poured on her clothing which was then fired. When her clothes had burned off, a sharp instrument was taken and she was cut open in the middle, her stomach being entirely opened. Her unborn child fell from her womb, gave two cries, and was then crushed by the heel of a member of the mob. Her body was then riddled with bullets from high-powered rifles until it was no longer possible to recognize it as the body of a human-being." Armstrong, *Mary Turner*, 38, 53–57.

33. Pitch, *Last Lynching*, locs. 3168–3192 of 5025, Kindle.
34. Organizer, interview.
35. Dewan, "Group Lynching Is Re-created."
36. Armstrong, *Mary Turner*, 6–8.
37. Harvey, interview.
38. Armstrong, *Mary Turner*, 169.
39. Oreskes and Conway, *Merchants of Doubt*.
40. Rushdy, *End of American Lynching*; Conquergood, "Lethal Theatre."
41. Waldrep, "Lynching and Mob Violence," 306–10; Hale quoted in Rushdy, *End of American Lynching*, 181.
42. A silent-era film historian emailed me that though he could not point to specific documents, he was "very confident [the sound presented in the exhibit] was not of the lynching itself." I also remember reading some years ago a story about the production of the sound for this exhibit being done at Edison's studios in New Jersey, but I have not been able to track down the reference. In any case, phonography equipment was widely distributed in the early 1900s, so the recording could have been re-created closer to the time and place of the lynching. Personal email, May 21, 2020.
43. Quoted in Goldsby, *Spectacular Secret*, 14.
44. Goldsby, *Spectacular Secret*, 16.
45. The essay collection *Sound Objects* (2019) offers a welcome theorization of recorded sound as object-like and yet bearing characteristics different from corresponding images in cinema and performance. The book aims to fill a gap in both post-structuralist theory and textual analysis of sound, starting from the work on "reduced listening" by Pierre Schaeffer and carried on in psychoanalytic film theory and sound studies by Michel Chion. I use this line of thinking in subsequent portions of this chapter and chapter 4 to help interpret representations of racial terror in the work of Black artists, which tends to emphasize sound objects rather than visualizations of violent events. See Steintrager and Chow, *Sound Objects*.
46. Rushdy, *End of American Lynching*, 80.
47. Wood, *Lynching and Spectacle*, 11.
48. Ibid., 8.
49. Friedberg, *Window Shopping*, 1993.
50. B. Lewis, "Decorated Death," 117.
51. Wood, *Lynching and Spectacle*, 10.
52. From Michele Faith Wallace's account: "After the election [of 1898], a white mob burned Alexander Manly's press [the *Daily Record*, the only Black daily in the state], hunted down prominent Blacks, and either shot them or ran them out of town. The Wilmington Light Infantry soon swelled the ranks of the mob. By the end of the day, ten Blacks were dead and Alfred Moore Waddell [leader of the armed Wilmington White Government League] had seized the mayor's office. As presented in *The Birth of a Nation*, the point had been to scare Blacks into never trying to vote again." For further details on voter suppression

in Wilmington and its devastating effects on the ideals of Reconstruction and the Black community there, see Wallace, "Good Lynching," 99–101. On "classical Hollywood style," see Bordwell, Staiger, and Thompson, *The Classical Hollywood Cinema*, 1–87.

53. Keeling, *Witch's Flight*, 3.

54. Michele Wallace argued for continuing to decode the film nearly one hundred years after the release because its "aesthetic legacy" remains salient as an object of critique. "Griffith defined the basic components of the melodramatic modern movie: a light realistic touch combined with unfathomable pathos," in her terms. She identifies one damaging aspect of the film in the lack of a narrative about white racial terror and the demise of Reconstruction in popular culture. Wallace, "Good Lynching," 88. For an introduction to analyses of racial stereotypes of Black people in American film, see Bogle, *Toms, Coons*.

55. B. Lewis, "Decorated Death," 118.

56. Markovitz, *Legacies of Lynching*, xvi.

57. Rushdy, *End of American Lynching*, ix.

58. Allen, Woody, and Nathan, *Without Sanctuary*, 12.

59. The PBS Independent Lens documentary *Birth of a Movement: The Battle against America's First Blockbuster* (2016) tells the story of William Monroe Trotter and his resistance to the theatrical release of Griffith's film in the city of Boston. Gray and Cram, *Birth of a Movement*.

60. Wallace, "Oscar Micheaux's within Our Gates," 61.

61. Mitchell, *Living with Lynching*, 1.

62. For detailed accounts of studio films about lynching in this period, see especially Wood, *Lynching and Spectacle*, 223–60; E. Scott, *Cinema Civil Rights*, 152–60.

63. See the newsreel clip California Pioneers of Santa Clara County, "Kidnapers Lynched."

64. Wood, *Lynching and Spectacle*, 244.

65. The newsreel shots reappear at the murder trial to disprove the denials of every townsperson that the white defendants were in fact participants in the lynching.

66. Wood, *Lynching and Spectacle*, 245.

67. E. Scott, *Cinema Civil Rights*, 155.

68. Wood, *Lynching and Spectacle*, 262.

69. See, for instance, the anecdote about such archival absences in the introduction to Armstrong, *Mary Turner*.

70. Wood, *Lynching and Spectacle*, 263–64. For an expansive, transnational exploration of the fraught mobilization of Black American culture makers during the Cold War, see Poiger, *Jazz, Rock, and Rebels*.

71. King, "Kick Up Dust."

72. The most thorough archival treatment of the history of the lynching and subsequent court case is in Pitch, *Last Lynching*.

73. Torres, *Black, White, and in Color*, 26.

74. Bodroghkozy, *Equal Time*, 2.

75. Torres, *Black, White, and in Color*, 30–31; Madrigal, "When the Revolution Was Televised."

76. I revisit the sit-ins in the conclusion of this book. See Cerese and Channing, *February One*.

77. Gray, "Remembering Civil Rights"; Bodroghkozy, *Equal Time*, 4.

78. Bodroghkozy, *Equal Time*, 2.

79. Ibid., 5.
80. Fairclough quoted in Bodroghkozy, *Equal Time*, 146; Torres, *Black, White, and in Color*, 28.
81. Kennedy, "Radio and Television Report."
82. Bodroghkozy, *Equal Time*, 7.
83. Young's insights on the geographies of violence in the South proved to have merit. Part of the reason SNCC and CORE workers in Mississippi decided to recruit white college student volunteers in 1964 was to ameliorate the systemic, unchecked, intransigent violence they had faced outside of the national spotlight since they began voter registration activities in the state in 1961. Led by Bob Moses, activists hoped to draw national attention to Mississippi by bringing the children of powerful northern whites to the state, a strategy that proved to be grimly successful after the disappearance and murder of James Chaney, Andrew Goodman, and Michael Schwerner that June. Torres, *Black, White, and in Color*, 24; Belfrage, *Freedom Summer*.
84. Hurley is quoted in Torres, *Black, White, and in Color*, 23–24.
85. Torres, *Black, White, and in Color*, 32; Chion, "From 'The Voice in Cinema,'" 263.
86. Bodroghkozy, *Equal Time*, 128.
87. Mary Anne Doane's writing on "crisis" in her article "Information, Crisis, Catastrophe" (1990) was picked up by both Torres and Bodroghkozy in their interpretations of footage recorded during Bloody Sunday in Selma. Doane, "Information, Crisis, Catastrophe"; Torres, *Black, White, and in Color*, 34–35; Bodroghkozy, *Equal Time*, 128–30.
88. Torres, *Black, White, and in Color*, 31.
89. Bodroghkozy, *Equal Time*, 115–32.
90. Hadley, "Eyes on the Prize," 100.
91. Brooks, *Reflections on Georgia Politics*.
92. S. Parks, *America Play*, 4.
93. Newman, "U.S. to Reopen Investigation."
94. Mitchell, *Living with Lynching*, 6.

FOUR

ESTABLISHING A BLACK AFFECTIVE INFRASTRUCTURE

From Lynching Performance in the Hollywood of the South to *Always in Season* (2019)

FORMER GEORGIA REPRESENTATIVE TYRONE BROOKS kicks off the 2019 Moore's Ford Lynching Reenactment with a promise. At the end of the day, he tells the small crowd gathered at the First African Baptist Church in Monroe, "You will see the lynching of the Malcoms and the Dorseys, and you will see the lynch mob cut the fetus out of Dorothy Malcom." Though many of the speakers and actors are the same as in 2012, the atmosphere of the reenactment is different. A lawyer working pro bono to secure the release of grand jury transcripts from the 1946 case has traveled from New Jersey to address the group, and it is access to these documents rather than arrest and prosecution that provides the rationale for the reenactment this year. Some present say that all the suspects in the 1946 lynching have died, while others insist that a few are still alive in Walton County. Just over twenty people hear the day's initial speeches (more come later), and over half of them film as they listen. I film them filming. Smartphones, handicams, DSLRs, and prosumer rigs with lights and specialty microphones float above the pews in the Baptist church to record speakers and performers. Some livestream segments to groups on Facebook, others record for documentary film projects, and a few photograph with DSLRs for local activist organizations or personal storytelling side projects on behalf of activist causes. Whereas spectators to the event in 2012 photographed on offline personal digital cameras, in 2019 many broadcast what they see in real time or close to it on social media platforms from their phones. Camerawork is less about capture than projection, less about archiving than affiliation, augmentation, and witnessing. The Moore's Ford Lynching Reenactment has become a social media happening as well as a live event. And we the audience make this

Figure 4.1. The cast and crew for the Moore's Ford Lynching Reenactment in Monroe, Georgia, on July 27, 2019. Photograph by the author.

happen. But our motives are complex. More than the civil rights movement of the 1960s, the lynching reenactment has come to depend on actors, theater directors, singers, and dancers to function as documentary vessels (fig. 4.1).

Georgia is now well positioned to provide such talent. In 2017, more of the one hundred top-grossing feature films were made in Georgia (sixteen) than in California (twelve), a transformation attributed to expansive tax credits the state began to offer film studios in 2008.[1] Drawn as well by the proximity of Atlanta to mountains, beaches, warehouse districts, forests, distribution hubs, and abandoned postindustrial towns (like those featured on the zombie-apocalypse-themed television series *The Walking Dead*), the film and television industries increased spending in the state from $93 million in 2007 to over $2 billion in 2016, leading *TIME* magazine to dub Georgia "the Hollywood of the South" in a 2018 feature article. Unlike other states, which have offered short-term incentives to production companies, Georgia placed no end date on their tax credit policies. They give a 20 percent incentive to films working with a budget greater than $500,000 with an additional 10 percent if they include the Georgia peach logo in the end credits. Large studios have taken notice. Marvel moved its base of operations to Georgia in 2016, where the studio produced much of *The Black Panther, Avengers: Infinity War,* and *Ant-Man and the Wasp,* and Atlanta has become a hub of Black film and television production headlined by the Tyler Perry Studios.[2] The growth of film and media work has had an ancillary impact on what civil rights activism such as the lynching reenactment can mean and be in Georgia. Attuned to Georgia's broader media context, this chapter aims to trace how the affective sentiments annually conjured by the lynching reenactment functioned in 2019.

I first want to emphasize that the organizers of the reenactment and longtime actors are still committed activists. They seek justice, protections for voters, passage of antilynching laws, and deathbed confessions from the killers or their kin. Some also dabble or work in media, and they do not see a contradiction between these two identities. Indeed, they embrace the synergy across activism and media work and the opportunity to bring activists and professional actors together to stage the reenactment. Some though not all of the actors who joined the cast over the last three years think of themselves as activists. At the same time, all the Black actors who participated in the reenactment in 2019 aspire to work in the Georgia media industry as actors, models, or back-end logistical personnel. They told me with excitement about successful auditions for their roles in the reenactment as well as small parts in crime dramas, daytime soaps, and Netflix series. One of the white actors playing a Klansman for the first time in 2019 wants to work as a model while also volunteering for civil rights groups; he moved from Ohio to Atlanta to better prepare for his part. All added their role in the reenactment to an acting résumé. For their part, longtime activist participants who appeared in Jacqueline Olive's *Always in Season* traveled to film festivals across the country in 2019 for question-and-answer sessions about the film and the case, building contacts while also offering forceful commentary on the unresolved legacies of lynching for often white-majority audiences. This group models what it means for a filmmaker and community to nurture dialogues about difficult subjects. But the culture industry ethos long associated with New York and Los Angeles now suffuses Atlanta and the surrounding area, where young hopefuls grind away at service-industry jobs while pursuing their big break. It filters how they see everyday life, structures conversations and bonds of affiliation, and reshapes the landscape. And in this right-to-work state, it leaves such workers precarious. They are hungry for media attention and also sometimes hungry. They must hustle while they do good.

In this dynamic environment, the organizers of the reenactment have won something across their fourteen years of commitment. The ritual of the reenactment still curates moments of poignant liveness and through those extends—even creates—an affective infrastructure that can function in flexible ways for a media world less controlled by large broadcasting institutions than was true in prior eras. It mobilizes political affect for a variety of potential endeavors focused on justice and advocacy. It keeps the story of the lynching alive for a historian such as Anthony Pitch, who revisited the crime in *The Last Lynching* (2016) and found the grand jury transcripts from the case mislabeled in a federal archive. These became the center of a legal case to make the transcripts public for reasons of historical interest.[3] It coaxes a small number of white locals such as Wayne Watson to recollect on videotape the stories he heard from relatives, alternately provocative and unbelievable, including fantastical details about Dorothy Malcom's seven-month-old fetus being secreted away to be raised by a white family in Atlanta after the lynching.[4] Radio and TV reporters from Georgia and beyond can continue to write fresh stories about the case through changes in focus offered by the reenactment, which increasingly bends toward Brooks's version of the story rather than Laura Wexler's.[5] It offers director Cassandra Greene the opportunity to add a scene to the annual reenactment about voter suppression in 1946, thereby involving more Black actors and creating a space for discussion about ongoing voter disfranchisement in Georgia, especially in light of Stacey Abrams's gubernatorial campaign in 2018. She can start work on a documentary about her life in which her role as the director of the reenactment plays a prominent part, creating acting, directing, and editing opportunities for longtime participants.[6] Someone like Olive can film this reenactment and use it to create meanings for other stories about lynching by dint of metonymic juxtaposition. The reenactment on film creates the possibility for montage in Sergei Eisenstein's understanding of this term, in which the collision of times and disparate incidents can construct social meanings not otherwise accessible to direct observation.[7]

This chapter analyzes *Always in Season* to illustrate the political potential latent in an affective infrastructure such as the Moore's Ford Lynching Reenactment in an era of ubiquitous media. I aim to answer a question about what happens to the political qualities of the repertoire for those who do not have access to the archive, to use Taylor's framing, when those groups find their way through recursive performance into searchable, documented media forms. I argue that in the case of the Moore's Ford Lynching Reenactment (and others like it by extension), the organizers create an affective infrastructure—in this case, a structure for interpreting counterhistories of racial violence in the US South. In writing about infrastructure, media studies scholars have tended to focus on qualities such as scale, materials, and distribution. This move, part of writing in the broader area of New Materialism, proposed to center the field of media studies on concerns about the environmental impact of media production and consumption, on the difficult task of educating the public about the mechanics of highly technical systems so as to better advocate for progressive policies and regulations on issues such as bandwidth allocation, and on better understanding the contours of distribution within a field historically focused on spectatorship, audience reception, and production. Studies about undersea cables, broken pipes, ferroconcrete, satellite infrastructures, online network protocols, algorithmic bias, and content moderation, among many others, have answered this call and offered a wealth of new ways to think about media.[8] I see this chapter building on the broader conversation about media infrastructure by centering on the dynamics of race in the construction of what I am calling an *affective infrastructure*. Rather than identify infrastructure in materials that industry extracts from ground, sea, or online activity, I focus here on the affective infrastructure built up over time by the recurring and recursive reenactment at the Moore's Ford Bridge. If infrastructure becomes ethical when it is accessible for even small and relatively marginalized users, as Susan Leigh Star and Karen Ruhleder proposed in 1996, then the affective affordances of the Moore's Ford Lynching Reenactment do function like indexical "pipes," if you will, for new media makers like Olive to tell a story about a contemporary lynching.[9] She has said as much in public reflections on the film. "It's been really important for me to give context, because that doesn't happen often enough in mainstream media," Olive explained in an interview in 2020 with Good Docs: "That's the whole point of making a film about these communities; it gives context so that you better understand what is going on in Bladenboro and you understand it from the perspective of someone who is African-American, who understands that there are connections historically that have been overlooked, stories that have been overlooked."[10]

To recenter a story framed by white officials as suicide through the lens of lynching, in other words, is to expose an affective infrastructure long broken but never repaired in towns with histories of egregious complicity with racial violence and sympathy (sometimes seemingly unconscious) to white supremacist ideology. Black residents of such places see the break. Olive's film intended to make such orientations more generally accessible.

But in seeking to facilitate justice, reconciliation, and repair, Olive cannot simply show footage of a lynching reenactment and expect the representation to bring these outcomes about. The ways that people identify with or objectify materials they see on screen create complexities for the broader mission of exposure to and identification with an antiracist point of view here. The goal is not stress inoculation, to refer back to the rationale for displays of blood and gore in the military training simulations discussed in chapter 2, but rather broadened empathy for the victims of unjust violence. With this goal in mind, Olive's aesthetic choices about when and how to show lynching imagery engage the tension between shock and empathy from her vantage as both a Black and female filmmaker. Touching back to the footage of the Selma march in 1965 discussed in chapter 3, Olive chooses an acousmatic approach to the representation of lynching. She uses a simulated crisis-coverage aesthetic and shows images of witnesses watching the reenactment rather than the moment of execution in the performance. Viewers of the film and spectators at the reenactment alike hear the sounds of actors' voices and gunshots as the scene unfolds. In this way, Olive's repetition-and-revision approach to representation and her clever reappropriation of shot–reverse shot scene construction in these scenes diverges from the naturalist approach taken in the reenactment. But the film shares with—and gleans from—the way that the organizers of the reenactment frame the story of the lynching itself. It is an invaluable context, to use Olive's term, through which to interpret Lennon Lacy's death.

REPRESENTING THE CONTEXT OF LYNCHING: PRACTICES OF LOOKING IN *ALWAYS IN SEASON* (2019)

Always in Season recounts the story of the racially suspicious death of seventeen-year-old Lennon Lacy, who was found hanging from the swing set behind his family's trailer in Bladenboro, North Carolina, in the early morning of August 29, 2014. Though it was ruled a suicide after a cursory investigation by the local police, details emerged in the following weeks that cast their conclusion into doubt, especially for Black residents in the town. When Olive first learned about Lacy's death, she was nearing the end of editing her documentary about restorative justice rituals then occurring in towns with histories of lynching. Olive's initial idea for a film followed her seeing the *Without Sanctuary* exhibit in the early 2000s, which moved her to seek out stories about the victims as well as the white spectators shown in the lynching postcard photographs. "I began to realize that the spectators in those photographs could have been my neighbors," she recalled during an interview in 2020. "They had faces like those of my friends, and I wanted to know more about how they came to be in the midst of the violence, as well."[11] Over eight years of research, filming, and editing, she identified the descendants of persons lynched and the communities from which they came, and she filmed enough material to tell a story about interracial efforts to address long-standing silences in several cases. By 2014, the rough cut of her film intercut the stories of three present-day communities in which the descendants of perpetrators and victims of lynchings were trying to create rituals together for justice and reconciliation, one of which was the Moore's Ford Lynching Reenactment. The film centered on retelling suppressed stories of lynching incidents; confronting legacies of silence, shame, and fear; and working through the vestiges of intergenerational trauma lingering in the present.

However, when Olive began to see patterns in the Lacy case parallel to those she had researched for her film, she changed her plans and traveled to Bladenboro to film Lacy's family and members of the community. Here was a contemporary, unresolved case in which white neighbors who looked like those featured in the lynching postcard photographs could speak (or decline to speak, in many cases) about their proximity to a potential lynching. Moreover, Olive had a son who was about Lacy's age at the time, and she connected with Lacy's mother, Claudia, over her loss. Claudia's partnership with the NAACP to pressure for a federal investigation lent the film both urgency and narrative structure. The concept, cases, and footage that had constituted the entirety of Olive's film about restorative justice came to serve as contextual material—an affective infrastructure—for a social issue, investigative documentary centered on interpreting the "death" of Lennon Lacy through the lens of lynching history.

Situated in the longer context of racially motivated hate crimes including the Moore's Ford lynching, *Always in Season* foregrounds patterns of intimidation, official silence, tacit terror, and aching sorrow in keeping with other lynching incidents so that general audiences might intuit something of what it is like for the Lacy family to live with the uncertainties surrounding Lennon's death. The film draws from widely accepted and accessible techniques, including sit-down interviews, animation and graphics over archival materials, and participant-observation of the Lacy family's search for answers in the present. Olive said that no Bladenboro official agreed to be interviewed, including the chief of police, the district attorney, the coroner, and the medical examiner at the time of Lacy's death.[12] Like the one-act lynching plays that Koritha Mitchell describes, Olive's film emphasizes the humanity of a young Black man and the struggle for the family to survive after a racially suspicious death, suturing camera gaze and audience identification from the first scene to the way Claudia looks at photographs of her late son (fig. 4.2).[13] "Think about it as if it were your son, or your daughter," Claudia's voice implores the viewers, even before they hear a suggestion about how he died in the next scene's disturbing 911 call reporting a boy who "hung himself."

Montage scenes that piece together Bladenboro's white supremacist id are less sympathetic. Given how quickly officials deemed Lacy's death a suicide, conversation snippets with residents about town life reveal alarming

Figure 4.2. Claudia Lacy (*top*) looks at a yearbook photo of her son Lennon Lacy (*bottom*) in the first scene of *Always in Season* (2019). Photography by Rodrigo Dorfman. Courtesy Jacqueline Olive.

continuities with other lynching locales. Emblematic is a scene about an annual town celebration called Beast Fest after a tradition of hunting a mysterious "almost human-like, cat-like combination," in the words of the white docent at the town's history museum. As he speaks, we see a newspaper drawing of "the beast" framed on the museum wall that looks a lot like a black panther. It was said to have emerged from the swamp to kill local livestock in 1954 (a year often cited as the start of the civil rights movement with the *Brown v. Board of Education* decision). The smiling former town mayor, Rufus Duckworth, explains without a hint of self-consciousness that "everybody wanted to be the one to get their picture in the newspapers that they captured the beast." The image track here shows a black panther statue adorning a plantation-style home in the town today. A Black reverend notes icily that none of his congregation participated in Beast Fest and that the area described as the beast's swamp in this white myth happened to be the part of town where enslaved persons once resided and many Black residents still lived. A Black female resident who lived through the civil rights era tells the crew that "Bladenboro's got the skeletons. And if you open the door they will scare you to death! Some things that you see, you keep it to yourself. You will live longer." This is the context in which white local officials quickly deemed Lennon's death a suicide. Lennon's brother Pierre reflects that "honestly, it looked like it was a display, like it was a message," as if summarizing the key point of it all, "like it was a back in the day lynching."

Expanding out from the Bladenboro storyline here, the film explicates contexts in which lynchings occurred historically. It is the first of three such extended scenes. Interviews with subject experts Sherrilyn Ifill, president and director counsel of the NAACP Legal Defense Fund, and Bryan Stevenson, subject of the narrative feature film *Just Mercy* (2019) and executive director of the Equal Justice Initiative and the first national museum on lynching, provide frameworks for interpretation.[14] Recurring parallel stories in these segments focus on the brutal lynching and dismemberment of Claude Neal by white Floridians in 1934, as told through readings of public articles, statements by witnesses, and transcripts of interviews with Neal's descendants by Danny Glover, as well as contemporary preparations in Georgia for the reenactment of the Moore's Ford quadruple lynching. The film parses each case out in these sections as if they are their own three-act play, with setup, event, and aftermath mapping the interpretive terrain for what we will soon see in Bladenboro.

In an inversion of the longing expressed in the eyeline match between Claudia's gaze and the portrait photographs of Lennon featured early in the film, sections on lynching history show the faces of spectators captured looking toward the camera in lynching postcard photographs from the early 1900s featured in the *Without Sanctuary* exhibit. They appear here to look at us viewers from their proximity in past time to the bodies of the lynched, disturbing for an ordinariness and banality that viewers might find relatable in other contexts. Ifill reminds us that the public circulation of such objects is damning evidence about the complicity of white townspeople where such events occurred. One photograph uncontextualized by place or date shows the three men lynched in Duluth, Minnesota, the catalyst in Olive's rough cuts up to 2014 for a twenty-five-minute segment on the descendants of lynchers and lynched depicted in it. The use of these photographs at the climactic moment of the Moore's Ford Lynching Reenactment, which I analyze in more detail below, again refracts the meaning of these looks by intercutting images of the faces of Black reenactment attendees in the present, whose faces express shock and horror, with those of individuals in lynch mobs from the archival photographs, whose faces seem to express unconcern, anger, or even glee. This is quite different from the gestural recollection-objects created in *In Country* as discussed in chapter 1. There, the juxtapositions of reenactment footage and archival imagery from Vietnam function to evoke the reenactors' desires for the presence of intense war experiences of the past. In *Always in Season*, the contrast in looks indexes the ongoing presence of overwhelming horror, somehow always just beyond visibility in the present. The film does not in fact show the moment of execution play out in the reenactment. Instead, these sections focus on what it means to look at lynching representations and to think about the ongoing impacts of this history now. Olive profiles the motivations of various actors who participate, including director Greene; Paula Logan, the actress who portrayed Dorothy Malcom from 2009 to 2011; Olivia Taylor, a woman remorseful about having grown up in a high-ranking Klan family in the 1950s; and Walter, the native Georgian who used his family pedigree to infiltrate white supremacist meetings on behalf of civil rights organizations. The scene of a rehearsal that I filmed with Olive in 2012 provides a thirty-second segue between Walter's infiltration story, told as he walks his dog through a trail in the woods while wearing a T-shirt that reads, "Careful, or you'll end up in my novel," and him reperforming the Talmadge stump speech in the reenactment described in the introduction. Greene, for her part, credits her participation to "social issues that I saw that needed to be addressed" and emphasizes how significant it was to show that "a baby was taken out of [Dorothy's] body." This way, the audience can understand that "this was some sick stuff." The film allows her statement to stand as definitive.

These interludes prime viewers to better understand the frustration of Black citizens in Bladenboro and function to propel the main storyline forward. As if to connect this past to the present, the Lacy family discovers that Lennon's grave site has been vandalized. In keeping with character-based, social documentaries such as *The Invisible War* (2012), *Bully* (2011), and *A Place at the Table* (2012), protagonists in *Always in Season* undergo a transformation from victims to activists. They model what we viewers, too, should do. Black anger at official accounts of Lacy's death lead Claudia and her sympathizers to seek out truth and justice. Standing alongside the thunderous civil rights leader

William Barber, Claudia and Pierre lead thousands of marchers through the streets of Bladenboro. F. W. Newton, the Black mortician who prepared Lacy's body for burial, states that Lacy "looked as if he'd been in a fight.... I know this is a murder." Archival clips of the Klan marching in the town underscore comments about the region's notoriously corrupt police force and give way to contemporary news clips of public Klan rallies staged within thirty minutes of Bladenboro less than three weeks after Lennon Lacy's death. NAACP lawyer Heather Rattelade reveals that while investigating Lacy's case, she found many other news stories about Black men described as committing suicide by hanging in public parks. She and Claudia persuade the FBI to open an investigation into Lennon's death.

After another return to Georgia for that year's reenactment, and as if running parallel to the imagined FBI investigation, the last section of the film details the troubled interracial relationship possibly central to Lacy's case—quite often the explicit rationale for lynchings in the past. Again, footage from the Moore's Ford reenactment, Glover's readings, and Ifill's commentary set to newspaper headlines about lynchings establish the historical context for this scene. Ifill explains that though even the appearance of being "uppity" could lead to lynching, "most Black men were lynched because they were accused of sexually assaulting a white woman." Dehumanizing language established the belief "that the Black man had to be physically restrained, that he was oversexualized, that he was naturally and inherently violent, or something that's not human," and laid the groundwork for whites to stand by amid racial terror. Black men were "always in season" for lynching, says Stevenson. Recontextualized as the title of the film, the phrase frames history as cyclical rather than linear. Lynching is an ongoing problem, not a relic of the past. It is a frame that primes viewers to regard contemporary disavowals—even or especially the polite ones—with suspicion. When the film returns to Bladenboro, there is a key interview with the white local newspaper editor, whose phrasing about the need to move on from the case betrays subtle vestiges of those processes of dehumanization to which Ifill referred. Softly, he tells Olive's crew that he believes the investigation was proper, that the town accepts it will be ruled a suicide, and that "the sooner the better to get this behind us." He insists that he lacks the staff to investigate Lacy's death and suggests that "the other side to the coin" in this case is the "family unit, and negligence, and that kind of thing." The music fades out here, cueing a provocative reveal: "You know, [there was] the fact that this teenage boy at fifteen or sixteen years old was involved with a thirty-year-old woman in the neighborhood, that he was regularly out after midnight on school nights. So those are the kinds of things that started to percolate as this went on during that first year." There is a straight cut to white, feminine hands holding photographs of Lennon Lacy and a white woman kissing, again echoing the film's opening, in which Claudia looks at the boyhood photos that represented Lennon to her. "From the time I met Lennon, it kind of just felt like it was meant to be," says the voice of Michelle Brimhall, identified in an interview frame in the next shot.

Further revelations pepper this section of the film as it accelerates to the conclusion. Brimhall struggled with drug addiction. She and her three kids were staying in the trailer neighboring the Lacy home with a drug-dealing white supremacist named Dewey Sykes, his girlfriend Carla, and Carla's son Trey—described earlier in the film as a friend of Lennon's. The night Lennon died, there was a dispute and a fight over Brimhall's new boyfriend, and Lennon punched a hole in the fence. Sykes disapproved of the relationship and called Lennon "n----r." The Sykes family moved out, says a neighborhood friend of Lennon's, "like they were running away from something" shortly after Lennon's death. Brimhall thinks Lennon was murdered but seems to restrain herself from saying all she knows in the interview with Olive.

The film concludes when the Lacy family receives a letter from the FBI, which reports in pro forma language of finding no evidence of a homicide. The Lacy family members express frustration and exhaustion as they read portions of the one-page document on camera. It appears that the lack of closure in the Neal and Moore's Ford lynchings will repeat and fester in Bladenboro as well. Glover reads the transcript of a 2011 interview with Neal's nephew, Orlando Williams, to illustrate the intergenerational trauma associated with lynching. Williams recalled his mother leaving without explanation for months at a time and drinking heavily to cope with the pain. "She went through hell and put us through hell," he states. We are left to imagine how Claudia will cope over time with Lennon's death and to consider the broader, less visible social and interpersonal effects of the shroud of silence around lynching, still with us today. The film concludes somewhat as it began, with a meditation on photography and its capacity to humanize as well as objectify the dead. Claudia attends the graduation for Lennon's class at Bladen High School holding a framed portrait of her son, posing for pictures with groups of his friends. Brief, slow-motion snippets of Lennon walking through the frame of home videos from family gatherings testify that he lived. The Lacy family organizes a candle-lighting vigil for Lennon near the place of his death. And the film gives the last word and image to Claudia, who stands in the doorway of her home with the laundry line visible in the background. "The more they understand, that's my way of grieving," she says.

THE OPPOSITIONAL ACOUSMETRE: A STRATEGY FOR REPRESENTING LYNCHING

While Olive uses the annual ritual of the Moore's Ford Lynching Reenactment as an affective infrastructure for interpreting Lacy's death, she does not reproduce that event's representational politics. Most notably, she does not show the moment of execution or feature Brooks as an interview subject.[15] But Olive's decisions about what to include and exclude from the film also show her commitment to the lives, actions, sensibilities, and struggles of female participants, especially Black female participants. Lacy, Greene, and Logan are, after all, key actors in this story, even if not heretofore the faces of their respective movements. Olive's film has changed this.

I interpret her decisions on how to represent the lynching reenactment itself as part feminist, following on Laura Mulvey's classic case for denying the spectator's voyeuristic pleasure, and part a visual expression of what bell hooks called "the oppositional gaze" in a trenchant critique of Mulvey's tacitly white positionality. More specifically, I revisit Olive's treatment of the lynching reenactment as emblematic of "the acousmatic," the peculiar power of the off-screen voice. While Michel Chion focused on films that withheld visual representations of individual speaking subjects, such as the murderer Hans Beckert played by Peter Lorre in Fritz Lang's classic murder mystery *M* (1931), the relation he identified between power and the invisible voice applies to Olive's use of off-screen collective voice to signify lynching in *Always in Season*. I use the term *oppositional acousmetre* to describe the complex operations of power entailed in Olive's representation of lynching and the gaze in these two scenes.[16]

Interestingly, the documentary even features a rogue balloon ascending away from the town much like the one in the famous opening scene from *M* analyzed in Chion's article, though here in the context of Claudia pondering the fact that the murderer remains at large in the community, off screen and unknown. While working at the supermarket deli, Claudia recalls, "It dawned on me as I looked to the dining area there that somewhere in this crowd is a murderer." The visuals of white families walking together in the Bladenboro town square on a sunny day (perhaps Beast Fest?) give way to several peculiar shots of a pink helium balloon floating in the sky, first handheld and captured from a distance, then up close and likely staged. The juxtaposition calls to mind the opening scene of *M*, in which the murderer appears in shadow and from behind as he purchases a balloon for an unsuspecting girl to lure her away from the public street. As the day proceeds like any other for children coming home from school, the mother of the girl looks out the window and checks the empty hallway. The image of the balloon entangled in street wires and then blowing away out of the frame signifies the girl's murder. Olive's film mirrors this moment, and indeed the balloon signals thematic consistencies across the two films. Her crew recorded a continuity close-up of a pink balloon (not the pink balloon from the previous shot) rising through the composition of a tripod, high-angle view of the town surrounded by woods. The privileged aerial optics here obfuscate rather than reveal the information we want to know, the identity of the murderer. No one is visible in the frame as the balloon exits upward and Claudia's voice continues, as if reenacting the premise of *M* in a documentary form: "And that day was the day that I realized there is still someone out here that is responsible," says Claudia's voice-over. It is the only shot staged in such a way in the entirety of the film.

The fact that Chion and Olive both refer to the metaphor of the balloon floating away is striking, but the political meaning of its evocation in Olive's documentary differs. The murderer's visual absence in *Always in Season* does not heighten suspense or set up an eventual downfall, as it does in *M*. For Claudia, the uncertainty is now a life condition. There seems to be no closure on offer for her or for the Black residents of Bladenboro and beyond. There is no object on which to focus the gaze, no visible, tangible entity indicted or prosecuted. As with the Moore's Ford lynchings and so many others, there is no witness testimony, photographic proof of events, or sure knowledge. Depressed about the death of an uncle and the loss of his girlfriend, Lennon may have committed suicide. The uncertainty creates a dangerous space where ideology must fill in gaps, but it is also a common one for the survivors of white-on-Black racial violence. And Olive's film interpolates its audience—in ways unsettling for those who identify as white—into Claudia's uncertainty. The balloon scene suggests the film's central dynamic, the play between photographic objects, absence, and off-screen sound. With Olive's handling of the lynching scene at the Moore's Ford reenactment, the film also leads viewers to witness unfolding events through an oppositional lens and perhaps a feminist one.

In her watershed essay "Visual Pleasure and Narrative Cinema" (1975), Mulvey proposed that scopophilia melded in classical narrative film with the unreciprocated gaze of the spectator to produce the toxic condition of voyeurism. The combination of voyeurism and the division of labor in narrative structure between the "man of action" and "the woman as bearer of the look" reproduced and naturalized inequitable gender positions as central to psychic coherence and desire for the interpolated male spectator. It was the project of a feminist cinema, then, to reject realist narrative continuity and identification in favor of formalist and reflexive filmmaking projects that explored female subjectivity, perhaps best illustrated in Mulvey's own trajectory in *Riddle of the Sphinx*

(1977). More on the realist side of the feminist realist debates among 1990s feminist documentary scholars, *Always in Season* employs techniques such as continuity editing, three-act structure, and character identification regularly critiqued in canonical feminist film theory.[17] Yet in representing moments of lynching, the film also disavows spatial continuity characteristic of realism in keeping with a tenet of feminist film theory. These scenes reflect on the gaze itself, disrupting narrative flow and whatever pain or pleasure it might induce to see the recreated execution of Black sharecroppers Roger and Dorothy Malcom and George and Mae Murray Dorsey.

In remaking the gaze in this way, Olive's film gives visual expression to what hooks called "the oppositional gaze" in her influential article about a viewing practice that Black women had to employ when watching Hollywood fare. In her critique of psychoanalytic feminist film theory, hooks argued that the viewing position assumed within Mulvey's critique tacitly reinscribed whiteness. While hooks praised Mulvey's call for formal experimentation, she took issue with her concept of the male gaze. The feminine object of the gaze in Hollywood films through the 1980s (and beyond), hooks noted, was white. There was no position within such films for Black female viewers to recognize self or imagine incorporation with dignity into the world viewed. Neither mammies nor tragic mulattoes passing for white nor the white women in films that featured no Black characters offered spiritual sustenance for her. Instead, she concluded, Black female viewers of that era had to bring an oppositional gaze to the experience of screening films. That is, they had to find pleasure in reading such films against the grain, as evidence of an ideology to oppose and overthrow when and where possible rather than as points of potential or partial identification. She suggested in the end that films such as Julie Dash's *Illusions* (1982) offered a possible site for transformative collective-making, as this was a space in which Black women could express a plausible form of agency and resistance.[18]

Especially in the two scenes that represent lynching, Olive's documentary takes up hooks's call. In one, Logan, the actress who played Dorothy Malcom in three reenactments, watches and hears footage of the reenactment for the first time (fig. 4.3). The frame presents her in three-quarter close-up as she looks at a television screen, but viewers never see the object of her gaze. They do, however, hear along with her the collective voices and sounds meant to signify white supremacist terror on the recording, somewhat as in the 1965 TV news crisis coverage of violence in Selma, Alabama, discussed in chapter 3. In the second scene of the lynching reenactment, the viewer sees the faces of horrified Black spectators looking on, intercut with black-and-white stills of white spectators in lynching postcard photographs who looked toward the camera, above a continuous soundscape of reenactors' yells, screams, and gunshots. As

Figure 4.3. Reenactor Paula Logan plays Dorothy Malcom in 2011 (*top*) and watches footage of that reenactment for the first time in 2012 (*bottom*). Frame grabs from *Always in Season*. Photography by Geoff Davis (*top*) and S. Leo Chiang (*bottom*). Courtesy Jacqueline Olive.

in the Selma newscast, the relative invisibility of the sources of sound augments audience anxiety. In Olive's film, however, this is an intentional aesthetic choice rather than the side effect of uncontrolled crisis coverage.

And this aesthetic is somewhat at odds with the logic of visibility central to the reenactment. Perhaps anticipating some majority-white cinema audiences, *Always in Season* hedges against the possibility that such scenes might spark the inklings of unconscious pleasure in its viewers or the shutting down of reflective thought. In this way, Olive's documentary film about a simulation scenario differs sharply from a film such as *Full Battle Rattle* (2008), discussed in chapter 2, which reproduces the spectacular scenes of violence in a military training simulation scenario as well as the ideological orientation of the military itself. If the simulation of death in fiction cinema plays a key role in spectatorial pleasure, fascination, and identification in general, then eliding the visibility of violent death and focusing on its consequences may rupture those well-worn circuits in favor of new thinking. Moreover, as John Protevi has noted, fear and anger lead perceiving subjects to focus on their own psychic survival and in-group identification rather than reflect on possibilities for empathic mutuality.[19] *Always in Season* expresses a consciousness of these affective dilemmas in its form. Below, I describe and then analyze the way that evidence functions in these two scenes, which alternately subvert the ideal of witnessing and remake the concept as an oppositional interpretive practice. The film uses the relation of gazes in these scenes, in other words, to teach viewers how to interpret the world like the Black women on screen and possibly to interrogate their own practices of looking.[20]

As with *Murder in Black and White*, the lynching reenactment footage in *Always in Season* first appears in the guise of crisis coverage. Using the raw footage of the 2009 reenactment recorded by the Atlanta-based independent journalism organization Creative Loafing for a three-minute YouTube story, Olive's editing team eschews settled framings for handheld floating, whip pans, quick zooms, and breathing focus. Though the finished, three-minute short uploaded to YouTube by Creative Loafing bears all the marks of professional advocacy video making—intentional compositions; on-site interview soundbites from key players in three-quarter framing; intertitles on message with the reenactment organizers' goals; branded lower-third titles for on-camera speakers; sophisticated sound mixing with singing, gunshots, and interview clips; and tightly edited narrative flow for an online audience—the footage that Olive uses in her film strips the context away.[21] The messiness of the raw footage takes center stage instead. A lone white male in a suit and straw hat walks up the road toward the camera, which breathes in and out of focus and wobbles from being handheld at such a distance. Two white reenactors wait by the side of the road, fidgeting with a rope fashioned into a noose. The white man in the straw hat arrives at the scene and slams the hood of the car with his right palm, yelling, "We want that n----r, Roger!" It is a past version of the scene Olive and I had recorded in rehearsal and performance for the 2012 reenactment. Screaming ensues as the mob pulls the four victims from the car and hustles them through the woods to the grassy area by the shore of the river. Camerawork struggling to track the transition from car to grass illustrates the crisis, even becomes crisis coverage of this acted event. In fact, for viewers seeing this scene for the first time, it is possible that they are not even aware that it is a reenactment, a possibility that Olive's team exploits much like the makers of *In Country* and *Full Battle Rattle* discussed previously. We see whip-panned blurry footage of trees; handheld, out-of-focus feet walking down the embankment; the end of a stick; the camera itself seeming to float down toward the grass as if expressing the view of one of the victims or (more likely) documenting the cameraperson's hustling and ignoring the image for a moment upon realizing that they need to be in front of the action moving toward the riverbank. The cameraperson's intention was for the editor to cut this part out that we now see. After another whip-pan through the trees, the white man in the straw hat reappears, out of focus and in extreme low angle this time. "Get them n----rs tied up!" he shouts. The camera zooms out and pauses on him for a beat. The simulated crisis coverage ends at this point. The film cuts to a tripod close-up of a Black woman in a quiet interior space who watches the footage we have just seen, on a screen off frame to the right. In this sense, the scene toys with shot–reverse shot construction; viewers of the Black woman watching intuit that she sees the next part of the reenactment on her screen here. The screams from the reenactment remain audible, though we no longer see its image. Instead, we watch this woman watch the reenactment. The climax of the reenactment, in other words, is an acousmetre, an off-screen sonic presence of screams, yells, and epithets that we do not see. The female viewer furrows her brow, shakes her head in disbelief, and raises her eyebrows as she watches. A female reenactor's voice emanating from the TV yells, "Please don't kill us!" and then film viewers and the woman watching the reenactment hear the sound of gunshots. Two tears run down the face of the woman who watches. She wipes them away. The straight cut back to the reenactment footage shows a final volley of gunfire into the fallen victims—the only one shown in the entire film—and then close-ups of the reenactors lying "dead" on the ground. The focus breathes. "This good, boss?" says an off-screen voice as the camera pans to its source. One of the reenactors playing a lyncher holds a Black baby doll above her head. "That's real good," the boss responds. As the camera zooms out, the lyncher throws the baby doll down among the other victims. The boss asks the reenactor playing Loy Harrison if he has seen anyone he knows here. Loy responds no, and the two reenactors move in opposite directions, briefly revealing the audience in the background standing behind yellow crime-scene tape. The camera jostles, but the image shows a group that appears to be multigenerational and entirely Black. A woman in the front row holds a child around the age of four, and preteen girls stand next to her. Older men and women point cameras toward the scene, mostly digital point-and-shoot-style models rather than smartphones. The film cuts back to the woman in close-up, watching the footage. She sighs. A title card appears in the dark space to the right of her face reading, "Paula Logan, Lynching Reenactor." "I don't think I've watched it since I did it," she says. Back at the site of the reenactment, the Creative Loafing interview with Logan plays. "You can feel the spirit of those that died out here," she says. But in the town, there is "this feeling of, nobody should say anything. We don't want to talk."

Following a montage of white and Black actors crying and hugging at the reenactment, *Always in Season* presents archival photographs and newspaper headlines to contextualize the quadruple lynching in Monroe. There is a photograph from the funeral parlor with the victims' bodies laid out under blankets, radio reports about the lynching reenactment, and newspaper clippings that advertise substantial rewards for anyone who would come forward with information that might lead to the arrest and prosecution of members of the lynch mob. Then the film returns to Logan, now walking across the bridge as a contemporary civilian with the actress who played Mae Murray alongside her in 2009. They are alone on the bridge, asked by the filmmaker to return and remember. Logan obliges: "I didn't remember until we came here today that we went up under this bridge, and there was writings that the Ku Klux Klan had put under this very bridge that we're standing on." The film cuts to an image of the spray-painted KKK graffiti under the bridge. The image seems to validate her voice.

At first glance, this moment of suturing authoritative voice to Logan's body seems to double down on the most recognizable marker of the documentary mode. "Documentary's difference from fiction is frequently articulated in terms of its reliance on sound rather than image," writes Pooja Rangan in her contribution to *Sound Objects*, "The Skin of the Voice." She cites Bill Nichols's argument that the spoken word lends documentary a sober-minded reality principle distinct from fiction, as with Frank Capra's narrated *Why We Fight* series and any number of episodic documentaries by Ken Burns. Individual voices testifying to feelings, perspectives, and evidence indeed constitute the bulk of *Always in Season* and contribute to its sense of urgency to resolve a crime and expose vestiges of white supremacist terrorism. But Rangan departs from the view that voice necessarily grounds anti-illusionistic documentary gravitas or even that this might be a desirable outcome for filmmakers from marginalized groups. Following feminist and postcolonial critiques of the acousmatic "Voice of God," long a staple of sober documentary, she insists that "anti-illusory cinematic forms can end up concealing the discriminatory perceptual frames of voicing and listening, even when they aim to achieve the opposite." That is, following Laura Marks's line of argument in *The Skin of the Film* discussed in chapter 1, voices in documentary that encode the identities, perceptive orientations, or life experiences of historically marginalized peoples tote their bodies along into the image, whether or not they appear visibly on screen. The sonic presence of racialized and gendered experiences calls into question the notion that "reduced listening" suggested by Pierre Schaeffer and taken up by Chion allows for the objective attunement to sound, as if unencumbered by a visible embodied cause. The primal acousmatic scene that Chion described, she points out, was the master of the Pythagorean sect, lecturing to his pupils for five years from behind a veil to avoid illusionistic distraction. This form of "perceptual disciplining," in Rangan's interpretation, tacitly encoded the white male "vocalic body" as that acceptably authoritative, serious, divine, and sober. When issued from otherwise racially coded bodies, Rangan points out, voices remain subjective. Therefore, the argument that reduced listening avoids issues of discrimination or illusion falls into a trap. The image formed on screen as well as in the viewer's mind inevitably bears a relationship to off-screen sound, coloring its perceptual and embodied expressivity. She proposes instead a "ventriloquial mode of cinematic looking-listening" attuned to discriminatory frames within which documentary voices tend to operate.[22]

What, then, are we to make of the peculiar acousmatic scenario presented in *Always in Season* as Logan watches the repurposed archival footage of the simulation in which she played a key role? As Rangan suggests, the image we see in this scene frames how we perceive the voices whose source remains out of view. Or perhaps, given that one of the sources of screams we hear in the din is likely Logan playing Dorothy Malcom, it is more accurate to say that the voices of pain, fear, struggle, and rage were performed live in a different time and location than the interior space in which Logan looks at the TV screen. These two times nonetheless touch in the film's present. Liveness here is about Logan's listening to a recording that emanates from a television. She comes to stand in for us viewers at the cut from archival footage to the image of her watching. The effect of this ventriloquial act is not, however, to produce or expose an illusion. We know that the performance we hear is a reenactment and that the sounds of anguish and anger do not come from an original source, per se. As a simulation, origins in reenactment are beside the point, and events are not singular. Rather, viewers must cast back into their own presumptions about narrative logic and the politics of the image here.

If the function of the reenactment, in A. Susan Owen and Peter Ehrenhaus's terms, is to create a space for "moral witness" to the crime, then the function of this cinematic rendition of witnessing complicates the nature of the ethics. The film does not permit gazing at the moment of execution and instead turns away from it, like the cinematic equivalent of what Eve Sedgwick called the "peri-performative utterance" in her critical analysis of the heteronormative, nuptial performative "I do." "Do not do it on my account," Sedgwick responds as a queer witness in peri-performative response.[23] The cut to Logan watching expresses as much about the lynching reenactment. "Do not watch this on my account," the film-body asserts. Instead, watch this individual experience a ghoulish "film souvenir," to use Vivian Sobchack's term for the mode of reception of home movies.[24] Be close enough to her to sense intergenerational trauma. Be uncomfortable in white skin, having expected the scene to conclude elsewhere. The film here offers an oppositional aesthetic because it refracts gazing at this key moment, even while it invests in the power of the gaze and identification in many other scenes, as when Claudia Lacy gazes with longing at photographic images of her late son. To see Logan watch this footage is to recenter the narrative of lynching on what it means for Black Americans to survive, endure, and respond both as individuals and as a group. In this juxtaposition, Logan's two tears stand in for "the skin of the voice," to paraphrase Rangan's argument.

Tears, cinema theorist of affect Eugenie Brinkema cautions, are not the cinematic gateway to authentic soul on the other end of the lens. They are forms rather than signs of affect, and she argues that scholars should distrust them for the touchy-feely value system they reintroduce to the study of cinema. The phenomenological turn overindulged the most artful performances of the spectator's intensity of feeling, she argues. The water droplets on the dead body of Marion Crane after the shower scene in *Psycho*, for instance, look like tears but are impossible to read as such in this context. The shower makes everything wet, and the dead do not tear. Water droplets on the face are forms, not signs of emotion.[25]

Yet in this scene in Olive's documentary film, Logan's tears must be read as such. She is not a form, and her tears are not just symbolic or formal. Viewers see them shed. They express involuntary touch with something between that tape and Logan's memory of playing that role and living as a Black woman in Georgia. The simulation at the center of the moment we see as viewers does not invalidate or compromise the gravity of the tear. It is a moment of truth worth taking seriously in this way. Something of the contingency prized by documentarians of the 1960s remains in this shot and in this scene, even though it denies the quality of being there usually associated with the ethic. Rather, it creates a sense of being with her or maybe being near as indexical referent. The acousmatic form of the collective voices off screen expresses power not as divine or even reduced exactly but rather as untenable for visibility. The film settles on an ethics of lynching representation centered on watching Logan watching. The vocalic body in this case emerges as a combination of anguished sounds from the recording, the image of Logan's steady gaze, and the event of her falling tears after she hears (and viewers hear) the sound of gunshots. The shift in perspective forced on the spectator from an action-violence schema to the thin recollection-image of Logan watching startles. It remakes spectators across the disjuncture of the cut and the tear, indexing like the thunderclap rather than the footprint. For those spectators who do not cry, this moment of beholding Logan's tears indexes like the man with the rolling gait that Peirce deduces to have probably been a sailor. But the difference between the perceiving subject and the object perceived as evidence here redounds with poignancy and urgency. If Logan cries and I do not, then I am compelled to think through this difference. I am indexed, as it were. I am changed. And though I the viewer do not know it yet, I will be changed again.

Logan's tears embed in me a memory that, forty-five minutes later, will reverberate as a gestural recollection-image when the second reenactment scene unfolds. The second reenactment echoes the first but truncates the events leading up to the execution and tweaks the dynamic of the oppositional acousmetre. It includes brief comments from members of the Dorsey and Malcom families as they walk to the site of the reenactment and then presents just enough detail of the performance to recognize Logan being dragged once again from the car and to expand on Greene's final pep talk to the reenactors, who momentarily freeze in the woods this year to allow spectators to make their way from the road to the cordoned-off area in the grass by the site of the lynching. Greene wears a radio mic, and we hear her up close though the camera is distant. "Please give me everything y'all got," she tells her actors. Quietly, she calls action. As the sounds of screams ensue, the edited sequence again turns attention away from images of the reenactors and toward witnesses of lynching—two different audiences this time. Mirroring the earlier scene with Logan watching the television, we see Black spectators at what appears to be the live reenactment event, including children, grandmothers, and middle-aged men who look on in horror. They wince and occasionally turn their heads away. A Black grandmother figure dabs her eyes with a handkerchief in her left hand while embracing a child around the shoulders with her right. These figures share this section of the film with the white participant-observers of lynchings depicted in those haunting postcard photographs of the late 1800s and early 1900s, who betray an opposite set of emotions frozen in time: anger, joy, resentment, and stone-faced determination (fig. 4.4). The montage progresses like the lynching scene in Lang's *Fury* discussed in chapter 3, with the continuous off-screen sounds of screams and yells rather than crackling fire. Children regularly appear as well in these black-and-white photographs in Olive's film, looking on with expressions of amusement and curiosity at portions of lynched bodies jutting into the cropped frames presented in the film. The stern white faces looking at the camera appear with especial prominence over the sound of gunshots from the reenactment. At the conclusion of the reenactment, as volunteers lift Logan's body into the back of a hearse, we hear Olive ask her a question in the interview frame seen previously, in the scene that first introduced the Moore's Ford Lynching Reenactment forty-five minutes ago. "Some people would ask, 'Why would you even do the reenactments? Whey even go there? It's history,'" Olive says. "That's why," Logan responds after a pause. "Because it's history. To bring the history to them." As if acting out Logan's rationale, Glover reads the account of a white witness to the Neal lynching. "First, they cut off his penis, and he was made to eat it," he states, echoing rumors of what happened to Roger Malcom as noted in Beauchamp's film about Moore's Ford, *Murder in Black and White*.

The idea to intercut spectators with the sounds of the reenactment occurred to Olive after her first two trips to film. In 2012, we filmed the event as vérité camerapersons tend to do, focusing on actors, the director, family members, and key events such as the stages of the reenactment. While we recorded a few cutaways of the crowd at the Moore's Ford Bridge—again for shot–reverse shot scene construction and time compression options in the editing—neither of us camerapersons filmed the images of spectators featured in the film. These were recorded in 2013 on a tripod, with what seems to have been a smaller crowd looking on. Logan, moreover, did not participate in the 2012 reenactment as an actress. A different actress took her place when she had to leave for a family emergency. The images of Logan participating in this reenactment were recorded in 2011, but they were vital to include given her place in the film's narrative. So though this scene actually includes shots from three different reenactments, the changes from one shot to the next are nearly imperceptible to spectators of the finished film. This backstory again highlights the way that reenactments and simulations on film can blur temporal distinctions across iterations of slightly different live performances. And even though I recorded some of the images in this scene, I did not catch the cross-temporal stitching, so to speak, when I first viewed the film. Neither of us camerapersons filming this scene nor Olive herself discussed the possibility of not showing the morbid conclusion of the reenactment in the finished film. We just filmed it.

Figure 4.4. *Always in Season* juxtaposes images of Black audience members watching the Moore's Ford Lynching Reenactment (*top*) with photographs of white attendees at actual lynchings in the early 1900s (*bottom*). Frame grabs from *Always in Season*. Photography (*top*) by Patrick Sheehan. Courtesy Jacqueline Olive.

In the previous chapter, I discussed the default way that my camerawork in 2012 ended up positioned with the reenactors playing the lynch mob. It is worth asking how the codes of the kind of camerawork I and many others practice tend to be out of step with the logic of the oppositional acousmetre that Olive deployed here in the finished film. Again, the sound of the lynching reenactment plays with a montage of images of spectators. But the twist here disallows the audience to identify in an unproblematic way with a spectator like Logan. Instead, the images of white faces looking toward the camera meld with the sounds and the images of contemporary Black spectators looking at the reenactment—with expressions of nearly opposite affects. Again, the impact of the scene is to startle the viewer, and especially the white viewer, to rethink their processes of perception. They must visibly confront their mirror in those postcards, must experience the cognitive dissonance of identifying bits of self in the faces and bodies of lynchers past, and feel the vestiges of those acts as pain in the present of the reenactment. It propels the awkward dissonance of being complicit by dint of quietly accepting whiteness as a fact of life, like those people who look like neighbors. The montage of two times, two sets of spectators framed in the image in similar ways, generates the indexical jolt of a third thing, a code remade.

What does the photographic evidence of lynching events index at this moment in Olive's film? Combined with off-screen sound of the lynching reenactment, the archival lynching photographs are neither indices of past events alone nor symbols of ongoing violence. Combined, they shift attention. In two times, actual people attended a well-publicized event. In both, the event itself used the modern technologies of mechanical reproduction to spread the feelings of the event beyond the bounds of locality. The disavowal of watching a lynching manifest in the film's form does not offer white viewers an easy out from a sense of accountability for lynching itself—indeed, it coerces the white viewer momentarily into the subject position of Klansman lyncher, the very role I had tried to avoid in my fieldwork. Such viewers can hear that accountability well enough through the simulation of its sound. The oppositional acousmetre unfolds across the interstices of sounds heard off screen and fused images of gazing, presented alternately for the purposes of acknowledging pain and affirming complicity in racial terrorism by silence, by the default position of the spectator in the darkened theater.

CONCLUSION: REVIEWING THE FILM AND REENACTMENT

Reviewers of the film have noted these scenes as a catalyst for uncomfortable affective experiences. "I consider myself a hardened, even cynical viewer of staged violence and yet I was shaken," wrote Odie Henderson of RogerEbert.com. One reviewer in attendance at the Sundance premiere recalled sitting afterward with Olive "in the basement of this bougie house in a room with *Star Wars* posters on the wall." She had sat between Claudia and Pierre Lacy during the film and found the perspective presented within it to be shattering in ways that she struggled to put into words. "I am awkward and fumbling in my interview," she wrote in the present tense, as if reliving the moment. "Olive's research—Lennon Lacy's story—is too much for me to process. I feel angry that we are even having this conversation—that people in the race I am identified with can be so abhorrent."[26] Conservative-learning white viewers in our polarized time are unlikely to take this particular conclusion from the film, but in an in-depth, nationwide study of reception in *Always in Season* community screenings conducted in 2020 by the team of documentary impact scholars at American University's Center for Media and Social Impact, 99 percent of survey participants "who live in counties reflecting demographic, geographic and political diversity" agreed that the "documentary provided a true portrayal of a real problem." Around 90 percent reported that they found themselves "wondering how they would feel and behave if they were in any one of the characters positions."[27] Significantly, and I believe largely because of the way the film blends narrative conventions with strategic oppositional disruptions, viewers from across the political spectrum can see lynching and racial violence in the film as "can be" rather than "was." It is an opening for a dialogue in the present, and one that Olive and her team worked diligently to expand in the months after the film's release and national PBS broadcast. The outcome of these conversations is yet to be determined in a context after the murder of George Floyd that ignited a national conversation about race, camerawork, and white-on-Black violence. But the form of the film in these key moments of representation is instructive. Neither reproducing the aspirational realism of the Moore's Ford Lynching Reenactment nor focusing narrowly on the Lacy case as a story about an individual murder, *Always in Season* taps into the affective infrastructure offered by the reenactment to frame the interpretation of the contemporary instances of racially suspicious death. The film testifies, ironically, to the ongoing value of the live reenactment performance at Moore's Ford Bridge.

    I do not believe any of the lynch mob will be prosecuted, but there is no quicker way to defang the political affect bound up in this unresolved lynching cold case than to stop reenacting it. To give up on the reenactment, even if all the members of the lynch mob have died, would be to abandon all the advantages for media strategy of reenacting the event on location in Georgia distant enough from Atlanta to avoid severe repercussions for those playing key roles (as has been the case for locals) but not so far away as to be an undue burden to organize, attend, and participate for Atlanta-based progressives. The failure to address discrepancies between archival evidence, memories, and performance, especially on disputes about the Malcom pregnancy, may discredit the reenactment for some, but genuine disagreements over such details need not derail the efforts to continue performing this story. Black Georgia residents, moreover, grow media savvier by the year. They need places to learn and practice acting, recording, distributing, and discussing media representations better attuned to issues they deem important than playing South African extras, for instance, on an Adam Sandler and Drew Barrymore destination rom-com filmed in Georgia.[28] As an affective infrastructure, the Moore's Ford Lynching Reenactment continues to provide tools for intervening in and perhaps repairing legal, economic, and political infrastructures that operate in Georgia under the guise of neutrality. Organizers include descendants of the Dorseys and the Malcoms, and at least some seem pleased to learn about this story and channel it into politics. For its part, *Always in Season* models how to use this simulation documentary without reproducing the most troubling aspects of a realist representation of lynching history, how to document a protest that features spectacle and sensationalism without reproducing too many of those effects, and how to teach perception practices around Black death to audiences who are not so reliably Black.

NOTES

1. Galuppo, "Feature Film Production."
2. Dockterman, "How Georgia Became."
3. Bell and Shivas staff, "Knocked Down, but Not Out."
4. Democracy Now!, "Unsolved Case of Racial Terror."
5. See, for instance, Bailey, "Moore's Ford Massacre."
6. Greene, interview.
7. Eisenstein, "Cinematographic Principle."
8. For an overview of writing on media infrastructures, see L. Parks and Starosielski, *Signal Traffic*.
9. Star and Ruhleder, "Ecology of Infrastructure."
10. Olachea and Olive, "ALWAYS IN SEASON Filmmaker."
11. Ibid.
12. Ibid.
13. Mitchell, *Living with Lynching*.
14. Stevenson is the executive director of the Equal Justice Initiative. This nonprofit organization operates the Legacy Museum, an indoor exhibit hall that traces legacies of racial terror from enslavement to mass incarceration, and the National Memorial for Peace and Justice, an outdoor installation space that acknowledges those 4,400 Black Americans known to have been lynched between 1877 and 1950. Both are located just outside of Montgomery, Alabama. The Equal Justice Initiative website states that before the opening of the memorial in 2018, there was "no national museum acknowledging the victims of racial terror lynchings." See Equal Justice Initiative, "Legacy Museum."

15. Unrelated to Olive's editorial choice, Brooks fell from his public position as Georgia state representative in late 2015. Convicted of tax, mail, and wire fraud for transferring funds donated to a literacy nonprofit he oversaw to a personal bank account (he said that he was guilty of "bad bookkeeping" and questioned why he was targeted), Brooks resigned from the Georgia Congress and spent time in federal prison. See Cook, "Former State Rep."

16. Mulvey, "Visual Pleasure and Narrative Cinema"; Chion, "From 'The Voice in Cinema'"; hooks, "Oppositional Gaze."

17. As Alexandra Juhasz pointed out, the "feminist realist debates" across this period led to the canonization of avant-garde and formalist makers such as Mulvey, Chantal Ackerman, and Yvonne Rainer at the expense of feminist filmmakers who worked in a realist mode. This prioritization, Juhasz argued, inadequately considered the ways that "realism and identification are used as viable theoretical strategies toward political ends within these films." Juhasz, "They Said We Were Trying," 194.

18. It is worth noting that Dash's *Illusions* in fact centers on the production of an acousmatic cinema moment, unacknowledged as such. In the film, Mignon Dupree comes to a Hollywood studio in 1942 to dub over the flubbed audio-recording of a white actress singing a love song. The cut from Dupree in close-up in the studio to the close-up of the white actress on screen singing with what we now understand to be Dupree's voice exposes a kind of discriminatory ventriloquism, in Pooja Rangan's characterization. Rangan delves into the second ventriloquism in this fiction film, the use of Billie Holliday's recording to dub over the performance of Marlon Dupree, a kind of double surrogacy. I return to her analysis of ventriloquism and voice in documentary in subsequent sections. Rangan, "Skin of the Voice."

19. Protevi, *Political Affect*, 46–50.

20. This phrase is indebted to the title of Sturken and Cartwright, *Practices of Looking*.

21. See the published short made from this footage at Creative Loafing Atlanta, "Moore's Ford Bridge Lynching Reenactment."

22. Rangan, "Skin of the Voice," 137–38.

23. Owen and Ehrenhaus, "Moore's Ford Lynching Reenactment," 72; Sedgwick, *Touching Feeling*, 69–70.

24. Sobchack, "Toward a Phenomenology," 247.

25. Brinkema, *Forms of the Affects*, 1–8.

26. Henderson, "Always in Season Movie Review"; Thatcher, "Facing the Past."

27. Conrad, Borum Chattoo, and Aufderheide, *Breaking the Silence*.

28. One reenactor whom I interviewed in 2019 credited serving as an extra on the film *Blended* (2014) with exposing him to the possibilities of working in logistics for films made in Georgia. Though the film was set largely on a resort in South Africa, many scenes were recorded at locations in Georgia, including a cricket scene filmed at a baseball stadium. See Brett, "Drew Barrymore and Adam Sandler."

CONCLUSION

Toward an Embodied Social Cinema, or From Point of View to Social Sense

THIS BOOK HAS BUILT ON documentary theory about camerawork and film spectatorship to explore the context of recursive, embodied, cinematic reenactments of history, which I have referred to as simulation documentaries. Akin to the reenactors who seek out revelations about past lives through performance, camerapersons seek out affective moments in the present to create films through which future audiences might experience revelations. But such moments tend not to be visible in simulation documentaries. Generative concepts in critical race theory and affect theory intimate an area in documentary studies focused on how such affective moments renew ritual performances of traumatic historical events and then shape media interpretations and discourses about them. The case studies in this book—on reenactments entailed in filming performed evocations of the Vietnam War, military training simulations that treat cultural performance as a new kind of weapon, and civil rights activists balancing reenactment performance, dignified witnessing, and broad media coverage of a racial atrocity—are emblematic of issues worthy of scholarly attention within a film studies approach to political affect.

I have charted out three major arguments applicable to ongoing conversations in the fields of documentary studies and performance studies. First, as I argued in the introduction and chapter 1, the concept of indexicality as filmic inscription is too narrow and too grounded in a technological understanding of the term to account for the role of affect in the embodied perception of evidence. Key to indexicality when cameras are common is not celluloid or digital medium but rather the startling, ephemeral experience of perceptive orientation being remade. I have drawn insights from affect theory and used the methods of media phenomenology to offer new spaces for theorizing indexicality. I apply insights on indexicality from documentary studies to a particular object: the ephemeral break in the continuity of routine wrought by the overwhelming sense of lost history. Tuning into these breaks is central to the affective labor of documentary camerapersons and reenactment performers alike.

Second, I have argued that thinking about documentary as resemblance to historical events is too cynical. The idea that indexicality no longer matters or is possible in the digital age because the image is made of binary code like a computer program ignores social use, material costs inherent to the manipulation of moving images, and the significance of numbers of cameras for reframing our collective orientation to time and feeling. It is too cynical because resemblance is also the centerpiece of simulation theory, which disavows the very possibility of documentary. I agree that the rise of mass media played a role in changing the meaning, scope, and scale of symbolic exchange, and simulation theory applies aptly to the military's conception of culture investigated in chapter 2, for instance. It is a useful theory to keep in mind when thinking about reenactments like those analyzed in chapter 1, where personal nostalgia for martial masculinity inhibits clear-eyed structural critique of colonial war-making in Vietnam. But writing before the proliferation of cameras and distribution platforms, simulation theorists looked past phenomenology as a method that could offer insight into material relations that structure the social. Whether or not our human world is heading toward a nihilistic end (and evidence does not allow for explicitly ruling out this possibility), there are limitations to the kind of hyperbolic, masculinist writing that this tradition emphasizes, as Vivian Sobchack has pointed out.[1] Reenactment rituals can generate mutual accountability, spontaneity, vulnerability, and hybrid identities in a variety of ways, including through practices in theater, psychodrama, cultural history, and nonfiction filmmaking. These shared departures into imagined history in the present can constitute critical knowledge, dialogue, and strength for a collective.

Third, I offered instead to consider embodiment as the location of indexicality, with case studies focusing on the dynamics of race in creating and perceiving evidence. I find this a promising direction for three reasons. First, in the digital context, recording technologies are widely distributed, cheap, and small. They are more like parts of the everyday lived body than technologies reserved for professionals. Because photographic media are woven into everyday life, their capacity to register subjective perception and expression matters as much as their older capacity to serve as evidence of events external to subjectivity. Second, embodiment is promising for media production that welcomes intersubjectivity and hybridity like *Always in Season*, an increasingly relevant orientation toward everyday life considering processes of globalization and practices of media sharing. Third, analyzing embodiment helps trace the iterative internalization and projection of cinematic affects, which I aimed to tease out in all case studies. Reenactments are ritual performances of activities collectively understood to be of the past that nonetheless change subtly in the context of the present. Though sometimes regressive, they can offer a forum for working through or confronting injustice. Reenactments can trouble linear time. They can open new spaces for developing agency, expressing doubt, and practicing politics attuned to the dynamics of simulation and the ubiquity of cameras.

When everyone has a camera, in short, the stories we tell about documentary's origins can change. In this context, I am trying to imagine a story about embodied documentary practice rooted in ephemeral feelings of connection to the past rather than images or papers created in a previous time. The past is always with us in this way but reveals itself only in certain places, at certain times. It catches us and startles, sometimes grooving habits of expectation or intensifying a sense of connection. From this vantage, the story of documentary need not center on white men who used the advanced technologies of their time to treat the actuality of others creatively.

As I wrote this conclusion, the world convulsed in reaction to the ten-minute, single-take citizen smartphone video of Minneapolis police officer Derek Chauvin employing a knee-on-neck hold to asphyxiate George Floyd. The long-take camerawork technique deployed to create this video had been honed by community activists associated with Black Lives Matter, Copblock, WEcopwatch, Cop Block, and NYC Resistance to provide a way for citizens to witness and legally record unfolding encounters with police and then rapidly disseminate the records online through social media sharing. Such single-shot documentary videos aimed both to record unfolding events and to shape the behaviors recorded across an evolving, interpersonal interaction. Jeffrey Skoller argued that in this present-tense documentary form, camerapersons used their cameras first and foremost for "shifting the dynamic of power in the interaction" and "momentarily denaturalizing the terms of power" between officer and Black citizen.[2] When filmer and subject share a somewhat common understanding of potential future implications for a recorded interaction once shared, the record-in-making can function performatively to alter the unfolding present. For the Black cameraperson, it is also a partial safety mechanism that was not available to previous generations of activists, who had to hope for and rely on the presence of professional TV news crews at demonstrations. In some respects, organizing campaigns and events for news cameras in the civil rights movement of the 1960s gave way to this kind of citizen smartphone recording of incidents involving police. When recording fails to alter the present, however, the liveness of the inequitable power dynamic and failure of police to serve constituents seems to store up in the video, so to speak, for future unleashing on vastly different terms. The long-take recording will not necessarily save the life of the citizen recorded, in other words, but it will augment the political power of the record when it does not. The future replay and reenactment of the moment of recording contains a poignant seed of contradiction that cannot be let go, though Chauvin ignored or misinterpreted such implications. This was "nothing less than a public lynching," reflected Black UK Labour parliamentarian Clive Lewis, echoing in words the visual aesthetic so central to Olive's representation of lynching in *Always in Season*: "Like countless lynchers before, murder suspect Derek Chauvin looks calmly into the lens of the camera, with the self-assurance of someone who has done this before and will do it again, with impunity."[3]

I must note that it took me a week to build up the courage, tolerance, ethical rationale—something—just to watch the video of Floyd's murder at the center of national uprisings. Others have also grappled with the "choice" about whether or not to look at videos of police killings of Black men and women, which can reproduce trauma especially in Black viewers and elicit strong negative affective responses that do not necessarily translate, Alex Juhasz points out, to "the larger ethical and political needs of movements for social justice."[4] Jennifer Malkowski notes that "death's limitless repetition in time and multiplication in space" via YouTube distribution can numb viewers to the shock of such imagery and end up exploited as a commodity in an attention economy in which graphic depictions of violent actual death garner more views (and company profits) but not necessarily appropriate justice.[5] For similar reasons, the NAACP circulates images or videos depicting Black death infrequently and only when doing so serves a clear policy goal.[6] But given that police kill Black Americans at a rate comparable to the number of lynchings documented during the early twentieth century, Kimberly Fain insists that "we should acknowledge and absorb the pain captured in these videos" to spur policy change. She and others write about these images as sacred for their power to create a liminal space and hail a new kind of collective. "When viral Black death transforms the white cultural gaze from perceived Black criminality toward shared racial empathy," Fain concluded in her 2016 reflection on the videotaped police killings of Philando Castile and Alton Sterling, "interracial efforts for reforming policing in America seem within our grasp."[7] To actualize "seem" in these potentially transformative moments of mediatized liminality is to resist the pitfalls of empathy as consumption.

The video is devastating. It is not an occasion to celebrate, and I worry for the seventeen-year-old cameraperson, Darnella Frazier. The police harassed

Ramsey Orta, the young man who filmed the police killing of Eric Garner on Staten Island on July 17, 2014, for a year afterward. "The cops had been following me every day since Eric died, shining lights in my house every night," he told a reporter several years later. Police ultimately arrested him on weapons and drug possession charges, which he claims were false. He claimed that wardens physically and psychologically abused him once he was in prison and may have tried to poison his food.[8] We should note with care and attention what happens to Frazier in the coming years and do what we can to support and protect her. She should have the opportunity to grow up without fear of police reprisal and with resources to help deal with the trauma of what she recorded and its fallout.

Before posting the video of Floyd's murder, Frazier had used her smartphone camera to live-broadcast a view out of a window of her house so she could talk through the incident with her high school friends. Camerawork here functioned as the backdrop for a multimodal interaction, as she told her story and answered questions posted as comments on the Facebook live feed. At least for the time being, it is all archived on her page as an ever-present historical documentary artifact of sorts, created in the liminal time between private knowledge and public outrage. The handheld, vertical image centers through a window screen on out-of-focus, flashing emergency lights in the distance surrounded by the darkness of night. We presume that Frazier could see the location where Floyd had been murdered from her home as she talks. "At first, they said he wasn't fittin' to die," she reflects for her friends as a new set of lights merges with the others in the distance. "He was just fittin' to get knocked out or whatever, but then they still here, and if it wasn't a murder they wouldn't still be here." Frazier posted the entire ten-minute video soon thereafter and hoped that Facebook would not take it down for violating the platform's terms of service.[9]

I learned something important from her video. Having read newspaper accounts of the "involuntary manslaughter" charge against Chauvin, I had assumed that this was an incident of police procedure gone wrong, of a mistake that required reform, retraining, cultural change, and better measures of accountability among police. It is difficult to watch the entirety of the clip and not consider the possibility that Chauvin intended to kill Floyd. Frazier recorded from the sidewalk among other bystanders who repeatedly implored Chauvin, his two trainee officers pressing on Floyd's back and legs, and lookout officer Tou Thou to get off Floyd and check his pulse. As with Olive's film and the footage of the Selma march in 1965, some of the most compelling evidence in the recording is acousmatic, heard but not seen. One off-screen voice yelled at Chauvin that he practiced jujitsu and recognized the pressing on the neck as a technique to stop an opponent's breathing. In one instance after Floyd had lost consciousness, Frazier and others on the sidewalk took a step toward Chauvin. Thou aggressively demanded that they retreat, and Chauvin pulled out his mace and pointed it at the camera while keeping his knee on Floyd's neck. Given the urgent and insistent commentary of the five or so off-screen speakers pleading with the police officers, it is simply not tenable that the officers were unaware that Floyd had lost consciousness. When the emergency medical technician finally arrived, Frazier's video reveals their cursory check of Floyd's pulse. His body was briskly moved into the back of an unlit ambulance without any effort at resuscitation, as if they already knew that he was dead. The technological indexicality of the video allows all of these contingent details to pass through Frazier's recording to viewers and speaks to why documentary studies has valued this kind of indexicality as a grounding concept. The details I mention are undeniable and verifiable. But Frazier was neither scientist nor observer here; turning on the camera had to do with the connection she felt to Floyd.[10]

Perhaps as poignant as Frazier's video was the fact that before she posted it—and just hours after she recorded the video of the murder—the Minneapolis Police Department issued a press release titled "Man Dies after Medical Incident during Police Interaction." This link no longer leads to a story, however—just a "page not found" notice. "Medical incident???" Frazier posted at 2:10 a.m. that morning. "Watch outtt they killed him and the proof is clearlyyyy there!!" The police report made its way to local news organizations, who published it as "Man Dies of Medical Incident in Police Custody," which Frazier reposted and reframed at 5:25 a.m. "They are literally lying!! Pls watch the video on my page!" she wrote.[11] By May 31, the *New York Times* had compiled surveillance footage and other bystander clips to fill out details absent from Frazier's recording, which began after Floyd had already been pinned to the ground. Floyd had not resisted arrest. The police had instructed a second citizen cameraperson, who had a view from the opposite side of the patrol car, to stop recording. Independent autopsy reports concluded that the cause of death was homicide.[12]

Across the two weeks following Floyd's death, Frazier's Facebook page became a forum for expressions of solidarity, gratitude, disbelief, and anger. Twenty thousand comments testified to the breadth and scope of this distant but meaningful form of bearing witness. "Because of this the world can see our plight," read one that concluded with a Black Lives Matter hashtag. "They can't deny it anymore." Contributors hailed from Sudan, China, England, Zambia, Brazil, Germany, Nigeria, France, Australia, and many (if not all) of the states in the United States. "This is exactly the cruelty we were facing during apartheid," wrote a contributor from South Africa. Other Black Americans expressed concern for Frazier. "Watch your back girl," wrote one in this vein. "Ain't easy to wage war on cops. Never be alone. May God protect you always." Some recommended that Frazier start seeing a therapist to help deal with the trauma of recording the video and then coping with the fallout. "You are the bravest 17-year-old out there. Be sure to take care of yourself and be safe out there," wrote a woman from New York. "Seek counseling ASAP! You are blessed. There are so many people standing with you!!"[13]

And apropos of the project of this book, debate about the documentary framing of Frazier's video began within days of its release. Film critic Ross Johnson published an ill-advised interpretation of Frazier's "cinematography" soon after it emerged online, anointing her "the most influential filmmaker of the century." He worked this attempt at homage from within the auteur school, describing subtleties of movement that kept Frazier's subject in frame as if she were reinventing structural filmmaking or cinema vérité rather than documenting a murder. Tonja Renée Stidhum's blistering response summarized the core problem with Johnson's approach: "Frazier's recording isn't 'truth cinema' in the pretentious sense of film analysis, in so much that it served as a significant step in the ongoing journey toward securing justice for Floyd."[14] And while Johnson's take borders on caricature, there is something in Stidhum's response worth noting about elitist considerations of nonfiction aesthetics and the liberatory politics attributed to long-take art documentary.

In a historical moment in which digital citizens have cameras that can function as extensions of their bodies and subjectivities, ironically, I want to suggest rethinking the techno-historicist mode through which documentary studies has long framed its subject. In Bill Nichols's canonical telling, the expository mode of the 1930s and 1940s roughly gave way to observational and participatory forms of cinema from the 1950s to the 1970s, which roughly gave way to reflexive filmmaking that questioned the apparatus of claiming reality itself in the 1980s and 1990s. An interactive mode that employed user selection within online platforms and nonlinear engagements with media then emerged in the 2000s, and he described "performative documentary" as sort of mushing across these times to refer to documentaries that would "have us feel or experience the world in a particular way as vividly as possible."[15] In this story about how documentary evolved, watershed moments in technological development fueled the emergence of new documentary modes, even as the older ones lingered on and the new ones kept returning to ancient forms of rhetoric. From beginning to end, "introduction to documentary" is about films.

Few moments were more significant to documentary, in this story, than the development of synch-sound technology around 1960, which facilitated direct cinema and cinema vérité experiments in being there for the professional journalists and documentarians excited about leaving behind the studio's expensive, bulky cameras and managerial oversight. The 1960s and 1970s fascination with being there, spontaneity, and the indexical in art dovetailed with the broader countercultural zeitgeist for turning away from the bureaucratic institutions of governance, corporate capitalism, and militarization and toward transcendence, empathy, and spontaneity. To be there with a camera, in that moment, was not so far off from participating in a hallucinogenic be-in or a performance art happening. All expressed a faith or a hope that technologized extensions of self could transcend the time and space of the individual body-consciousness to shatter its preconceptions and remake community on new ground.[16] To counter cliché industrial cinema, one could mobilize the long take to challenge habits of perception and embrace contingency. Durational recording might even render the mundane into a what P. Adams Sitney described as "mystical contemplation of a portion of space" in which "time will enter as an aggressive participant in the viewing experience," as Warhol aimed to do with the six-hour *Sleep* (1964) and eight-hour *Empire* (1964).[17] A similar logic is still at the center of the slow cinema movement and the argument for long-duration recording in ethnographic nonfiction art cinema. To look at something for a long duration is to perceive a pace of life or the texture of work, space, or interaction rather than symbolic capital within a fast-cutting commercial documentary regime. For proponents, expressing "duration as material form" opposes conventional media pace without recourse to verbal or written critique, making new affective knowledge through old practices of skillful recording that still provide "a condition of possibility for intrinsically ethical acts, such as recognition, reflection, imagination and empathy."[18] Detractors have come to regard this "way of simulating older cinematic styles" as "profoundly nostalgic and regressive," however. Steven Shaviro prefers oppositional media practices that better engage with the twenty-first-century media environment, arguing that "you cannot change a situation if you are unwilling to have anything to do with it."[19]

The long-take smartphone videos of encounters with police, though on the street and created out of the unscripted copresence between filmer and subject, have little to do with this documentary tradition. Frazier was a seventeen-year-old kid, not an acolyte of Fred Wiseman or Andy Warhol. The impetus to record had less to do with fascination or understanding or transcendence than civil disobedience. The camera is inseparable from the body behind it and here from the oppositional impulse entangled in recording. In this light, we might rather recast this documentary history as originating in another watershed "technology" of 1960, the embodied lunch-counter sit-ins that started in Greensboro, North Carolina, to "document" racist laws. I read the sit-ins as a simulation documentary. This first direct-action campaign of the civil rights movement was repeatable, recursive, adaptable to different spatial and political circumstances but tied to locations, youthful, seductive for news cameras, and focused on creating a public narrative about Black dignity and equal rights. It both simulated and embodied racist contradictions embedded in law and culture through long-duration aesthetics, here the daily performance from opening to closing of sitting at the lunch counter of a local drug store. The script for spontaneity went viral. Sit-ins spread across dozens of cities across the South in a matter of days and everywhere occupied space in ways that startled copresent whites uncomfortably, compelling some to allyship and others to revealing resistance. Connections across protesters were transcendent through number, solidarity, and ideological position rather than shared experience of technology or time spent in a cinema seat with others watching ice melt on screen. Participants in sit-ins nonetheless determined—even compelled—the copresence of professional camerapersons who followed their oppositional action. It transformed those who participated in it into leaders such as John Lewis and Diane Nash and garnered the attention of national television news crews who created films about it. The movement used these television films in turn to train new recruits in nonviolent resistance techniques, and Henry Hampton based an episode of *Eyes on the Prize* on the successful sit-in campaign in Nashville in part because this footage allowed him to do so.[20]

It is interesting to note that the four young men who conducted the first sit-in, Ezell Blair Jr. (now Jibreel Khazan), David Richmond, Franklin McCain, and Joseph McNeil, did not contact the press about what they were doing, as they thought of the action as an assertion of dignity. The manager would not allow the one press photographer who heard what they were doing to enter the store. There is one photograph of the four young men walking down the street after they exited the F. W. Woolworth drugstore, but it was only published ten years after this era-shaping event, as the Greensboro paper did not want to promote the protest by granting it too much attention.[21] The photograph is included in *Eyes on the Prize*, but the Greensboro story is reduced to a line, a segue to the Nashville story. It strains credulity to imagine a public protest failing to generate photographs and footage in a twenty-first-century context, when nearly every participant has a camera at the ready. In this light, Frazier's smartphone long-take functions as a twenty-first-century sit-in as much as a documentary record. What would it mean to reimagine the history and future of documentary from this trajectory? What would it mean to consider the work of documentarians as expressive of an embodied social sense rather than a point of view?

This is a project for another book, but Allissa Richardson's monograph suggests a starting point. She emphasizes a long tradition of witnessing among Black people centered on the collective, communal South African philosophy of Ubuntu, "I am because *we* are." Black witnessing, in Richardson's telling, is more complex than simply watching tragic images on TV or recording violent incidents on a phone: "When most African Americans view fatal police shooting videos, something stirs at a cellular level. They want to *do* something with what they just saw." When few have the resources to travel to sites to film events or direct access to broadcast their footage on mass media channels, they must act as "distant witnesses" encumbered by the "weighty baggage" of identification with victims, Richardson argues. Protest practices such as marches, speeches, and reenactments answer the question about how to be there from a distance, how to think about indexical touch as cellular rather than celluloid.[22]

Part of the reason for the difference in response to the video of Floyd's death is that the affective infrastructures established in the Black Lives Matter movement starting in 2013—and in annual events such as the march in Selma and the Moore's Ford Lynching Reenactment—facilitate broad, pointed, consistent, medially flexible direct action on long-standing questions about structural racism. The pathway from indexical artifact of camerawork to the embodied indexical performance of outrage in response constitutes and builds on these affective infrastructures. Quickly, as invocations of the name George Floyd functioned to reinforce—and in some cases create—a sense of collective community identity in public demonstrations, indexicality came to function as affective more than observational, as subjective positioning in gestures of solidarity rather than represented event. There is a kind of momentum to this sort of response, an affective spread that buoys hope as well as danger. A particular insistence on generating fearful, angry affective surges, after all, played a role in the 2016 election and the insurrection at the Capitol after the 2020 election, as well. But this may reflect the shifting terrain of materiality from the visible to the performative rather than the inevitable primacy of fear or cynicism in our politics.

The indexicality of the embodied performances, as with the simulation documentaries I have described in this book, generates complex forms of accountability. Frazier's camerawork and then embodied performance catalyzed recursive, unfolding chains of witnessing, perceiving, and categorizing that have, in the end, more to do with a perspective from which to look and think than a singular event.

A week after the posting of Frazier's video, student activists in my small Ohio town organized a march for Black dignity and mourning for Floyd and countless other Black men and women killed by white vigilantes and police. They led a group of 250 Black and white community members, local politicians, professors, and students to the police station and then on to the courthouse, chanting "Say his name, George Floyd! Say her name, Breonna Taylor!," "No justice, no peace, no racist police," and "Black Lives Matter!" along the way. On the sidewalk and parking spaces in front of the city's courthouse building, the group then staged a reenactment of sorts, an eight-minute, forty-six-second "die-in" to touch the amount of time that Floyd had been pressed into the pavement. It was a spectacle in the sense of drawing attention to and affective investment in our presence on the street and in the media, and it was a simulation in the sense of looking like Floyd's body without the immanence of bodily harm. But the new thoughts and affects that circulate as collective effervescence among a diverse group performing this memorial for the first time are generative, uncomfortable, and shared. Such moments are potentially ruptures, affective starting points for listening well and then seeking out the slow, unrecognized, grinding kind of public service that a healthy democracy requires. Such moments carry the activist spirit of documentary traditions dating to the sit-ins, spreading across the country as instructions, then photographs, and then news stories and citizen videos. Hundreds of thousands of bodies document in their reenactment a will for remaking policing or perhaps the social itself—a will, sadly, that comes and goes. Regardless, if a sustainable body of practices emerges from this generative simulation documentary, it will focus less on being there than on the documentary acts we can do from where we already are.

NOTES

1. Sobchack, "Beating the Meat."
2. Skoller, "IDocument Police."
3. C. Lewis, "George Floyd Was Lynched."
4. Richardson, *Bearing Witness While Black*, xvi; Juhasz, "How Do I (Not) Look?"
5. Malkowski, *Dying in Full Detail*, 170.
6. Richardson, "Cellphone Videos."
7. Fain, "Viral Black Death."
8. C. Jones, "He Filmed the Killing."
9. Frazier, "They really killed."
10. Frazier, "They killed him."
11. Frazier, "Medical incident"; Frazier, "They are literally lying."
12. Hill et al., "Video."
13. Frazier, "They killed him."

14. Stidhum, "George Floyd Homicide Video."

15. Nichols explicitly rejects the framing of performative documentary along the lines of J. L. Austin's definition of performative. "Performance here draws more heavily on the tradition of acting as a way to bring heightened emotional involvement to a situation or role," he says. I have written in this book about performative in documentary along Austinian lines, closer to the approach taken by Stella Bruzzi. Nichols, *Introduction to Documentary*, 151; Bruzzi, *New Documentary*.

16. Turner, *From Counterculture to Cyberculture*, 41–68; Murphy, *Rewriting Indie Cinema*, 282–85; Krauss, "Notes on the Index."

17. Sitney, *Film Culture Reader*, 330.

18. Grønstad, "Slow Cinema," 274.

19. Shaviro, "Slow Cinema vs Fast Films."

20. Vecchione et al., *Eyes on the Prize*; H. Scott, *Younger Than That Now*, 18–32.

21. The photograph and contextual detail are published at Moebes, "David Richmond, Franklin McCain." The documentary *February One* features interviews with these four men and this photograph but uses docudrama-style reenactment footage to simulate the sense of the first sit-in on the eponymous day in 1960. Cerese et al., *February One*.

22. Richardson, Bearing Witness While Black, 5.

FILMOGRAPHY

Allan, Diana, dir. *Terrace of the Sea = Jal al-bahr.* Cambridge, MA: Harvard University, Film Study Center, and Cinema Guild, 2014.
Annaud, Jean-Jacques, dir. *Enemy at the Gates.* Hollywood, CA: Paramount Pictures, 2001.
Attie, Mike, and Meghan O'Hara, dir. *In Country: Reenacting the Vietnam War.* Oregon and San Francisco: Oscar-Alpha Mopic and BOND/360, 2015.
Bacon, Lloyd, dir. *The Frisco Kid.* Burbank, CA: Warner Brothers, 1935.
Bagwell, Orlando, dir. *Eyes on the Prize.* Episode 3, "Ain't Scared of Your Jails (1960–1961)." Boston: Blackside. Aired February 4, 1987, on PBS. http://www.aspresolver.com/aspresolver.asp?MARC;4684723.
Barbash, Ilisa, and Lucien Castaing-Taylor, dir. *Sweetgrass.* Cambridge, MA: Grasshopper Film, 2009. https://www.kanopy.com/product/sweetgrass-0.
Beauchamp, Keith, dir. *The Untold Story of Emmett Louis Till.* Brooklyn, NY: Till Freedom Come Productions, 2005. https://youtu.be/bvijYSJtkQk.
Beauchamp, Keith, and Barnard Jaffier, dir. *Murder in Black and White.* Episode 1, "Moore's Ford Lynching." Brooklyn, NY: Till Freedom Come Productions. Aired October 5, 2008, on TV One. https://vimeo.com/121519485.
Bigelow, Kathryn, dir. *The Hurt Locker.* Hollywood, CA: Voltage Pictures, 2008.
Burns, Ken, and Lynn Novick, dir. *The Vietnam War.* Walpole, NH: Florentine Films. Aired September 17–28, 2017, on PBS. https://www.pbs.org/kenburns/the-vietnam-war/.
Capra, Frank, dir. *Why We Fight.* NYX Channel, 2019. https://uwo.kanopy.com/node/5459116.
Castaing-Taylor, Lucien, and Verena Paravel, dir. *Leviathan.* Cambridge, MA: Films We Like, 2012. https://torontopl.kanopy.com/node/6554379.

Cerese, Rebecca, and Steven Channing, dir. *February One: The Story of the Greensboro Four*. San Francisco: California Newsreel. Aired February 1, 2005, on PBS Independent Lens.
Coogler, Ryan, dir. *Black Panther*. Atlanta, GA: Marvel Studios, 2018.
Coppola, Francis Ford, dir. *Apocalypse Now*. San Francisco: Omni Zoetrope, 1979.
Coraci, Frank, dir. Featuring Adam Sandler and Drew Barrymore. *Blended*. Los Angeles: Happy Madison Productions, 2014.
Cretton, Destin Daniel, dir. *Just Mercy*. Beverly Hills, CA: Endeavor Entertainment, 2019.
Dash, Julie, dir. *Illusions*. Los Angeles: Women Make Movies, 1982. Distributed on Kanopy, 2021. https://www.kanopy.com/product/illusions-0.
Dick, Kirby, dir. *The Invisible War*. Los Angeles: Chain Camera Pictures, 2012.
Drew, Robert, Richard Leacock, D. A. Pennebaker, Albert Maysles, dir. *The Kennedy Films of Robert Drew and Associates*. Aired 1960–1964 on ABC. Distributed on DVD by the Criterion Collection, 2016.
Dunye, Cheryl, dir. *The Watermelon Woman*. New York: First Run Features, 1996.
DuVernay, Ava, dir. *Selma*. Hollywood, CA: Paramount Pictures, 2015.
Favreau, Jon, dir. Featuring Robert Downey Jr. and Gwyneth Paltrow. *Iron Man*. Los Angeles, CA: Marvel Studios, 2008.
Figgis, Mike, dir. Featuring Jeremy Deller and the National Union of Mineworkers. *A Mike Figgis Film of Jeremy Deller's The Battle of Orgreave*. London: Artangel Media, 2001.
Fincher, David, dir. *Fight Club*. Century City, CA: Twentieth Century Studios, 1999.
Gerber, Tony, and Jesse Moss, dir. *Full Battle Rattle*. New York: Market Road Films and Mile End Films, 2008.
Goldovskaia, Marina Evseevna, dir. *The Prince Is Back*. Los Angeles: Goldfilms, 2000.
Gray, Susan, and Bestor Cram, dir. Based on the book by Dick Lehr. *Birth of a Movement: The Battle against America's First Blockbuster*. Boston: Northern Light Productions. Aired on February 6, 2017, on PBS.
Greaves, William, dir. *Symbiopsychotaxiplasm: Take One*. New York: Take One Productions, 1968. Distributed by Kanopy, 2014. http://ucsb.kanopystreaming.com/node/113042.
Greene, Robert, dir. *Bisbee '17*. New York: Grasshopper Film, 2018. https://deschutes.kanopy.com/node/6251215.
Griffith, D. W., dir. Featuring Lillian Gish and Mae Marsh. *The Birth of a Nation*. Hollywood, CA: David W. Griffith Corp. and Epoch Producing Corp., 1915.
Har'el, Alma, dir. *Bombay Beach*. Los Angeles, CA: Focus Features, 2011.
Hawks, Howard, dir. *Barbary Coast*. San Francisco: Samuel Goldwyn Productions and United Artists, 1935.

Hirsch, Lee, dir. *Bully*. New York: Cinereach, 2011. https://canterbury.kanopy
.com/node/1290373.
Hitchcock, Alfred, dir. *Psycho*. Universal City, CA: Universal Studios, 1960.
Jarecki, Andrew, dir. *The Jinx: The Life and Deaths of Robert Durst*. New York: HBO Documentary Films and Blumhouse Television, 2015.
Johnson, Kirsten, dir. *Cameraperson*. New York: Fork Films, Big Mouth Productions, and Criterion Collection, 2016.
Kiarostami, Abbas, dir. *Kluz ap, numa-yi nazdik = Close-Up*. Iran: Kanoon and Celluloid Dreams, 1990. Distributed on DVD by the Criterion Collection, 2010.
Kotcheff, Ted, dir. Featuring Sylvester Stallone. *Rambo: First Blood*. Los Angeles, CA: Orion Pictures, 1982.
Kramer, Stanley, dir. *Judgment at Nuremberg*. Germany: Roxiom Films, 1961.
Kubrick, Stanley, dir. *Full Metal Jacket*. London: Natant, 1987.
Lang, Fritz, dir. *Fury*. Hollywood, CA: Metro-Goldwyn-Mayer, 1936.
———. *M*. Berlin, Germany: Nero-Film A.G. and Vereinigte Star-Film, 1931. Distributed on DVD by the Criterion Collection, 2004.
———. *Metropolis*. Berlin, Germany: UFA and Parufamet, 1927. https://www.kanopy.com/en/video/114333.
Laurence, John, dir. *The World of Charlie Company*. New York: CBS. Aired July 14, 1970, on CBS.
LeRoy, Mervyn, dir. *They Won't Forget*. Burbank, CA: Warner Brothers, 1937.
Levin, Marc, dir. Featuring Anna Deavere Smith. *Twilight—Los Angeles*. New York: Offline Entertainment Group and WNET, 2000.
Lusztig, Irene, dir. *Yours in Sisterhood: A Collective Portrait of Feminist Conversations from Ms. Magazine*. Santa Cruz, CA: Women Make Movies, 2018. https://uwo.kanopy.com/node/5880746.
Maitland, Keith, dir. *Tower*. Austin, TX: Tower Documentary, Independent Television Service, and Kino Lorber, 2016.
Marzynski, Marian, dir. *Patriots Day*. Boston: American Experience. Aired April 19, 2004, on PBS. https://vimeo.com/86734113.
Micheaux, Oscar, dir. *Within Our Gates*. Chicago, IL: Micheaux Book and Film Company, 1920. https://www.kanopy.com/en/miamioh/video/278620.
Morris, Errol, dir. *The Thin Blue Line*. Santa Monica, CA: Metro Goldwyn Mayer Home Entertainment, 1988. Distributed by IFC Films, 2005.
Mulvey, Laura, and Peter Wollen, dir. *Riddles of the Sphinx*. London: BFI Production Board and Women Make Movies, 1977. https://docuseek2.com/wm-rots.
New York Times. "The Ferguson Case, Verbatim." Op-Docs, *New York Times*, August 6, 2015. https://www.youtube.com/watch?v=pQXbEUEtf2U.
———. "Verbatim: What Is a Photocopier?" Op-Docs, *New York Times*, April 28, 2014. https://www.youtube.com/watch?v=PZbqAMEwtOE.

Olive, Jacqueline, dir. *Always in Season*. San Francisco: Tell It Media, 2019.
Oppenheimer, Joshua, dir. *The Act of Killing*. Copenhagen, Denmark: Final Cut for Real, 2012.
Paravel, Véréna, and J. P. Sniadecki, dir. *Foreign Parts*. Cambridge, MA: Harvard Sensory Ethnography Lab, 2010.
Reed, Peyton, dir. *Ant-Man and the Wasp*. Atlanta, GA: Marvel Studios, 2018.
Rice, Andy, dir. *About Face! Reenacting in a Time of War*. Cambridge, MA, and San Diego, CA: AndyRiceFilms. YouTube, 2012. https://www.youtube.com/watch?v=6jRl1pnsZ_E.
Rithy Panh, dir. *S21: The Khmer Rouge Killing Machine*. Brooklyn, NY: First Run/Icarus Films, 2003.
Ross, RaMell, dir. *Hale County This Morning, This Evening*. Hale County, AL: Doc and Film International, 2018. https://canterbury.kanopy.com/node/6520421.
Russo, Joe, and Anthony Russo, dir. *Avengers: Infinity War*. Atlanta, GA: Marvel Studios, 2018.
Scott, Ridley, dir. *Black Hawk Down*. Hollywood, CA: Columbia Pictures, 2001.
Silverbush, Lori, and Kristi Jacobson, dir. *A Place at the Table*. Los Angeles: Participant Media, 2013.
Sniadecki, J. P., and Joshua Neves, dir. *Tie dao = The Iron Ministry*. Cambridge, MA: DGenerate Films, 2014. http://docuseek2.com/df-iro.
Sommers, Stephen, dir. *G.I. Joe: The Rise of Cobra*. Hollywood, CA: Paramount Home Entertainment, 2009.
Spielberg, Steven, dir. Featuring Tom Hanks. *Saving Private Ryan*. Los Angeles, CA: DreamWorks Pictures and Paramount Pictures, 1998.
Stefanov, Ljubomir, and Tamara Kotevska, dir. *Honeyland*. North Macedonia: Trice Films and Apolo Media, 2020.
Tajiri, Rea, dir. *History and Memory*. Chicago: Video Data Bank, 2018.
Vecchione, Judith, Steve Fayer, Orlando Bagwell, Callie Crossley, James A. DeVinney, and Madison Davis Lacy, dir. Executive produced by Henry Hampton. *Eyes on the Prize*. Boston: Blackside. Aired January 21–February 25, 1987, on PBS.
Wellman, William, dir. *The Ox-Bow Incident*. Hollywood, CA: Twentieth Century Fox, 1947.
Warhol, Andy, dir. *Empire*. New York: Warhol Films, 1965.
Winterfilm, Vietnam Veterans against the War, and Milliarium Zero. *Winter Soldier*. Harrington Park, NJ: Milliarium Zero, 1972. Distributed by New Yorker Video, 2006.
Yezbick, Julia, dir. *Into the Hinterlands*. Cambridge, MA: Harvard University, Sensory Ethnography Lab, 2018.
Zwick, Edward, dir. Featuring Matthew Broderick, Denzel Washington, and Morgan Freeman. *Glory*. Culver City, CA: Freddie Fields Productions and Tri-Star Pictures, 1989.

BIBLIOGRAPHY

Ackerman, Spencer. "Rare Photographs Show Ground Zero of the Drone War." *Wired*, December 12, 2011. https://www.wired.com/2011/12/photos-pakistan-drone-war/?pageid=63671&pid=999&viewall=true.
Aguayo, Angela J. *Documentary Resistance: Social Change and Participatory Media*. New York: Oxford University Press, 2019.
Allen, James, Jack Woody, and Arlyn Nathan. *Without Sanctuary: Lynching Photography in America*. Santa Fe, NM: Twin Palms, 2000.
Anable, Aubrey. *Playing with Feelings: Video Games and Affect*. Minneapolis: University of Minnesota Press, 2019.
Anderson, Jay. *Time Machines: The World of Living History*. Nashville, TN: American Association for State and Local History, 1984.
Ang, Ien. *Watching Dallas: Soap Opera and the Melodramatic Imagination*. London: Routledge, 1991.
Armstrong, Julie Buckner. *Mary Turner and the Memory of Lynching*. Athens: University of Georgia Press, 2011.
Atlanta Journal-Constitution. "Clinton Adams Recalls the Lynching at Moore's Ford." YouTube, December 28, 2017. https://www.youtube.com/watch?v=DOpPPxu649I.
Attie, Mike. Phone interview by Andy Rice, May 27, 2015.
Aufderheide, Patricia, Peter Jaszi, and Mridu Chandra. *Honest Truths: Documentary Filmmakers on Ethical Challenges in Their Work*. Center for Social Media, September 2009. https://doi.org/10.17606/2XGP-DF57.
Auslander, Mark. "Contesting the Roadways: The Moore's Ford Lynching Reenactment and a Confederate Flag Rally, July 25, 2015." *Southern Spaces* (blog), August 19, 2015. https://southernspaces.org/2015/contesting-roadways-moores-ford-lynching-reenactment-and-confederate-flag-rally-july-25-2015/.

———. "'Give Me Back My Children!': Traumatic Reenactment and Tenuous Democratic Public Spheres." *North American Dialogue* 17, no. 1 (2014): 1–12.

———. "'Holding on to Those Who Can't Be Held': Reenacting a Lynching at Moore's Ford, Georgia." *Southern Spaces* (blog), November 8, 2010. https://southernspaces.org/2010/holding-those-who-cant-be-held-reenacting-lynching-moores-ford-georgia/.

Auslander, Philip. *Reactivations*. Ann Arbor: University of Michigan Press, 2018.

Azoulay, Ariella. *The Civil Contract of Photography*. Translated by Rela Mazali and Ruvik Danieli. New York: Zone Books, 2008.

Bailey, Chelsea. "Moore's Ford Massacre: Activists Reenact Racist Lynching as a Call for Justice." NBC News, August 2, 2017. https://www.nbcnews.com/news/nbcblk/moore-s-ford-massacre-activists-reenact-racist-lynching-call-justice-n787831.

Balsom, Erika. "The Reality-Based Community." *E-Flux Journal*, no. 83 (June 2017). https://www.e-flux.com/journal/83/142332/the-reality-based-community/.

Baron, Jaimie. *The Archive Effect: Found Footage and the Audiovisual Experience of History*. New York: Routledge, 2014.

Barrett, Lisa Feldman. *How Emotions Are Made: The Secret Life of the Brain*. Boston: Houghton Mifflin Harcourt, 2017.

Barthes, Roland, and Richard Howard. *Camera Lucida: Reflections on Photography*. New York: Hill and Wang, 1981.

Bates, Christopher. "'Oh, I'm a Good Ol' Rebel': Reenactment, Racism, and the Lost Cause." In *The Civil War in Popular Culture: Memory and Meaning*, edited by Lawrence A. Kreiser and Randal Allred, 191–222. Lexington: University Press of Kentucky, 2014.

Baudrillard, Jean, and Sheila Faria Glaser. *Simulacra and Simulation*. Ann Arbor: University of Michigan Press, 1994.

Baudrillard, Jean, and Mark Poster. *Jean Baudrillard: Selected Writings*. Stanford, CA: Stanford University Press, 2001.

Baudrillard, Jean, and Chris Turner. *America*. New York: Verso, 1989.

Bazin, André. *What Is Cinema?* Translated by Hugh Gray. Berkeley: University of California Press, 1967.

Belfrage, Sally. *Freedom Summer*. Charlottesville: University Press of Virginia, 1990.

Bell and Shivas staff. "Knocked Down, but Not Out: Fighting for Answers to a Lynching That Shocked America." *Morristown Green*, April 27, 2020. https://morristowngreen.com/2020/04/27/commentary-knocked-down-but-not-out-fighting-for-answers-to-a-lynching-that-shocked-america/.

Bellman, Beryl, and Bennetta Jules-Rosette. *A Paradigm for Looking: Cross-Cultural Research with Visual Media*. Norwood, NJ: Ablex, 1977.

Belton, John. "The World in the Palm of Your Hand: Agnes Varda, Trinh T. Minh-ha, and the Digital Documentary." In *Film Theory and Criticism: Introductory Readings*, edited by Leo Braudy and Marshall Cohen, 8th ed., 744–56. New York: Oxford University Press, 2016.

Berlant, Lauren. "The Commons: Infrastructures for Troubling Times." *Environment and Planning D: Society and Space* 34, no. 3 (2016): 393–419.

Blatner, A. "Morenean Approaches: Recognizing Psychodrama's Many Facets." *Journal of Group Psychotherapy, Psychodrama and Sociometry* 59, no. 4 (2007): 159–70.

Blue, James. "One Man's Truth: An Interview with Richard Leacock." In *The Documentary Tradition*, edited by Lewis Jacobs, 406–19. New York: W. W. Norton, 1979.

Bodroghkozy, Aniko. *Equal Time: Television and the Civil Rights Movement*. Urbana: University of Illinois Press, 2012.

Bogle, Donald. *Toms, Coons, Mulattoes, Mammies, and Bucks: An Interpretive History of Blacks in American Films*. 5th ed. New York: Bloomsbury Academic, 2016.

Bordwell, David, Janet Staiger, and Kristin Thompson. *The Classical Hollywood Cinema: Film Style and Mode of Production to 1960*. New York: Columbia University Press, 1985.

Boyle, Brenda M., and Jeehyun Lim. *Looking Back on the Vietnam War: Twenty-First-Century Perspectives*. New Brunswick, NJ: Rutgers University Press, 2016. https://www.degruyter.com/isbn/9780813579962.

Boyle, Deirdre. "Shattering Silence: Traumatic Memory and Reenactment in Rithy Panh's S-21: The Khmer Rouge Killing Machine." *Framework: The Journal of Cinema and Media* 50, no. 1–2 (2009): 95–106.

Brandt, Marisa Renee. "Simulated War: Remediating Trauma Narratives in Military Psychotherapy." *Catalyst: Feminism, Theory, Technoscience* 2, no. 1 (2016): 1–42.

Brave Heart, Maria Yellow Horse, and Lemyra DeBruyn. "The American Indian Holocaust: Healing Historical Unresolved Grief." *AIANMHR American Indian and Alaska Native Mental Health Research* 8, no. 2 (1998): 60–82.

Brett, Jennifer. "Drew Barrymore and Adam Sandler Here for 'Blended.'" *Atlanta Journal-Constitution*, July 26, 2013. https://www.ajc.com/entertainment/movies/drew-barrymore-and-adam-sandler-here-for-blended/NwKlJ4N9MLlVas4yDwfzdK/.

Brinkema, Eugenie. *The Forms of the Affects*. Durham, NC: Duke University Press, 2014.

Brooks, Tyrone. *Reflections on Georgia Politics*. Interview by Bob Short, Atlanta, GA, September 2, 2009. Richard B. Russell Library for Political Research and Studies University of Georgia Libraries and Young Harris College. http://russelllibrarydocs.libs.uga.edu/ROGP-085_Brooks.pdf.

Bruzzi, Stella. *New Documentary: A Critical Introduction*. London: Routledge, 2000.

California Pioneers of Santa Clara County. "Kidnapers Lynched by Enraged Crowd after Jail Battle—San Jose, 1933." YouTube, July 21, 2014. https://www.youtube.com/watch?v=LUoZesLvbYE.
Cartwright, Lisa. "The Hands of the Projectionist." *Science in Context* 24, no. 3 (2011): 443–64.
———. *Moral Spectatorship: Technologies of Voice and Affect in Postwar Representations of the Child*. Durham, NC: Duke University Press, 2008.
Cerese, Rebecca, Daniel Blake Smith, Leslie Blair, Steven A. Channing, David Richmond McCain, Franklin, Jibreel Khazan, and Joseph McNeil. *February One: The Story of the Greensboro Four*. San Francisco: California Newsreel, 2004.
Childers, J. P. "Transforming Violence into a Focusing Event: A Reception Study of the 1946 Georgia Lynching." *Rhetoric and Public Affairs* 19, no. 4 (2016): 571–600.
Chion, Michel. "From 'The Voice in Cinema.'" In *Film Theory and Criticism: Introductory Readings*, edited by Leo Braudy and Marshall Cohen, 8th ed., 263–74. New York: Oxford University Press, 2016.
Clough, Patricia Ticineto, and Jean O'Malley Halley. *The Affective Turn: Theorizing the Social*. Durham, NC: Duke University Press, 2007.
Conquergood, Dwight. "Lethal Theatre: Performance, Punishment, and the Death Penalty." *Theatre Journal* 54, no. 3 (2002): 339–67.
Conrad, David, Caty Borum Chattoo, and Patricia Aufderheide. *Breaking the Silence: How Documentaries Can Shape the Conversation on Racial Violence in America and Create New Communities, a Participatory Research Study on the Film Always in Season*. Center for Media and Social Impact, October 2020.
Cook, Rhonda. "Former State Rep. Tyrone Brooks Sentenced." *Atlanta Journal-Constitution*, November 9, 2015. https://www.ajc.com/news/local-govt--politics/former-state-rep-brooks-sentenced-prison-prosecution-satisfied/kkow7mta2xzGX7owR8KaNO/.
Cooley, Heidi Rae. *Finding Augusta: Habits of Mobility and Governance in the Digital Era*. Hanover, NH: Dartmouth College Press, 2014.
Cousineau, Matthew. "The Surveillant Simulation of War: Entertainment and Surveillance in the 21st Century." *Surveillance and Society* 8, no. 4 (2011): 517–22.
Crane, Stephen, and Henry Binder. *The Red Badge of Courage: An Episode of the American Civil War*. New York: W.W. Norton, 1999.
Creative Loafing Atlanta. "Moore's Ford Bridge Lynching Reenactment." YouTube, July 29, 2009. https://www.youtube.com/watch?v=1GCQi2jhre4.
Cross, Emily S., Antonia F. de C. Hamilton, and Scott T. Grafton. "Building a Motor Simulation de Novo: Observation of Dance by Dancers." *NeuroImage* 31, no. 3 (2006): 1257–67. https://doi.org/10.1016/j.neuroimage.2006.01.033.
Cubitt, Sean. *Simulation and Social Theory*. London: Sage, 2001.

Cullen, Jim. *The Civil War in Popular Culture: A Reusable Past*. Washington, DC: Smithsonian Institution Press, 1995.
Cuningham, Henry. "Training Leader: Army Changing Focus." *Fayetteville Observer*, April 13, 2006.
Damasio, Antonio R. *The Strange Order of Things: Life, Feeling, and the Making of Cultures*. New York: Pantheon Books, 2018.
Delgado, Richard, and Jean Stefancic. *Critical Race Theory: An Introduction*. 3rd ed. New York: New York University Press, 2017. https://doi.org/10.2307/j.ctt1ggjjn3.
De Luca, Tiago, and Nuno Barradas Jorge. "From Slow Cinema to Slow Cinemas." In *Slow Cinema*, edited by Tiago De Luca and Nuno Barradas Jorge, 1–22. Edinburgh: Edinburgh University Press, 2016.
Democracy Now! "An Unsolved Case of Racial Terror: FBI Probes 1946 Moore's Ford Bridge Lynching in Georgia." YouTube, February 20, 2015. https://www.youtube.com/watch?v=hqNs6xveUJM.
Der Derian, James. *Virtuous War: Mapping the Military-Industrial-Media-Entertainment Network*. Hoboken, NJ: Taylor and Francis, 2009.
Dewan, Shaila. "Group Lynching Is Re-created in a 'Call for Justice.'" *New York Times*, July 26, 2005. https://www.nytimes.com/2005/07/26/us/group-lynching-is-recreated-in-a-call-for-justice.html.
Doane, Mary Ann. *The Emergence of Cinematic Time: Modernity, Contingency, the Archive*. Cambridge, MA: Harvard University Press, 2002.
———. "Indexicality and the Concept of Medium Specificity." *Differences* 18, no. 1 (2007): 128–52.
———. "Indexicality: Trace and Sign—Introduction." *Differences* 18, no. 1 (2007): 1–6.
———. "Information, Crisis, Catastrophe." In *Logics of Television: Essays in Cultural Criticism*, edited by Patricia Mellencamp, 251–64. Bloomington: Indiana University Press, 1990.
———. "The Object of Theory." In *Rites of Realism*, edited by Ivone Margulies, 80–90. Durham, NC: Duke University Press, 2003.
Docherty, Bonnie. *"More Sweat . . . Less Blood": US Military Training and Minimizing Civilian Casualties*. Cambridge, MA: Carr Center for Human Rights Policy at Harvard University, 2007.
Dockterman, Eliana. "How Georgia Became the Hollywood of the South." *Time*, July 26, 2018. https://time.com/longform/hollywood-in-georgia/.
Doidge, Norman. *The Brain That Changes Itself: Stories of Personal Triumph from the Frontiers of Brain Science*. New York: Penguin Books, 2016.
Dorsey, Jack. "The Government Has Spent $6 Billion Fighting IEDs . . . but as Casualties Mount, Are the Efforts All in Vain?" *Virginian-Pilot*, November 1, 2006.

Durkheim, Émile. *The Elementary Forms of the Religious Life*. New York: Free Press, 1967.

Eatman, Megan. "Loss and Lived Memory at the Moore's Ford Lynching Reenactment." *Advances in the History of Rhetoric* 20, no. 2 (2017): 153–66.

Eisenstein, Sergei. "The Cinematographic Principle and the Ideogram." In *Film Theory and Criticism*, 8th ed., edited by Leo Braudy and Marshall Cohen, 12–23. Oxford: Oxford University Press, 2016.

Eitzen, Dirk. "The Duties of Documentary in a Post-Truth Society." In *Cognitive Theory and Documentary Film*, edited by Catalin Brylla and Mette Kramer, 93–112. Cham, Switzerland: Palgrave Macmillan, 2019.

Elsaesser, T. "Freud as Media Theorist: Mystic Writing Pads and the Matter of Memory." *Screen* 50, no. 1 (2009): 100–113.

Equal Justice Initiative. "Legacy Museum and National Memorial for Peace and Justice." Legacy Museum and National Memorial for Peace and Justice, accessed April 7, 2022. http://museumandmemorial.eji.org/.

Fain, Kimberly. "Viral Black Death: Why We Must Watch Citizen Videos of Police Violence." *JSTOR Daily*, September 1, 2016. https://daily.jstor.org/why-we-must-watch-citizen-videos-of-police-violence/.

Filkins, Dexter, and John F. Burns. "Mock Iraqi Villages in Mojave Prepare Troops for Battle." *New York Times*, May 1, 2006. https://www.nytimes.com/2006/05/01/world/americas/01insurgency.html.

Foucault, Michel. *The Essential Foucault: Selections from Essential Works of Foucault, 1954–1984*. Edited by Paul Rabinow and Nikolas S. Rose. New York: New Press, 2003.

Frank, Adam, and Elizabeth A. Wilson. "I: Like-Minded." *Critical Inquiry* 38, no. 4 (2012): 870–77. https://doi.org/10.1086/667428.

Franklin, John Hope. "A Century of Civil War Observance." *Journal of Negro History* 47, no. 2 (1962): 97–107.

Frazier, Darnella. "Medical Incident??? Watch Outtt They Killed Him and the Proof Is Clearlyyyy There !!" Facebook, May 26, 2020. No link available.

———. "They Are Literally Lying !! Pls Watch the Video on My Page !" Facebook, May 26, 2020. No link available.

———. "They killed him right in front of cup foods over south on 38th and Chicago!!" Facebook, May 26, 2020. https://www.facebook.com/darnellareallprettymarie/posts/1425398217661280/.

———. "They really killed than man bro." Facebook, May 26, 2020. https://www.facebook.com/100005733452916/videos/1425381660996269/.

Friedberg, Anne. *Window Shopping: Cinema and the Postmodern*. Berkeley: University of California Press, 1993.

Frosh, Paul. "The Gestural Image: The Selfie, Photography Theory, and Kinesthetic Sociability." *International Journal of Communication* 9 (2015): 1607–28.

Gabriel, Teshome H. *Third Cinema in the Third World: The Aesthetics of Liberation.* Ann Arbor: University of Michigan Research Press, 1982.
Gaines, Jane. "Introduction: 'The Real Returns.'" In *Collecting Visible Evidence*, edited by Jane Gaines and Michael Renov, 1–18. Minneapolis: University of Minnesota Press, 1999.
———. "Political Mimesis." In *Collecting Visible Evidence*, edited by Jane Gaines and Michael Renov, 84–102. Minneapolis: University of Minnesota Press, 1999.
Galuppo, Mia. "Feature Film Production in Georgia Outpaced California Last Year, Study Says." *Hollywood Reporter*, May 23, 2017. https://www.hollywoodreporter.com/news/general-news/feature-film-production-georgia-outpaced-california-last-year-study-says-1006912/.
Gill, Zack Whitman. "Rehearsing the War Away: Perpetual Warrior Training in Contemporary US Army Policy." *TDR: The Drama Review* 53, no. 3 (2009): 139–55.
Ginsburg, Faye. "Decolonizing Documentary On-Screen and Off: Sensory Ethnography and the Aesthetics of Accountability." *Film Quarterly* 72, no. 1 (2018): 39–49.
Godmilow, Jill. "Kill the Documentary as We Know It." *Journal of Film and Video* 54, no. 2/3 (2002): 3–10.
Goldman, Alvin I. *Simulating Minds: The Philosophy, Psychology, and Neuroscience of Mindreading.* Oxford: Oxford University Press, 2006.
Goldovskaya, Marina. *Woman with a Movie Camera: My Life as a Russian Filmmaker.* Austin: University of Texas Press, 2006.
Goldsby, Jacqueline Denise. *A Spectacular Secret: Lynching in American Life and Literature.* Chicago: University of Chicago Press, 2006.
González, Roberto J. *Militarizing Culture: Essays on the Warfare State.* London: Routledge, 2016.
Gray, Herman. "Remembering Civil Rights: Television, Memory, and the 1960s." In *The Revolution Wasn't Televised: Sixties Television and Social Conflict*, edited by Lynn Spigel and Michael Curtin, 349–58. New York: Routledge, 1997.
Greene, Cassandra. Personal interview by Andy Rice, Atlanta, GA, July 28, 2019.
Greg. Personal interview by Andy Rice, San Diego, CA, February 3, 2012.
Gregg, Melissa, and Gregory J. Seigworth, eds. *The Affect Theory Reader.* Durham, NC: Duke University Press, 2010.
———. "An Inventory of Shimmers." In *The Affect Theory Reader*, edited by Gregory J. Seigworth and Melissa Gregg, 1–28. Durham, NC: Duke University Press, 2010.
Grimshaw, Anna, and Amanda Ravetz. *Observational Cinema: Anthropology, Film, and the Exploration of Social Life.* Bloomington: Indiana University Press, 2010.
Grønstad, Asbjørn. "Slow Cinema and the Ethics of Duration." In *Slow Cinema*, edited by Tiago De Luca and Nuno Barradas Jorge, 273–84. Edinburgh: Edinburgh University Press, 2016.

Gross, Larry P, John Stuart Katz, and Jay Ruby. *Image Ethics in the Digital Age.* Minneapolis: University of Minnesota Press, 2003.

———. *Image Ethics: The Moral Rights of Subjects in Photographs, Film, and Television.* New York: Oxford University Press, 1988.

Gutierrez, Scott. "Training Stop on the Way to Iraq—Fort Lewis Troops Practice in California." *Olympian*, February 26, 2006.

Guynn, William Howard. *Unspeakable Histories: Film and the Experience of Catastrophe.* New York: Columbia University Press, 2016.

Hadley, Elizabeth Amelia. "Eyes on the Prize: Reclaiming Black Images, Culture, and History." In *Struggles for Representation: African American Documentary Film and Video*, edited by Phyllis Rauch Klotman and Janet K. Cutler, 99–121. Bloomington: Indiana University Press, 1999.

Hagood, Mack. "Emotional Rescue." *Real Life*, December 3, 2020. https://reallifemag.com/emotional-rescue/.

———. *Hush: Media and Sonic Self-Control.* Durham, NC: Duke University Press, 2019. https://doi.org/10.1515/9781478004479.

Hale, Grace Elizabeth. *Making Whiteness: The Culture of Segregation in the South, 1890–1940.* New York: Pantheon Books, 1998.

Handler, Richard, and William Saxton. "Dyssimulation: Reflexivity, Narrative, and the Quest for Authenticity in 'Living History.'" *Cultural Anthropology: Journal of the Society for Cultural Anthropology* 3 (1988): 242–60.

Harris, Jack. "A Short History of Fort Irwin." Richard Jones Photography, accessed April 6, 2022. http://rsjphoto.net/jaeger/memorial/irwin.html.

Harris, Mike. "Fillmore Couple's Firm Tapped for Honor: Lexicon Provides Language, Cultural, Military Training Noticed by National Media." *Ventura County Star*, November 26, 2010.

Harvey. Personal interview by Andy Rice, Social Circle, GA, July 19, 2012.

Hayles, N. Katherine. *How We Became Posthuman: Virtual Bodies in Cybernetics, Literature, and Informatics.* Chicago: University of Chicago Press, 1999.

Henderson, Odie. "Always in Season Movie Review." RogerEbert.com, September 20, 2019. https://www.rogerebert.com/reviews/always-in-season-movie-review-2019.

Hill, Evan, Ainara Tiefenthäler, Christiaan Triebert, Drew Jordan, Haley Willis, and Robin Stein. "Video: How George Floyd Was Killed in Police Custody." *New York Times*, June 1, 2020. https://www.nytimes.com/video/us/100000007159353/george-floyd-arrest-death-video.html.

hooks, bell. "The Oppositional Gaze." In *Film Theory and Criticism: Introductory Readings*, edited by Leo Braudy and Marshall Cohen, 8th ed., 681–93. New York: Oxford University Press, 2016.

———. *Sisters of the Yam: Black Women and Self-Recovery.* Boston: South End, 1993.

Hutchins, Edwin. *Cognition in the Wild.* Cambridge, MA: MIT Press, 1995.

Jane. Personal interview by Andy Rice, Fort Irwin National Training Center, February 15, 2012.

Jones, Amelia, and Adrian Heathfield. *Perform, Repeat, Record: Live Art in History*. Chicago: Intellect Books, 2012.

Jones, Chloé Cooper. "He Filmed the Killing of Eric Garner—and the Police Punished Him for It." *Verge*, March 13, 2019. https://www.theverge.com/2019/3/13/18253848/eric-garner-footage-ramsey-orta-police-brutality-killing-safety.

Juhasz, Alexandra. "Ceding the Activist Digital Documentary." In *New Documentary Ecologies: Emerging Platforms, Practices and Discourses*, edited by Kate Nash, Craig Hight, and Catherine Summerhayes, 33–49. New York: Palgrave Macmillan, 2014.

———. "How Do I (Not) Look? Live Feed Video and Viral Black Death." *JSTOR Daily*, July 20, 2016. https://daily.jstor.org/how-do-i-not-look/.

———. "They Said We Were Trying to Show Reality—All I Want to Show Is My Video: The Politics of the Realist Feminist Documentary." In *Collecting Visible Evidence*, edited by Jane Gaines and Michael Renov, 190–215. Minneapolis: University of Minnesota Press, 1999.

Jurgensen, John. "Stress under Fire: To Keep Soldiers Mentally Fit to Fight, Army Providing Psychiatric First Aid on the Front Line." *Hartford Courant*, April 9, 2003.

Kahana, Jonathan. "Introduction: What Now? Presenting Reenactment." *Framework: The Journal of Cinema and Media* 50, no. 1–2 (2009): 46–60.

Kamber, Michael, and Tim Arango. "4,000 U.S. Deaths, and a Handful of Images." *New York Times*, July 26, 2008. https://www.nytimes.com/2008/07/26/world/middleeast/26censor.html.

Kammen, Michael G. *Mystic Chords of Memory: The Transformation of Tradition in American Culture*. New York: Vintage Books, 1993.

Kaplan, E. Ann. *Trauma Culture: The Politics of Terror and Loss in Media and Literature*. New Brunswick, NJ: Rutgers University Press, 2005.

Kasic, Kathy. "Sensory Vérité." In *The Routledge International Handbook of Ethnographic Film and Video*, edited by Phillip Vannini, 173–82. New York: Routledge, 2020.

Kazim, Hasnain. "Drone War in Pakistan: Photos from the Ground Show Civilian Casualties." *Der Spiegel*, July 18, 2011. https://www.spiegel.de/international/world/drone-war-in-pakistan-photos-from-the-ground-show-civilian-casualties-a-775131.html.

Keeling, Kara. *The Witch's Flight: The Cinematic, the Black Femme, and the Image of Common Sense*. Durham, NC: Duke University Press, 2007.

Kennedy, John F. "Radio and Television Report to the American People on Civil Rights, 11 June 1963." JFK Library, June 11, 1963. https://www.jfklibrary.org/asset-viewer/archives/JFKWHA/1963/JFKWHA-194-001/JFKWHA-194-001.

Kimmel, Ross. "My Recollections as a Skirmisher during the Civil War Centennial: Or, Confessions of a Blackhat." Wesclark.com, accessed April 6, 2022. http://wesclark.com/jw/k_1961.html.

King, Martin Luther Jr. "'Kick Up Dust': Letter to the Editor, Atlanta Constitution." In *The Papers of Martin Luther King, Jr.*, vol. 1, *Called to Serve, January 1929–June 1951*, edited by Clayborne Carson, Ralph Luker, and Penny A. Russell, 121. Berkeley: University of California Press, 1992. https://kinginstitute.stanford.edu/publications/papers-martin-luther-king-jr-volume-i-called-serve-january-1929-june-1951.

Kinney, Joel. "Mission Statement." PNWHG, accessed October 11, 2021. http://www.pnwhg.com/1stCav/mission.htm.

Kipper, David. "The Emergence of Role Playing as a Form of Psychotherapy." *Journal of Group Psychotherapy, Psychodrama and Sociometry* 49, no. 3 (1996): 99–119.

Kirschenbaum, Matthew G. *Mechanisms: New Media and the Forensic Imagination*. Cambridge, MA: MIT Press, 2008.

Klay, Phil. "Ken Burns Never Knew How Wrong He Was about the Vietnam War." *Mother Jones*, October 2017. https://www.motherjones.com/politics/2017/09/ken-burns-the-vietnam-war-lynn-novick-documentary/.

Knox, Hannah. "Affective Infrastructures and the Political Imagination." *Public Culture* 29, no. 2 (2017): 363–84.

Komarow, Steven. "Cybersoldiers Test Weapons of High-Tech War." *USA Today*, March 6, 1997.

———. "Unexpected Insurgency Changed Way of War." *USA Today*, March 21, 2005.

Krauss, Rosalind. "Notes on the Index: Seventies Art in America." *October* 3 (1977): 68–81.

LaFlore, John. "On-the-Scene Story of Butchery." *Chicago Defender*, August 3, 1946, sec. 2.

Laine, Tarja. *Shame and Desire: Emotion, Intersubjectivity, Cinema*. Brussels: P.I.E. Peter Lang, 2007.

Lancaster, John. "At Army's Training Center, the Bad Guys Still Fight Like Soviets." *Washington Post*, January 21, 1992.

Lavell, Kit. "Advances in Training Help Revolutionize the Military." *San Diego Union-Tribune*, March 9, 2003.

Lazic, Elena. "Irene Lusztig: 'To Me, Conflict Is as Important as Empathy.'" *Seventh Row*, March 14, 2018. https://seventh-row.com/2018/03/14/irene-lusztig-yours-in-sisterhood/.

Lee, Toby. "Beyond the Ethico-aesthetic: Toward a Re-valuation of the Sensory Ethnography Lab." *Visual Anthropology Review* 35, no. 2 (2019): 138–47. https://doi.org/10.1111/var.12184.

Levins, Harry. "War." *St Louis Post-Dispatch*, October 28, 1990.

Lewis, Barbara. "Decorated Death and the Double Whammy." In *Violence Performed: Local Roots and Global Routes of Conflict*, edited by Patrick Anderson and Jisha Menon, 101–25. Basingstoke: Palgrave Macmillan, 2011.
Lewis, Clive. "George Floyd Was Lynched." *OpenDemocracy*, June 6, 2020. https://www.opendemocracy.net/en/opendemocracyuk/george-floyd-was-lynched/.
Leys, Ruth. *The Ascent of Affect: Genealogy and Critique*. Chicago: University of Chicago Press, 2018.
———. "The Turn to Affect: A Critique." *Critical Inquiry* 37, no. 3 (2011): 434–72.
Lippit, Akira Mizuta. *Atomic Light (Shadow Optics)*. Minneapolis: University of Minnesota Press, 2005.
Losh, Elizabeth. "The Palace of Memory: Virtual Tourism and Tours of Duty in *Tactical Iraqi* and *Virtual Iraq*." In *Proceedings of the 2006 International Conference on Game Research and Development*, 77–86. Murdoch, Australia: Murdoch University, 2006.
Lucas, Martin. "Resistance and Public Art: Cultural Action in a Globalized Terrain." *Afterimage* 34, no. 1/2 (2006): 18–21.
MacDonald, Scott. *American Ethnographic Film and Personal Documentary: The Cambridge Turn*. Berkeley: University of California Press, 2013.
MacDougall, David. *The Corporeal Image: Film, Ethnography, and the Senses*. Princeton, NJ: Princeton University Press, 2006.
MacDougall, David, and Lucien Castaing-Taylor. *Transcultural Cinema*. Princeton, NJ: Princeton University Press, 1998.
Madrigal, Alexis C. "When the Revolution Was Televised." *Atlantic*, April 1, 2018. https://www.theatlantic.com/technology/archive/2018/04/televisions-civil-rights-revolution/554639/.
Magelssen, Scott. *Living History Museums: Undoing History through Performance*. Lanham, MD: Scarecrow, 2007.
———. "Rehearsing the 'Warrior Ethos': 'Theatre Immersion' and the Simulation of Theatres of War." *TDR* 53, no. 1 (2009): 47–72.
———. *Simming*. Ann Arbor: University of Michigan Press, 2014.
Malkowski, Jennifer. *Dying in Full Detail: Mortality and Digital Documentary*. Durham, NC: Duke University Press, 2017. https://doi.org/10.1215/9780822373414.
Mamber, Stephen. *Cinema Verite in America: Studies in Uncontrolled Documentary*. Cambridge, MA: MIT Press, 1974.
Manovich, Lev. "What Is Digital Cinema?" *Balkanmedia* 7 (1998): 1–16.
Margulies, Ivone. "Exemplary Bodies: Reenactment in *Love in the City*, *Sons*, and *Close Up*." In *Rites of Realism*, edited by Ivone Margulies, 217–44. Durham, NC: Duke University Press, 2003.

Markovitz, Jonathan. *Legacies of Lynching: Racial Violence and Memory.* Minneapolis: University of Minnesota Press, 2004.

Marks, Laura U. *The Skin of the Film: Intercultural Cinema, Embodiment, and the Senses.* Durham, NC: Duke University Press, 2000.

Massumi, Brian. *99 Theses on the Revaluation of Value: A Postcapitalist Manifesto.* Minneapolis: University of Minnesota Press, 2018.

———. *Parables for the Virtual: Movement, Affect, Sensation.* Durham, NC: Duke University Press, 2002.

Matheson, Kathy. "Flashy Army Recruitment Center in Pa. Mall Closing." *San Diego Union-Tribune,* June 10, 2010. https://www.sandiegouniontribune.com/sdut-flashy-army-recruitment-center-in-pa-mall-closing-2010jun10-story.html.

Mayer, Emeran A. *The Mind-Gut Connection: How the Hidden Conversation within Our Bodies Impacts Our Mood, Our Choices, and Our Overall Health.* New York: Harper Wave, 2018.

Mbembe, Achille. *Out of the Dark Night: Essays on Decolonization.* New York: Columbia University Press, 2021.

McCalman, Iain, and Paul A. Pickering. *Historical Reenactment: From Realism to the Affective Turn.* Basingstoke: Palgrave Macmillan, 2010.

McFate, Montgomery. "The Military Utility of Understanding Adversary Culture." *Joint Force Quarterly* 38, quarter 3 (2005): 42–48.

Minh-ha, Trinh T. "The Totalizing Quest of Meaning." In *Theorizing Documentary,* edited by Michael Renov, 90–107. New York: Routledge, 1993.

Mitchell, Koritha. *Living with Lynching: African American Lynching Plays, Performance, and Citizenship, 1890–1930.* Urbana: University of Illinois Press, 2011.

Moebes, Jack. "David Richmond, Franklin McCain, Ezell Blair, Joseph McNeil, Are Seen Leaving the Woolworth Store on February 1, 1960." The Sit-In Students Captured on Film, Smithsonian National Museum of American History. https://objectofhistory.org/objects/extendedtour/lunchcounter/index.html%3Forder=4.html.

Montfort, Nick. "Continuous Paper: The Early Materiality and Workings of Electronic Literature." Talk given at the MLA Convention, Philadelphia, PA, December 28, 2004. https://nickm.com/writing/essays/continuous_paper_mla.html.

Morris, Meaghan. "Banality in Cultural Studies." In *Logics of Television: Essays in Cultural Criticism,* edited by Patricia Mellencamp, 14–43. Bloomington: Indiana University Press, 1990.

Mossner, Alexa Weik von. "Engaging Animals in Wildlife Documentaries: From Anthropomorphism to Trans-species Empathy." In *Cognitive Theory and Documentary Film,* edited by Catalin Brylla and Mette Kramer, 163–79. Cham, Switzerland: Palgrave Macmillan, 2019.

Mueller, Chuck. "'Graduate-Level Training.'" *Sun, San Bernardino,* April 14, 2006.

———. "Preparing for Urban Warfare." *Sun, San Bernardino*, April 9, 2006.
Mulvey, Laura. "Visual Pleasure and Narrative Cinema." In *Film Theory and Criticism: Introductory Readings*, edited by Leo Braudy and Marshall Cohen, 8th ed., 620–31. New York: Oxford University Press, 2016.
Murphy, J. J. *Rewriting Indie Cinema: Improvisation, Psychodrama, and the Screenplay*. New York: Columbia University Press, 2019.
NBC News. "Looking behind Tragedy at Moore's Ford Bridge." July 24, 2006. https://www.nbcnews.com/id/wbna13905047.
Newman, Maria. "U.S. to Reopen Investigation of Emmett Till's Murder in 1955." *New York Times*, May 10, 2004. https://www.nytimes.com/2004/05/10/national/us-to-reopen-investigation-of-emmett-tills-murder-in-1955.html.
Nichols, Bill. *Introduction to Documentary*. 3rd ed. Bloomington: Indiana University Press, 2017. https://iupress.org/9780253026859/introduction-to-documentary-third-edition/.
———. *Representing Reality: Issues and Concepts in Documentary*. Bloomington: Indiana University Press, 1991.
North-South Skirmish Association. "About the N-SSA." Accessed October 11, 2021. http://www.n-ssa.org/about-nssa.
O'Connell, P. J. *Robert Drew and the Development of Cinema Verite in America*. Carbondale: Southern Illinois University Press, 1992.
Odendahl-James, Jules. "A History of U.S. Documentary Theatre in Three Stages." *American Theatre*, August 22, 2017. https://www.americantheatre.org/2017/08/22/a-history-of-u-s-documentary-theatre-in-three-stages/.
O'Hara, Meghan. Personal interview by Andy Rice, Santa Cruz, CA, May 17, 2015.
O'Hara, Meghan, and Mike Attie. "They Think the Vietnam War Never Ended." *Daily Beast*, April 12, 2015. https://www.thedailybeast.com/they-think-the-vietnam-war-never-ended.
Olachea, Barbara, and Jacqueline Olive. "ALWAYS IN SEASON Filmmaker Jacqueline Olive on Promoting Justice and Reconciliation through Documentary Film." Good Docs, March 28, 2020. https://gooddocs.net/blogs/behind-the-camera/jacqueline-olive-interview.
Oliver, Kelly. *Witnessing: Beyond Recognition*. Minneapolis: University of Minnesota Press, 2001.
———. "Witnessing, Recognition, and Response Ethics." *Philosophy and Rhetoric* 48, no. 4 (2015): 473–93. https://doi.org/10.5325/philrhet.48.4.0473.
Oreskes, Naomi, and Erik M. Conway. *Merchants of Doubt: How a Handful of Scientists Obscured the Truth on Issues from Tobacco Smoke to Global Warming*. New York: Bloomsbury, 2010.
Organizer. Personal interview by Andy Rice, Atlanta, GA, July 24, 2012.
Ott, Brian L. "Affect in Critical Studies." *Oxford Research Encyclopedia of Communication*, July 27, 2017. https://doi.org/10.1093/acrefore/9780190228613.013.56.

Owen, A. Susan, and Peter Ehrenhaus. "The Moore's Ford Lynching Reenactment: Affective Memory and Race Trauma." *Text and Performance Quarterly* 34, no. 1 (2014): 72–90. https://doi.org/10.1080/10462937.2013.856461.

Paglen, Trevor. "Limit Telephotography." Accessed April 6, 2022. https://paglen.studio/2020/04/22/limit-telephotography/.

Parks, Lisa. "Coverage, Media Space, and Security after 9/11 for Drones at Home." Conference presentation for "Drones at Home—Phase 2," University of California, San Diego, May 11–12, 2012.

Parks, Lisa, and Nicole Starosielski, eds. *Signal Traffic: Critical Studies of Media Infrastructures*. Urbana: University of Illinois Press, 2017.

Parks, Suzan-Lori. *The America Play, and Other Works*. New York: Theatre Communications Group, 1995.

Pavsek, Christopher. "Leviathan and the Experience of Sensory Ethnography." *Visual Anthropology Review* 31, no. 1 (2015): 4–11.

Paylor, Terez. "Replicating Iraq: Guard Trains for Combat at Kentucky Site." *Lexington Herald-Leader*, June 30, 2005.

Pearlman, Karen. "Documentary Editing and Distributed Cognition." In *Cognitive Theory and Documentary Film*, edited by Catalin Brylla and Mette Kramer, 93–112. Cham, Switzerland: Palgrave Macmillan, 2019.

Peirce, Charles S. *Philosophical Writings of Peirce*. Edited by Justus Buchler. New York: Dover, 1955.

Phelan, Peggy. *Unmarked: The Politics of Performance*. London: Routledge, 1993.

Pitch, Anthony. *The Last Lynching: How a Gruesome Mass Murder Rocked a Small Georgia Town*. New York: Skyhorse, 2016.

Poiger, Uta G. *Jazz, Rock, and Rebels: Cold War Politics and American Culture in a Divided Germany*. Berkeley: University of California Press, 2000.

Porges, Stephen W. "Emotion: An Evolutionary By-Product of the Neural Regulation of the Autonomic Nervous System." In *The Integrative Neurobiology of Affiliation*, 62–77. Annals of the New York Academy of Sciences. New York: New York Academy of Sciences, 1997.

Prince, Stephen. *Digital Visual Effects in Cinema: The Seduction of Reality*. New Brunswick, NJ: Rutgers University Press, 2014.

Protevi, John L. *Political Affect: Connecting the Social and the Somatic*. Minneapolis: University of Minnesota Press, 2009.

Public affairs officer. Personal interview by Andy Rice, Fort Irwin National Training Center, April 7, 2007.

———. Phone interview by Andy Rice, 2012.

Rainwater, Lee, and William L. Yancey. *The Moynihan Report and the Politics of Controversy: A Trans-action Social Science and Public Policy Report*. Cambridge, MA: MIT Press, 1967.

Rangan, Pooja. *Immediations: The Humanitarian Impulse in Documentary*. Durham, NC: Duke University Press, 2017. https://doi.org/10.1215/9780822373100.

———. "The Skin of the Voice: Acousmatic Illusions, Ventriloquial Listening." In *Sound Objects*, edited by James A. Steintrager and Rey Chow, 130–48. Durham, NC: Duke University Press, 2019.

Rather, Dan, and nomorenarcissism. "U.S. Military Future 1: BOGsters, Bombers, BattleGroups, Bribery or Bankruptcy?" YouTube, December 13, 2008. https://www.youtube.com/watch?v=nR-KJRVegSg.

Razsa, Maple John. "Beyond Riot Porn: Protest Video and the Production of Unruly Subjects." *Ethnos: Journal of Anthropology*, 2013. doi:10.1080/00141844.2013.778309, 1–29.

Rehak, Bob. *More Than Meets the Eye: Special Effects and the Fantastic Transmedia Franchise*. New York: New York University Press, 2018. https://www.degruyter.com/isbn/9781479866823.

Renov, Michael. *The Subject of Documentary*. Minneapolis: University of Minnesota Press, 2004.

———. "Toward a Poetics of Documentary." In *Theorizing Documentary*, edited by Michael Renov, 12–36. New York: Routledge, 1993.

Rice, Andy. "Salvaging the Bees: Honeyland and the Paradox of the Observational Fable." In *Honeyland: A Docalogue*, edited by Jaimie Baron and Kristen Fuhs, 9–26. New York: Routledge, 2022.

———. "The Sense of Feminism Then and Now: *Yours in Sisterhood* (2018) and Embodied Listening in the Cinema Praxis of Irene Lusztig." *Senses of Cinema*, December 2018. http://sensesofcinema.com/2018/feature-articles/the-sense-of-feminism-then-and-now-yours-in-sisterhood-2018-and-embodied-listening-in-the-cinema-praxis-of-irene-lusztig/.

Richardson, Allissa V. *Bearing Witness while Black: African Americans, Smartphones, and the New Protest #journalism*. New York: Oxford University Press, 2020.

———. "Why Cellphone Videos of Black People's Deaths Should Be Considered Sacred, like Lynching Photographs." *Conversation*, May 28, 2020. https://theconversation.com/amp/why-cellphone-videos-of-black-peoples-deaths-should-be-considered-sacred-like-lynching-photographs-139252.

Rini, Regina. "Deepfakes Are Coming. We Can No Longer Believe What We See." Opinion, *New York Times*, June 10, 2019. https://www.nytimes.com/2019/06/10/opinion/deepfake-pelosi-video.html.

Rizzolatti, Giacomo, and Maddalena Fabbri-Destro. "Mirror Neurons: From Discovery to Autism." *Experimental Brain Research* 200, no. 3 (2010): 223–37. https://doi.org/10.1007/s00221-009-2002-3.

Rodowick, David Norman. *The Virtual Life of Film*. Cambridge, MA: Harvard University Press, 2007.

Rogers, Keith. "Nevada Soldiers Help in Training." *Las Vegas Review-Journal*, February 27, 2005.
Role-Player 1. Personal interview by Andy Rice, April 8, 2007.
Rony, Fatimah Tobing. *The Third Eye: Race, Cinema, and Ethnographic Spectacle*. Durham, NC: Duke University Press, 2004.
Rose, Phil. "Silvan Tomkins as Media Ecologist." *Explorations in Media Ecology* 12, no. 3 (2013): 217–27.
Rosen, Philip. *Change Mummified: Cinema, Historicity, Theory*. Minneapolis: University of Minnesota Press, 2006.
Ross, RaMell. "Renew the Encounter." *Film Quarterly* 72, no. 3 (2019): 17–19.
Rouch, Jean, and Steven Feld. *Ciné-Ethnography*. Minneapolis: University of Minnesota Press, 2003.
Rowan & Martin's Laugh-In. "Sock It To Me | Rowan & Martin's Laugh-In | George Schlatter." YouTube, June 9, 2017. https://www.youtube.com/watch?v=n6HIzYXZzIo.
Rushdy, Ashraf H. A. *The End of American Lynching*. New Brunswick, NJ: Rutgers University Press, 2012.
Samuel DuBois Cook Center on Social Equity at Duke University. "13th (2016) Film Question and Answer Session with Hans L. Charles." YouTube, April 17, 2017. https://www.youtube.com/watch?v=L0ux59fGfvU.
Santos Aquino, Rowena. "Necessary Fictions: From Cinéma Vérité to Ciné, Ma Vérité(s)." *CINEJ Cinema Journal* 1, no. 2 (2012): 51–61.
Santschi, Darrell R. "Uncertain Future: Base Closures; Fort Irwin Fights to Stay on Duty." *Press-Enterprise*, November 29, 2004.
Schmitt, Eric. "U.S. Tripling Fund to Stop Homemade Iraq Bombs." *New York Times*, February 6, 2006. https://www.nytimes.com/2006/02/06/world/americas/06iht-military.html.
Schneider, Rebecca. *Performing Remains: Art and War in Times of Theatrical Reenactment*. Abingdon: Routledge, 2011.
Scott, Ellen C. *Cinema Civil Rights: Regulation, Repression, and Race in the Classical Hollywood Era*. New Brunswick, NJ: Rutgers University Press, 2015.
Scott, Holly V. *Younger Than That Now: The Politics of Age in the 1960s*. Boston: University of Massachusetts Press, 2016.
Sedgwick, Eve Kosofsky. "Paranoid Reading and Reparative Reading, or, You're So Paranoid, You Probably Think This Essay Is about You." In *Touching Feeling: Affect, Pedagogy, Performativity*, 123–52. Durham, NC: Duke University Press, 2003.
———. *Touching Feeling: Affect, Pedagogy, Performativity*. Durham, NC: Duke University Press, 2003.
Sedgwick, Eve Kosofsky, and Adam Frank, eds. *Shame and Its Sisters: A Silvan Tomkins Reader*. Durham, NC: Duke University Press, 1995.

Sewall, Sarah, John Nagl, David Petraeus, and James Amos. *The U.S. Army and Marine Corps Counterinsurgency Field Manual*. Chicago: University of Chicago Press, 2007.

Shaviro, Steven. "Slow Cinema vs Fast Films." *Pinocchio Theory* (blog), May 12, 2010. http://www.shaviro.com/Blog/?p=891.

Simblist, Noah. "Dread Scott's Struggle to Reclaim Collective Memory." *ARTnews.Com* (blog), June 30, 2020. https://www.artnews.com/art-in-america/features/dread-scott-john-akomfrah-slave-rebellion-reenactment-reclaim-collective-memory-1202693023/.

Sitney, P. Adams. *Film Culture Reader*. New York: Cooper Square, 2000.

Skoller, Jeffrey. "iDocument Police: Contingency, Resistance, and the Precarious Present." *World Records* 1, no. 4 (2018): 1–17.

Smaill, Belinda. *The Documentary: Politics, Emotion, Culture*. Basingstoke: Palgrave Macmillan, 2010.

Smith Broady, Arlinda. "Hanging Near Social Circle Spawned Strife." *Atlanta Journal-Constitution*, February 19, 2014. https://www.ajc.com/news/local/hanging-near-social-circle-spawned-strife/UGnpA9l5WarGiGGkBtBoYO/.

Sobchack, Vivian. *The Address of the Eye: A Phenomenology of Film Experience*. Princeton, NJ: Princeton University Press, 1992.

———. "Beating the Meat/Surviving the Text, or How to Get Out of the Century Alive." *Carnal Thoughts: Embodiment and Moving Image Culture*, 165–78. Berkeley: University of California Press, 2004.

———. *Carnal Thoughts: Embodiment and Moving Image Culture*. Berkeley: University of California Press, 2004.

———. "Toward a Phenomenology of Nonfictional Film Experience." In *Collecting Visible Evidence*, edited by Jane Gaines and Michael Renov, 241–54. Minneapolis: University of Minnesota Press, 1999.

Stahl, Roger. *Militainment, Inc.: War, Media, and Popular Culture*. New York: Routledge, 2010.

Stanley, Jason. *How Fascism Works: The Politics of Us and Them*. New York: Random House, 2018.

Stanton, Cathy, and Stephen Belyea. "Their Time Will Yet Come: The African American Presence in Civil War Reenactment." In *Hope and Glory: Essays on the Legacy of the Fifty-Fourth Massachusetts Regiment*, edited by Martin Henry Blatt, Thomas J. Brown, and Donald Yacovone, 253–74. Amherst: University of Massachusetts in association with Massachusetts Historical Society, Boston, 2001.

Star, Susan Leigh, and Karen Ruhleder. "Steps toward an Ecology of Infrastructure: Design and Access for Large Information Spaces." *Information Systems Research* 7, no. 1 (1996): 111–34.

Steele, Dennis. "Decisive Action Training: 'Old School without Rotations: Going Back in Time.'" *Army*, February 2013, 26–37.

Steintrager, James A., and Rey Chow. *Sound Objects*. Durham, NC: Duke University Press, 2019. http://catalog.hathitrust.org/api/volumes/oclc/1042078342.html.

Sterenfeld, Ethan. "Army Seeks to Expand National Training Center Facilities." Inside Defense, May 24, 2021. https://insidedefense.com/insider/army-seeks-expand-national-training-center-facilities.

Stevenson, Lisa, and Eduardo Kohn. "'Leviathan': An Ethnographic Dream." *Visual Anthropology Review* 31, no. 1 (2015): 49–53.

Stidhum, Tonja Renée. "The George Floyd Homicide Video Is Not Cinéma Vérité—WTF Is Wrong with You, Ross Johnson?" *Root*, June 10, 2020. https://www.theroot.com/the-george-floyd-homicide-video-is-not-cinema-verite-wt-1843978072.

Strategic Operations. "Medical Products." Accessed April 6, 2022. https://www.strategic-operations.com/category-s/169.htm.

Sturken, Marita, and Lisa Cartwright. *Practices of Looking: An Introduction to Visual Culture*. Oxford: Oxford University Press, 2001.

Suchman, Lucy. "Configuring the Other: Sensing War through Immersive Simulation." *Catalyst: Feminism, Theory, Technoscience* 2, no. 1 (2016): 1–36.

Summerhayes, Catherine. "Web-Weaving: The Affective Movement of Documentary Imaging." In *New Documentary Ecologies: Emerging Platforms, Practices and Discourses*, edited by Kate Nash, Craig Hight, and Catherine Summerhayes, 83–102. New York: Palgrave Macmillan, 2014.

Taylor, Diana. *The Archive and the Repertoire: Performing Cultural Memory in the Americas*. Durham, NC: Duke University Press, 2007.

Technician. Personal interview by Andy Rice, Fort Irwin National Training Center, February 15, 2012.

Thatcher, Autumn. "Facing the Past and Present with 'Always in Season.'" KRCL, January 31, 2019. https://krcl.org/blog/facing-the-past-and-present-with-always-in-season/.

Thevenot, Brian. "Duty Calls: Louisiana National Guardsmen Are Training Furiously in California, Preparing for the Front Lines of Iraq." *Times-Picayune*, September 12, 2004.

Tomkins, Silvan S. *Affect Imagery Consciousness: The Complete Edition (Two Volumes)*. New York: Springer, 2008.

Torchin, Leshu. *Creating the Witness: Documenting Genocide on Film, Video, and the Internet*. Minneapolis: University of Minnesota Press, 2012.

Torres, Sasha. *Black, White, and in Color: Television and Black Civil Rights*. Princeton, NJ: Princeton University Press, 2003.

Trachtenberg, Alan. "Albums of War: On Reading Civil War Photographs." *Representations*, no. 9 (1985): 1–32. https://doi.org/10.2307/3043765.

Turner, Fred. *From Counterculture to Cyberculture: Stewart Brand, the Whole Earth Network, and the Rise of Digital Utopianism*. Chicago: University of Chicago Press, 2006.

United States and Civil War Centennial Commission. *The Civil War Centennial: A Report to the Congress*. Washington, DC: US Government Printing Office, 1968.

US Army. "NTC Community Box Tours." National Training Center and Fort Irwin, accessed April 6, 2022. https://home.army.mil/irwin/index.php/about/visitor-information/ntc-tours.

Van der Kolk, Bessel A. *The Body Keeps the Score: Brain, Mind, and Body in the Healing of Trauma*. New York: Viking, 2014.

Vargo, Joe. "Destination Iraq: Inland Base Trains Troops for Intense Situations." *Press-Enterprise*, June 15, 2007.

Vertov, Dziga, Annette Michelson, and Kevin O'Brien. *Kino-Eye: The Writings of Dziga Vertov*. Berkeley: University of California Press, 1984.

Virilio, Paul. *Desert Screen: War at the Speed of Light*. London: Continuum, 2002.

Vizzo, Emily. "Purposeful Chaos: Local Company Sets Up Realistic Training for Combat, Drug Houses and Ship Seizures." *San Diego Union-Tribune*, May 10, 2011.

Wahlberg, Malin. *Documentary Time: Film and Phenomenology*. Minneapolis: University of Minnesota Press, 2008.

Waldrep, Christopher. "Lynching and Mob Violence." In *Encyclopedia of African American History, 1619–1895: From the Colonial Period to the Age of Frederick Douglass*, edited by Paul Finkelman, 307–14. Oxford: Oxford University Press, 2006. https://www.oxfordreference.com/view/10.1093/acref/9780195167771.001.0001/acref-9780195167771.

Walker, Janet. *Trauma Cinema: Documenting Incest and the Holocaust*. Berkeley: University of California Press, 2005.

Wallace, Michele Faith. "The Good Lynching and 'The Birth of a Nation': Discourses and Aesthetics of Jim Crow." *Cinema Journal* 43, no. 1 (2003): 85–104.

———. "Oscar Micheaux's within Our Gates." In *Oscar Micheaux and His Circle: African-American Filmmaking and Race Cinema of the Silent Era*, edited by Pearl Bowser, Jane Gaines, and Charles Musser, 53–66. Bloomington: Indiana University Press, 2001.

Walters, William. "Parrhēsia Today: Drone Strikes, Fearless Speech and the Contentious Politics of Security." *Global Society* 28, no. 3 (2014): 277–99. https://doi.org/10.1080/13600826.2014.900741.

Ward, Geoffrey C., Ken Burns, Lynn Novick, Salimah El-Amin, Lucas B. Frank, and Maggie Hinders. *The Vietnam War: An Intimate History*. New York: Knopf, 2017.

Watanabe, Theresa. "When Time Allows, 1992 Riots Are Poignant Lesson in L.A. Schools." *Los Angeles Times*, April 15, 2012. https://www.latimes.com/local/la-xpm-2012-apr-15-la-me-riots-schools-20120415-story.html.

Waugh, Thomas. "Lesbian and Gay Documentary: Minority Self-Imaging, Oppositional Film Practice, and the Question of Image Ethics." In *Image Ethics: The Moral Rights of Subjects in Photographs, Film, and Television*, edited by Larry P. Gross, John Stuart Katz, and Jay Ruby, 248–72. New York: Oxford University Press, 1988.

Wexler, Laura. *Fire in a Canebrake: The Last Mass Lynching in America*. New York: Scribner, 2003.

Whissel, Kristen. *Spectacular Digital Effects: CGI and Contemporary Cinema*. Durham, NC: Duke University Press, 2014.

Williams, Linda. "Film Bodies: Gender, Genre, and Excess." In *Film Theory and Criticism: Introductory Readings*, edited by Leo Braudy and Marshall Cohen, 8th ed., 537–51. New York: Oxford University Press, 2016.

Winston, Brian. "The Documentary Film as Scientific Inscription." In *Theorizing Documentary*, edited by Michael Renov, 37–57. New York: Routledge, 1993.

Winston, Brian, and Hing Tsang. "The Subject and the Indexicality of the Photograph." *Semiotica* 2009, no. 173 (2009): 453–69.

Winston, Brian, Gail Vanstone, and Chi Wang. *The Act of Documenting: Documentary Film in the 21st Century*. New York: Bloomsbury Academic, 2017.

Wood, Amy Louise. *Lynching and Spectacle: Witnessing Racial Violence in America, 1890–1940*. Chapel Hill: University of North Carolina Press, 2009.

Zimmerman, Patricia R., and Helen De Michiel. *Open Space New Media Documentary: A Toolkit for Theory and Practice*. New York: Routledge, 2017. https://www.taylorfrancis.com/books/e/9781351762090.

INDEX

Page references in italics refer to illustrations.

Abernathy, Ralph, 150
About Face! Reenacting in a Time of War (2010), 31n35, 46–48; reenactors' bodies in, 46; voice-over in, 48
Abrams, Stacy: gubernatorial defeat (2018), 26, 169
abstractions, power of, 3–4
Abu Ghraib scandal (2003), 81, 83, 86; staged photos at, 105
Acconci, Vito: *Blinks*, 79n46
accountability: complex forms of, 203; cultural mores about, 74; in documentaries, 63; national dialogue about, 153; in oppositional film, 33n73; political, 20, 137; in queer film, 73
acousmetre (off-screen voice): oppositional, 27, 178–90, 191; power of, 149
actor network theory, 20
Adams, Clinton: witnessing of Moore's Ford lynching, 160nn1–2
affect: in childhood, 20; cinema's generation of, 16; circuit breakers for, 18; in human evolution, 102; humanist positions on, 20; in humanities, 3; in media indexicality, 12, 13; in military simulation training, 81, 88, 90, 99, 103; negative, 104–5; performed for camera, 21–22; political, 83; in relationship with material forms, 161n11;

self-corrective, 19; sensorial interplay in, 18; in simulation documentaries, 7; in social sciences, 3; Spinoza on, 32n50; surprise-startle, 18; technology and, 102; transfer of presence in, 55; universal system of, 19
affect system, 70, 86; hardwired, 33n61; image of, 103; sensorial interplay in, 18; sensory-affect-memory feedback loop in, 102; simulation and, 102; universal, 19
affect theory, 161n11, 194; applications of, 16; on camerawork, 15–16; cognitive sciences and, 18; critical language in, 20; in critical theory tradition, 19; Deleuzian, 16–17, 19, 21; political accountability in, 20; psychoanalytic theory and, 16; reimaginative, 16; weak/strong, 70
Afghanistan: civilian fatalities in, 100; IED use in, 97; military failures in, 83; secret prisons in, 119n87
afterimage, nineteenth-century belief in, 51
agency, distributed, 17
Aguayo, Angela, 28n6
Al Hadr (Iraq), Princess of Hatra Statue, 111, *114*
Allen, James: *Without Sanctuary* exhibit, 155–56, 171, 174

Always in Season (2019), 3, 4, *181*; Abrams's campaign and, 26; absence in, 179; aesthetic choices of, 171; affective infrastructure of, 191; antiracist point of view, 170–71; archival material in, 184; audience of, 179, 189–90; balloon imagery, 178–79; Beast Fest in, 173–74; being there and, 186–87; Black female participants in, 175, 178, 180, 184; Black spectators in, 180, 187, 189, 190; camerawork for, 125, 171, 182–83; cognitive dissonance experience for, 190; community screenings of, 191; consent protocols of, 34n76; context making in, 170; continuity editing in, 180; creation of meaning, 169; Creative Loafing footage in, 182, 183; descendants of lynchers in, 175; facilitation of justice in, 170; the gaze in, 172, 174, 177, 178, 182; indexical referents in, 186–87, 190; intergenerational trauma in, 186; interviews in, 174, 176, 177; Ku Klux Klan footage in, 176; Lacy hanging in, 171; liveness in, 185; lynching reenactment footage, 181, 197; majority-white audience of, 181; metonymic juxtaposition in, 123–24; modeling of simulation documentaries, 192; montage scenes, 172, 189–90; Moore's Ford reenactment in, 174–76, 178, 182–83; narrative conventions of, 191; official silence in, 172, 177; off-screen collective voice of, 178; oppositional acousmetre of, 27, 178–90, 191; oppositional lens of, 179; parallel stories in, 174; participants in, 168, 175, 178, 180, 184; patterns of intimidation in, 172; PBS broadcast of, 191; photographic objects in, 179; politics of image in, 185; practices of looking in, 171–77; premiere of, 190; process of perception for, 190; protagonists' transformation in, 175; recollection-image of, 187; reviewers of, 190–91; reworking of linearity, 153; shot-reverse shot scene construction, 171; simulated crisis coverage in, 182, 183; soundscape of, 180–81, 185, 189–90; spectator montage, 189–90; tears in, 186–87; three-act structure of, 174, 180; title of, 176; urgency in, 184; white accountability in, 160; white community in, 178. *See also* Olive, Jacqueline

Ang, Ien, 91; *Watching Dallas*, 117n25
Anthropocene, ontological poetics of, 76n9
anthropology, visual: salvage anthropology and, 27n1; sensory ethnography in, 22; transcultural cinema in, 38
Apple, Final Cut Pro software, 11
Arab-Israeli War, tactical decisions in, 93
Armstrong, Julie Buckner, 133, 136
Army Experience Center (Philadelphia), 107, 118n75
Arundell-Latshaw, Jamie, 97
Atlanta, GA, Black film production in, 168
atrocity, documentary imaging of, 88–89
Attie, Mike, 37; on *In Country* production, 62; observational camerawork of, 36; reenactment by, 36, 38, 61, 62. *See also In Country*
audiences: affective jolts for, 137; camerapersons as, 35; recording of reenactments, 157, 166–67; revelations through film, 194; of sensory cinema, 9. *See also* spectatorship
Aufderheide, Pat, 33n71
Auslander, Mark, 133; on reenactment, 121
Auslander, Philip, 79n46
Austin, J. L., 205n15
automata, computerized, 102
Azoulay, Ariella, 5

Barber, William, 176
Baron, Jamie: "archive affect" theory, 40, 42, 57, 79n44; on consciousness, 48; on metonymy, 65; on temporal disparity, 54, 67
Barrett, Lisa Feldman, 33n65
Barthes, Roland: on the punctum, 53
Baudrillard, Jean: *America*, 93; *Consumer Society*, 15; phenomenology of, 15; *Simulacra and Stimulation*, 93
Baumgartner, Hayden "Bummy": reenactment by, 44

Bazin, André: *What Is Cinema?*, 9–10
Beauchamp, Keith: *Murder in Black and White* series, 26, 153–54, 159; *The Untold Story of Emmett Louis Till*, 153
Behram, Noor: drone strike photographs, 88–89, 115; exhibition of photographs, 117n20
being there, 204; *Always in Season* and, 186–87; in documentaries, 35, 201; in *In Country*, 36, 41, 65; in observational cinema, 36, 201; in reenactment, 48
Berlant, Lauren, 27; on the commons, 161n11
Birmingham, AL: Project C desegregation campaign, 146; racial violence in, 147
Birth of a Movement (documentary, 2016), 164n59
Black activism: bearing witness in, 7; reenactment in, 26, 168, 191; strategies of representation, 139; white camerapersons and, 146; witnessing, 203. *See also* civil rights movement
Black bodies, dehumanization of, 155
Black celebrities, in popular culture, 144
Black death: circulation of images, 197; movement struggles against, 160; perception practices around, 192; in South, 27, 128, 130; videotapes of, 27, 196, 197–98; white cultural gaze on, 197. *See also* lynchings; violence, racial
Black dignity: advocacy for, 26, 120; public narrative about, 202; student activists for, 204
Black Hawk Down (film), 97
Black history: cameras' interpretation of, 126; loss of, 151
Black Lives Matter movement, 204; affective infrastructures of, 203; camerawork in, 27; George Floyd murder and, 199, 204
Black males, dehumanization of, 140, 176
Blackness, in affective reenactment, 121
Blackside Films, Inc.: *Eyes on the Prize*, 150
Black women: participants in *Always in Season*, 175, 178, 180, 184; practices of looking, 182; resistance by, 180; spaces of healing for, 128
Bladenboro, NC: Beast Fest in, 173–74, 178; white community of, 178
Bladenboro, NC, hanging, 124, 156, 171; Black anger at, 175; continuity with lynching locales, 173; FBI investigation of, 176, 177; interviews with officials, 172; justice for, 175, 179; Ku Klux Klan rally following, 176; Moore's Ford Lynching Reenactment and, 178; parallel stories, 174. *See also Always in Season*; Lacy, Lennon
Blair, Ezell, Jr., 202
Bloody Sunday (Selma, AL, 1965): commemorative reenactments of, 150; crisis coverage of, 180; footage of, 148–49, 171; televised brutality of, 148–50; voices in, 149
bodies: cinematic code and, 22–23; "constitutive outside" of, 86; documentation by, 204; indexicality of, 8–14, 26; medium specificity, 59; perceiving, 59; permeability with screen, 17; self-preservation of, 83; spectacular photographability of, 122
bodies, performing: as civil political space, 5; as documentary, 5; indexicality of, 73, 115; in long-duration art, 55; in military simulation training, 95–96; in simulation documentaries, 21; spectacular photographability of, 122; witnessing by, 7. *See also* performance, embodied; reenactors
bodies, traumatized, 33n65; the trace in, 12. *See also* trauma
Bodroghkozy, Aniko, 146, 147, 165n87; on Selma violence, 149
Bordwell, David, 140
Born into Brothels (2004), 20
Boyle, Brenda, 46
Boyle, Deirdre, 6
Brady, Matthew: battlefield photography of, 84
brain, simulation of motor action response, 14

INDEX

Brandt, Marisa, 109

Brimhall, Michelle, 177

Brinkema, Eugene: on cinematic tears, 186; *The Form of the Affects*, 20

Brooks, Tyrone: approach to politics, 150; and Moore's Ford Lynching Reenactment, 129, 134, 150, 166; tax fraud conviction, 193n15

Brown v. Board of Education, 173–74

Bruni, Stella: *New Documentary*, 78n37

Burdett, Samuel, 138; *A Test of Lynch Law*, 139

Burns, Ken: on storytelling, 76n10; use of spoken word, 184; war films of, 40. See also *The Vietnam War*

Bush, George W., 88

Butler, Judith, 52, 86

Cambodia, genocide of 1970s, 6

camcorders, low-cost, 11

camera: affect performed for, 21–22; inseparability from body, 201

camerapersons: affective experiences of, 4, 54; affective labor of, 195; as audience, 35; Black, 196; conjoined experience with reenactors, 16; copresence with subject, 6, 35, 201; experience as reenactors, 46–47; field of perception, 21; interpersonal interactions of, 21; participation in live performance, 41; participatory techniques of, 11; perception of present, 53; reenacted practices of, 64; as surrogate witnesses, 21; Vietnam-era, 38

camerapersons, white: Black activists and, 146

camerawork: affective, 2, 3, 20–21, 53; affect theory on, 15–16; at be-ins, 201; in Black Lives Matter movement, 27; capture of unpredictability, 21; cinematic lures for, 21; crisis coverage, 60–64, 149; decoupling from finished film, 11; documentary theory on, 194; embodied experiences of, 7; gesture of, 57; indexical artifacts of, 203; multimodal interaction in, 198; of 1960s/1970s, 201; noninterventionist, 23; perception in, 21, 53, 61; as performance, 11, 38; phenomenology of, 22, 34n76; reframing of collective orientation, 195; representation of spectacle lynchings, 123; role in antilynching, 142; in simulation documentaries, 20, 28n6, 42, 49; structural change through, 125. See also filmmaking

camerawork, common-cause: civil rights subjects and, 145–51

camerawork, documentary: affective flow in, 2; close-ups in, 152; continuity editing principles in, 152; orientation to time, 152; as public relations tool, 7; repetition/revision structure of, 151–53; shot–reverse shot scene construction in, 152, 153, 156–60

camerawork, ethnographic: media phenomenology in, 22

camerawork, observational, 8; crisis aesthetic of, 38, 154; epistemology of, 36; everyday activities in, 61; in *In Country*, 24, 35–75; lived experience in, 39; neutrality in, 63; nimble, 36; performative, 39; photographic index and, 51; presence in, 24; proximity to subjects, 61; as recollection-object, 42–43, 57, 73; recreation of martial psyche, 41, 43; as reenactment, 73; relationship to archival materials, 42; at Sensory Ethnographic Lab, 38; as severed index, 61; temporality in, 24, 39; transcendence of self through, 51; vérité methods, 36, 38, 41; of Vietnam War, 38; voltmeter in, 39, 61, 76n9. See also reenactment

Capitol insurrection (January, 2020), generation of anger for, 203

Capote, Truman: *In Cold Blood*, 131

Capra, Frank: *Why We Fight*, 184

Cartwright, Lisa, 32n44

Castile, Philando: videotaped killing of, 197

catastrophes, televised indices of, 59

Charles, Han, 8

Chauvin, Derek, 27, 196, 197; involuntary manslaughter charge against, 198

Chion, Michel, 149, 163n45, 179; on voices, 178, 185

cinema: anti-illusory, 185; common-sense filters for, 84, 106; Deleuze on, 16–17; direct, 38, 63; expressive units of, 17; feminist, 179; generation of affect, 16; military action films, 107; repetition in, 152; slow, 201; transcultural, 38
cinema, digital: computer graphics of, 10; image manipulation in, 10–11, 14; "trauma," 12
cinema, Hollywood: Black characters in, 180; Black female viewers of, 180; Hayes Code (1934), 142; lynching depictions, 142–44; military simulation training and, 81, 82, 92, 100; racial stereotypes in, 141
cinema, intercultural: sensory effect of, 17
cinema, observational, 9, 22; being there in, 36, 201; ethics of, 76n9; long takes in, 39; sensory qualities of, 27n1
cinema, postwar: space in, 17; traumatic memory in, 17
cinema, sensory: affective experience in, 9; embodied reenactment in, 8–9; media phenomenology and, 22–23; observational recording in, 9; techniques of, 9; theory of, 8
cinema, social: distributed authorship of, 27; intersubjectivity of, 27
cinephilia, 78n34
citizens, smartphone use by, 196, 200. See also Frazier, Darnella
citizenship, decoupling from soldiering, 116n9
civilians, US: identification with soldiers, 86–87
civil rights movement: American image abroad and, 147; camerawork following, 202; in cities, 148, 150; common-cause camerawork of, 145–51; crisis coverage of, 149, 154; group demonstrations, 148; media strategy of, 122, 145, 148, 150; reenactment and, 47, 150, 194; television coverage of, 123, 145–51, 202; violence against television coverage, 148; voter registration during, 148; white copresence in, 202. See also Black activism; Bloody Sunday

civil rights subjects, national audience for, 146
Civil War: commemorations of, 78n23; photography in, 84; reenactment of, 47, 77n23, 123
Clark, Jim, 148
Clayton, Elias: lynching of, 156
climate change, scientists' denial of, 136–37
Cold War, military training for, 94
commemoration, ethics of, 24, 43
common sense: in experience of white-on-Black violence, 121; filters for cinema, 84, 106; in media consumption, 91, 116n11; among soldier trainees, 85, 99
Cone, Robert, 100–101
consciousness: cinematic, 106; documentary mode of, 48; effect of autonomous nervous system on, 32n61; feedback mechanisms of, 18; simulation of, 101–3
consumption: collective nature of, 15; in experience economy, 23
Conway, Erik: *Merchants of Doubt*, 136–37
Cooley, Heidi Rae, 31n40
counterculture: documentaries, 3; of 1960s/1970s, 201
Count Five, "Psychotic Reaction," 44
Crane, Stephen: *The Red Badge of Courage*, 67
Creative Loafing (journalism organization), Moore's Ford Lynching Reenactment footage, 182, 183
crises, condensation of temporality, 60
Crisis: Behind a Presidential Commitment (1963), 80n62
crisis coverage, 165n87; of Bloody Sunday, 180; camerawork for, 60–64, 80n62, 149; of civil rights movement, 149, 154; in *In Country*, 60–64; simulated, 182, 183
critical cultural theory: of Frankfurt School, 15; on hidden forces, 19; simulation theory in, 14–15
critical media theory, 9
cultural awareness: military shift away from, 119n85; in military simulation training, 83, 91–92, 97, 107, 111, 114

INDEX

culture, American: Black celebrities in, 144; desert as symbol of, 93; racist contradictions in, 202; simulation in, 93
Cvetkovich, Ann, 126

daily life, observational recording of, 36, 62
Dallas (television program), European fans of, 117n25
Darensburg, Lucien "Doc": PTSD of, 44, 71, 72; reenactment by, 71, 72
Dash, Julie: *Illusions*, 180, 193n18
death: collective coping with, 127; documentary representation of, 127–28; "down home," 128; filming of, 127; repetition in time/space, 197; temporality of, 13; traditional rituals of, 128
death, natural: cinematic representation of, 127
death, violent: in fictional filmmaking, 127; indexical signs of, 127–29; media representations of, 127. *See also* Black death; lynchings; violence, racial
deepfakes, 30n29
Deleuze, Gilles, 141; affect theory of, 16–17, 19, 21; *Cinema 1–2*, 16
De Michiel, Helen, 31n37
Der Derian, James, 84
Desert Storm, desert training for, 95
digital culture: indexicality in, 17; reenactment in, 38; the trace in, 12
digital media: binary data of, 10, 195; embodied performance and, 115; footage of death in, 11; medium specificity and, 10, 49; Neo-Marxist theorists on, 10; resemblance in, 10
digital technologies: creation of communities, 31n37; recording, 195; use in *In Country*, 49
distributed cognition (DC), 28n8
Doane, Mary Anne: on the crisis, 60, 165n87; on digital media, 49; on the index, 52. Works: *The Emergence of Cinematic Time*, 50–51; "The Object of Theory," 78n34
Docherty, Bonnie: on Fort Irwin training, 106–7; "More Sweat...Less Blood," 106

documentaries: accountability for ethics in, 63; being there in, 35, 201; Black production of, 28n6; cinema-vérité styles, 54, 201; connection to past in, 196; consent protocols in, 33n73, 34nn75–76; contingency in, 186; counter-cultural, 3; cultural insight in, 35; daily life in, 3, 36; death in, 127–28; digital camera use in, 10–11; documentary theater and, 29n12; effect on power relations, 196–97; embodied social sense in, 203; ethics in, 7; indexicality of, 54, 59, 67; long-take, 197; of 1960s, 3; online distribution platforms for, 11; performative, 10, 205n15; present-tense, 196; proximity to subjects in, 115; reliance on sound, 184, 185; single-shot, 196; social actor, 29n11; social media sharing of, 196; synch-sound technology for, 200–201; technological developments in, 200; true representation in, 115; voice-of-God narration in, 115, 184–85
documentary theater, archival reenactments by, 5, 29n12
documentary theory: about camerawork, 194; on digital imagery, 49; historical understanding in, 48; on indexicality, 8, 52; Neo-Marxist, 10; photography and, 60
Dorsey, George, 27n1; gravesite of, 130, 133; lynching of, 1, 120; military background of, 136
Dorsey, Mae Murray: gravesite of, 130, 133; lynching of, 1, 120; reenactor playing, 184
Drew, Robert, 63, 75n4
drone strikes, US military, 84; photography of, 88–89
dualism, mind-body, 54–55
Du Bois, W. E. B., 141
Duckworth, Rufus, 174
Duluth, MN, lynching, 156, 174
Dunbar-Nelson, Alice, 142
Dunye, Cheryl: *The Watermelon Woman*, 40
duration, representation of, 51
Durkheim, Émile: *Elementary Forms of Religious Life*, 80n68
Duvernay, Ava: *Selma*, 150; *13th*, 8

Easy Rider (1969), 45
Eatman, Megan, 133
Edmund Pettis bridge, reenactment of march at, 129
Edwards, Willie: lynching of, 153
Ehrenhaus, Peter, 121, 161n8; on "moral witness" space, 186
Eisenstein, Serge: montage of, 169
Eitzen, Dirk, 30n16; on storytelling, 161n5
Ekman, Paul, 19; Facial Action Coding System (FACS), 33n65
elections, US (2016): Russian influence operations in, 115
embodiment: of cinematic effects, 195–96; indexical, 49–60, 195, 203; in listening, 29n11; in reenactment, 8–9, 11, 15, 35
Emmett Till Unsolved Civil Rights Crime Act (2008), 153
emotion: "basic emotions" theory, 19; hardwired, 33n65
empowerment, Black female, 77n18
Equal Justice Initiative, 174, 192n14
ethics, oppositional, 73–74
ethnography: filmmaking in, 3, 76n9, 201; reverse participant, 46–48; sensory, 22
exchange, Neo-Marxist theorists on, 14
experience, commodification as media object, 15
Eyes on the Prize (1986), 150, 202

Facial Action Coding System (FACS), 33n65
Fain, Kimberly, 197
Fairclough, Adam, 147
FBI: investigation of Lacy hanging, 176, 177; investigation of Moore's Ford Bridge lynching, 129, 135, 144, 161n18
Felton, Rebecca Latimer, 141
feminism: Black liberation, 141; film phenomenology tradition, 22
fetishes: as memory, 54; temporal, 57
Fight Club (1999), 77n18
film: contingency in, 78n34; diasporic, 17, 54; oppositional ethics of, 73; reenactment of past, 51

film, ethnographic, 3; Cambridge turn in, 76n9; nonfiction, 201
film, fictional: ventriloquism in, 193n18
film, narrative: male gaze in, 91; scopophilia in, 179
film, nonfiction: archival footage in, 40; diasporic makers of, 17; elitist consideration of, 200; ethnographic, 201; precision in, 11; sensory orientation in, 76n9
film-body, 186; perception of, 82; space with viewer, 86; as system of being, 82
filmmaking, fictional: abrupt death in, 127; continuity in, 152
filmmaking, postcolonial: sensory cinema in, 9
film phenomenology, simulation-body and, 84–87
film studies, textual analysis in, 20
film theory, black, 8
film theory, feminist: phenomenology of, 22; realism in, 180, 193n17
Floyd, George, 191; Black dignity march for, 204; *New York Times* reporting on, 199; police press release on, 199; recording of murder, 27, 196, 197–200, 201, 202. *See also* Frazier, Darnella
Ford, Charles "Tuna": reenactment experiences, 44, 45
Forman, James, 147
Forrest Gump (1994), 10
Fort Irwin National Training Center (NTC): Box Tours of, 113, 119n83; camera operators at, 82; civilian visitors to, 83, 87, 95, 110, 111; Cold War training at, 94; control of journalism, 87; critique of realism at, 106–11; decisive action training at, 119n85; development of simulation at, 102–3; environmental stresses at, 95; immersive environments at, 91; journalists at, 83–84, 87, 89, 95, 98, 99–100, 106, 110–11, 113, 114, 116n9; military training at, 25; mock villages at, 82, 87–91, 96, 111, 112, 113; news reports on, 85; public relations at, 34n75, 83, 87, 92, 98, 113–14, 125; realism at, 106–11, 116n19; rules of

Fort Irwin National Training Center (NTC) (*Cont.*)
  engagement at, 106; screen metaphor for, 96; simulation-bodies of, 86; simulation of Saddam Hussein's army, 94; TCs (tactical controllers) at, 88, 113, 114, 116n18; tests of technology at, 94; visual violence records at, 85, 90. *See also* simulation training, military; soldier trainees
Fort Leavenworth, Kansas: counterinsurgency training at, 97
Foucault, Michel: on biopolitics, 46; "Society Must Be Defended," 77n20
Frank, Adam, 19, 33n65; *Shame and Its Sisters*, 16
Frankfurt School, critical theory of, 15
Franklin, Aretha, 77n18
Franklin, John Hope, 47
Frazier, Darnella: documentary framing by, 200; Facebook posts, 198–99; video of Floyd murder, 27, 197–99, 201, 202
Freedom Riders, violence against, 148
Freedom Summer, media coverage of, 148
Freud, Sigmund, 105; "mystic writing pad," 72
Fridlund, Alan, 33n65
Friedberg, Anne: *Window Shopping*, 41
Frosh, Paul, 11
Full Battle Rattle (2008), 4, 85, 111; ideological orientation of, 182

Gaines, Jane, 10; on political mimesis, 11
gaze: on Black death, 197; fused images of, 190; oppositional, 178, 180; unreciprocated, 179
gaze, cinematic: consumer desire and, 41; feminine object of, 180
gaze, male, 180; in narrative film structure, 91, 179
genocide, Cambodian: documentaries of, 6; traumatic memories of, 6
Georgia: film industry in, 26–27, 166–68, 193n28; media industry in, 123, 167; voter suppression in, 3
Georgia Association of Black Elected Officials (GABEO), sponsoring of Moore's Ford Lynching Reenactment, 129, 130
Georgia Bureau of Investigation, investigation of Moore's Ford lynching, 129
Gerber, Tony: *Full Battle Rattle*, 4, 85, 111, 182
Gill, Zack Whitman, 106; on warrior ethos, 105
Glover, Danny, 156, 174, 176
Goldovskaya, Marina, 31n33
Goldsby, Jacqueline, 139
Gramsci, Antonio: *Prison Notebooks*, 116n11
Greaves, William: *Symbiopsychotaxiplasm: Take 1*, 70
Greene, Cassandra, 169, 175, 178, 187
Greensboro, NC, sit-ins (1960), 202, 205n21
Gregg, Melissa: *The Affect Theory Reader*, 16
grief, historical unresolved, 28n6. *See also* trauma
Griffith, D. W.: *The Birth of a Nation*, 28n6, 140–42, 163n52; Griffith's defense of, 164n54; resistance to, 142, 164n59; spectacle lynching in, 140–41, 142
Grimké, Angelina Weld, 142
Gross, Larry, 33n71
Guynn, William, 5

Hale, Grace Elizabeth, 138
Hampton, Henry, 150, 202
happenings, of 1960s/1970s, 201
Harrison, Loy, 131, 160; reenactor playing, 183
Hayes Code (1934), 142
Hemmings, Sally, 136
Henderson, Odie, 190–91
Hester, Barnett, 135; stabbing of, 130
Hill, Flosse, 135
Holliday, Billie, 193n18
Holmes, Jack, lynching of, 143
hooks, bell: on "down home" death, 128; on oppositional gaze, 178; on white male gaze, 180
Howard, Bobby, 161n4
humanities, affect in, 3
Hurley, Ruby, 148
Hurt Locker, The (2008), 67
Hutchines, Edwin, 28n8

INDEX 239

Ifill, Sherrilyn, 174, 176
imagery, war: of atrocities, 89–90; ceding to entertainment industry, 90–91; entertainment cinema clichés in, 85
images: of affect system, 103; binary code, 195; connection with subject, 49; in everyday lives, 52; indexicality of, 38, 49, 63; materiality of, 49; punishing, 103; representation of events, 49
images, digital: discontinuous, 31n37; in documentary theory, 49; manipulation of, 10–11, 14
improvised explosive devices (IEDs): casualties from, 96; in military simulation training, 82, 83, 87, 92, 96–99, 104; neutralization efforts for, 96
In Country (Attie and O'Hara, 2014), 4, 36; absent pasts in, 64, 69; absent time in, 73; affect in, 44; archival footage use, 40, 44, 45, 65, 66–68; archive affect of, 40, 69; archived repertoire of camerawork, 64–70; being there in, 36, 41, 65; commemoration ethic of, 74; continuity-disjuncture in, 70; continuum of time in, 65; crisis coverage in, 60–64; cultural memory in, 56; daily life in, 44, 45, 62, 66; dialogue in, 43; digital technology use in, 49; drama of accumulation in, 153; editing of, 64, 69, 71; filmmakers/subjects copresence, 62; indexicality in, 41, 52, 60, 63, 65; Iraq War footage in, 80n67; manhood in, 66, 67, 70; memory in, 44, 45; metonymy in, 56, 58, 65, 69; montages of, 43, 56, 65, 66; narrative structure of, 44; nimble cameras of, 36; nonintervention in, 73, 125; observational footage in, 41, 52, 56; opening of, 43–44; outdoor aesthetics of, 63; the past in, 52, 64, 69; perceptual orientation of, 49; performance in, 24; psychic repair in, 24, 70–72; recollection-objects of, 56–57, 175; reenacting camerawork in, 24, 35–75; reparative dynamic in, 71; replica use in, 60; representation in, 49; role-play in, 43; situation in present, 40–41; slurs used in, 45, 75; synopsis of, 43–49; temporality of, 71–72, 74; temporal rupture in, 65, 69; traces of recording in, 60–72. *See also* reenactors (*In Country*)
the index: Peirce on, 18, 50, 52–53, 58, 73, 79n37; photographic, 51; situated theory of, 59; taxonomy of, 52
indexicality: of *Always in Season*, 186–87, 190; in art, 201; of behavior, 52–53; of body, 8–14, 26; in body of perceiver, 13; bond with object, 9; in digital culture, 17; of documentaries, 54, 67; documentary theory on, 8, 52; as embodied experience, 59, 195; of embodied performance, 203; in film theory, 9–10, 52; of images, 38, 49, 63; in *In Country*, 41; mechanical reproduction in, 51, 63; in media phenomenology, 58; perceptive orientation in, 194; in performance theory, 58; performative, 14; of performing bodies, 73, 115; as photochemical trace, 52; of power relations, 119n87; in reenactment, 13–14, 48, 59, 127–28; as sensory unit of, 13; in simulation documentaries, 17, 41, 203; of spectacle lynchings, 138–39; thunderbolt effect of, 58, 65, 149. *See also* signs, indexical
indexicality, media, 9, 58; affective, 12, 14; in the body, 12–13; as processual, 12; technological understanding of, 50
infrastructure, affective, 161n11
institutions, state: authorizing power of, 40
Iraqis, perspectives on Iraq War, 25
Iraq War: civilian fatalities in, 100; cultural awareness training in, 75; documentary images of, 89–90; embedded reporting on, 61; IEDs in, 96; Iraqi perspectives of, 25; military failures of, 83; performance for cameras during, 92; photographic media of, 84–85; television coverage of, 95

Jackson, Elmer: lynching of, 156
Jackson, Jimmie, 148
Jackson, Lynn McKinley: possible lynching of, 130, 162n19
Japanese, incarcerated, 55
jazz, repetition and revision structure of, 151

Jinx, The (HBO series), 161n5
Johnson, Kristen: *Cameraperson*, 152
Johnson, Ross, 200
Juhasz, Alexandra, 193n17
justice, restorative: for lynchings, 3, 156, 169, 171; in simulation documentaries, 3, 5, 25
Justice Department, US: reopening of Till case, 153
Just Mercy (2019), 174

Kahana, Jonathan, 29n11
Kammen, Michael: on heritage syndrome, 47
Keeling, Kara, 84, 91, 105, 161n4; on rise of cinema, 141; *The Witch's Flight*, 116n11
Kennedy, David, 156
Kennedy, John F.: on civil rights, 147
Kim, Jihoon, 31n37
King, Martin Luther, Jr.: on Georgia lynchings, 144; Moore's Ford Bridge lynching and, 129; use of television coverage, 145–46
King, Rodney: video of beating, 29n12
Kinney, Joel: motives for reenactment, 73–74; recollection-object of, 56–57; reenactment by, 44, 45, 46; slurs used by, 45, 75
Kinney, Matt: reenactment by, 44–45
Klein, Melanie, 105
knowledge, embodied, 54; through reenactment, 57
Knox, Hannah, 161n11
Kohn, Eduardo, 76n9
Kubrick, Stanley: *Full Metal Jacket*, 45
Ku Klux Klan: in *Always in Season*, 176; firebombings, 161n4; lynchings by, 138, 141, 190; merchandise, 156; in Moore's Ford Lynching Reenactment, 124, 156–58, 158, 168; rise of cinema and, 141

Lacy, Claudia, *173*, *177*, *178*; at *Always in Season* premiere, 190–91; justice for, 179; partnership with NAACP, 172; photographic gaze of, 174, 177, 186
Lacy, Lennon, *173*; community of, 172; family of, 172; family's vigil for, 177; grave site, 175; hanging of, 124, 156, 171; interracial relationship of, 176–77; 911 call for, 172; photographic gaze of, 174; suicide ruling for, 171, 174, 175; uncertainties over, 172. See also *Always in Season*; Bladenboro, NC, hanging
Lacy, Pierre, 174, 176; at *Always in Season* premiere, 190–91
Laine, Taj: on space of collective experience, 85
landscape, in American culture, 93
Lang, Fritz: *Fury*, 142–43, 164n65; *M*, 178, 179
Leacock, Ricky, 36; on observational camerawork, 35, 64
Lee, George, lynching of, 153
Lee, Jeehyun, 46
Legacy Museum (Montgomery, AL), 192n14
Leigh, Susan, 170
Leviathan (2015), 76n9
Lewis, Clive, 197
Lewis, John: as civil rights icon, 150; on television apparatus, 149
Lexicon, Inc.: military simulation training business of, 97
Leys, Ruth, 16, 33n65; affect theory of, 19–20, 32n51; *The Ascent of Affect*, 19
Lincoln, Abraham: assassination myth of, 151; Black reenactors of, 151
listening, embodied, 29n11
Logan, Paula: in Moore's Bridge reenactment, 175, 178, 180, 184; tears of, 186–87; watching archival footage, *181*, *185*, 186–88, 190
logophobia, 76n9
Lorre, Peter, 178
Losh, Elizabeth, 110
loss, perception of, 58
Lucas, Martin, 132
Lusztig, Irene, 29n11
Lynch, Charles, 137
lynchings: acquittals for, 134–35; actuality film of, 155; affective infrastructure of, 170; affective understanding of, 126; annual reenactments of, 1–4, *2*, 25–26;

"Black brute" figure in, 140; cinematic indictment of, 142; civic pride in, 139; cold-case investigations, 153–54; conflation of stories, 136; connection to racial prejudice, 138; ethics of representation, 187; FBI investigation of, 27n1; historical contexts of, 174; Hollywood depictions of, 142–44; hybrid stories of, 133; intergenerational trauma of, 122, 177, 186; lack of closure for, 177; as martyr archetypes, 133; mob violence at, 142–43; pamphlets promoting, 139; private, 138; prosecution of perpetrators, 129; protest efforts, 142; racial terrorism, 137; racist ideology of, 128; rationales for, 176; reenactment for politics, 126; reenactments of purported crime, 121–22; reported as suicides, 176; representation of context, 171–77; restorative justice rituals for, 3, 156, 169, 171, 172; Revolutionary War, 137; silence about, 131, 171, 172, 177; southern disavowal of, 144; state trials for, 138; strategies for representing, 178–90; unpunished, 144–45; unreported, 136, 161n4; unresolved legacies of, 168, 172; vigilantes, 137–38; white accountability for, 190; white Americans' interpretation of, 144; by white supremacists, 138, 143. *See also* Black death; Moore's Ford Lynching Reenactment; violence, racial

lynchings, spectacle, 26, 121, 122; in *The Birth of a Nation*, 140–41; camerawork depicting, 142; carnival show displays of, 139; complicity of spectators, 139, 190; early, 138; indexicality of, 138–39; mass protests against, 145; meaning of community in, 138; modern technology in, 138; Moore's Ford Lynching Reenactment and, 131; national scrutiny of, 144; news media on, 144; numbers of, 141; panoptic visual experience of, 142; participant-witnesses to, 139; performativity of, 140; photographic representations of, 123, 137–45, 159, 190; photographic souvenirs of, 140; postcards of, 155, 156, 171, 172, 180, 190; publicizing of, 138; response to social change in, 140; sonic experience of, 138–39, 163n42; white spectators at, 139, 171, 172, 180, *189*

lynching victims: cinematic identification with, 142; communities of, 171–72; descendants of, 171–72; families of, 155, 187; memorialization of, 1, 25, 156; of Moore's Ford Bridge, 1, 120; surrogate bodies of, 122

Lynch's Law (1780), 137

MacDonald, Scott, 76n9
MacDougall, David, 61
Malcom, Dorothy: gravesite of, 130, 133; lynching of, 1, 13, 120; marriage of, 135; pregnancy of, 130, 133–37, 159, 166, 169, 175, 192; reenactor playing, 13, 159, 175, 185
Malcom, Roger: gravesite of, 130, 133; jail site of, 131; lynching of, 1, 120; marriage of, 135; stabbing of landlord, 130
males, white: gaze of, 180; vocalic body of, 185
Malkowski, Jennifer, 197; *Dying in Full Detail*, 11
Manley, Alexander: burning of press, 163n52
Manovich, Lev, 10
Marguiles, Ivonne, 29n11
Marks, Laura U., 16, 57; analysis of *History and Memory*, 55–56; explanatory power theory, 56; on the fetish, 54; "recollection-object" theory, 24, 42, 54, 69, 73; *The Skin of the Film*, 17, 185
Marvel industry, Georgia productions in, 167–68
mass media: distribution networks of, 15; symbolic exchange in, 195
Massumi, Brian, 32n51
Mbembe, Achille, 3–4
McCain, Franklin, 202
McFate, Montgomery, 82
McGhie, Isaac: lynching of, 156
McIntosh, Francis: murder of, 138
McNeil, Joseph, 202

media: nonlinear engagements with, 200; oppositional practices of, 201. *See also* digital media

media consumption: collective understanding in, 116n11; environmental impact of, 170; shaping of worldviews, 91; status economies in, 15

media infrastructure, 32n60, 160; marginalized users of, 170

media phenomenology, 194; in ethnographic camerawork, 22; indexicality in, 58; sensory cinema and, 22–23

media spectatorship, embodied experiences of, 22

memory, fetish as, 54

memory, traumatic: in postwar cinema, 17; repression of, 32n61. *See also* trauma

Merleau-Ponty, Maurice: *The Address of the Eye*, 17; on perception of stimuli, 86

metonymy: in *History and Memory*, 55; in *In Country*, 56, 58, 65, 69; metaphor and, 79n44; in Moore's Ford Lynching Reenactment, 169; of reenactment, 121

Micheaux, Oscar: *Within Our Gates*, 142

Middle Passage: "slave tourism" sites for, 133

military, US: all-volunteer, 116n9; control over images, 90; decisive action training, 119n85; demographic of, 107; embedded reporting on, 116n9; gaming experience in, 107; internalization of the cinematic, 115; professional videographers, 113; recruitment depots, 107

military training, US: for Cold War, 94; cultural awareness, 75, 81, 82, 91–92, 97, 107; force-on-force, 81, 86, 100; warrior ethos of, 74, 82; for World War II, 93–94; XCTCs (exportable combat training centers), 97. *See also* simulation training, military; soldier trainees

Miller, Zoriah, 117n21

Minow, Newton, 146

mirror neurons, in simulation theory of mind, 14

Mitchell, Koritha, 142, 155, 172

Mobley, Mamie Till, 145

Mojave Desert: Desert Storm training in, 95; environmental stresses at, 95; as metaphor for simulation, 93; screen metaphor for, 95; World War II training in, 93–94. *See also* Fort Irwin National Training Center

Monfort, Nick, 32n60

Montgomery Bus Boycott, television coverage of, 145–46

Moore's Ford Bridge lynching (Monroe, GA), 120; archives of, 136; Black news media coverage, 134; FBI investigation of, 129, 135, 144, 161n18; first filmed reenactment, 153; grand jury transcripts for, 166; lack of closure, 177; Martin Luther King and, 129; in *Murder in Black and White* series, 153–54, 159; NAACP and, 134–36; as national embarrassment, 144; perpetrators of, 1, 25, 120, 122, 125, 172, 191; rumors concerning, 162n18; scandal of, 144; site of, 131; surviving suspects, 120, 131, 166; victims of, 1, 120; wall of silence about, 131; witnesses to, 160nn1–2

Moore's Ford Lynching Reenactment, 1–4, *2*; absence in, 120; as act of love, 127; affective infrastructure of, 27, 123, 169–70, 178, 192; affective significance of, 121, 133, 136, 137; archival materials for, 137; aspirational realism of, 191; Atlanta activists in, 168, 191; audience, *134*, *183*, *187*; audiences' recording of, 157, 166–67; Black spectators of, 150, 180, 187, *189*, 190; camerawork in, 115, 122, 123, 150, 151–60, 189; car caravan in, 131; cast and crew (2019), *167*; community cohesion in, 136; continuity of, 123; documentary videos of, 131; duration of, 131; ethical rationales for, 120; as ethical space, 127–28; ethics of opposition in, 25; events comprising, 129–31; evolution of, 120, 169; feminism in, 178; first filming of, 153; foreground-background relationships in, 157–58; as funeral procession, 121; GABEO sponsorship of, 129, *130*; gazing at death in, 127; Google results for, 123; gunshot in, 157, 158–59; healing through, 121; image making for, 123, 137; indexical landscape in, 127–28; indexing of sadness, 128; information about perpetrators following, 129; international profile for, 122; KKK graffiti at, 184; liminal ritual space of, 121; linearity of, 153; livestreaming to Facebook, 166; martyr archetypes of, 133; media artifacts of, 121; media coverage of, 169; media strategy of, 125, 137, 191; memory in, 26; metonymic juxtaposition in, 169; news media coverage of, 129; ongoing value of, 191; organizers of, 168; origin of, 129; photographic record of, 122; political affect of, 169, 191; political purpose of, 153; power of media objects for, 126; purpose of, 120; realism of, 159; realtime projections of, 166; recollection-objects in, 127; rehearsals, 156–57, 175, 182; repetition/revision in filming of, 151–60; representational politics of, 178; reproduction of perpetrators' view, 125; as ritual, 121, 128, 136, 168–69, 172; scholarship on, 132–33; shaping of public perceptions, 26; shot-reverse structure camerawork, 153, 156–60, *158*, 188; as simulation documentary, 122; as social media happening, 166; sounds of, 188; speakers at, 130, 167; spectacular simulation in, 139; spiritual singing at, 131, 132; stabbing scene in, 130; symbolism of, 120; synopsis of, 129–37; therapeutic function of, 133; tools for intervention in, 192; as urban legend, 136; vérité filming of, 188; as vernacular public art, 132; victims' families and, 187, 192; voter suppression in, 131; white criticism of, 132. *See also* reenactors (Moore's Ford Lynching Reenactment)

Moore's Ford Memorial Committee (MFMC), 129, 133, 153; white members of, 135

Moreno, J. L., 70

Morris, Errol: *The Thin Blue Line*, 30n14

Morris, Meaghan: "Banality in Cultural Studies," 59

Moses, Bob, 164n76

Moss, Jesse: *Full Battle Rattle*, 4, 85, 111, 182

movement, representation of, 51

Moynihan Report, The, 67

Ms. Magazine, 29n11

Mulvey, Laura: *Riddle of the Sphinx*, 179–80; "Visual Pleasure and Narrative Cinema," 179; white positionality of, 178

the mundane, durational recording of, 201

Murder in Black and White (television documentary series), 182; *Moore's Ford* episode, 153–54, 159; structure of white supremacy in, 154

Musgrave, John, 74, 75

myths, national: reinterpretation of, 151

NAACP: antilynching lobbying, 155; circulation of Black death images, 197; and Lacy hanging, 172; Moore's Ford Bridge lynching and, 134–36

Nash, Diane, 202

National Great Blacks in Wax Museum (Maryland), 133

National Memorial for Peace and Justice (Montgomery, AL), 192n14

Neal, Claude: descendants of, 174; lynching of, 142, 156, 177

nervous system, autonomous: effect on consciousness, 32n61

New Historicism, use of archives, 40

New Materialism, 169

NewsBank: Access World News database, on simulation training, 116n14

Newton, F. W., 176

Nguyen, Vinh: reenactment of Vietnam War, 44, 45, 74

Nichols, Bill, 49, 200; on spoken word, 184

nostalgia: power over political movements, 74; reenactors', 71, 81

Novick, Lynn, 24. *See also The Vietnam War*

Obama, Barack: commemoration of Selma violence, 150

objectification, witnessing of, 7

O'Hara, Meghan, 37, 67; on *In Country* production, 62; on *In Country* temporality, 71–72; reenactment by, 36, 38, 61, 64;

INDEX

O'Hara (Cont.)
  on reenactment process, 38; role as filmmaker, 35. See also *In Country*
Olive, Jacqueline, 3, 190; interviews by, 159; partnership with Rice, 125, 156; research of, 191; restorative justice forum of, 156; and *Without Sanctuary* exhibit, 156, 171, 174. See also *Always in Season*
Oliver, Kelly, 7–8
O'Neal, Patrick, 95
Oreskes, Naomi: *Merchants of Doubt*, 136–37
Orta, Ramsey: police harassment of, 198
otherness, sensory experiences of, 108
Ott, Brian, 16
Ottley, Roi, 142
Owen, A. Susan, 121, 161n8; on "moral witness" space, 186

Paglen, Trevor, 117n20; photographs of Afghanistan prisons, 115, 119n87
Parks, Lisa, 115; repetition/revision of, 151, 152
Parks, Suzan-Lori, 153; *The America Play* as recollection-object, 151; Black subjectivity in *The America Play*, 151; "Elements of Style," 151
passion plays, Judeo-Christian: reenactments and, 133
the past: absent, 64, 69; documentaries' connection to, 196; performance of, 4; reenactment in film, 51
Patriot's Day (2004), 77n19
Patton, George: desert training by, 93
Pavsek, Christopher, 76n9
Peirce, Charles Saunders, 9; on the afterimage, 51; on the index, 18, 50, 52–53, 58, 73, 79n37; semiotics of, 50; on subjective perception, 42; "The Theory of Signs," 50
perception: accumulated affect in, 55; afterimage of, 51; in camerawork, 21, 53, 61; chained acts of, 53; ephemeral experience of, 194; of film-body, 82; indexical, 58–59; of loss, 58; in performance, 57; processes for reenactment, 190; subjective, 42; visual inadequacies, 50–51

performance: acting tradition of, 205n15; camerawork as, 11, 38; copresence in, 123; in Iraq War, 92; perception in, 57; in politics, 203; recursive, 4; ritual, 80n68; as simulation-body, 82; weaponization of, 84. See also reenactment
performance, embodied: digital media and, 115; indexicality of, 203; of outrage, 203; in reenactment, 9, 121. See also bodies, performing
performance documentation, scholarship on, 6
performance theory: on indexicality of image, 38; "repertoire" in, 41
Petraeus, David, 97
Phelan, Peggy, 5, 71; on metonymy, 55, 79n44
photographic media: in everyday life, 195; indexicality of, 9–10; of Iraq War, 84–85
photography: of American casualties, 117n21; composite, 50; consent protocols for, 117n21; documentary theory and, 60; evidentiary connection to world, 51–52
photography, digital: immateriality of, 50
Pitch, Anthony, 134, 135; *The Last Lynching*, 169
Pittard, Dana, 101
police violence: videos of, 7, 27, 196, 197–99. See also violence, racial
postcards, of spectacle lynchings, 155, 156, 187; spectators in, 171, 172, 180, 190
Poston, AZ: Japanese internment at, 55–56
power: of abstractions, 3–4; claims to neutrality in, 63; explanatory, 56; of nostalgia, 74
power relations: asymmetrical, 5; effect of documentaries on, 196–97; indexicality of, 119n87
presence: in observational camerawork, 24; in simulation documentaries, 24; transfer of, 55
present, instantaneous, 51
Primary (1960), 80n62
protest practices, distance sharing of, 203

Protevi, John, 4; political affect theory, 28n8, 83; on psychic survival, 182
Psycho, shower scene of, 186
psychodrama, reenactment of, 70
Puritans, public executions of, 137

racial discrimination, affective understanding of, 126
Rangan, Poojah, 20, 193n18; "The Sound of the Voice," 184; on "Voice of God" narrative, 184–85
Rattelade, Heather, 176
Razsa, Maple, 31n38
reading, surrogacy in, 29n11
realism: commercial forms of, 98; commonsense, 91; in feminist film theory, 180, 193n17; in military simulation training, 87, 91–92, 98–101; procedural, 108
realism, affective, 101, 106–11; in public-relations material, 106
realism, cinematic: contradicting of social facts, 92; spectator investment through, 91–92
recollection-objects, 55–56, 59; camerawork as, 57, 73; in *In Country*, 56–57
Redneck Shop (Laurens, SC): KKK merchandise at, 156
reenactment: accumulated time in, 54; activist scholarship on, 125–26; affective infrastructure of, 126; American identity in, 47; archive affect of, 56, 65; of battles, 11; being there in, 48; camaraderie in, 48; camerawork as, 8, 35–75; civil rights movement and, 47, 150, 194; "collective effervescence" in, 80n68; in digital culture, 11, 38; in direct action campaigns, 11; effect on structural racism, 203; embodied knowledge through, 57; empowerment in, 155; ethics of, 14, 23–26; evocation of white supremacy, 155; films about, 30n14, 36; function of, 186; of Greensboro sit-in, 205n21; as healing space, 71; "heritage syndrome" in, 47; for imagined viewers, 5; indexicality in, 13–14, 48, 59, 127–28; linear time and, 196; materiality of, 8; materialization of feelings in, 31n40; metonymic expansiveness of, 121; modes of consciousness for, 48; "moral witness" space of, 186; mutual accountability in, 195; noninterventionist camerawork in, 23; passion plays and, 133; past/present in, 5, 48, 196; performative repertoire of, 122; political accountability for, 137; possession in, 155; psychic experience of, 53; of psychodrama, 70; in PTSD recovery, 109; public interest issues in, 29n12; in public spaces, 137; of public speeches, 129; as reactionary social movement, 47; recursive practices of, 22; relationship to activism, 123–24, 126; rhetoric *in situ* of, 133; ritual, 128, 196; scholarship on, 6, 30n20; shared performance in, 49; and simulation of trauma, 104; spectators' camera use at, 11, 157, 166–67; of subject positions, 70; as temporal fetish, 57; temporality in, 74, 188; of Vietnam War, 4, 24, 35, 36, 39, 52, 294; visceral responses to, 126. *See also* camerawork, observational; performance
reenactment, Civil War, 47, 77n23, 123; Confederate, 47; ethnographic study of, 33n71
reenactment, embodied, 9, 121; decoupling from finished film, 11; material qualities of, 15; in military simulation training, 81, 83; performance practices of, 9; in sensory cinema, 8–9
reenactors: affective experiences of, 4; affective labor of, 195; cathartic experiences of, 5; collective identity of, 9; conjoined experience with camerapersons, 16; dealing with trauma, 9; discriminatory, 47; lived experiences of, 48; military veterans, 44–45, 47–48, 67; motives for, 58; "period rush" among, 48; recollection of trauma, 23–24; revelation about past lives, 194; social ties among, 47. *See also* bodies, performing
reenactors (*In Country*, 2014), 24, 35, 72; daily life of, 44, 45, 62; embodied

reenactors (Cont.)
  mimesis of, 35; interviews with, 44; media consumption by, 41; memories of, 44; montages of, 65; motivations of, 44; nostalgia among, 71, 81; observational footage of, 44; performance of individual personhood, 46; playing Vietcong, 45, 61, 63; PTSD among, 44; social authority of, 68–69; veterans, 44–45, 67; weapons of, 66
reenactors (Moore's Ford Lynching Reenactment), 193n28; Black, 124–25, 168; Black female, 128, 183; indexicality of, 13–14; Klansmen, 124, 156–58, 158, 168; lynch mob, 157, 189; performing bodies of, 5; repercussions for, 191; trauma among, 124; white performers, 124, 125
reenactors (Revolutionary War): following 9/11, 77n19; motives of, 47; strategies of, 47
referentiality, drama of, 11
Revolutionary War, reenactment of, 11, 24, 31n34, 41, 46–48, 77n19
Richardson, Allissa, 7, 203; on Black witnessing, 203
Richmond, David, 202
"riot porn," collective viewing of, 31n38
Rithy Panh, S21: The Khmer Rouge Killing Machine, 6–7
Rodowick, David, 49
Ross, RaMell: Hale Country This Morning, This Evening, 28n6
Rouch, Jean, 54
routine, ephemeral breaks in, 195
Rowan and Martin's Laugh-In (television show), "Sock It To Me" motif, 77n18
Ruhleder, Karen, 170
Rushdy, Ashraf, 139
Rusk, Richard, 133

Safina-Massey, David "Cricket": reenactment by, 44–45, 67, 69–70, 75
Santos-Aquino, Rowena, 29n11
Scales, Robert, 96
Schaeffer, Pierre, 163n45; on "reduced listening," 185

Schneider, Rebecca, 61
school segregation, direct cinema films about, 63
screen essentialism, 32n60
Second Life (online role-playing world), restorative justice forum in, 156
Sedgwick, Eve, 19, 20, 21; on paranoid position, 105; on peri-performative utterance, 186; Shame and Its Sisters, 16; on "strong affect theory," 70, 105
self, technologized extensions of, 201
selfies, documentary practice of, 11
Selma (Alabama). See Bloody Sunday
Selma (documentary, 2014), 150
sensation: photographic mediation of, 59; in simulation documentaries, 4–5
Sensory Ethnography Lab (Harvard), 24, 76n9; observational camerawork at, 38
sensory vérité, 22
September 11 attacks, Revolutionary War reenactment following, 77n19
Shaviro, Steven, 201
Siegworth, Gregory: The Affect Theory Reader, 16
signs, indexical: continuity with object, 51; performative aspect of, 52; of reenactment, 59; sudden perception of, 58; of trauma, 12; of violent death, 127–29. See also indexicality
simulation, 14–15; affect system and, 101–6; agency of, 86; in American culture, 93; in computer programs, 14; of consciousness, 101–2; excess in design of, 99; of the human, 101–3; modeling of events, 14; in Neo-Marxist theory, 14; recursive practices of, 4, 22; role in empathy, 14; traces left by, 86; of trauma, 104; value-neutral, 106
simulation-body: affective strategy of, 86; film phenomenology and, 84–87; perception of stimuli, 86; performance as, 82; political affect in, 115; variables in, 86
simulation design, human experience and, 81

simulation documentaries: affect in, 7; camerawork in, 20, 28n6, 42, 49; distributed agency in, 17; distributed cognition and, 28n8; encouragement of justice, 7, 115; generation of social practices, 204; indexicality in, 17, 41, 203; justice-oriented, 115; key voices in, 75; noninterventionist cinema in, 24; performing bodies of, 5, 21; presence in, 24; purposes of, 4; recursive performance in, 4; restorative justice in, 3, 5, 25; sensation in, 4–5; support for racial justice, 147; temporality in, 24; trauma reenactment in, 4, 5; viewer emotion at, 7

simulation theory, 15; mirror neurons in, 195; resemblance in, 195

simulation training, military, 4, 7, 25; academics' viewing of, 110, 114; action-cinematic, 84, 100; for adversary culture, 84; affective power in, 103–4; affective realism in, 106–11; affective responses to, 81, 88, 90, 99, 116n7; affective strategy of, 101, 114; Afghan American actors in, 81, 84, 109, *110*; amputee actors in, 98; Arabic speakers in, 97, 109; assessment of efficiency, 87; avoidance strategies in, 105; awareness of consequences in, 108; battle fatigue from, 100; cinema-industry tropes in, 81, 85; cinematic affect in, 105–6; cinematic culture in, 91–92, 116n7; cinematic-theatrical production needs, 97; civilian casualties in, 107; civilian figure in, 86; consent protocols of, 34n75; for counterinsurgency, 82, 83, 84, 97, 114; cultural awareness in, 83, 91–92, 97, 107, 111, 114; cultural performance in, 114–15, 194; diasporic subjects in, 83; dimensionality of, 87; documentation of, 83, 84, 85; domination/control in, 83; efficacy of, 106; embodied reenactment in, 81, 83; enemy figure in, 86; entertainment paradigms in, 95; ethics of, 25; expense of, 98; fear in, 103; habituation in, 103; Hollywood studios' work in, 81, 82, 92, 100; humanitarian law and, 106; hypermasculine filmmaking in, 113; immersive, 25, 81; improvised explosive devices (IEDs) in, 82, 83, 87, 92, 96–98, 104; incremental changes to, 98; indexing of war, 100; industries supporting, 97–98, 99; intersubjectivity in, 83, 85; Iraqi American actors in, 25, 81–82, 84, 87–89, 92, 106; journalistic coverage of, 83–84, 87, 89, 95, 98, 99–100, 106, 110–11, 116n9; LAPD input into, 97; martial endurance trials in, 80n65; medical dummies in, 87; mock villages in, 82, 87–91, 96, 111, *112*, 113; negative affect in, 104–5, 109; neutral evaluation of, 86; official interpretations of, 108; outside evaluation of, 108; participants' stories, 81–82; Pashto speakers in, 109; as permanent rehearsal, 106; political affect of, 81, 115; present/future in, 81; prior life experiences during, 83; procedural realism in, 108; pyrotechnics for, 98; realism in, 87, 91–92, 98–101, 116n19; recursive, 81; reduction of civilian casualties in, 106; reiterative scenarios of, 25; role-playing in, 25; screen metaphor for, 95; sensations of touch in, 92; stage directions in, 113; stimulation of contempt, 104; stress in, 99–101, 103; SWET (Sewage, Water, Electricity, and Trash) procedures, 97; tactical controllers (TCMs) in, 87, 88; tank warfare, 94, 95; three-dimensional, 81; "unnecessary" killing in, 100; for urban insurgency, 82; variety for, 106; video evaluations of, 88; visceral reactions to, 108; visualization of wounds in, 92, 98, 109–10, *110*; warrior ethos in, 105; women actors in, 108–10. *See also* Fort Irwin National Training Center; soldier trainees

"Sit In" (*White Paper* documentary, 1960), 146

sit-ins: documentary traditions of, 204; Greensboro (NC), 202, 205n21

Sitney, P. Adams, 201

Skoller, Jeffrey, 196

Slave Rebellion Reenactment (Scott and Akomfrah), 29n11

smartphones: citizens' use of, 196, 200; long-take recordings, 197, 201. *See also* Frazier, Darnella
Smith, Anna Deveare, 29n12
Smith, Henry: lynching of, 138–39
Smith, Lamar: lynching of, 153
Snipes, Maceo: lynching of, 130
Sobchack, Vivian, 16, 85, 195; on cinematic consciousness, 106; on consciousness, 48; on documentary space, 127; documentary theory of death, 127, 128; on "film body," 86; on home movie reception, 186; phenomenology of, 17
social life: hidden forces determining, 70; inclusiveness in, 144
social sciences, affect in, 3
soldier trainees (Fort Irwin National Training Center): affective hardening of, 99, 116n7; affective realism and, 107; battle fatigue among, 100; common-sense orientation of, 85, 99; expressive experiences of, 88; interviews with, 85; opinions of simulation training, 107; performing of affect among, 88; preexisting attitudes of, 107–8; recognition of insurgents, 106; recruiting of, 107; review of training footage, 113; video game playing, 107, 108; war imagery for, 85. *See also* Fort Irwin National Training Center; simulation training, military
sound: cameras', 149; documentaries' reliance on, 184, 185; embodied expressivity of, 185; objective attunement to, 185
sound, recorded: as object-like, 163n45
Sound Objects (essay collection, 2019), 163n45
South, US: interracial class alliances in, 140; sit-ins, 202, 204, 205n21. *See also* civil rights movement; lynchings; violence, racial
Southern Christian Leadership Conference (SCLC), 148; media strategy of, 150
spectatorship: embodied experiences of, 22; film, 194; theories of, 18. *See also* audiences

Spinoza, Baruch: *Ethics*, 32n50
Stahl, Roger, 90–91; on "militainment," 116n9
Staiger, Janet, 140
state power, reproduction in subject body, 46
Steele, Charles, 129, 150
Sterling, Alton: videotaped killing of, 197
Stevenson, Bryan, 174, 176, 192n14
Stevenson, Lisa, 76n9
Stidhum, Tonja René: on Floyd murder video, 200
Stoney, George, 29n11
storytelling, emotional experience of, 161n5
Strategic Operations (company), military simulation training business of, 97–98, 113, 118n53
Student Nonviolent Coordinating Committee (SNCC), 129; white volunteers in, 165n83
Stu Segall Productions, military simulation training business of, 97–98
subjects: camera's objectification of, 28n6; civil rights, 146; connection with images, 49; reproduction of state power in, 46; state control of, 77n20
Suchman, Lucy, 86
suicide bombings, photographs of, 117n21
Summerhayes, Catherine, 31n37
Sweetgrass (Barbash and Castain-Taylor, 2008), long time of, 39
Sykes, Dewey: and Lacy hanging, 177

Tactical Iraqi (virtual-reality training game), 110
Tajiri, Rea: *History and Memory*, 79n46; recollection objects in, 55–56, 60, 127
Talmadge, Eugene, 27n1; reenactment of speech, 1, 124, 130; stump speech (Georgia, 1946), 1, 131
Taylor, Breonna, 204
Taylor, Diana, 122, 160, 169; on the archive, 64; on embodied performance, 121; performance theory of, 41
Taylor, Olivia, 175
tears, in *Always in Season*, 186–87

television: acousmetre use, 149; camera sounds in, 149; civil rights movement coverage, 123, 145–51, 202; coverage of Montgomery Bus Boycott, 145–46; effect on white power structure, 147; indexing of catastrophes, 59, 149; Iraq War coverage, 95; manifestation of modernity, 147; Martin Luther King Jr.'s use of, 145–46; shot–reverse shot scene construction in, 152; as vast wasteland, 146; white perspective of programming, 147

temporality: of death, 13; in observational camerawork, 24, 39; in reenactment, 57, 74, 188; in simulation documentaries, 24

Thompson, Kristin, 140

Thou, Tou, 198, 199

Thurmond, Thomas: lynching of, 143

Till, Emmett: justice for, 153; lynching of, 145, 153

time: absent, 73; cinematic structures of, 2; circular conceptions of, 151; representation of, 51; sensory units of, 13

Tomkins, Silvan: *Affect, Imagery, Consciousness*, 18; affect system of, 18–21, 70, 101, 104–5, 106; on automata, 102; on autonomous nervous system, 32n61; basic emotions theory, 32n51; critical theorists and, 33n65; on humiliation, 104; "ideo-affective orders" concept, 25; psychological research of, 19; on simulation, 101

Torres, Sasha, 145, 154; on crisis coverage, 149, 154, 165n87; on Montgomery Bus Boycott, 145; on television / civil rights connection, 146, 149

training games, virtual-reality, 110

trauma: American Psychological Association on, 28n6; bodily responses to, 33n65; fields of perception in, 12; historical, 28n6; indexical signs of, 12; among oppressed groups, 28n6; racial, 14; recollection-images of, 121; in reenactment, 23–24, 104; reproduction in killing videos, 197; ritual performances of, 194; simulation of, 104

trauma reenactment, 9; in simulation documentaries, 4, 5; simulation of death, 5

Trotter, William Monroe, 164n59; and *Birth of a Nation*, 141

Trumpism, exploitation of viewers, 30n15

truth, emotional representation of, 7

Turner, Hayes, 162n32

Turner, Mary: lynching of, 135–36, 162n32

Ubuntu (South African philosophy), 203

United States, collective memory in, 75

United States v. Harris (1882), 138

U.S. Army and Marine Corps Counterinsurgency Field Manual (2007), 116n10

Vann Nath, 6

Vertov, Dziga, 21

video: advocacy, 182; editing software, 11

video games, military-sponsored, 107

Vietnam, anticolonial struggles of, 46

Vietnam War: authentic feeling about, 35–36; collectable material of, 56; collective memory of, 39; indexical documents of, 41; journalistic coverage of, 83–84; medics, 72; parallels with Afghanistan, 39; popular films about, 48; public-relations strategies following, 86; racism in, 75; reenactment of, 4, 24, 35, 36, 39, 52, 294; "Sock It To Me" motif in, 77n18; veterans' memories, 44; video archives of, 39, 40, 56, 64, 68, 68, 72, 175. See also *In Country*; reenactors

Vietnam War, The (Burns and Novick), 24, 39–40, 56, 69, 75; interviews in, 74, 80n67; popular reception of, 40

viewers, cinema: reconstituted space for, 85

viewers, generation of meaning, 3

violence, racial: antebellum, 138; cinematic depiction of, 140–42; common-sense experience of, 121; contemporary, 130; counterhistories of, 169; funds for investigation of, 153; graphic depictions of, 155; lack of evidence for, 179;

violence, racial (Cont.) memorialization of, 121; photographic reproductions of, 155, 156; police, 136; silence concerning, 190; television's recording of, 147, 148–50; uncertainty in, 136; unpunished, 120; white complicity with, 162n32, 170, 190. See also Black death; lynchings; police violence

Virilio, Paul: *Desert Screen*, 95

Virtual Iraq (virtual-reality training game), 110

vision, human: inadequacies of perception, 50–51

Visual Anthropology Review (journal), 76n9

voices: male, 185; in simulation documentaries, 75; subjectivity of, 185. See also acousmetre; sound

voltmeters, participation in observational cinema, 39, 61, 76n9

voter suppression, Black, 3

Voting Rights Act (1965), effect of television coverage on, 148, 150

voyeurism: pleasure of, 178, 184; toxic, 179

Waddell, Alfred Moore, 163n52

Walker, Jane, 12

Walker, Wyatt, 147

Wallace, George, 47, 62n80; and Selma violence, 148

Wallace, Michelle, 142, 164n54

war: civilian deaths in, 100, 115; covert, 115; habituation to, 103; images' communication of, 117n21; journalistic reports of, 114–15; low-intensity, 116n10; masculine heroes of, 90–91; post-9/11 discourses on, 11; proxy discussions of, 31n34; reenactment of, 63, 67; storytelling of, 76n10. See also military, US; simulation training, military; Vietnam War; World War II

Warhol, Andy: durational recordings of, 201

Watson, Wayne, 169

Waugh, Thomas: on oppositional ethics, 73–74

Weiner, Norbert: on cybernetics, 18

West, Cornel, 126

Wexler, Laura, 134, 162n22, 169; *Fire in a Canebreak*, 131–32, 160n2

White, Walter, 135; antilynching efforts, 142, 143; on *Fury*, 142; investigation of lynchings, 162n32

white supremacists: contested ideology of, 139–40; infiltration of, 175; lynchings by, 138, 143; unpunished, 144

Willeman, Paul, 78n34

Williams, Linda: on "body genres," 99

Williams, Orlando, 177

Williams, Robin, 45

Wilmington, NC, racial violence in, 141, 163n52

Wilson, Elizabeth, 33n65

Wilson, Tim, 96

Winter Soldier (1972), 74, 80n74

Wiseman, Frederick, 62, 201; factory scenes of, 152

Without Sanctuary: Lynching Photography in America (exhibit, 2000), 155–56, 171, 174

witnessing: mediation by race, 8; by performing bodies, 7

Wollen, Peter: *Signs and Meaning in the Cinema*, 9

Wood, Amy Louise: on *Fury*, 142; *Lynching and Spectacle*, 139–40

World of Charlie Company, The (1970), 66

World War II: geopolitical strategy in, 144; incarcerated Japanese during, 55; military training for, 93–94; novel footage of, 57

XCTCs (exportable combat training centers), 97

Yellow Horse Brave Heart, Maria, 28n6

Young, Andrew, 148, 165n83

Young, Dan, 135

Zavattini, Cesar, 29n11

Zimmerman, Patricia R., 31n37

ANDY RICE is Assistant Professor of Film Studies and Media and Communication in the Department of Media, Journalism & Film at Miami University in Ohio. He has written for venues including the *Journal of Film and Video*, *JumpCut*, *The Scholar and Feminist Online*, and *Senses of Cinema*. He also coproduced, shot, and edited the award-winning historical documentary *Spirits of Rebellion: Black Independent Cinema from Los Angeles* on the LA Rebellion film movement.

www.ingramcontent.com/pod-product-compliance
Lightning Source LLC
Chambersburg PA
CBHW021139230426
43667CB00005B/182